RESEARCH METHODS
for
GENERALIST SOCIAL WORK

Third Edition

Christine R. Marlow
New Mexico State University

D0165197

BROOKS/COLE

THOMSON LEARNING

Australia · Canada · Mexico · Singapore · Spain · United Kingdom · United States

Social Work Editor: *Lisa Gebo*
Assistant Editors: *JoAnne von Zastrow, Susan Wilson*
Marketing Manager: *Caroline Concilla*
Marketing Assistant: *Jessica McFadden*
Project Editors: *Teri Hyde, Marlene Vasilieff*
Print Buyer: *Barbara Britton*
Permissions Editor: *Bob Kauser*
Production Service: *Hockett Editorial Service*

Text Designer: *Carolyn Deacy*
Copy Editor: *Regina Knox*
Illustrator: *MacArt Design*
Cover Designer: *Bill Stanton*
Cover Images: *Francisco Cruz/Super Stock; Leslie Parr*
Cover Printer: *Von Hoffmann Press*
Compositor: *G&S Typesetters, Inc.*
Printer: *Von Hoffmann Press*

Printed in the United States of America
1 2 3 4 5 6 7   04 03 02 01 00

Wadsworth/Thomson Learning
10 Davis Drive
Belmont, CA 94002-3098
USA

For more information about our products,
contact us:
**Thomson Learning Academic Resource
Center**
1-800-423-0563
http://www.wadsworth.com

International Headquarters
Thomson Learning
International Division
290 Harbor Drive, 2nd Floor
Stamford, CT 06902-7477
USA

UK/Europe/Middle East/South Africa
Thomson Learning
Berkshire House
168-173 High Holborn
London WC1V 7AA
United Kingdom

Asia
Thomson Learning
60 Albert Street, #15-01
Albert Complex
Singapore 189969

Canada
Nelson Thomson Learning
1120 Birchmount Road
Toronto, Ontario M1K 5G4
Canada

Library of Congress Cataloging-in-Publication Data

Marlow, Christine.
    Research methods for generalist social work / Christine Marlow. — 3rd ed.
       p.   cm.
    Includes bibliographical references and index.
    ISBN 0-534-52571-7
    1. Social service—Research—Methodology.   I. Title.

HV11.M3493   2000
361'.0072—dc21   00-037920

Contents

5

Designing Needs Assessments   71

6

Designing Program Evaluations   85

7

Designing the Evaluation of Practice   109

8

Selecting the Participants in the Research   131

9

Collecting the Data   155

10 Organizing the Data   195

Analysis of Qualitative Data   207
With Colin Collett van Rooyen, M.Soc.Sc.

Analysis of Quantitative Data: Descriptive Statistics   227

13

Analysis of Quantitative Data: Inferential Statistics   249

14

Research Writing   267

15

Using Research Findings in Practice and Evaluating Research With Patricia Sandau-Beckler, M.S.W.   291

Appendixes

My reason for writing this text is not unusual. After several years of seeking a social work research methods text and unsuccessfully trying a new text each year, I gave up and started to write. From teaching the same course repeatedly, I had developed a number of ideas of what a text needed. These ideas became crystallized through many discussions with students and colleagues and through my experiences with the Council on Social Work Education (CSWE) accreditation process. This text is intended for both undergraduate and graduate students taking a research methods course for the first time.

THEMES AND ORGANIZATION

A focus on generalist practice. Undergraduate and foundation graduate courses in social work programs usually are taught from a generalist perspective. Research methods must also be taught within this framework; consequently, the text includes examples from generalist practice. The relevance of research to the rest of the curriculum is thereby increased.

Emphasis on the practice-research link. When the parallels between generalist practice and research are emphasized, research becomes more accessible because practice is often perceived as more intuitive and understandable. Consequently, the text illustrates these parallels. Throughout the text, examples emphasize the link between research and practice by presenting real-life social work studies.

Discussion of production and consumption. The text presents research methods from the perspective that social workers can be both producers and consumers of research. This also ensures compliance with the CSWE accreditation requirements for the research curriculum.

Agency focus. In line with ensuring the relevance of research methods, the text discusses the application of research methods in agency rather than academic settings, because agencies are where the majority of social work graduates will be employed.

Ethics content. Ethical issues are included for each stage of the research process; that is, they are integrated into each chapter and not viewed as separate, discrete topics.

Human diversity content. Similarly, issues concerning human diversity as they relate to research methods are included. Although partly addressed through discussions of alternatives within and to the scientific method, this content (as with the ethics content) is considered for each stage of the research process.

Discussion of the different approaches to research.   This text includes coverage of different research approaches: the more traditional approaches (in this text called positivist) and alternative approaches (here designated interpretist). The use of these terms is somewhat arbitrary, and they are used here in a general sense. The term *positivism* is used in a general sense to include its variants, such as *post-positivism* and *quantitative methods; interpretism* is similarly used in this general sense to include *constructivism* and *qualitative methods.* Some may find this distinction rather elementary. A beginning text in research methods cannot engage in epistemological debates; what is important for the student to understand is that research can be conducted using different methods and within different paradigms.

International content.   As universities become increasingly conscious of internationalizing their curricula, social work programs are also adopting global perspectives. Thus this text incorporates some content from outside the United States, particularly in the examples.

Content on participatory approaches to research.   Recent years have seen increased use of research methods that empower clients and research participants through their engagement in the research process. These approaches vary in name and form; they include action research and empowerment research. This text includes content on these approaches.

The book is written so that each chapter can stand independently if necessary. The statistics chapters (Chapters 11 and 12) may be omitted if students have already completed statistics courses. Important terms appear in the text in **boldface** type and are defined there. These terms also are included in the glossary at the back of the text. Each chapter includes a reference section, as well as a summary and study/exercise questions. If possible, students should complete the exercises as a group; a group effort often provides a richer educational experience.

The third edition includes updated examples, an increased emphasis on the strengths approach, access to the InfoTrac College Edition, more content on qualitative data analysis, and an instructor's guide that includes powerpoint slides for each chapter.

ACKNOWLEDGMENTS

Completion of this new edition depended on many people (too many for me to name them all), but I would like to thank the following specific individuals and groups: Pat Sandau-Beckler, associate professor at New Mexico State University, co-authored Chapter 15; Donnelyn Curtis, reference librarian at University of

Nevada, Reno, contributed the bulk of the literature review and library web resource material. Joelle Meckel, who has now graduated with her MSW but at the time was my teaching assistant, made significant contributions to this edition by searching for interesting examples of the concepts covered in this text.

The reviewers of the manuscript contributed critical comments as the book progressed, and I would like to thank Michel Coconis, Grand Valley State University; Debbie Holt, Mississippi College; Sherrie Koussoudji, University of Michigan; John Nasuti, University of North Carolina, Wilmington; Frank Sansone, University of Western Florida; and Bob Siegler, University of Alabama. Special thanks go to Colin van Rooyen at the University of Natal, Durban, South Africa. He helped me shift from being too "U.S.-centric" to adopting more of an international perspective; he also offered many practical suggestions. In addition he is responsible for contributing to Chapter 11. Thank you also to the social work students at the University of Natal who offered several of the research study examples.

Other contributors include all the students who have enrolled in the research methods courses I have taught over the years in the United States and in Zimbabwe where I was a Fulbright Scholar in 1994. In many ways, the students wrote the book by teaching me how the material could be presented so that it would make sense to them.

Lisa Gebo at Brooks/Cole was wonderfully understanding and supportive. I would like to thank Leslie Parr, Loyola University, New Orleans, for the superb photographs. Leslie and I have been friends for many years; her photography continually reminds us that social work research has to do with people rather than numbers.

Finally, to my family: sons, Sam and Michael, and partner, Mike. Thanks for your great patience and support.

Science and Social Work

*"The social work research methods course was the one
I dreaded the most. I didn't want to take it."*

— social work student

INTRODUCTION

T he attitude reflected in this student's statement is not unusual in social
work classrooms. Social workers often express inherent suspicion, or even
a phobia, about research. Have you ever skimmed over articles in social work
journals because you were intimidated by the language and the displays of results? Have you ever shuddered at the thought of undertaking a research project?
If so, you are not alone. Because research is typically associated with mathemat-
ics, you may not be enthusiastic about applying what is perceived as a cold, im-
personal approach to human needs and problem solving. After all, most social
workers want to work with people, not numbers. Research, however, is simply a
means of gaining knowledge, and in social work practice, we need all the knowledge we can muster if we are to be optimally responsible to ourselves, our clients,
and our agencies.

Once you understand the research process, you will have access to a vast
amount of information in the literature. Articles that once eluded you with discussions of "validity" and "correlation coefficients" not only will become accessible, but will make available information that you can apply to your practice.

When you are equipped with the knowledge and skills to apply research
methods, you will also know how to answer many of the questions that arise in
your role as a generalist social worker, such as these:

- Are my visits to Mrs. Garcia really helping her cope with the death of her
  husband? What was her experience with the grief counseling?

- How effective is program X in providing services that support and protect
  victims of domestic violence? What are the experiences of the clients receiving these services?

- What are the needs of adolescent fathers in City Y? What is it like to be a
  teenage father in City Y?

This book emphasizes the strong links between the processes of research and
practice, helping you answer these types of questions and understand social
work research. The steps of generalist social work practice have their equivalents
in social work research.

Thus, the following chapters help you learn the steps of research in a process
similar to the way you learn the steps of practice.

Certain themes of this text will help explain research methodology and its
relevance to your practice as a generalist social worker:

- The research process and generalist practice are connected.

- You may be either a consumer or producer of research.

- Research examples throughout the book are those you will encounter as a generalist researcher.

- Different research approaches may apply depending upon the type of question being asked.

- Special issues are involved when you conduct research in agencies.

- Ethical issues are associated with each stage of the research process.

- Human diversity issues are also involved with each stage of the research process.

These overlapping themes support the mission of the book: to present research methods within a generalist social work framework.

Many new concepts are introduced in this book. These terms are boldfaced in the text where they are first defined; they are also listed in the glossary at the end of the book. Each chapter includes an overview, a summary, study/exercise questions, and a section called Infotrac College Edition. This chapter will discuss the following topics:

- common types of understanding
- conceptions of science
- the positivist approach to science
- the interpretive approach to science
- the choice of a scientific approach in social work

COMMON TYPES OF UNDERSTANDING

In our attempt to understand the world, we have developed many different ways of understanding and thinking about human behavior. These types of understanding include using values, intuition, past experience, authority, and the scientific approach. Social work can involve any or all of these types of understanding, and it is important to know about them and the role they play in generalist social work practice.

Values. **Values** are beliefs about what is right and wrong. They are closely tied to our respective cultures. For example, among many cultures, a strong value is placed on children's having respect for their elders. Among some groups, formal education is highly valued, whereas among others education within the family is emphasized.

Values can be institutionalized by religion. For example, certain values characterize Christianity, such as the Protestant belief that work is a means of gaining societal and individual worth, and the Catholic belief in the forgiveness of sins. Buddhists value reincarnation, and this belief affects how people live their present lives. Other religions involve a form of ancestor worship, whereas others strongly value the natural world around them, revering the plants and animals that make up their worlds.

Although values may be fundamental to a culture's tradition, these traditions can change over time. For example, in a number of cultures, many people now recognize that women should have the same career opportunities as men. This was not the case a hundred years ago, or even ten years ago in some countries.

Social work as a profession is based on certain values. These include fundamental notions about the most desirable relationships between people and their environment. Social work values include respect for the individual's dignity and uniqueness; recognition of the client's right to self-determination; and confidentiality.

Intuition. **Intuition** can be defined as a form of insight: when we intuitively know something, we understand it without recourse to specialized training or reasoning. Intuition may also be based on past experiences. In some cultures, intuition is a powerful tool for understanding and explaining the world. People with strong intuition may be seen as having magical powers. If they also exhibit experience and skills, they may enjoy special status in a culture. An example is the *curandera,* a woman who is perceived to possess healing powers in the Hispanic culture in the Southwest and Mexico. Similarly, in South Africa among the Zulu people, the *sangoma* is thought to be able to understand the world using special intuitive powers.

Sometimes we call upon intuition in social work practice, and it is a valid source of professional understanding (Allen-Meares & DeRoos, 1994). Although it's unlikely that we would act on intuition alone, we might use it to give ourselves leads to investigate further. For example, we might have an intuition that a child is being sexually abused. It may be hard for us to explain this feeling rationally, but the insight can provide a base or starting point for gathering information, which may or may not support the intuition.

Experience. **Experience** can be defined as firsthand, personal participation in events that provide a basis for knowledge. You often use this experience to guide present and future actions, particularly when the experience had a successful outcome (even though you may not understand why it was successful). Clearly, these experiences vary from individual to individual and according to the type of situation. Experience is highly valued in most cultures. Elders are often highly regarded because of their experience; employers often use experience as a criterion for assessing job applicants. In the practice of social work, this experience is often referred to as practice wisdom. Although highly valuable as a source of knowledge, it is risky to use practice wisdom as the sole guide to practice and as the only resource for making practice judgments.

Authority. Sometimes events and circumstances are understood by referring to outside sources of knowledge or to an **authority** on specific topics. The authority is credited with an understanding we do not directly possess. Thus, in lieu of direct understanding—whether obtained through values, intuition, or experience—we accept an explanation by virtue of our confidence in authorities.

Who or what the authority is depends upon the nature and context of the problem.

In practice, social workers rely on authority in a number of ways. We identify experts in different fields of practice and seek their opinions and knowledge, either by consulting with them personally or by reading their publications. There is vested authority in the social work professional organizations, such as the National Association of Social Workers (NASW) in the United States and the National Institute of Social Work in Great Britain. We use their authority to direct us in different areas, for instance, in adhering to a prescribed code of ethics.

Science.   Specific characteristics of science distinguish it from the other forms of understanding discussed in this section. **Science** refers to both a system for producing knowledge and the knowledge produced from that system. It is guided by a set of norms that include the following (Neuman, 1994).

Universalism.   Regardless of who conducts scientific research or where it is conducted, it is judged solely on its scientific merit.

Organized skepticism.   All scientific evidence should be challenged and questioned.

Disinterestedness.   Scientists should be able to accept other scientific evidence that runs against their position.

Communalism.   Scientific knowledge must be shared with the public, including the methods used.

Honesty.   Scientists demand honesty in all research.

As well as being characterized by these norms, science consists of theories and research methods. **Theories** describe or explain logical relationships among phenomena in our world. Theories help guide our thinking about many aspects of social work practice and include theories of human behavior, such as developmental theories, and theories underlying practice, such as systems theories. Theories are to be distinguished from values, which are concerned with what should be rather than what is. Instead, theories attempt to understand and explain logical and persistent patterns in phenomena.

Theories cannot stand alone in science, however. They need to be supported by the other component of science: **research methods.** Research methods adhere to the following principles:

1. Information is collected from *observing* the world. This observation can be carried out in different ways, but it is different from philosophizing or speculating.

2.   The steps of the research process are *systematic,* not random or haphazard.

3.   Studies should be *replicated;* repeating studies a number of times determines whether the same results will be found.

People think about the relationship between research methods and theory in different ways. Just as different types of theories explain different phenomena, so different research methods may apply to different topics. These different methods and ways of conceptualizing science will be discussed in the next section of this chapter.

Science is the focus of this text because it is the dominant type of understanding today. Many individuals and organizations throughout the world depend on science. For example, the medical profession relies on knowledge derived from the application of science. Businesses use scientifically based theories and strategies. Social work is no exception; the profession has historically recognized the contributions of the scientific approach.

Before proceeding with a more detailed description of the scientific method, it is important to note that although the scientific approach dominates the thinking in many countries, this has not always been the case. For example, Greek rationalism once dominated Western thought, offering logic as the test of truth and not relying on scientific evidence. Even today, scientific thinking is not dominant in all cultures. For example, in some American Indian cultures, direct experience of an event is the primary means of explanation. Among some other groups, including the Zulu, scientific explanations are not always accepted. For example, existence of HIV (the human immunodeficiency virus) in the body is not always seen as evidence of a person's being HIV positive (van Rooyen & Engelbrecht, 1995).

CONCEPTIONS OF SCIENCE

Although science is unified by its shared norms, the actual doing of science varies. Up until about 25 years ago, this was not the case. One model or approach was used in the social sciences; this model was broadly referred to as positivism. (Variations and other terms include logical positivism and empiricism.) **Positivism** rests on a number of different principles about how science should be done. One central principle is that science depends upon the collection of observations that support theories. These observations need to be made objectively. **Objectivity** refers to the condition in which, to the greatest extent possible, researchers' values and biases do not interfere with their study of the problem. Another principle is that the theories and observations remain separate. A theory ultimately needs to be supported by observations, resulting in laws and rules that help make sense of the world.

Over the years, however, the positivist approach and its principles have been questioned. Throughout the social sciences, including social work, positivism's claim to be the same thing as the scientific method and empirical science has raised skepticism. The questioning derives from two major sources: first, students of the history of science; and second, people who traditionally have been excluded from the scientific community, members of diverse, often minority groups, including women. Each of these sources will be discussed.

Thomas Kuhn explores the issue of values in *The Structure of Scientific Revolutions* (1970). From studying the history of science, Kuhn concluded that other factors besides specific observations and theoretical necessity lead to the emergence and acceptance of the "best theory." These other factors include values. Kuhn wrote about paradigms, defining a paradigm as "the entire constellation of beliefs, values, techniques and so on shared by members of a given [scientific] community" (Kuhn, 1970). Paradigms function as maps, directing us to the problems that are important to address, the theories that are acceptable, and the procedures needed to solve the problems. Kuhn proposed that paradigms shift over time. Paradigms reflect changing values, countering the idea that a fixed reality exists out there to be objectively observed. Objective reality appears to change as paradigms change.

An example of a paradigm shift occurred in social work during the last 50 years. In the 1920s and 1930s, the prevailing paradigm or framework for social work practice was psychoanalytic and was tied closely to a medical model. In the 1960s, a more ecological systems framework was adopted. This paradigm shift has important implications not only for how social workers conceptualize their practice but also for how research is conducted. Research questions deriving from a medical model differ substantially from those deriving from a systems perspective.

The views of diverse groups, which previously had been virtually denied access to the traditional scientific paradigm, have had an increasing impact on how science is perceived. Many argue that the types of questions asked are influenced by the social context of the researcher (Kuhn's point) and that different groups bring different experiences to the research, influencing the types of questions asked.

Many **feminist researchers** have also affected how science is viewed. They argue that men and women experience the world differently, and that the objective model of science is more compatible with men's ways of thinking. Because women see the world more in terms of relationships and interaction, feminists think that a relationship is formed between the researcher and subject, which results in the formation of a constructed reality between them. Thus, according to feminist researchers and many others, no facts exist out there that can be objectively observed (Morawski, 1997).

This questioning of the principles underlying the positivist approach to science resulted in the adoption of alternative research models by people in the social sciences, including social work. Positivism has not been rejected, but alternatives to positivism are now considered also to be part of the scientific norm. Just as positivism embraces a number of different variations, for example, postpositivism, so several models have also been developed as alternatives to positivism. **Interpretism** is the term used here to denote these alternatives. In the next two sections, the positivist and interpretist approaches will be examined, and the different principles guiding the two approaches will be discussed.

THE POSITIVIST APPROACH TO SCIENCE

Positivism is traditionally equated with science and is the approach predominantly used in the natural sciences. Some principles of this approach were described in the previous section; here positivism will be presented in more detail.

According to positivism, observations of the world can and must be carried out objectively. Biases and values must be eliminated as much as possible. Positivist research methods are designed for this purpose. Many of these methods rely on a clear distinction between the researcher and the subject, with any contact between the two being strictly formalized. In positivist research, the subject actually becomes the object of study. The science is researcher-driven (Guba, 1990); the subjects have little say about how the research is carried out.

The goal of positivist science is to search for causes of phenomena. Such a search is possible because it is assumed that the world has an order that can be discovered, such that you can explain and predict what goes on in the world. In other words, positivist researchers strive to identify factors that lead to certain events. For example, if a family lives in a rural area, has more than four children, and is headed by a single parent, there is a greater likelihood that there will be parental involvement with the children's school system. Obviously these kinds of research findings can be very useful to social work practice.

Causality means that changes in some factor or factors (A) produce variations in another factor or factors (B). The following conditions have to exist in order to infer the existence of a causal relationship:

- A statistical association has to exist between the factors. (The intricacies of statistical association will be explained later.)

- Factor or factors A must occur prior to factor or factors B.

- The relationship between the factors A and B must not be spurious. In other words, the relationship must not disappear when the effects of other factors are taken into consideration.

A deductive approach is used to build knowledge. **Deduction** involves drawing conclusions from the general to the particular. A theory generates questions; these questions are then compared with observations. For example, various researchers have investigated whether Piaget's theory of child cognitive development is valid across different cultures (Mangan, 1978), testing through observation whether Piaget's theory describes what occurs in different cultures. The results are then fed back into the theory.

Quantitative data are usually collected. To gather quantitative data, categories of the phenomena under study are created prior to investigation. Numbers are assigned to these categories, which are then statistically analyzed.

The positivist approach requires studying large numbers of subjects, because a central concern is that one should be able to **generalize** the results of the research to as large a group as possible. Findings from a study can be generalized if they can be applied to other groups rather than being specific to those in the current research. For the findings to be generalized, the subjects being studied need to be representative of the groups to which the researcher wants to generalize the findings. Certain techniques in positivist research ensure this representativeness. Large groups are also needed because the statistical tests used to analyze the quantitative information usually gathered by positivist research are designed for large numbers of subjects.

As discussed earlier, the positivist approach has come under increasing criticism in recent years, particularly in the social sciences. In general, critics have questioned whether a positivist approach is applicable when studying human beings. Recently there has even been some question about whether positivism can be used as the only research approach in the natural sciences. One main group of alternative approaches to science is offered in the next section.

A Positivist Study

Kim and Harrison (1999) examined factors influencing the quality of Korean working wives' marital relationships. The authors used data drawn from a national survey of randomly sampled adults. There were 251 women in the sample: they were all married, working, and did not have any female adult in the household except their children. They had their own incomes. Data were collected using a marital satisfaction scale and scales investigating the wife's perception of fairness in division of housework, the husband's participation in housework, and the wife's attitudes on the male provider/female housekeeper role. Marital quality was most affected by the perception of fairness on the division of housework.

THE INTERPRETIVE APPROACH TO SCIENCE

There are several branches of interpretive science, including hermeneutics, ethnomethodology, constructionism, phenomenology, naturalistic inquiry, and qualitative methods. Here we need not be concerned about the distinctions among these approaches (see Patton, 1990, for a good discussion), but rather with their overall assumptions and methods of interpretation.

For the interpretive researcher, reality is based on people's definitions of it, rather than on something externally present. The **subjective** experience is what needs to be studied, rather than the objective one. For the interpretists, observation takes on a different quality than it does for the positivists. People's behavior cannot be observed objectively; instead, the researcher and subject create a reality through their interaction. Because reality is perceived as interactive and constructed, the subject's role in the research process is more active. Instead of being researcher-driven as in the positivist approach, the research process is subject-driven. Subjects become partners with the researchers and are empowered in the process. In addition, interpretists explicitly acknowledge the researcher's biases and values. These are stated explicitly rather than ignored.

Interpretists are primarily interested in **description** rather than explanation. Because of the assumption that reality is socially constructed and is in a state of being mutually shaped, causes cannot always be definitively established. Instead the interactive reality is discovered and described.

Interpretists usually build knowledge inductively. **Induction** uses observation to examine the particulars of a phenomenon and then develops generalizations to explain or describe relationships among the particulars. Inductive reasoning involves finding patterns common to separate phenomena. For example, certain similarities may be seen in children with behavioral problems in school. After collecting case examples, a theory is developed that states the children have other characteristics in common besides the behavior problems. The majority may be found to be new immigrants whose parents do not speak English, and their behavioral problems may result from teachers' failures to appreciate the children's difficulty in making the transition from home to school. Thus, a theory is built from observations, rather than developed through generating questions that are then answered through observations.

Interpretive researchers usually collect **qualitative data.** Qualitative information involves the nonnumerical examination of phenomena, using words instead of numbers, and focuses on the underlying meanings and patterns of relationships. Often these underlying patterns are disguised if categories are formed before numerical observations are made. Analysis of qualitative information

Interpretive Research in Social Work

In Sweden Hyden (1994) studied 20 couples in which the husband repeatedly beat the wife. Hyden learned about the two parties' characterizations of the situation, their reflections on what happened, and their interpretations of the meaning of the events for their marriage. Hyden collected data over two years through intensive, detailed interviews. She then analyzed these narratives, with the focus on describing and understanding the couples' experiences.

consists of creating categories after the verbal material has been collected. When qualitative information is collected, the number of subjects in the study is often small, because the focus is on collecting in-depth information from each subject so as to understand the subject's subjective experience of the phenomena under study.

See Figure 1.1 for an illustration of the relationship between the interpretist and positivist approaches. Remember that the distinction made between the two approaches here is a fairly crude one. As mentioned earlier, different terms are

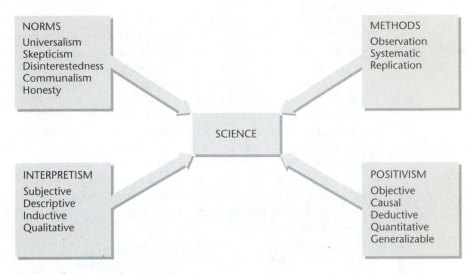

Figure 1.1   ***Different approaches to science***

often used in different ways, and what they denote is subject to considerable debate. The complex field of the philosophy of science is beyond the scope of this book.

THE CHOICE OF A SCIENTIFIC APPROACH IN SOCIAL WORK

Having described two basic approaches to science, how do you reach a decision about which one to use for social work? Over the last few years there has been quite a debate in social work about this very question. Some argue that social work will lose its credibility as a social science if it abandons the positivist approach, and that positivism is the only method that develops sound knowledge on which to base social work practice (Schinke & Nugent, 1994). Others defend and promote alternative perspectives, arguing that only they can capture the essence and meaning of social work (Heineman-Pieper, 1994; Gilchrist & Goldstein, 1994), reminding us that human behavior is complex and not always observable and measurable. Their argument is that the basic principles underlying the interpretive, alternative approaches are more compatible with social work in that they empower the subjects and reflect more accurately the diversity of opinions and perspectives within the field.

The position behind this book is that both positivism and interpretism offer the potential to build knowledge in social work. Just as different models exist to guide practice, each offering its strengths and weaknesses, so in research, different methods have advantages and disadvantages. Each is a response to different perceptions of reality. Neither positivism nor interpretism can offer the ultimate "truth."

Since both approaches offer advantages, the question becomes which one to use when. The decision depends on the type of question being asked. Some questions are more suited to a positivist research method, and some to an interpretive one. Take the three sets of questions at the beginning of this chapter. The first part of each question is asking for information that goes beyond the particular to the general. The answers need to be as generalizable as possible. The focus, at least in the first two questions, is on explanation—in other words, whether and how the programs and interventions are working. The intent of these questions is to produce information that is as objective as possible in order that funding decisions can be made and programs developed.

The second part of each question is a very different matter. The second part focuses more on the subjects' experiences, and the goal is to understand rather than explain. These questions are less concerned with objectivity and the ability to generalize the findings.

Sometimes the type of question to ask and subsequently the type of approach to use depends upon the level of knowledge we have about the area under study. For example, suppose the phenomenon under study is battered women. Initially, Walker's (1979) theory, that "learned helplessness" can explain why battered women stay in violent relationships, was developed using an interpretist approach. It was only after the theory was developed through interpretist observation that the theory was tested using a positivist approach. Thus the generation of knowledge can be seen to be cyclical, with both approaches integral to the development of concepts and theories.

In this book, both approaches will be described, and you will be given guidance about times when one might be more appropriate than the other. Both approaches require specific skills, experience, and planning. The appropriate choice depends upon the question under study and the overall purpose of the research. As with practice—where, for example, behavioral interventions require a different knowledge base and are appropriate to different circumstances from psychodynamic interventions—no one approach is always better or right.

SUMMARY

This chapter introduces the themes in this book. Different types of understanding are based on sources of knowledge including values, intuition, experience, authority, and science. The positivist and interpretist approaches to science can both offer advantages in addressing the different types of research questions asked in generalist social work.

STUDY/EXERCISE QUESTIONS

1. List the five different types of understanding presented in this chapter and discuss how you use each of them in your practice.

2. Go to a public place and observe the people for 15 minutes. Report back to your class. Note the similarities and differences in what each student

observed. Discuss the implications of these observations for the concept of objectivity.

INFOTRAC COLLEGE EDITION

1. Search for *positivism* and examine how the articles refer to and use this term.
2. Search for *feminist research* and discuss this concept in class and its use in social work research.

REFERENCES

Allen-Meares, P., & DeRoos, Y. S. (1994). Are practitioner intuition and empirical evidence equally valid sources of professional knowledge? In W. W. Hudson & P. S. Nurius (Eds.). *Controversial issues in social work research*. Boston: Allyn & Bacon.

Gilchrist, L. D., & Goldstein, H. (1994). Is research training important to the development of analytic reasoning and critical judgment in social work? In W. W. Hudson & P. S. Nurius (Eds.). *Controversial issues in social work research*. Boston: Allyn & Bacon.

Guba, E. G. (Ed.). (1990). *The paradigm dialog*. Newbury Park, CA: Sage.

Heineman-Pieper, M. (1994). Science, not scientism: The robustness of naturalistic clinical research. In E. Sherman and W. J. Reid (Eds.). *Qualitative research in social work*. New York: Columbia University Press.

Hyden, M. (1994). Woman battering as a marital act: Interviewing and analysis in context. In C. K. Riessman (Ed.). *Qualitative studies in social work research*. Newbury Park, CA: Sage.

Kim, Y., & Harrison, D. F. (1999). Housework, general role attitudes, perceived fairness, and marital quality of Korean working wives. *Aretê, 23* (2), 21–32.

Kuhn, T. (1970). *The structure of scientific revolutions*. Chicago: University of Chicago Press.

Mangan, J. (1978). Piaget's theory and cultural differences: The case for value based modes of cognition. *Human Development, 21,* 170–189.

Neuman, W. L. (1994). *Social research methods*. Boston: Allyn & Bacon.

Patton, M. Q. (1990). *Qualitative evaluation and research methods*. Thousand Oaks, CA: Sage Publications.

Schinke, S. P., & Nugent, W. R. (1994). Are some research methodologies inherently more worthy of professional endorsement than others? In W. W. Hudson & P. S. Nurius (Eds.). *Controversial issues in social work research*. Boston: Allyn & Bacon.

van Rooyen, C., & Engelbrecht, B. (1995). The impact of culture on HIV/AIDS social work service delivery: Emerging themes from a study in progress. *Social Work Practice, 3.95,* 2–8.

Walker, L. (1979). *The battered woman*. New York: Harper & Row.

Research and Generalist
Social Work Practice

■

O ne problem in understanding the research process is that it is often viewed in isolation rather than being closely linked to practice. In this chapter the link between research and practice will be explored, and close parallels between the practice process and the research process will be examined. This chapter discusses the following:

- generalist practice
- the purpose of research in generalist social work practice
- research roles in generalist practice
- research and generalist practice processes
- values and ethics in research and practice
- research and human diversity

GENERALIST PRACTICE

Before discussing how research is linked to generalist practice, we need to explain what is meant by **generalist social work practice.** From its inception social work has been committed to addressing individual competencies and implementing social change. Today generalist practice is the form of social work practice taught in undergraduate programs in the United States and in many other parts of the world as a basis for professional social work education.

Over the years various views have developed about what constitutes generalist practice. Several writers have tried to clarify its components and have proposed different conceptualizations. Miley, O'Melia, and DuBois (1998) suggest that the generalist approach rests on four major premises:

- Human behavior is closely connected to the physical and social environment.
- Enhancing human functioning depends upon changing the system itself and altering other systems.
- Work with any level, whether macro or micro, involves similar social work processes.
- Generalist social workers have a responsibility to work for just social policies and to conduct and apply research.

THE PURPOSE OF RESEARCH IN GENERALIST SOCIAL WORK PRACTICE

As generalist social workers, why do we need to be concerned with research? Given that the dominant way of understanding the world is through science, building a strong research base for practice helps legitimize the profession and gives it credibility to others. Relying on research, however, does not mean dismissing other forms of understanding. Beyond its legitimizing role, research fulfills a number of other functions by promoting a strong knowledge base, fiscal and ethical responsibility, and empowerment of clients. Each of these will be discussed in turn.

Scientific Knowledge

Scientific knowledge is built by using research methods to develop and refine theories. In the last chapter two different research approaches were discussed. Each builds knowledge rather differently than the other. The positivist approach generally uses the deductive method of building theory, deducing premises from the theory and testing those premises. The interpretist approach uses the inductive method, in which observations are made. From those systematic observations, theories are built.

The development of knowledge through research is a central function of research in social work. This knowledge about the extent, nature, and causes of social problems, and the effectiveness of various interventions and programs, significantly enhances social work practice. Without this research-based knowledge, social workers would have to rely on the other sources of understanding described in the last chapter. Although each of these sources has its own contributions to make to the generalist practice, this form of social work would suffer without scientifically based knowledge.

For example, if you were employed in Child Protective Services as an investigator, a critical part of the way in which you would make decisions on family intervention would be based on assessment tools. These tools, such as Structured Decision Making (Myers, 1999), are based on previous research and are tested using scientific methods. Without such tools, your decision might be based on your authority as an investigator, your intuition, your values, or your past experience with similar situations—all important components in the final decision but weakened by the absence of the scientific component.

Entire programs are developed on the basis of research. For example, early intervention programs for new parents are based on research that indicates that parent training and support can help reduce the incidence of child abuse and neglect. The training itself is based on theories of child development that are supported by research.

On a larger scale, major welfare reform decisions need to be based on information gathered from previous studies. For example, Chilman (1995) critically reviewed studies concerning the working poor. As a result of this review, she proposed further legislation to help move welfare recipients from economic dependency to self-sufficiency through employment.

Ethical Issues

Social workers need to be knowledgeable about research for ethical reasons. Social workers are ethically responsible for providing the best possible services to their clients. In the United States, the NASW (1997) Code of Ethics specifically addresses this issue.

- Social workers should educate themselves, their students, and their colleagues about responsible research practices.

- Social workers should monitor and evaluate policies, the implementation of programs, and practice interventions.

- Social workers should promote and facilitate evaluation and research to contribute to the development of knowledge.

- Social workers should critically examine and keep current with emerging knowledge relevant to social work and fully use evaluation and research evidence in their professional practice.

To abide by the NASW Code of Ethics, the social worker needs to be proficient in social work research methods.

Fiscal Accountability

As long as social work practice is predominantly funded by government and charitable contributions, accountability will be a critical issue in the field. In recent years, fiscal accountability has become even more important. Funds allocated to the human services are decreasing rapidly, and different organizations must compete for smaller and smaller pools of money.

Two aspects of social accountability must be considered. First, social workers are expected to demonstrate that they are spending money responsibly—this in-

Ensuring Fiscal Responsibility through Research

Hagen and Lurie (1995) examined the Job Opportunity and Basic Skills Training Program (JOBS) introduced as part of the Family Support Act of 1988, which attempted to help move welfare organizations from promoting welfare dependency to self-sufficiency. The study examined the views of frontline workers and found that they strongly support the JOBS program and its goals. They did have reservations about the program's effectiveness, suggesting that education and training services were inadequately funded and that their local communities lacked employment opportunities.

cludes the assurance that a social program's goals are being met and that funds are being distributed in the most efficient way to meet those goals. The agency or the individual practitioner may be responsible for this accountability. Second, generalist social workers are often called upon to establish new services and programs, particularly in rural areas. To do so, and to solicit funds for this purpose, you need to substantiate your claim by providing clear evidence of need and a strong basis in research for the proposed program.

Empowering Clients

Not only can research be indirectly empowering to clients—through building knowledge and ensuring fiscal and ethical accountability—but certain research methods can be directly empowering as well. Subjects (often clients) can be directly involved in the research process from planning to implementation. Some research strategies involve clients more than others. We discussed in the last chapter how the interpretive approach tends to be more subject- rather than researcher-driven. This tendency derives in part from the assumption that meaning emerges from the interaction of subject and researcher rather than from the researcher's objective observations alone. Through use of the interpretive approach, clients become empowered because they are not being used as subjects but instead as direct participants in the research.

Another opportunity for clients' involvement in research, and subsequent empowerment, is through **participatory action research.** This approach to research has three aims, all intended to empower clients. The first is to produce knowledge and action directly useful to groups of people. A second aim is to encourage people to construct and use their own knowledge for empowerment. The third aim is to promote collaboration throughout the research process. Participatory action research originated and grew in developing countries, where it continues to be a standard approach to research. Increasingly, participatory action research is being adopted in other parts of the world. In the United States, corporations have used this type of research as a way of motivating workers to adopt new productivity strategies. For example, in a case study of Xerox Corporation, White (1991) demonstrated how labor, management, and the researcher worked as a team to help increase productivity, instead of the researcher simply going in with a plan and recommendations from management's perspective. Participatory action research is particularly compatible with generalist social work in that the approach emphasizes empowering systems of different sizes, from individuals to whole communities. Usually, the people under study participate actively with the researcher throughout the research process, from the initial design to the final presentation and dissemination of results. Note that a number of different research methods can be used within the participatory action research framework, including either the positivist or interpretist approach.

RESEARCH ROLES IN GENERALIST PRACTICE

As we have seen, generalist social work practice is based in research, and practitioners must be able to assess or examine their own practice in terms of research. To accomplish this goal, the generalist social worker needs to adopt two roles with respect to research: the consumer and the producer.

The Consumer

As was discussed earlier, the scientific approach is essential in building a knowledge base for social work. To use this knowledge in an informed manner, social workers need to understand research methods so that they can evaluate the extent of a theory's research base. Even if the theory has apparently been validated and supported by research, there is no guarantee this research is of high quality. A social worker who is knowledgeable about research can better evaluate the quality of that research base. In their users' guide to social science research, Causer, Cook, and Crouch (1991) point out that many mistakes and errors occur even in published research. Your research instructor can undoubtedly confirm this statement.

Critical analysis of research is also useful in the social worker's assessment of specific practice techniques. For example, home-based services are commonly provided by generalist practitioners, and there exists a whole body of literature and research about these services. The practitioner informed about research can turn to this research for practice guidelines. Using research in this way, the practitioner may be able to answer a question such as "How do I know whether home visits to 85-year-old Mrs. Garcia will help prevent her being placed in a nursing home?" This ability to evaluate theories is known as the consumer function of research knowledge. See Chapter 15 for details of how to consult research to enhance practice.

The Producer

The second reason social workers need to know about research methods is the most obvious one. Armed with this knowledge, social workers can then use the methods directly in their own practice to answer questions that arise. This ability to use research methods is vital whenever answers cannot be found in the existing literature, as is frequent in social work, whether or not the social worker is engaged in generalist practice. Social workers often need to carry out their own research on the effectiveness of many interventions they use. In addition, generalist social workers are often required to demonstrate the need to provide new services or to improve existing services. Clearly, this type of inquiry also demands a knowledge and implementation of research methods.

In sum, generalist social workers, acting as producers of research, can begin to build new knowledge for practice. Though such a task may seem overwhelming to you at this point, this book will describe how to produce research step-by-step. You will be provided with the tools to become not only a producer of research, but also a critical and intelligent consumer.

Remember that social workers use many of the skills and techniques described in this book routinely, without formal research training or education.

Social workers act as consumers of the literature, for example, when they read reports and gather relevant information. As producers, social workers gather data from multiple sources. In addition, they document progress toward clients' goals, write reports, and engage in many other activities that, as we will see, are all included in the larger activity of research.

RESEARCH AND GENERALIST PRACTICE PROCESSES

Social workers are often intimidated by research, in part because they think it involves types of knowledge and skills that are very different from those of practice. In fact, as we are about to see, the processes of practice and research are very similar, particularly for generalist social work practice.

Although the generalist perspective is conceptualized in different ways, authors of generalist social work texts are in basic agreement on a general process for practice. This process is usually conceptualized sequentially, as consisting of progressive stages leading to certain goals. This concept originated with one of the founding mothers of social work practice theory, Helen Harris Perlman (1957), who proposed "operations" as part of the practice process. Others later modified these operations; for example, Pincus and Minahan (1973) described "guideposts for the process"; Schulman (1992) and Egan (1994) proposed "stages" or "phases"; and O'Neil McMahon (1996) discussed the "general method." The practice process itself was generally referred to as the "problem-solving process"—now generalist writers have reframed the idea as *empowerment-based practice* (Miley, O'Melia, & DuBois, 1998) that focuses on strengths rather than problems. The empowerment-based practice approach and its associated steps follow very closely those of research.

Forming Partnerships

A critical step in social work practice is the building of the relationship between the social worker and the client, a relationship that respects the uniqueness of the client. Miley, Omelia, and DuBois (1998) state that forming partnerships is "the process whereby a worker and client System define their working relationship in ways which reflect the purposes of social work and standards of ethical codes. For the process to be empowering, social workers and client systems resolve power and authority dilemmas by defining their relationship in an egalitarian way, maximizing their respective contributions" (pp. 101–102). This establishment of a relationship is also critical in social work research. As stated earlier, one of the purposes of research is to empower clients, and one way of accomplishing this is to involve the clients directly through participatory action research. Participatory action research is rapidly becoming the preferred approach to social work research. For example, if your agency wants to assess some of the problems and difficulties faced by children with AIDS, an important first step is to establish relationships with some of the professionals and family members who work and live with these children. In this way they can become partners in your research.

Articulating Challenges

Social workers used to refer to this as the preliminary statement of the problem, but now we tend to conceptualize problems in social work as "challenges." In this stage of the practice process clients and social workers develop a mutual understanding of the situations that bring the clients to seek help. Similarly, in research, the first step after developing a relationship with the client is to *decide on the question*. For example, consider the issue of children with AIDS. Instead of simply conceptualizing the question as "the problem of children with AIDS," seek greater clarity. For example, the question might be stated: "To what extent are the needs of children with AIDS being met?" And then framing from a strengths perspective, "What are some of the strengths of this population?" As we proceed with the research, new insights occur and new information is gathered, which in turn may lead to a reformulation of the challenge. For example, the question may change to focus on evaluating the services of a specific agency: "To what extent is program X serving the needs of children with AIDS?" This question may then become even more specific: "How effective is program X in advocating for children with AIDS?" Or from more of a strengths perspective: "What are some of the characteristics of programs that successfully serve children with AIDS?" This issue of deciding on the question is discussed further in Chapter 3.

Defining Directions

The next step in practice is for the worker and client to "orient their work together toward a specific purpose" (p. 102). This helps establish a specific direction for their work together. The process of definition also occurs in research and is known as the *developing the question* stage. Clear definitions of terms and explicit statements of the assumptions that underlie the research question help reduce bias. This is an important consideration whether one is adopting the objective stance of positivism or the empathic neutrality of interpretism. Although assumptions can be made at all stages of the research process, clearly stating what is assumed during the initial stages of the research is particularly useful. One strategy is to state very carefully the nature of the question and to identify its different components. In our example on children with AIDS, we would need to define the term *advocating*. We may have a number of different assumptions about this function of social work, but how does the agency see this role and how can it be defined so that all concerned are in agreement? What do we mean by effective or successful? That all children with AIDS referred to the agency receive advocacy services? Half the children? How are children with AIDS defined? Are we concerned with children who are infected with the HIV virus or those with AIDS symptoms? What ages will be included in this study? (This issue of assumptions will be further discussed in Chapter 4.)

Identifying Strengths

In practice, the social worker collects this information recognizing that the identification of client strengths is critical if change is to occur. Strengths can be found in interpersonal relationships, culture, organizational networks, and community connections. In research the collection of information is also critical. It consists of three tasks: *data collection, sampling,* and *design.* For the project concerning children with AIDS, data collection might include interviewing or administering questionnaires to the children's caretakers. The sample might be relatively small, perhaps only ten or so caretakers, and thus their selection will need careful consideration. The research design might include a comparison group of caretakers of children with AIDS who do not receive services from program X, which provides services specifically to those with AIDS, but instead receive services from a more generic type of agency. Each of these research steps will be discussed further in Chapters 5, 6, 7, 8, and 9.

Analyzing Resource Capabilities

In practice, this stage is often known as assessment and includes examining the information or data collected. Workers and clients jointly assess personal, interpersonal, familial, group, organizational, community, societal, and political systems looking at the interrelationships within the environment. Miley, O'Melia, and DuBois (1998) state, "This analysis transforms the abundant information generated through assessment into a coherent, organized foundation of information on which to construct a plan of action" (p. 103).

The next step in research is known as *analysis* and involves a process similar to that undertaken in practice. If quantitative data are collected, statistical techniques are used. However, with qualitative data, the information is sorted and categorized so that meanings will emerge. As in practice, the analysis step needs to be carried out systematically and conscientiously to avoid misinterpreting the results. Specific techniques are used to ensure bias-free results. Results often generate new questions and issues much as plans are generated in practice.

Analysis of the data about children with AIDS may reveal that those in program X thought they had received more advocacy services than those from the comparison program Y, but that those in program X were less satisfied with the types of medical services available to them. Another phase of the research might include examining the source of this dissatisfaction and investigating whether this dissatisfaction extends to the adults with AIDS who receive services from program X. Organization of data and data analysis will be further discussed in Chapters 10, 11, 12, and 13.

Framing Solutions

In practice, the social worker takes the results of the assessment and develops a plan of action that often involves the formulation of goals.

The comparable step in research is the writing of the report, which formally presents the analyzed results along with a description of the research method. The research report includes recommendations for further research, a logical extension of the process in which analysis of results generates new questions. An important part of the report in social work research is the section on the implications of the research for practice: How can the findings help social workers in the field? The researcher may recommend further research into reasons for the dissatisfaction with medical services, and, more specifically, into the medical needs of children with AIDS. Report writing is further discussed in Chapter 14.

Activating Resources, Creating Alliances, and Expanding Opportunities

This stage in practice is often known as *intervention* or the *implementation of the plan*. Implementation is the "action" part of social work practice. Part of this process involves developing alliances through collaboration with clients and between the clients themselves. Also, the worker continues to create opportunities at the macro level, including creating resources that address social justice. Unfortunately, this step tends to be downplayed in research, although research findings are of little use unless they are implemented in some way. In research this stage is known as the *utilization of research*.

Ideally, going back to our example, workers in program X would take the findings from the research and try to monitor more closely their medical referrals for the children, perhaps undertaking a more thorough follow-up with the families to ensure that the children's medical needs are being met. Chapter 15 discusses the various ways in which research can be utilized.

Recognizing Success and Integrating Gains

The last step in practice is often known as *evaluation* and *termination*. Miley, O'Melia, and DuBois (1998) refer to it as recognition of success and integrating gains. Perhaps because it comes last, this stage is often given little attention. We may find ourselves simply moving onto the next case instead. In research this step involves evaluating the research by discussing its limitations and generally assessing its overall quality.

For example, one problem with the project concerning children and AIDS might have been that the caretakers were influenced in their questionnaire answers about satisfaction with medical treatment. Wanting to please the researcher, the caretakers might have covered up some of the problems they experienced in caring for the children. Thus the answers might have been biased, making the program appear to be more effective than it was.

This step of evaluating the research will be further discussed in Chapter 15. See Table 2.1 for a comparison of these steps of research and practice.

VALUES AND ETHICS IN RESEARCH AND PRACTICE

Besides the similarities in the processes of research and practice, there is a similarity in their values and ethics. Values relating to social workers' conduct and responsibilities to their clients, colleagues, employers, profession, and society are all reflected in social workers' ethical codes. In the United States, the NASW Code of Ethics (1997) includes ethical standards that apply to research. Many of these

Table 2.1   **The relationship between research and practice**

Practice	Research
Forming partnerships	Using participatory methods
Articulating challenges	Deciding on the question
Defining directions	Developing the question
Identifying strengths	Collecting the data, sampling, and design
Analyzing resource capabilities	Organizing and analyzing the data
Framing solutions	Research writing
Activating resources, creating alliances, and expanding opportunities	Utilization of research findings
Recognizing success and integrating gains	Evaluation of research

ethical standards are directly related to the values that underlie practice, values such as confidentiality, privacy, and self-determination. Some of these standards were listed earlier in this chapter. Here are the remaining standards:

■   Social workers engaged in evaluation or research should carefully consider possible consequences and should follow guidelines developed for the protection of evaluation and research participants. Appropriate institutional review boards should be consulted.

■   Social workers engaged in evaluation or research should obtain voluntary and written informed consent from participants, when appropriate, without any implied or actual deprivation or penalty for refusal to participate; without undue inducement to participate; and with due regard for participants' well-being, privacy, and dignity. Informed consent should include information about the nature, extent, and duration of the participation requested and disclosure of the risks and benefits of participation in the research.

■   When evaluation or research participants are incapable of giving informed consent, social workers should provide an appropriate explanation to the participants, obtain the participants' assent to the extent they are able, and obtain written consent from an appropriate proxy.

■   Social workers should never design or conduct evaluation or research that does not use consent procedures, such as certain forms of naturalistic observation and archival research, unless rigorous and responsible review of the research has found it to be justified because of its prospective scientific, educational, or applied value and unless equally effective alternative procedures that do not involve waiver of consent are not feasible.

- Social workers should inform participants of their right to withdraw from evaluation and research at any time without penalty.
- Social workers should take appropriate steps to ensure that participants in evaluation and research have access to appropriate supportive services.
- Social workers engaged in evaluation or research should protect participants from unwarranted physical or mental distress, harm, danger, or deprivation.
- Social workers engaged in the evaluation of services should discuss collected information only for professional purposes and only with people professionally concerned with this information.
- Social workers engaged in evaluation or research should ensure the anonymity or confidentiality of participants and of the data obtained from them. Social workers should inform participants of any limits of confidentiality, the measures that will be taken to ensure confidentiality, and when any records containing research data will be destroyed.
- Social workers who report evaluation and research results should protect participants' confidentiality by omitting identifying information unless proper consent has been obtained authorizing disclosure.
- Social workers should report evaluation and research findings accurately. They should not fabricate or falsify results and should take steps to correct any errors later found in published data using standard publication methods.
- Social workers engaged in evaluation or research should be alert to and avoid conflicts of interest and dual relationships with participants, should inform participants when a real or potential conflict of interest arises, and should take steps to resolve the issue in a manner that makes participants' interests primary.

These values and ethics guiding research will be discussed throughout the book. Each chapter will include a section on ethics and how ethical standards relate to the topic being discussed in that chapter.

RESEARCH AND HUMAN DIVERSITY

By human diversity we mean the whole spectrum of differences among populations, including but not limited to gender, ethnicity, age, and sexual orientation. In practice we recognize the importance of understanding and appreciating group differences so we will not impose inappropriate expectations; we must also account for these differences in research. We discussed earlier that an important step in both research and practice is to clarify our assumptions. If we are not aware of our assumptions regarding certain groups, these assumptions can be disguised and undisclosed, causing biases in the research itself. Clarifying assumptions is only one way in which human diversity issues should be considered in the research process. As with ethics, each chapter in this book will discuss human diversity issues as they relate to research.

SUMMARY

In conclusion, research and practice follow parallel processes in approaching problems. When research methods are viewed in this way, they appear far less intimidating. We all know that practice can be frustrating; in truth, so can research. Just as practice has its great rewards, however, so does research. The road at times is a rocky one, but ultimately we all benefit.

STUDY/EXERCISE QUESTIONS

1. Discuss some of the ways you may find yourself engaged in research as a generalist social worker.

2. Select a research article from a social work journal. How could the findings from this research help you in your practice?

3. Select a research article from a social work journal. How would you change the research to make it more participatory?

4. Imagine you were asked to evaluate the program in which you were working (use your field placement as an example). How would you justify the importance of this research to a fellow student?

INFOTRAC COLLEGE EDITION

1. Search for *participatory action research* and describe the advantages to both the researcher and the participant in conducting this type of research.

REFERENCES

Causer, J., Cook, K. H., & Crouch, W. W. (1991). *Evaluating information: A guide for users of social science research.* New York: McGraw-Hill.

Chilman, C. (1995). Programs and policies for working poor families: Major trends and some research issues. *Social Service Review, 69* (3), 515–544.

Egan, G. (1994). *The skilled helper: A problem management approach to helping.* Pacific Grove, CA: Brooks/Cole.

Hagan, J. L., & Lurie, I. (1995). Implements JOBS: A view from the front line. *Families in Society, 4,* 230–238.

Miley, K., O'Melia, M., & Dubois, B. (1995). *Generalist social work practice.* Boston: Allyn & Bacon.

Myers, B. (1999). Implementing actuarial risk assessment: Policy decisions and field practice in New Mexico. Proceedings from the Twelfth National Round Table of CPS Child Risk Assessment. American Humane Association, Boulder, Colorado.

National Association of Social Workers. (1997). NASW Code of Ethics. *NASW News, 25,* 24–25.

O'Neil McMahon, M. (1996). *The general method of social work practice.* Boston: Allyn & Bacon.

Perlman, H. H. (1957). *Social casework: A problem solving process.* Chicago: University of Chicago Press.

Pincus, A., & Minahan, A. (1973). *Social work practice: Model and method.* Itasca, IL: Peacock.

Schulman, L. (1992). *The skills of helping individuals, families, and groups.* Itasca, IL: Peacock.

White, W. (1991). *Participatory action research.* Thousand Oaks, CA: Sage.

Deciding on the Question

"**H**ow do I know whether this is a *real* research question? Is this what a research question should look like? I can't quite pin down what it is I need to find out." You will find yourself asking these kinds of questions when you are first confronted with the task of deciding on the research question. As a generalist social worker, you may not always participate in deciding on the question; this decision is often made within the agency prior to your involvement in the research. You need to be familiar with the procedure involved in deciding the question, however, so that you can understand (as in practice) how one step in the process leads to the next. You also need to learn this research stage so that you can evaluate your own practice, a process that is described later in this chapter.

As discussed in Chapter 2, the first step of the research process—deciding on the question—is equivalent to one of the first steps in practice, articulating challenges. This step, in research as in practice, is one of the most challenging. Often, this step is ongoing and involves continuously reworking and reevaluating the process.

This chapter will discuss the following topics:

- sources of questions
- research strategies
- types of questions
- the agency and deciding on the question
- ethical issues in deciding on the question
- human diversity issues in deciding on the question

SOURCES OF QUESTIONS

For generalist social workers, research problems or questions usually are determined by their agencies; these questions are directed at solving problems that arise in practice and are intended to produce practical outcomes. This type of research is known as **applied research.** When research is instead aimed at satisfying our intellectual curiosity, even if the results eventually will be applied to help solve practice problems, it is known as **pure research.**

An example will help clarify this definition. You are employed in an agency where a large proportion of the clients are victims of spousal abuse, and you see this as a growing problem. A pure research question would concern the causes of spousal abuse per se. As a generalist social worker employed in the agency, however, you would ask applied research questions, such as how well your agency serves the victims or what other services are needed by this client population.

If this distinction between pure and applied research still seems difficult to understand, some would argue that is because the distinction does not really exist in social work. Social work is in itself an applied field, so any question related to social work in any way will be some type of applied question. Some research, though, is more immediately applicable to social work practice than other research is. Rothman and Thomas (1994) actively promote forms of social work research called **developmental research** (also called **intervention research**). This type of research focuses on developing innovative interventions; research is used to design the interventions, test their effectiveness, and modify them based on recommendations that emerge from testing.

Developmental Research (Intervention Research)

Dore, Nelson-Zlupko, and Kaufman (1999) stated that they could not find any school-based interventions aimed at latency-aged children from drug-abusing families so they designed and tested a model curriculum to use with children in schools located in high drug-use communities. The authors found that the children needed strategies and skills for working with their environment. The group participants responded well to structure, predictability, and affirmation, and their classroom behavior improved and measures of self-worth increased.

Personal experiences also come into play in the formulation of research questions. For example, you may find yourself working with a number of physically challenged young adults in the agency in which you are employed. You become aware that some specialized type of housing needs to be established for these clients, and after consulting with your supervisor, you decide that it would make sense to carry out a needs assessment to determine the extent and type of need in the community. Your interest also may have stemmed in part from the fact that a member of your family is physically challenged.

The following is a checklist you can use to test whether the question you are thinking about can be successfully answered.

- Does this topic really interest me? For example, am I choosing this topic to please someone else or do I have a genuine interest in it?

- Do I think that this is a problem that is appropriate for scientific inquiry? For instance, if the question is along the lines of whether child abuse is morally wrong, the question may not be a suitable topic for scientific inquiry, as we discussed in Chapter 1.

- Do I have enough resources available to investigate this topic? For example, will the topic require large samples that will be costly to access or many time-consuming interviews? Do I or other people have the time and money to pursue the topic appropriately?

- Will this topic raise ethical problems? For instance, will the questions to be asked of participants arouse potentially harmful emotions? Will the subjects feel coerced to participate?

- Will I be able to secure permission—from the agency, community, clients, and so on—to carry out this research?

- Are the results of the research going to be useful and have implications for the practice of social work?

Chapter 3

RESEARCH STRATEGIES

Before you embark on the actual formulation of a research question, you need to identify the general research strategy that the question will adopt. The research strategy is determined by three factors: (1) the intent or goal of the research; (2) the amount of information we already have on the topic to be investigated; and (3) the intended audience. Two main strategies can be identified: descriptive and explanatory. Each of these will now be examined.

Descriptive Research

Descriptive research describes, records, and reports phenomena. Descriptive research can provide important fundamental information for establishing and developing social programs, but it is not primarily concerned with causes. Many surveys trying to determine the extent of a particular social problem—for example, the extent of child sexual abuse—are descriptive. In fact, an entire approach to research, called **survey research,** focuses on describing the characteristics of a group; this type of research will be discussed further in Chapter 5. Another example of descriptive research is students' recording their initial observations of an agency or case by keeping a log or journal. One method associated with descriptive research is **ethnography,** a method of describing a culture or society that is used in much anthropological research.

The interpretive approach lends itself very well to descriptive research. Because the interpretive approach generally uses words (qualitative data) rather than numbers or concepts that can be quantified (quantitative data), rich descriptions of phenomena can be produced. Often these descriptions emerge after carefully selecting the participants in the research—often, those who are best informed about the phenomenon being described. If the intention, however, is for the results to be generalized to wider populations and used as the justification for new or expanded services, the positivist approach would probably be more suitable. Here it would be more useful to collect relatively objective quantitative

Interpretive Descriptive Research

Gregg (1994) explored the perceptions of women about their pregnancies. She conducted 31 interviews with pregnant women. Gregg wanted to explore the experience of pregnancy from the women's perspective. First she found that many of the women she interviewed thought that it is after all possible to be a "little bit pregnant." They thought of pregnancy as starting prior to conception, when they were considering pregnancy. She also found that these women described pregnancy as resembling a "risk-laden obstacle course," rather than a relaxing, totally fulfilling experience. In this study new concepts emerged as a result of using an interpretive approach.

Positivist Descriptive Research

Whipple (1999) researched the effectiveness of a community-based parent education and support program that was aimed at reducing the risk factors for child physical abuse. Based on previous research, selected risk factors were examined in this study. Three unstructured programs and one ongoing support group, which differed in duration and intensity, were assessed. Data were collected using self-report questionnaires, staff assessments, and observational home visits over a 15-month period. Instruments were group administered to the participating parents by the program staff both before and after these parents participated in the program. Results revealed that parents who participated in the more intensive program made the strongest gains.

data describing the phenomena (rather than seeking people's subjective experiences) and to select the participants in the research according to how well they represent the population under study.

You will encounter descriptive research in social work journals. A considerable amount of policy evaluation and analysis is of this type. As a generalist practitioner, you may also be engaged in descriptive research. You could be asked to present some descriptive data relating to your agency (number of clients served, types of problems, and so forth) or to your community (the proportion of the population living below the poverty line, for example). Your supervisor may also require you to keep a journal describing your activities in the agency.

Explanatory Research

Explanatory research aims at providing explanations of events in order to identify causes. This type of research requires the formulation of a **hypothesis**—a statement about the relationships between certain factors. Hypotheses

A Hypothesis

Nash, Rounds, and Bowen (1992) studied the relationship between the level of parent involvement on early childhood intervention teams and social worker membership on the team. They stated: "This article hypothesizes that the presence of a social worker as a regular team member will be associated with a significantly higher level of parent involvement. It also hypothesized that this association will remain significant regardless of organizational or community setting" (p. 95). Both hypotheses were supported by the evidence resulting from the research.

Explanatory Research

Rittner and Dozier (2000) studied the effects of court-ordered substance abuse treatment in the cases of 447 children in kinship care while under child protective services supervision. The effects of court orders on the duration of service and on numbers of placements were studied. Results were mixed and indicated that levels of compliance with the mandated treatment did not influence rates of reabuse or duration of service. Court orders affected the number of caretakers and placement experienced by the children.

usually have an "if *x*, then *y*" structure: for example, "if the ethnicity of the group leader is the same as the client, then success in the group will be more likely."

As discussed in Chapter 1, the following conditions need to be met in order to establish causality, which is central to explanatory research. First, *two factors must be associated with one another*. Usually this association is established empirically. For example, you might determine that there is a relationship between the grade B.S.W. students received in the practice class and their grade in the field. That relationship, however, does not necessarily mean that the practice grade caused the success in the field. The other conditions of causality also need to be met. The second condition is that *the cause precedes the effect in time*. In our example, you would need to demonstrate that students completed their practice courses prior to entering the field. The third element of causality is that *the relationship between the factors cannot be explained by other factors*. In our example, it is possible that other factors, such as past experience, had as much impact on field performance as the practice course grade.

In each step of the research process, explanatory research tries to address these conditions of causality. In reality, meeting all three conditions is often extremely difficult; the best we can expect is that only one or two of the conditions will be met. A positivist approach is often most appropriate to use when testing hypotheses and carrying out explanatory research. Qualitative data, however, can often be used to add depth and detail to the findings and so assist in the acceptance or rejection of the hypothesis.

Explanatory research is found in the social work literature, and as generalist practitioners, you may be directly involved in such research. Usually, you would not undertake such research alone but would participate as a member of a team—for example, in determining the effectiveness of a particular program or agency.

Exploratory Research

Beyond the strategies of explanatory and descriptive research, another strategy, **exploratory research,** deserves mention. This strategy is undertaken when very little is known about the topic under study. Such studies can adopt either

Exploratory Research

Shongwe (1996) explored social workers' thoughts about their involvement in primary health care, that is, community-based preventive care, a feature of the new health care policy in South Africa. When the study was carried out, there had been increasing pressure to involve social workers in urban areas in primary health care, which represented a shift from previous social work practice. This research was an important exploratory step in finding out social workers' feelings about the issue.

an explanatory or a descriptive strategy. Either an interpretist or a positivist approach is appropriate with exploratory research, although exploratory research is often associated with the former. Exploratory research often determines a study's feasibility and raises questions to be investigated by more extensive studies using either the descriptive or the explanatory strategy.

For example, you might suspect that the ethnicity of a group leader is important for success in the support group you have organized for children of alcoholics. The group leader is Puerto Rican. After interviewing some of the clients in the group to get their opinions, you find that the Puerto Rican clients were more likely than the others to state that the group was successful. Based on these results from the exploratory study, you plan to undertake more extensive research to evaluate the impact of the group leader's ethnicity on clients' perceptions of success.

TYPES OF QUESTIONS

This section will explore the different types of applied research questions that are asked in generalist practice. The following questions from Chapter 1 provide examples of these different types of questions.

These questions evaluate the effectiveness of individual practice and are known as **practice evaluations.**

1. How effective is the grief counseling I am providing to Mrs. Garcia in helping her to cope with the death of her husband?
2. How is Mrs. Garcia experiencing the grief counseling I have been providing?

These questions evaluate the effectiveness of a program and are known as **program evaluations.**

1. How effective is program X in providing services that support and protect victims of domestic violence?
2. What are the experiences of the clients who receive services from program X?

These questions describe the extent of a social problem and are known as **needs assessments.**

1. What are the needs of adolescent fathers in city Y?
2. What is it like to be a teenage father in city Y?

Note that two examples are offered for each type of question. As we discussed in Chapter 1, the first example for each type of question is asked in a way that is more appropriate for a positivist approach—for example, "Program X received additional funding for next year. How can we show our program is effective and deserves more money?" The second example for each type of question is more appropriate for an interpretist approach—for example, "In what areas could our program be improved and what are our clients' experiences with the program?" The choice of which type of question to ask depends on the level of knowledge that already exists on the topic under study and the overall purpose of the research.

These types of questions, practice evaluations, program evaluations, and needs assessments, represent the different types of applied research encountered by generalist social workers in their practice. Although these questions appear diverse, they can be matched up with the three purposes of generalist social work as described by Baer and Federico (1978):

1. To enhance people's problem-solving, coping, and developmental capacities
2. To promote effective and humane operation of systems that provide people with resources and services
3. To link people with systems that provide them with resources, services, and opportunities

The question evaluating individual practice is the one asking about visits to Mrs. Garcia. This question examines our ability to enhance a person's (in particular, Mrs. Garcia's) problem-solving, coping, and developmental capacities. The program evaluation question addresses the issues of the effective and humane operations of systems that provide people with resources and services. The third question, a needs assessment question about teenage fathers, is involved with linking people to resources. We will now discuss the different types of questions in more detail.

Practice Evaluations

One type of research question that often occurs in social work practice is concerned with the effectiveness of an individual social worker's practice. As we have seen, this type of question directly relates to the enhancement of people's problem-solving, coping, and developmental capacities. Practice evaluations usually involve only one case, subject, or client system and require social workers to use specific criteria and methods in monitoring their own practice cases. For the generalist social worker, these cases include individuals, families, groups, or communities. Whatever the type of client system, only one is evalu-

A Practice Evaluation

Tyson (1996) reports on the use of intrapsychic humanism for crisis intervention and brief treatment for young children. The case study examines the process that evolves between the social worker and a three-year-old child. The social worker evaluated the treatment effectiveness through naturalistic approaches that included process recordings after sessions. To measure whether the treatment goals were being met, the social worker formulated change indices. The social worker also used the child's mother's descriptions of his functioning to assess changes. All measuress indicated that the child had made changes and progress over the course of the treatment.

ated in a practice evaluation. This type of research can be either descriptive or explanatory, and either interpretive or positivist.

Increasingly, practice evaluations are being recognized as an integral element of social work practice. In part, this recognition has resulted from social workers' seeking a method of evaluation that could be integrated into their practice relatively easily. In addition to being easily integrated into practice, practice evaluations offer the generalist practitioner the advantages of low cost and immediate feedback (to the client as well). Practice evaluations will be discussed more fully in Chapter 7.

Program Evaluations

Program evaluation research questions are asked extensively in generalist social work practice and involve assessing a program's overall functioning rather than an individual practitioner's effectiveness. This type of question relates directly to the generalist social work function of promoting the effective and humane operation of the systems that provide resources.

Program evaluations play an increasing role in today's social work practice. During the federal government's War on Poverty of the 1960s and early 1970s, funding for social programs was high. Unfortunately, however, there was little accountability to funding sources regarding social programs' effectiveness in meeting client needs. Fischer (1976) conducted a review of the casework practice in social work. He concluded that approximately half of the clients receiving casework services either deteriorated to a greater degree or improved at a slower rate than did subjects who did not participate in the programs. Fischer's study jolted social workers and others into the awareness that adequate funding did not ensure a program's effectiveness. Fischer's work also disclosed that many of the studies he reviewed contained various methodological problems. As a result, the profession realized the necessity for more sophisticated research methods to assess service effectiveness and to conduct program evaluations so that findings—positive or negative—would be reliable.

Program evaluation is primarily concerned with determining a program's effectiveness, which can be accomplished using any of three different strategies: formative, summative, or cost-benefit approaches. First, the **formative program evaluation** approach, or **process analysis,** examines a program's planning, development, and implementation. This type of evaluation is often performed as an initial evaluative step and is generally descriptive. Often the interpretive approach is used because it allows for a fuller understanding of the processes at work within the agencies and can address these processes from multiple perspectives—those of the client, the worker, and the administrator.

A Formative Program Evaluation

Miller (1997) reported on a parent education group for African-American parents who are clients of the child welfare system. In the article the author describes the unique needs of the population for a culturally responsive parenting group. Miller describes topics that were covered in the groups:

- Profile and context of effective African-American parenting
- Concerns and issues of single parenthood
- Social support systems and how to use them
- Developmental and psychosocial stages and issues of the child
- Factors influencing African-American child development
- Developing positive racial self-esteem in African-American children
- Racial socialization for African-American children
- History and mission of child welfare
- Effective utilization of social service network

The **summative program evaluation** approach, or **outcome analysis,** determines whether goals and objectives have been met and the extent to which program effects are generalizable to other settings and populations. This type of research is usually explanatory. Usually the positivist approach is more appropriate with summative evaluations, since the purpose is to establish causality (the

A Summative Program Evaluation

Hack, Osachuk, and De Luca (1994) evaluated the effectiveness of semistructured group work with adolescent boys who had experienced either extra- or intrafamilial sexual abuse. From pre- to postgroup, the boys experienced decreased anxiety, decreased depression, increased self-esteem, and decreased internalizing and externalizing behaviors.

program's effect). Often these types of evaluations are required by funding organizations, which are more interested in the kind of research evidence (generally quantitative) produced by positivist studies.

Cost-benefit or cost-effectiveness analysis can also be conducted. A **cost-benefit analysis** compares the program costs to the dollar value of the program results and computes a ratio of costs to benefits. A **cost-effectiveness study** compares program costs to some measure of program outcome and calculates a cost per unit.

The most comprehensive program evaluations combine a study of a program's implementation, outcomes, and cost-benefit aspects. As with summative evaluations, these types of studies usually require a more positivist approach, producing quantitative evidence. The design of program evaluations will be discussed in Chapter 6.

A Cost-Benefit Analysis Program Evaluation

Knobbe, Carey, Rhodes, and Horner (1995) conducted a cost-benefit analysis comparing services in community residences versus an institution for 11 individuals with severe mental retardation. Overall, the community-based program costs were lower and resulted in significant increases in the client's social networks, opportunities for integrated activities, and income.

Needs Assessments

Needs assessment questions are concerned with discovering the characteristics and extent of a particular social problem to determine the most appropriate response. This type of research is usually descriptive and, as previously mentioned, is also known as survey research. This kind of question is related to the practice function of linking people with systems.

An example of this type of needs assessment is the following: "I have talked to a couple of clients who need an alternative living situation for their adult developmentally delayed children. I wonder if there is a great enough need in the community to start a group home for the adult developmentally delayed?"

Reporting hearsay, citing individual cases, or simply acting on a hunch does not provide enough evidence for funding sources. Usually a funding source, whether a voluntary organization, a private foundation, or state government, requires documentation of the need for the program with evidence that the needs assessment has been performed scientifically.

Generally, a positivist approach is used for a needs assessment, since most needs assessments are concerned with generalizability of results rather than in-depth understanding of how people experience social problems. Sometimes, however, an interpretive approach can provide some important insights and

A Needs Assessment

Fredrikson (1999) studied the variety of family-care responsibilities experienced among lesbians and gay men. Thirty-two percent of the participants in the study provided some time of caregiving assistance. Lesbians were more likely to be caring for children and elders, whereas gay men were more likely to be assisting working-age adults with a disability. The author suggested that these findings have important implications for the development of family responsive services and policies.

new directions for assessing the needs of certain populations. Needs assessments can be designed in different ways; these design issues are discussed in Chapter 5.

Although the types of research questions appear quite different, they all follow essentially similar research steps and strategies. Some differences in approach are sometimes required, particularly in the design stage. Thus a separate chapter is devoted to each of the three types of research questions (Chapters 5, 6, and 7).

The three types of research questions described here are not the only types of research questions social workers ask. If you look through any social work journal, you will find other types of research questions. You may find some pure research questions or historical studies. In addition, some articles may be theoretical and conceptual rather than empirical in nature.

In this book we focus upon practice evaluation, program evaluation, and needs assessment questions simply because these are the types of research questions you will be most likely to encounter as generalist social workers. Remember, though, that many other types of questions are possible in social work.

THE AGENCY AND DECIDING ON THE QUESTION

As we discussed earlier, except when conducting practice evaluations, you may have little or no choice in the research you will be doing as a generalist social worker. The question may have already been decided, and your task instead may be to conduct a needs assessment to help build a case for developing a new program in your community. Or perhaps your program's funding source demands that an evaluation be undertaken for funding to continue. You may find that you often have little opportunity to decide on research strategies or types of questions.

Despite this tendency for you to have little choice in the research, in many respects you are in an ideal position for conducting applied research. As an agency-based generalist social worker who is knowledgeable about research and familiar with the agency's workings and the community's concerns, you are well

Collaboration Between a Researcher and a Practitioner

Galinsky, Turnbull, Meglin, and Wilner (1993) described an example of collaboration between researcher and practitioner to evaluate single-session groups for families of psychiatric inpatients. The article discussed some of the issues that can arise in this type of collaboration.

situated to conduct relevant research. You can also act as a resource person for outside researchers; when the opportunity arises, you may assist them in conducting research that is beyond the scope of your immediate responsibilities in the agency.

If you are asked to initiate a research study from the ground up, however, you must recognize that research is almost always a team effort, particularly at the stage of deciding on the question. Consult with agency staff, clients, and community to determine what they want from the evaluation or needs assessment. Don't forget to confer with those who are providing the funding for the project.

One strategy for ensuring that those who are affected by the research or its findings participate more fully in the research implementation is the use of **focus groups.** A focus group is a special group formed to help decide on the research question and the research method. A focus group is composed of people who are informed about the topic or will be affected by it in some way. A focus group can be used at any stage of the research process but is particularly useful in the beginning stages.

The focus group is informal. The researcher asks participants focused questions with the emphasis on sharing information. The empowerment or action approach to research often uses focus groups, since a focus group enables clients

The Use of Focus Groups

Drake and Washeck (1998) used focus groups comprised of both Child Protective Services (CPS) workers and CPS supervisors to construct an instrument that allows supervisors to receive feedback from the workers they supervise. Four worker groups included seventeen randomly selected workers and two groups included six supervisors. Attendance was voluntary, 38% of invited supervisors and 35% of the invited workers participated. The focus groups provided information on those factors most critical to a supervisor's ability to perform well. Six general areas of supervisory competency were identified: Availability, Knowledge, Tasks, Communication, Integrity, and Flexibility. Each area included between four and fourteen specific items.

to become directly involved in the research. For example, focus groups are an excellent way of involving community members in developing the research. The focus groups can themselves help identify other stakeholders and so expand the potential input.

In addition to focus groups, agencies often use **task forces** to help formulate research questions. Task forces are usually made up of representatives of the agency and sometimes representatives from the community, including clients. They often are charged with assessing needs or developing strategic plans, these activities often being the starting point for the development of research questions that are of concern to the agency.

Task Force

Pine, Warsh, and Maluccio (1998) developed a model to evaluate and improve an agency's family reunification services. The model included a task force comprised of administrators, supervisors, line staff, trainers, attorneys, staff members with financial responsibilities, foster parents, collateral providers, and birth parents. The goal of the task force was to conduct a self-assessment of the agency's service delivery systems and to develop an action plan for change. A positive impact that resulted was a set of 65 recommendations to improve family reunification services.

ETHICAL ISSUES IN DECIDING ON THE QUESTION

Two ethical issues are central to the stage of the research process concerned with deciding on the question: the question's applicability to social work practice and the availability of funding.

Applicability of the Question to Social Work Practice

One concern when you are deciding on a research question is whether and how the answer to the question is going to contribute to the field of social work. Usually applicability to practice is not too much of an issue, particularly for generalist social workers, because most questions derive directly from our practice in an agency. If your question has evolved from your personal experiences, however, you must ask whether answering the question is really going to assist the clients you serve. To determine the appropriateness of the question, discuss it with colleagues.

This issue presents another reason for adopting more participatory action research—it is rooted directly in clients' concerns, and they become active contributors.

Another strategy to ensure that the research is applicable to social work practice is to use a developmental or intervention approach to research. This ap-

Participatory Action Research

Mwansa, Mufune, and Osei Hwedie (1994) examined youth power and programs in Botswana, Swaziland, and Zambia. They used participatory research involving officials, academics, and the youths in the programs. The findings showed that most of the income-generating activities were inadequate, that teenage pregnancy was a serious problem, and that there were no viable programs for street children.

proach, which was discussed earlier in the chapter, uses research to help design and develop interventions. A number of different ways of conducting developmental research have emerged, but its basic principle is that effective interventions must be built systematically using the stages of design, continued testing, feedback, and modification. The focus is on using research to test and improve interventions—hence the alternative label *intervention research*.

Availability of Funding

In agencies, research projects may be conducted because funding is available for these projects. Certain issues may be a priority at the local, state, or federal level, and funds consequently become available. You should be aware of the reason you are conducting research on these particular issues—namely, at least in part, the availability of funds. Presumably, it has already been established that this topic is a deserving one, but you need to realize that other issues are probably equally deserving and should not be ignored because of the convenience of funding. In other words, you should continue to act as advocates for those issues, regardless of the extent to which they are receiving fiscal support.

In addition, you may sometimes want to confirm for yourself whether a research program deserves an investment of time and money. Again, the best source for this type of information is the literature and colleagues.

HUMAN DIVERSITY ISSUES IN DECIDING ON THE QUESTION

During the stage of deciding on the question, you need to pay attention to human diversity issues. You should be aware that researchers' characteristics can influence their research and that agencies may also promote biases.

Characteristics of the Researchers

Traditionally there has been a predominance of studies conducted by white, middle-class men, resulting in an inherent bias in the types of research questions. In an article about methodological approaches to research on Hispanics, Becerra, and Tambrana (1985) stated: "Clearly, the major advantage of having

Hispanics conduct research on Hispanics is that, it assumes, Hispanic researchers will be sensitive to and understand the cultural norms and language" (p. 43). The authors also pointed out, however, that "being Hispanic" does not ensure cultural sensitivity or knowledge. The researcher also needs to be aware of subgroups (for example, some Hispanic subgroups are Cuban, Mexican American, Spanish, and Puerto Rican), as well as the level of acculturation and socioeconomic class of those being studied.

Bowman (1983) addressed the issue of who conducts research, particularly with African-Americans, by using two concepts: significant involvement and functional relevance. Significant involvement means that members of the group under study have a central role in the research, including decision making at each stage of the research process. Functional relevance means that the study promotes the expressed needs and perspectives of the study population. Significant involvement need not necessarily result in functional relevance or vice versa. Bowman argued that both these concepts must be considered in conducting research with minorities to ensure that minority concerns are addressed in research studies.

Similar arguments are presented in support of more women-centered research. Women tend not to conduct research in social work (Davis, 1986); those who do tend to be white, middle-class women. Consequently certain questions are not asked, and the content of research questions is not necessarily relevant to women. For example, when studies were conducted on work satisfaction, it was unusual to consider family issues, which are often of primary concern to women, but traditionally are not for men. Thus a biased picture was developed depicting women's lives in a male framework.

To broaden the idea of diverse group representatives conducting research, community members need to be involved as much as possible in the development of projects so that participants are empowered. In other words, more participatory action research needs to be undertaken. The Cornell Empowerment Project (1989) suggested that evaluation should be as inclusive as possible, involving (1) people who develop and use the program (for example, funders, agency boards, program staff); (2) direct and indirect beneficiaries of the program; and (3) people who suffer a disadvantage related to the program.

Including Participants in the Research Design

Stevens (1998) used a participatory research approach to examine consultation in South African schools, with the intention of making consultations more relevant. Social workers were involved from the outset in planning the research, identifying what needed to be studied, and planning a workshop on consultation, as well as in the resulting evaluation. Focus groups were used in which the social workers were able to start thinking critically about what they were doing.

A final point concerning who conducts the research relates to the potential problem of people's studying themselves—an issue when members of an organization or agency evaluate their own performance. Although the input and participation of organization members are essential, these evaluations do need to be counterbalanced by outsiders' evaluations.

Bias in the Agencies

Most of our research questions derive from practice in agencies. We need to be aware that bias can also exist in agencies and that this bias can influence decisions about research questions.

For example, an agency's homophobic attitudes may result in ignoring the needs of lesbian clients, even though that group may require substantial social supports. Your supervisor may dismiss your request to carry out a needs assessment of this particular group. Watch for these biases; be aware that your agency's operation may be influenced by presuppositions and prejudices.

Including Diverse Populations and Their Issues in the Research Question

Gaston, Barrett, Johnson, and Epstein (1998) examined the role of the Bureau of Primary Health Care (BPHC) in meeting the health care needs of medically underserved women of color. They examined studies on Asian and Pacific Islander populations as well as African-American, Hispanic, and Native-American women. The authors suggest that "a special initiative, aimed at women of color, supported by BPHC and implemented at the local level could increase access to primary health care by low-income women of color and their families" (p. 91).

SUMMARY

This chapter described two research strategies: descriptive and explanatory. There is a distinction between applied research and pure research. Generalist social workers usually engage in three types of applied research: practice evaluations, program evaluations, and needs assessments.

Usually, in agencies, research questions have already been decided on, but it is important to ensure maximum input from those affected by the research and the resulting services. Focus groups are useful in ensuring this input, and participatory action research is recommended. Ethical issues in deciding on the research question include assessing the question's applicability to social work practice and availability of funding. Human diversity issues include the researcher's characteristics and the agency's biases.

STUDY/EXERCISE QUESTIONS

1. Look through a social work journal such as *Social Work Research and Abstracts* or *Affilia* and identify studies that adopt the research strategies described in this chapter (practice evaluations, program evaluations, and needs assessments). Discuss in class the reasons for your decisions.

2. If you are enrolled in a practicum or field placement, ask your supervisor about any program evaluations or needs assessments carried out by the agency. Find out why the evaluation or needs assessment was carried out. Who suggested it? Who was involved in that decision? Present the results of this discussion in class.

INFOTRAC COLLEGE EDITION

1. Search for *exploratory* research studies, and identify the purpose of these studies explaining why they are exploratory (rather than descriptive or explanatory).
2. Find a *program evaluation* and identify it as summative or formative.

REFERENCES

Baer, B. L., & Federico, R. C. (1978). *Educating the baccalaureate social worker: Report of the undergrad-social work curriculum development project.* Cambridge, MA: Ballinger.

Becerra, R. M., & Tambrana, R. E. (1985). Methodological approaches to research on Hispanics. *Social Work Research and Abstracts, 21* (2), 42–49.

Bowman, P. J. (1983). Significant involvement and functional relevance. *Social Work Research and Abstracts, 19* (4), 21–26.

Cornell Empowerment Project. (1989). Evaluation consistent with the empowerment process. *Networking Bulletin.* Ithaca, NY: Cornell University, Cornell Empowerment Project.

Davis, L. (1986). A feminist approach to social work research. *Affilia, 1,* 32–47.

Dore, M. M., Nelson-Zlupko, L., & Kaufmann, E. (1999). "Friends in need." Designing and implementing a psychoeducational group for school children from drug-involved families. *Social Work, 44* (2), 179–190.

Drake, B., & Washeck, J. (1998). A competency-based method for providing worker feedback to CPS supervisors. *Administration in Social Work, 22* (3), 55–74.

Fischer, J. (1976). *The effectiveness of social casework.* Springfield, IL: Charles C Thomas.

Fredriksen, K. I. (1999). Family caregiving responsibilities among lesbians and gay men. *Social Work, 44* (2), 142–155.

Galinsky, M. J., Turnbull, J. E., Meglin, D. E., & Wilner, M. E. (1993). Confronting the reality of collaborative practice research: Issues of practice, design, measurement, and team development. *Social Work, 38* (4), 440–449.

Gaston, M. H., Barrett, S. E., Johnson, T. L., & Epstein, L. G. (1998). Health care needs of medically underserved women of color: The role of the bureau of primary health care. *Health & Social Work, 23* (2), 86–95.

Gregg, R. (1994). Explorations of pregnancy and choice in a high tech age. In C. Riessman (Ed.), *Qualitative studies in social work research.* Newbury Park, CA: Sage.

Hack, T., Osachuk, T., & De Luca, R. (1994). Group treatment for sexually abused preadolescent boys. *Families in Society, 75* (4), 217–228.

Knobbe, C., Carey, S., Rhodes, L., & Horner, R. (1995). Benefit cost analysis of community versus institutional services for adults with severe mental retardation and challenging behaviors. *American Journal on Mental Retardation, 99* (5), 533–547.

Massat, C. R., & Lundry, M. (1998). "Reporting costs" to nonoffending parents in cases of intrafamilial child sexual abuse. *Child Welfare, 77* (4), 371–388.

Miller, D. B. (1997). Parenting against the odds: African-American parents in the child welfare system—a group approach. *Social Work with Groups, 20* (1), 5–17.

Morawski, J. (1997). The science behind feminist research methods. *Journal of Social Issues, 53* (4), 667–682.

Mwansa, L., Mufune, P., & Osei Hwedie, K. (1994). Youth policy and programmes in the SADC countries of Botswana, Swaziland, and Zambia: A comparative assessment. *International Social Work, 37* (3), 239–263.

Nash, J., Rounds, K., & Bowden, G. (1992). Level of parental involvement on early childhood intervention teams. *Families in Society,* 93–99.

Pine, B. A., Warsh, R., & Maluccio, A. N. (1998). Participatory management in a child welfare agency. A key to effective change. *Administration in Social Work, 22* (1), 19–31.

Rittner, B., & Dozier, D. C. (2000). Effects of court-ordered substance abuse treatment in child protective services cases. *Social Work, 45* (2), 131–140.

Rothman, J., & Thomas, E. (1994). *Intervention research.* New York: Haworth Press.

Shongwe, C. H. L. (1996). *The relationship between social work and primary health care: An urban based study.* Coursework master's thesis, in progress, University of Natal, Department of Social Work, Durban, South Africa.

Smith, L., Smith, J., & Beckner, B. (1994). An anger management workshop for women inmates. *Families in Society,* 172–175.

Stevens, L. A. (1998). Consultation as a social work method. In Gray, M. (Ed.), *Developmental social work in South Africa: Theory and practice.* Cape Town: David Philip Publishers.

Tyson, K. (1999). An empowering approach to crisis intervention and brief treatment for preschool children. *Families in Society, 80* (1), 64–77.

Whipple, E. E. (1999). Reaching families with preschoolers at risk of physical child abuse: What works? *Families in Society,* March–April, 148–159.

Developing the Question

Suppose your supervisor asked you to carry out a needs assessment to establish a health promotion program for a local business. You have some implicit assumptions about what the program will include—namely, seminars and information dispersal on wellness. After consulting with the staff of the business, however, you find that they are defining a health promotion program more broadly. Their idea of a health promotion program includes other services, such as revising the business's health insurance coverage and providing discounts to local health clubs, counseling information and referral, and so forth.

This chapter will describe the research stage of developing the question, which is equivalent to the practice stage of defining directions. Developing the question involves clarifying the research question once it has been initially formulated. This clarification can help make explicit some initial assumptions inherent in research, in much the same way as is necessary in practice.

Here the question will be examined more closely. The following will be discussed:

- the literature review
- units of analysis
- levels of measurement
- naming the variables and values
- the relationship of variables
- defining and operationalizing the variable
- the agency and developing the question
- ethical issues in developing the question
- human diversity issues in developing the question

As discussed in the last chapter, the research question often has been decided on prior to your involvement. For example, the agency may have been asked by one of their funding sources to carry out an evaluation of the services, and you are to help with planning and implementing the study. Similarly, many of the stages discussed in this chapter may already have been completed by the time you are involved. It is still important for you as a participant in the project to understand the rationale behind these stages and, if you have the opportunity, to develop them yourself.

THE LITERATURE REVIEW

When conducting applied research—whether a program evaluation, a needs assessment, or single system study—we need to consult other sources of information. Sometimes information can come from colleagues who have had experience with the questions we are trying to answer. Our usual source of other information, however, is written material.

Undertaking a **literature review** means consulting with the written material relevant to a research problem. This written material can be found in a variety of places including libraries, public and private; city, state, and federal buildings; social agencies; private collections; and political, professional, social, and interest group organizations such as the NASW.

In this section we will discuss the specific uses of the literature review, accessing the information, and writing the literature review.

Using the Literature Review

The literature review assists with developing the question in the following ways:

- connecting the research question to theory
- identifying previous research
- giving direction to the research project

Consulting the literature is useful not only in conducting research but in guiding practice, particularly if the literature is based on research. Using the research literature to guide practice is the focus of Chapter 15.

Connecting the Research Question to Theory

As discussed in Chapter 1, science consists of both theories and research methods. Consequently, in any research, the connection to theory has to be made clear. In pure research, connecting a question to theory is a fairly obvious step. For example, if you are investigating the causes of spousal abuse, you need to be apprised of the human behavior theories that attempt to explain spousal abuse. This theoretical base can be found in the existing literature. In applied research, however, this step is not so obvious and can be easily overlooked. This step will be clarified by giving illustrations of the use of the literature review for linking different types of social work research questions to theory.

Practice evaluations.   When evaluating your own practice, you need to understand the theoretical base underlying your use of a particular intervention. For example, if you are using positive reinforcement to help a parent learn disciplining skills, you need to be familiar with the theory behind positive reinforcement—namely, behavior theory. The literature on behavior theory can then be consulted. In addition, you need to understand the theoretical link between the use of positive reinforcement in disciplining children and its appropriateness and effectiveness for this purpose, again turning to the literature for this information.

Program evaluations.   You recall that program evaluation can take several forms: summative, formative, or cost-benefit analyses. For each form, we need to consider how the research question links to theory. For example, you may be examining whether the agency in which you are employed is meeting one of its goals in providing support services to homebound elderly. You consult the literature to ascertain the theoretical basis for this type of care and examine studies of this type that have already been carried out. You may also find some of this material in the initial program proposal.

**Connecting the Research Question to Theory:
Program Evaluation**

Schaffer and Lia-Hoagberg (1994) assessed the personal, family, and provider rewards and costs low-income pregnant women experienced in obtaining pre-natal care. Exchange theory provided the theoretical framework for this evaluation of prenatal services. The theory suggests that humans avoid relationships, inter-actions, and feeling states that are dissatisfying or costly and seek out experiences that are gratifying, pleasurable, or rewarding.

Needs assessments.   When assessing the need for a program, the literature can also be consulted to provide some theoretical substance. For example, in con-ducting a needs assessment to determine the number of homeless women and children in our community, a theoretical perspective and context can be gained by consulting the literature and determining the risk factors and problems expe-rienced by homeless women and children.

Identifying Previous Research

When you choose or are assigned a research question, it is useful to find out whether a similar or identical question has already been answered. If it has, you may wish to reconceptualize the research question. For example, in conducting your needs assessment, you may find a report on a survey conducted in your community two years previously. This information will probably be useful, since the survey was done so recently. If the survey had been conducted ten years ago, however, you would need to **replicate** or repeat the study. Similarly, in a pro-gram evaluation, you may find that other evaluations of comparable programs had already been conducted and thus your evaluation might not necessarily contribute new and useful knowledge. Alternatively, you may find that the eval-uations were conducted in communities very different from the one your agency serves, which would suggest that your evaluation would fulfill a useful purpose.

Note that when writing a thesis you will be required to include a section that includes a clear discussion of the relationship between your research topic and its theoretical framework.

Giving Direction to the Research Project

Although the concern here is primarily with the role of the literature review in developing the research question, you should also note that the literature review can give overall direction and guidance to the entire research project. You can, for example, review the literature to find out how researchers set up comparison groups in similar projects or to get ideas about how samples can be selected. Us-ing the literature review in this way, particularly in the early step of developing the question, can save considerable time later on and avoids "reinventing the wheel."

Accessing Information

As we discussed previously, several literature sources are available to the social worker. Libraries have always housed the most wide-ranging and extensive collection of these materials. Government agencies along with public and private organizations often maintain specialized collections of materials, and they are increasingly making their own publications available on the World Wide Web. The development of the Web allows the researcher access to a seemingly endless supply of information.

Libraries

Academic libraries have traditionally provided research literature and the tools (indexes, abstracts, databases) for accessing the literature. Although the Web has begun to transform the process of identifying and acquiring information, libraries still play an important role for researchers. To begin with, contrary to popular belief, all information on the Web is not free. Web-based indexes, reference materials, and journals to which the library once subscribed in print (or, in some cases, in CD-ROM format) are still paid subscriptions, made available through license agreements to authorized library users, through the library's Web site. The enormity of the Web gives the illusion that all information is available online (somewhere). However, a print source is often still the only way to satisfy an information need. In addition, libraries can provide effective navigation through the Web wilderness.

Library catalogs. Computerized library catalogs, which show what is available in a particular library, can usually be searched on the Web. They also provide direct links to the full text of information that is available to the library's users, in both online books and journals. Although different libraries have different systems, the general principles are similar. You can enter an author's name, a title, or subject words, or a combination of terms, and you can usually limit or modify a search by publication date or other criteria. The computer will retrieve a list of potential sources of information. One way to retrieve more relevant information when searching a library catalog is to limit your search to the "subject headings" category. First do a more general "keyword" search. If you find a good source among your results, use the subject headings, which have been assigned to that source, to conduct another search. Through the library catalog you can find journals, books, dictionaries, encyclopedias, and bibliographies that will lead to more information.

Government documents. Government documents are a great resource for social work researchers; these documents include census data, Congressional proceedings, agency information, and statistics. Although some library catalogs include listings for the government documents that are held in the library, other libraries provide a separate online system for finding them. Certain libraries are depositories for all published U.S. government information, but an increasing amount of government information is being disseminated only on the Web. Gateway sites for Web-based government information are listed in Appendix A.

Indexes and databases.   Indexes and abstracts, whether available on the Web or in the library in print or CD-ROM format, will help you identify specific articles, dissertations, chapters in books, or books and documents that will not necessarily be held in your library. You will usually need to use such an index to locate a literature review of your area of research. The list of references in a current literature review will lead you to further relevant resources.

Some of these indexes or databases are quite specific, defined by a subject area or type of material to which they provide access. Some databases provide "citations" or information about the resources that you will then need to locate in the library or obtain through interlibrary loan. Some databases will provide access to the full text of the actual articles or documents, and others include some citations, perhaps abstracts and some full text, or links to full text. Searching an electronic database is similar to searching a library catalog in that you will use keywords or subject terms and limit the search by various parameters. There are fewer ways to search a print index, which is usually organized by subject terms. Relevant indexes and abstracting databases are listed in Appendix A.

Access to Web-based library resources.   When a library subscribes to electronic books or journals, a license agreement usually limits the access to authorized members of the community served by the library, such as university faculty, staff, and students. Just as it is necessary to have a library card to check out a book, often that same library card will enable you, from any location, to have access to Web resources that are provided by a university or public library. Computers within the domain served by the library (such as those in the library building or on a university network) will usually have barrier-free access and, in most cases, anyone walking into a library can have free access to the library's Web-based subscriptions using computers provided by the library.

Interlibrary loan.   Indexes and databases often provide information about resources that are not available on the Web or in your local library. To get access to those books or articles, it is necessary to use your library's interlibrary loan or document delivery service. Libraries can borrow books or obtain photocopies of articles from other libraries or from a commercial supplier. Some libraries will subsidize all or part of the cost of this service, whereas others will pass along all or part of the cost to the borrower. Interlibrary loan can take days or in some cases, even weeks. Start your search early so that you will have time to receive articles and books that are not available locally.

Library staff.   When trying to access information, do not forget to consult with the library staff. They are professionally trained in every aspect of information management and can be a tremendous resource. They will save you time in the library and on the Web, and with their help you should find better resources.

The World Wide Web

More and more of the types of information social work researchers need is being made available only on the Web, which also provides unprecedented access to international information. However, it can be very time-consuming to wade through this vast amount of information, most of which is of little use to the researcher. Search engines lack precision, and hierarchical sites are designed with commercial interests at heart. It is sometimes difficult to evaluate the currency, authority, or accuracy of the information you retrieve. Your Web-searching efficiency and success will increase with practice, and tools are currently being developed that will help with the precision of future information retrieval. For example, the Google search engine (http://www.google.com) ranks results based on how many other Web sites are linked to the sites listed in your search results.

When you find a site that suits your needs, bookmark it for later use. It is often impossible to re-create a search or remember a circuitous path that led to good results. However, keep in mind that Web sites get reorganized, and URLs (Web addresses) change. Make use of gateway sites that provide organized and well-maintained access to Web sites of interest to a specialized audience. Social work gateways have been developed and maintained by schools and departments of social work, libraries that support them, and organizations of social workers. Some of these sites are listed in Appendix A. Also refer to Vernon and Lynch (2000) for guidance in using the Web in research and other aspects of social work practice.

Summary

1. State the topic, limit the range, and list all the relevant synonyms and keywords. Use background sources in Appendix A for help with terminology and scope.

2. Using the computer catalog in your library, use the keywords to access potential sources of information.

3. When you access a relevant item, look at its subject headings and use these words in the subject headings category to find similar items.

4. If relevant, locate other materials in government documents.

5. Use your keywords to search the online databases available through your library.

6. Use a print index if you have not found enough results in databases.

7. From your results, try to develop a literature review on your research topic. Consult the list of references for further resources.

8. Use gateway sites on the Web to track down other materials. Verify the source of Web-based information and evaluate it for accuracy, currency, and integrity.

9. If material that you have identified is not available locally or on the Web, use interlibrary loan through your local library.

10. Ask a reference librarian for other ideas and help, if you need it, for each of these steps.

Writing the Literature Review

Although writing up your research, including the literature review, is discussed in Chapter 14, some guidelines for writing the literature review will be given here. The literature review is usually the first section of the research to be completed and written. It should be completed before other stages of the research are undertaken. The literature review places the current research in its historical and theoretical context. It describes the background to the study and the relationship between the present study and previous studies conducted in the same area. The literature review should also identify trends and debates in the existing literature. It provides a link between past, present, and future, in addition to providing a context for the discussion of the results from the study. See Figure 4.1 for a checklist for writing the literature review (van Rooyen, 1996).

A literature review places the current research in its historical and theoretical context. It describes the background to the study and the relationship between the present study and previous studies conducted in the same area. It also identifies trends and debates in the existing literature.

The following are a few issues to consider when constructing a literature review (van Rooyen, 1996).

- Cite only research that you find specifically pertinent to the current study; be selective. Avoid reviewing or referring to sections of articles or texts that are not related to your study.

- Discuss and evaluate the literature you have selected.

- Show the logical continuity between existing literature and your study.

- Identify controversial issues or differences in the literature and your study.

- If there is a choice, cite the more recent literature, unless the older citations are needed for additional perspective.

- Write the literature review in the past tense.

- Refer to published studies for examples of literature reviews.

Figure 4.1   ***Literature review***

UNITS OF ANALYSIS

After examining the literature, it is important to further develop the question. One of the first steps in this process is to determine the **unit of analysis.** The unit of analysis refers to what or whom is being studied. Three types of units of analysis are used in social work research: individuals, groups, and social artifacts.

Individuals. These are the most common units of analysis. Descriptions of individuals are often aggregated to explain social group functioning. For example, in conducting a needs assessment for a community youth center, you may interview individual youths to assess their needs. This information would then be aggregated to document the needs of the group.

Groups. Groups can also be the unit of analysis. Groups are of different types and include families, organizations, and communities. Families are often the unit of analysis in social work. For example, in an evaluation investigating the impact of a program on family cohesion, although individuals will be studied, the family group would make up the unit of analysis.

Social artifacts. These are behaviors or products resulting from human activity. In social work, social artifacts may include books, divorces, birth practices, or ethical violations. For example, you are asked by your state NASW chapter to investigate unethical social work practice behavior. In the study, you look at the characteristics of those charged with such behavior: whether they are B.S.W.s or M.S.W.s, the field of practice in which they are employed, and so on. Here the unit of analysis is unethical social work practice.

LEVELS OF MEASUREMENT

Another step in developing the research question is considering the level of measurement. The **level of measurement** is the extent to which a variable can be quantified and subsequently subjected to certain mathematical or statistical procedures. Obviously, determining the level of measurement for a variable is only of concern if quantitative data are being collected, so the level of measurement usually is not considered in interpretive studies, where the data are generally qualitative. Quantification involves assigning a number to a variable; it depends, as you might guess, on how the variable is being operationalized. Using an example of measuring depression, we could count the number of hours the client sleeps each night, use an already developed measure such as the Generalized Contentment Scale, or have the client simply note each day whether she was depressed. Each measure involves assigning numbers in different ways, and consequently they result in different levels of measurement. Four different levels of measurement can be identified: nominal, ordinal, interval, and ratio (see Table 4.1).

⋀ *Table 4.1*   **Levels of measurement**

Level of measurement	Definition	Example
Nominal	Data are assigned to categories based on similarity or difference.	Ethnicity, marital status, yes/no response
Ordinal	Data are sequenced in some order.	Many attitude and opinion questions
Interval	Data are sequenced in some order, and the distances between the different points are equal.	IQ, GRE scores
Ratio	Data are sequenced in some order, the distances between the different points are equal, and each value reflects an absolute magnitude. The zero point reflects an absence of the value.	Years of age, number of children, miles to place of employment

Nominal measures classify observations into mutually exclusive categories, with no ordering to the categories. Phenomena are assigned to categories based on some similarity or difference (for example, ethnicity, gender, marital status). Numbers are assigned to nominal categories, but the numbers themselves have no inherent meaning. For example, 1 is assigned to Hispanic and 2 to African American, but the numbers could be reversed and no meaning would be lost. The use of numbers with nominal data is arbitrary. In the example of depression, the client recording the absence (no) or presence (yes) of depression each day would result in a nominal level of measurement, as would other yes/no responses to questions.

Ordinal measures classify observations into mutually exclusive categories that have an inherent order to them. An ordinal level of measurement can often be used when we are examining attitudes. Respondents to a survey might be asked whether they agree with a particular statement, with the alternatives as follows:

> strongly agree
> agree
> disagree
> strongly disagree

These responses are ordered in sequence from strongly agree to strongly disagree (or vice versa) and numbered 1 to 4. Nevertheless, although these values are placed in sequence and are meaningful in that sense, the distance between each of the values is not necessarily equal and may be somewhat arbitrary.

Interval measures classify observations into mutually exclusive categories with an inherent order and equal spacing between the categories. This equal distance differentiates the interval level from the ordinal level of measurement. A good example of an interval scale is the IQ test: The difference between an IQ of 120 and 130 is the same as between 110 and 120. Nevertheless, the interval level of measurement does not allow one to make any statements about the magnitude of one value in relation to another. It is not possible to claim that someone with an IQ of 160 has twice the IQ of someone with an IQ of 80.

Ratio measures possess all the characteristics of the interval level of measurement and reflect the absolute magnitude of the value. Put another way, at the zero point, the value is absent, or did not occur. Measurements of income, years of education, the number of times a behavior occurs—all are examples of ratio levels of measurement. In the depression example, counting the number of hours of sleep each night would result in a ratio level of measurement.

Note that most variables can be defined to allow different levels of measurement. Our example of depression is one case; anger is another. For example, a variable like anger can be measured at various levels. If the question "Do you think your child is angry?" is posed, and possible responses are yes and no, this constitutes a nominal level of measurement. But say the question is "To what extent do you think your child is angry?" and the respondent is offered the following scale:

> very aggressive
> aggressive
> not aggressive

This would be an ordinal level of measurement. If anger is measured as one component in a personality test such as the Minnesota Multiphasic Personality Inventory (MMPI), the resulting level of measurement would be interval. Finally, if anger is defined in behavioral components, for example, the number of times the child hit another in an hour, it would be possible to use a ratio level of measurement.

These levels of measurement have important implications for the statistical analysis of research results. These implications will be examined in Chapters 12 and 13.

NAMING THE VARIABLES AND VALUES

A **variable** is a characteristic of a phenomenon, and it is something that varies. Some common examples of variables often seen in social work research are income, ethnicity, and stress level. These characteristics vary or have different quantities, and these different quantities of variables are referred to as *values*. Note that our use of *value* in this context is not the usual meaning we assign to that term in social work practice, such as the social work value of self-determination. You can also think about values as being the potential answers to questions on, for example, a questionnaire.

Using the examples just given, possible values of income might include the following:

> under $15,000/year
> $15,000–$19,999/year

$20,000–$24,999/year
$25,000–$29,999/year
$30,000 and over/year

Ethnicity attributes might include the following:

white (non-Hispanic)
Hispanic
African American
Native American
other

Stress level values might include the following:

high
medium
low

Both the variables and the values that are used in research studies differ from study to study. In conducting a survey to assess the need for a day care center for developmentally delayed preschoolers, one variable might be income, so that you could assess the extent to which parents could pay for such a service. If you were carrying out the needs assessment in rural Kentucky, you might anticipate that incomes would be low. Consequently, the values included on the survey instrument would also be low; the levels presented in the above example might be too high. However, if the needs assessment were being performed in Santa Barbara, California, this categorization might be too low, and we would need to add much higher income levels.

In the same survey, ethnicity might also be considered a factor that would influence service need and consequently should be included in the study. As a variable, ethnicity is restricted in terms of the values that may be included, but there are still some choices. For example, if the study was carried out in New Mexico, the values for ethnicity listed earlier would need to be included. Alternatively, if the study was conducted in South Africa, completely different values would be used. Again, the values included depend on the purpose and context of the study.

One of the problems with naming values in this way is that information is lost in the process. For example, clustering all individuals in a category such as "Native American" leads to the loss of potentially critical information: the differences between different tribes, places of residence (on or off the reservation, rural or urban areas), and so on. This problem points to the importance of using the interpretist approach when appropriate, particularly when you are unsure about the nature of the values to be included in the study.

In interpretive studies the variables and values are not necessarily named prior to the research, but instead emerge from the study. For example, in the pregnancy study cited in Chapter 3, the author concluded after carrying out extensive interviews with women that the key values relating to pregnancy were not simply "pregnant" and "not pregnant," but instead "not pregnant," "pregnant," and "a little bit pregnant," with the last condition's not having been suspected prior to the research's being undertaken. Even in interpretive studies, however, you need to have some idea of what variables are to be studied, even if other variables and their values are to be added later. In this example, the major variable studied was pregnancy.

One note of caution is in order about deciding variables to include in a study: Beware of what is called **reductionism,** or the extreme limitation of the kinds and numbers of variables that might explain or account for broad types of behavior. Reductionism is particularly problematic with the positivist approach, in which all the variables are named prior to the study and little allowance is made for the discovery of additional variables. For example, in a study on spousal abuse you may take many perspectives to explain this phenomenon. You might focus on economic factors, biological factors, family dynamics factors, or psychological factors, to name a few. According to the literature, all appear to play some role in spousal abuse. Incidentally, the literature review is key in the selection of these variables. Time and money constraints, however, often force us to consider only one group of factors. In this case, you may opt for the economic factors because the literature review disclosed these as being in need of further investigation. Choosing economic factors above the others is not, in itself, necessarily a problem; however, if you then suggest that these are the *only* factors in explaining spousal abuse, you would be guilty of reductionism. When you select the variables for a study, these variables may represent only one perspective on the explanation; in discussing your results, you need to acknowledge this. Social workers study human behavior, and human behavior is very complex. You cannot expect to come up with a complete explanation; you need to be aware of this limitation from the early stage of question development to the final stages.

THE RELATIONSHIP OF VARIABLES

Variables have different functions in a research study. The major distinction is between the roles of the independent and dependent variables. Independent and dependent variables are of primary concern in an explanatory study where specific variables are identified as contributing to specific outcomes—in other words, the study attempts to establish causality. In descriptive studies, such as a needs assessment, independent and dependent variables are often not identified as such. Also, interpretist studies often do not identify independent and dependent variables because they are usually not concerned directly with causality.

The **independent variable** is the variable that can affect other factors in the research. If you were studying the impact of social isolation on child sexual abuse, the independent variable would be social isolation. In a program evaluation, the independent variable is the program itself.

You can think of the **dependent variable** as the outcome variable that has presumably been affected by the independent variable. In a summative program evaluation where you are interested in whether program's goals are being met, the dependent variable would be those goals. In the example of the study

Independent and Dependent Variables

Itzhaky and York (1995) studied the impact of apartment building committees in Israel. The house committees employed tenants as maintenance workers and administrators and also introduced professional workers. The researchers considered the dependent variable to be whether social activity of any kind for the residents of the building took place. One set of independent variables included the background variables of the number of families living in the apartment building and the community's typology. The second set included the functioning of the house committee, and such factors as how the committee was set up, how many meetings took place, and how dues were collected. A final independent variable considered whether a community social worker was in contact with the committee.

attempting to identify the factors leading to child sexual abuse in a community, child sexual abuse would be the dependent variable. For each study, there may be a number of independent and dependent variables. In the study of child sexual abuse, income level (in addition to social isolation) may be another independent variable, and different types of child sexual abuse might be identified as different dependent variables.

As with the identification of variables and values, the literature review is extremely important in identifying the dependent and independent variables. In the study of child sexual abuse, any related theories need to be found in the literature and additional variables identified.

As in the case of different values, variables are not fixed as dependent or independent; the nomenclature depends on the study's purpose and context. Although child abuse is identified as a dependent variable in the example just given, in a study examining the factors that determine teenage pregnancy, child sexual abuse might well be identified as an independent variable.

DEFINING AND OPERATIONALIZING THE VARIABLES

Variables need to be defined in a clear and unambiguous manner, in much the same way we need to define concepts in practice.

A central tenet of the positivist approach is that variables must be clearly defined so they can be measured. Definition is less of a priority when using the interpretist approach, in which the definitions of concepts or variables emerge as the topic of inquiry is explored. Nevertheless, the focus of an interpretist study still must be clearly defined. In a study exploring people's beliefs about mental illness, the researcher would have to be clear about defining *mental illness,* even if the study itself ultimately explores and expands this definition.

Many variables used in social work practice tend to be vague; they may seem open to a number of different interpretations depending on who is using them.

Defining Variables in an Interpretive Study

Margareta Hyden (1994), in her interpretive study of woman battering in Sweden, clearly defined at the outset of her research the definition of assault or aggravated assault where the woman was the victim and the husband the perpetrator. Her study involved interviewing women about their experiences and how they made sense of violent action within their marriages. What emerged were different definitions and interpretations of the concept of marriage.

In my first field practicum in a psychiatric hospital in Chicago, I was confused by such terms as *ego strength, depression,* and *independent living skills.* The definitions of these terms either were not provided or varied depending on who was doing the defining. In social work practice, we have to be careful that we clearly define our terms; otherwise confusion can result. A worker and client may think they both know what they mean by *independent living,* while their understandings are actually very different: The client may have in mind "living in my own apartment with no supervision," whereas the worker may mean "living in her own apartment with close supervision." In this example, no matter which definition is accepted, the term *supervision* will also need to be defined—perhaps as "the client's reporting to the social worker twice a week."

One danger of defining variables is that a definition appropriate in one culture may be inappropriate in another. So you have to be particularly careful about using definitions cross-culturally. Be especially careful with definitions when studying people in an unfamiliar culture (with *culture* not limited to describing nationality or ethnicity but also including groups of diverse types, such as single fathers or children of alcoholics). A more interpretive approach might even be advisable, so that definitions can emerge from the research.

As you did when naming the variables earlier, use the literature when defining variables. Consult both the previous research and theoretical writings on the topic for approaches to definitions.

Operationalizations

When using the positivist approach, the next step after defining the variables is to **operationalize** them—in other words, specifying how the variables are to be measured. This process is central to the positivist approach, where measuring and quantifying the study's variables is key. An interpretist approach is not concerned with this step, since the purpose of the study is to understand different dimensions of the variable.

Operationalizing becomes easier once variables have been formally defined. Even after definitions have been accepted, however, some ambiguities remain. For example, measuring the extent to which a client's independent living has been achieved would involve clarifying the issue of supervision. Would the client report by means of a telephone call or a face-to-face visit? How long would the client need to live independently in order to be considered successful? What kind of financial status would qualify as independent living? These are only a few of the questions that need to be answered before a satisfactory operational definition of the variable is achieved.

Measuring a variable could entail simply recording the presence or absence of a phenomenon. If reporting is defined as a telephone contact, either the contact was made or it was not. Or measurement might involve more elaboration, such as specifying the nature of the telephone contact. For example, if a prior arrangement was made regarding the time of the call and who was to initiate it, were these conditions fulfilled?

Operationalizing variables can be a challenge. Measuring a concept like depression may seem overwhelming to the social worker. A useful strategy in operationalizing a variable is to look in the literature and determine how others operationalized this concept. We refer to many variables in social work research over and over again. Depression is a good example; many measures of depression are available in the literature, including the Generalized Contentment Scale (Hudson, 1990), and the Depression Self-Rating Scale for Children (Birleson, 1981). Many of these measures can be adopted by social workers for evaluating their own practices.

Nevertheless, perhaps none of these measuring instruments is appropriate for the aspect of depression you are interested in examining. *Depression* is generally a label applied to specific behaviors being exhibited; to operationalize a variable like depression, often we must consider the behaviors that led to the label's original application. These behaviors might include excessive sleeping, loss of appetite, and so forth. A person's excessive sleeping is easier to measure than the person's level of depression. Excessive sleeping could be measured by the time spent sleeping.

The processes of defining and operationalizing the variables are closely related and can become circular. After defining a variable, the social worker may find that it is still difficult to operationalize the variable, and consequently the variable needs to be redefined. In fact, this circular process characterizes the entire research process, in the same way as it characterizes practice.

Operationalization

Cox (1995) compared the experiences of African American and white caregivers of dementia patients. Among the variables operationalized for the study were (1) attitudes toward caregiving, assessed by the extent to which elderly people should expect to receive care from their relatives and the extent to which relatives should be expected to provide such care; (2) patient status, assessed according to the level of cognitive functioning, disruptive behavior, social functioning, and physical functioning; and (3) caregiver stress, measured according to the caregiver's sense that his or her activities were restricted and relationships strained.

Defining and Operationalizing Goals and Activities

One type of defining and operationalizing that demands a separate discussion is when the generalist social worker conducts a summative program evaluation to determine whether a program has met its goals. As mentioned previously, the positivist approach might be the most appropriate here, and the program's goals and activities need to be defined and operationalized.

First, you need to specify what is meant by *goal* and *activity*. People use these terms in different ways, which confuses the matter. The term *goal* usually refers to the end product, "the end toward which effort is directed" (*Merriam-Webster's*, 1993). Occasionally, people use the terms *goal* and *objective* synonymously, or they use *goal* to refer to a long-term end product and *objective* to refer to a short-term end. *Activity,* in this context, refers to the means by which the goal is achieved.

The goals of a program called Adolescent Family Life might be to reduce the rate of high-risk babies born to adolescents and the rate of child abuse and neglect among teenage parents. The activities might include providing prenatal care and parenting classes to teenage parents.

The next step is to define and operationalize these goals and activities. The first goal, reducing the rate of high-risk babies born to adolescents, requires us to define *adolescents* and *high risk*. We might decide to define *adolescents* as those 18 years and under, and *high-risk babies* as low birth weight or premature infants. Of course, we would then need to operationalize these last two terms—*low birth weight* perhaps as under 5½ pounds at birth and *premature* as born after a pregnancy lasting 32 weeks or less. We would continue defining and operationalizing the other goals and the activities in a similar manner.

THE AGENCY AND DEVELOPING THE QUESTION

Much of the development of the research question occurs before you are involved. Variables may have already been identified, defined, and operationalized by those who initially conceived of the research question: our supervisors, the agency administrators, the funding organization, or individuals or groups in the community.

Don't be discouraged about not having had a role in that development. Work with what you have, and remember that this is only the beginning of the research. Often you can enhance the future development of the project through your research knowledge and your skills as an agency-based generalist practitioner. Don't forget that research is a team endeavor.

ETHICAL ISSUES IN DEVELOPING THE QUESTION

Giving Credit to Contributors

When drawing on information generated by others (for example, using a literature review or consulting with colleagues), you need to give credit to these sources of information when you write the research report. The technicalities of how to do this are discussed in Chapter 14. If you refer to someone else's ideas and do not give him or her credit, particularly if they are written ideas, you may be guilty of plagiarism.

Including Relevant Variables

The major ethical issue at the stage of the research process is determining what variables and values to include in the research question. You need to be certain you included all the important variables. In a needs assessment, it might be tempting to leave out some factors that you think may not support the need you are trying to document. In surveying a community to assess the need for an elder day care center, you want to leave out variables such as transportation need because, if such needs are great, the eventual funding of the project might be jeopardized. All variables perceived as important to the study should be included, however. Completeness is particularly critical when conducting positivist research, in which the variables are clearly defined before the research is undertaken. Including relevant variables is less of a problem with the interpretist approach, when the variables are often identified as part of the study.

Avoiding Reductionism

An associated issue that we discussed previously is reductionism. You need to avoid looking at only one type of variable (for instance, economic factors) and claiming, if an association is found, that this variable alone is responsible for the particular outcome. Reductionism can be a danger when carrying out program evaluations because you are tempted to look only at the variables associated with the program, rather than considering others. For example, if you are evaluating a program that is intended to enhance self-esteem among high school dropouts, you would undoubtedly include the program-related variables such as length of time in the program and so on. You may not consider measuring outside factors that could also influence self-esteem, however, such as involvement in a local sports activity. These other factors may turn out to have far more impact than the program itself, but you may be reluctant to include them because they jeopardize the demonstrated efficacy of the program. Again, this problem of reductionism is more apparent in positivist research. In fact, a tendency to reductionism is one of the major drawbacks of this research approach and provides one of the rationales for social work to use more interpretive studies when attempting to answer many of the questions confronting social workers.

HUMAN DIVERSITY ISSUES IN DEVELOPING THE QUESTION

In developing the question, you must look carefully at human diversity issues to ensure that you are not building in biases against certain groups. The last chapter described the possible bias that exists when only certain groups undertake research in social work. Here will be discussed the potential bias in the literature.

Bias in the Literature

McLaughlin and Braun (1998) discussed the differences between individualist and collectivist orientations in health care decisions. Americans tend to have individualist orientations, whereas Asians and Pacific Islanders tend to have collectivist orientations, meaning that many decisions are made by families and groups rather than by the individual. This is especially true concerning health care decisions. The authors note that the collectivist orientation is not well represented in the research and literature. They recommend that universities and health care settings provide education and training to promote cross-cultural practice and sensitivity.

Before you use materials to help guide a particular research project, you need to be aware of bias in the literature. Literature relating to human diversity issues has been scarce, although in recent years it has grown rapidly. For example, one social work journal is specifically devoted to human diversity issues: the *Journal of Multicultural Social Work*. Generally, though, we need to remember when consulting the literature that most social science research has been conducted by white, middle-class men; even when women have contributed, they have tended to be white, middle-class women. Overrepresentation of the views of these segments of the population, to the exclusion of others, constitutes a clear bias. Research questions developed by other groups may take a rather different course. For example, until relatively recently, few studies had been conducted on the relationship between women's work and family lives, particularly those of minority women and their families. Studies of family functioning often did not examine women's experiences but instead focused on role relationships or parenting practices.

Another human diversity issue in developing the research question is the influence of cultural factors on each of the processes presented in this chapter. For example, how a variable is defined is influenced heavily by the culture in which

Cultural Definitions

Lowery (1998) described American Indian perspectives on addiction and recovery, reaching beyond simply an intellectual understanding of "healing the spirit." The article was purposely organized to reflect the movement between "spirit and science" and included four concepts: (1) balance and wellness, (2) the colonization experience and addiction as a crisis of the spirit, (3) issues of abuse, including sexual abuse, and (4) a time of healing illustrated by a Lakota commemorative event. The author suggests that social workers must explore their definitions and perspectives on healing to enhance both their practice and research.

the definition occurs. One of the examples discussed earlier, *independent living,* is a culturally laden term. In some cultures, this may involve living with the family but being employed outside of the family setting, or living with the family and being married. The possible different definitions are as diverse as the number of cultures.

SUMMARY

A critical step in the research process is the literature review, which assists in the generation of questions, connecting the question to theory, identifying previous research, and giving direction to the project. The unit of analysis needs to be determined at this stage in the research process. Variables and values must be distinguished. The definition and operationalization of variables includes defining goals and activities. Another step in developing the question involves determining the level of measurement: nominal, ordinal, interval, or ratio.

Often the generalist social worker does not have much influence over development of the research question. Ethical issues include ensuring the identification of relevant variables and avoiding reductionism. Human diversity issues in the development of the question include identifying potential bias in the literature and understanding different cultural definitions.

STUDY/EXERCISE QUESTIONS

1. Look at research articles in *Social Work* and identify the unit of analysis used in the study. Also identify the independent and dependent variables when appropriate.

2. You are involved in an evaluation of a support group for parents of children with developmental disabilities.
    a. Identify some possible goals and activities of the group.
    b. Name at least five variables you would need to include in the evaluation.
    c. Define and operationalize these variables.

3. You have been asked to help design and implement a needs assessment for an elder day care facility in your community. Whom would you consult in the early stages of developing the assessment?

4. If you are in a field placement, talk to your supervisor; if not, talk to someone who is employed in a supervisory position in an agency in your community. Discuss with that person who they have involved in research projects at the agency and how they have involved those other people.

5. At your university library, meet with the social work reference librarian. Practice searching for a specific topic.

INFOTRAC COLLEGE EDITION

1. Identify three research articles that examine different aspects of domestic violence and compare the literature review sections. How are these reviews similar and different to one another?
2. In these same articles, identify the independent and dependent variables.

REFERENCES

Birleson, P. (1981). The validity of depression disorders in childhood and the development of a self-rating scale: A research report. *Journal of Child Psychology and Psychiatry, 22,* 73–88.

Cox, C. (1995). Comparing the experiences of black and white caregivers of dementia patients. *Social Work, 40* (3), 343–349.

Hudson, W. W. (1990). *The clinical measurement package.* Homewood, IL: Dorsey Press.

Hyden, M. (1994). Woman battering as a marital act: Interviewing and analysis in context. In Riessman, C. (Ed.), *Qualitative studies in social work research.* Newbury Park, CA: Sage.

Itzhaky, H., & York, A. (1995). The autonomous apartment block: Israeli house committees. *International Social Work, 38,* 355–364.

Lowery, C. T. (1998). American Indian perspectives on addiction and recovery. *Health & Social Work, 23* (2), 127–136.

McLaughlin, L. A., & Braun, K. L. (1998). Asian and Pacific Islander cultural values. *Health and Social Work, 23* (2), 116–126.

Merriam-Webster's Collegiate Dictionary, 10th ed. (1993). Springfield, MA: Merriam-Webster.

Schaffer, M., & Lia-Hoagberg, B. (1994). Prenatal care among low income women. *Families in Society, 75 (3),* 152–159.

van Rooyen, C. (1996). *Taking the leap: A guide to higher degree research study in the Department of Social Work at the University of Natal.* Durban, South Africa: The University of Natal, Department of Social Work.

Vernon, R., & Lynch, D. (2000). *Social Work and the Internet.* Pacific Grove, CA: Brooks/Cole Publishing.

Designing Needs Assessments

T his chapter will examine needs assessments, one of the three major types of research questions undertaken in generalist social work and first described in Chapter 3. Strengths assessments are concerned with discovering the characteristics and extent of a particular social situation to determine the most appropriate response.

Needs assessments are also known as **feasibility studies, front-end analyses,** or **strengths assessments.** Needs assessments were introduced in Chapter 3 as an important research strategy in social work. Social workers carry out needs assessments prior to designing a program, and for generalist social workers the need assessment is probably the most common type of research undertaken.

Needs assessments are often thought of as a type of survey research. Surveys measure people's attitudes, behaviors, or beliefs at one point in time; data are usually collected using questionnaires. In this chapter we will see that the survey is only one type of needs assessment design.

This chapter will include the following topics:

- reasons for conducting needs assessments
- types of designs for needs assessments
- the agency and designing needs assessments
- ethical issues in designing needs assessments
- human diversity issues in designing needs assessments

REASONS FOR CONDUCTING NEEDS ASSESSMENTS

Sometimes it may seem unnecessary to conduct a needs assessment, because it seems obvious that a particular program is needed. For example, a social worker working with families of children with mental retardation has heard parents for the last year maintaining that increased respite care would help considerably to relieve some of the stress for themselves and their families. So why not just go ahead and develop a program? The answer is that since the early 1970s, there has been an unofficial (and sometimes official) requirement that any program proposal be accompanied by a needs assessment that systematically, and as objectively as possible, provides a rationale for a program's initial or further development. Thus, although you think you know what the needs are, this presumed knowledge is only subjective opinion and will not carry much weight with your proposed program's potential funders.

There are a number of different reasons for conducting needs assessments that go beyond just trying to figure out how many people can benefit from a proposed program. Being clear about the reason for conducting the study is important because that can help you more accurately plan, design, and implement the needs assessment. Five different reasons can be identified (Royse & Thyer, 1996):

1. To determine whether services exist in the community
2. To determine whether there are enough clients
3. To determine who uses existing services

4. To determine what barriers prevent clients from accessing services
5. To document the existence of an ongoing social problem

Needs assessments may be conducted for only one of these reasons, or for several. Each will be described in turn using the example of respite care for the parents of mentally retarded children as an illustration.

Determining Whether Services Exist in the Community

Just because you do not know of an intervention or program does not mean that it does not exist. Obviously this is more likely to be the case if you work in a large metropolitan area than if you are employed in a rural setting.

In order to make this determination, use your networking skills, the Internet, or other resources to search for programs. If your community does not already have a directory of social service agencies and programs, create one. Use your research skills to put together a directory of services that are available on computerized databases. This can be either a community-wide resource, or one specifically addressing the needs and concerns of the client population with which you work. In our example, this step would involve documenting services that are already available for families with mentally retarded children in your community.

Determining Whether There Are Enough Clients

One of the more common reasons for conducting a needs assessment is to find out whether enough clients have a particular problem to justify a new program. You may hear the need expressed for respite care from the majority of your clients, but your clients may not constitute enough of a need to start a new program. Perhaps your clients are not representative of clients of other agencies or other workers; in other words, your clients may be a nonrepresentative sample. The extent of the need should be systematically documented.

A Needs Assessment Determining the Number of Clients with a Particular Problem

Singer, Bussey, Song, and Lunghofer (1995) investigated the psychosocial issues of women serving time in jail. The study involved interviewing 201 randomly selected female inmates incarcerated at a municipal jail to establish the needs of this population. Of the women, 64% were in the clinical range for mental health problems, 83% were in the substance abuse range, and 81% had been sexually victimized at some time in their lives.

The authors made nine recommendations for services, including drug and alcohol treatment services, mental health services, education on sexually transmitted diseases, medical services, dental services, and parenting education.

Determining Who Uses Existing Services

Just because an agency or community runs a certain program does not mean that those who could benefit from it use the program. Respite services may be available, but parents may think they are ineligible or may simply not have heard of the program. Certain parents may use the program, but others may not; for example, older parents may use the services more than younger parents.

A Needs Assessment Determining Who Uses Existing Services

Barnes, Given, and Given (1995) examined use of services by daughters giving care to their elderly parents. The researchers compared employed daughters, daughters who were never employed while caregivers, and daughters who ended their employment to continue caregiving. The authors found that although all the caregivers could benefit from social work services, special attention is required for employed daughters, particularly those who are conflicted about their employment and caregiving roles.

Determining What Barriers Prevent Clients from Accessing Services

Sometimes clients know about services and may be referred to them by social workers but for various reasons do not use the services. Identifying these barriers can start the process of redesigning services or developing supplementary services. Often factors such as transportation and child care work as barriers. In the example of parents of children with mental retardation, one barrier might be parents' feeling of guilt concerning their children, in which case counseling and support to the families might be necessary before the families would actually use respite care.

A Needs Assessment Determining the Existence of Barriers to Use of Services

Rittner and Kirk (1995) carried out a survey of low-income, elderly people who attended daytime meal programs. The authors examined sociocultural and quality of life variables as they affected use of health care and transportation services. Most of the respondents self-reported their health as poor or very poor, and more than half had no medical care during the preceding six months. Social isolation from family and support systems exacerbated problems with transportation. Most relied on public transportation to gain access to health care services, but expressed fear in using this form of transportation.

Documenting the Existence of an Ongoing Social Problem

Sometimes it is not clear what problems people are confronting. This is a more fundamental question than documenting how many need a service (which assumes the nature of the problem is already known) and focuses on the characteristics of the social problem. In the respite care example, it was not until the parents started speaking out and expressing their need for support and assistance in the care of their children that the need for respite was recognized.

A Needs Assessment Assessing the Nature of a Social Problem

Strober (1994) investigated the factors involved in the acculturation of Cambodian refugees in Los Angeles. Professionals involved in refugee services noted that Cambodian refugees were more severely psychologically distressed and slower to acculturate than other groups. The findings indicated that their adjustment difficulties were related to severe psychological distress. The Cambodian families and ethnic communities were ineffective at reducing this psychological distress, which the author suggested could be explained by the absence of a preexisting Cambodian community and the refugees' discomfort with existing culturally unfamiliar community agencies. (Note that this study also identified some barriers to existing service use.)

The author suggested that these refugees needed services that support family strengths, stronger worker-client bonds through more reciprocal interaction between the two, and greater worker community involvement.

TYPES OF DESIGNS FOR NEEDS ASSESSMENTS

A needs assessment is usually conceptualized as a descriptive survey, and as discussed in Chapter 3, does not require the types of explanatory designs needed for program evaluations. Some choices in design do need to be made, however. The first step is to understand why the study is being conducted. Use the options outlined in the previous section as a guide. Regardless of which of these questions is being addressed (with the exception of determining whether services already exist), almost all surveys, including needs assessments, rely on a probability sample from which results can be generalized. Since the primary purpose of a needs assessment is to document the need for services as accurately as possible, selecting the sample is critical. Refer to Chapter 8 for a full discussion of this aspect of the study.

The next step in deciding what type of design to use is to pose a number of questions.

1. Whose need is being assessed?
2. Who will have input into the design of the needs assessment?

3.   When will the needs assessment be carried out?
4.   What type of understanding of the need is required?
5.   What level of description is useful?

Each of these questions will be discussed next. (See Figure 5.1 for a chart depicting the different reasons for conducting a needs assessment and the different types of designs.)

Whose Need Is Being Assessed?

The first question, whose need the assessment is addressing, should be answered early on, since it determines who will be selected as participants in the research. Four different levels of needs can be studied: individual, organizational, community, and societal. Most needs assessments are concerned with individual needs of clients or potential clients, including basic needs such as food and shelter and needs for social services. A significant proportion of needs assessments carried out by social workers are concerned with organizational needs, the need for technical assistance, or training of some type—for example, the need for an employee assistance program.

Assessing an Organization's Need

Rycraft (1994) investigated factors that may influence some caseworkers to continue employment in public child welfare when so many are leaving. From interviews with 23 caseworkers, four factors of retention emerged: mission, goodness of fit, supervision, and investment.

Needs assessments are also carried out in communities, assessing the community's need for neighborhood development or services—for example, a community's need for a youth program. Societal needs are assessed at an even broader level—for instance, assessing the need for revisions in Social Security or in national policies related to services to the very old.

Who Will Have Input into the Design of the Needs Assessment?

As with program evaluations, early on you need to determine who will be involved in designing and implementing the needs assessment. Clearly, this determination is partly related to the answer to the previous question—whose need is being assessed. The decision then becomes whether and to what extent participants will have input into planning the project. This book stresses the importance of participatory or action research. Involving the participants in the study design ensures their "ownership" of the results. If participants are involved in designing and implementing a needs assessment, the results not only will have greater validity and relevance but also will be much more likely to be heard.

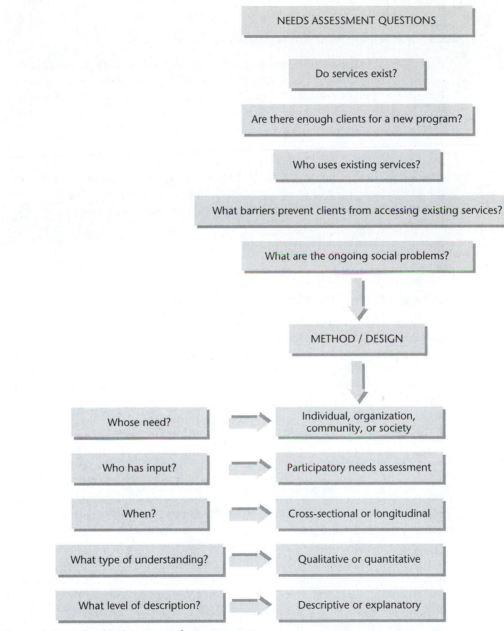

Figure 5.1   ***Designing a needs assessment***

Participatory Action Needs Assessment

Watt (1998) described work that was completed at the First Baltic-Polish Conference on Social Work Education in Lithuania in 1994. The conference participants consisted of indigenous social work educators, social work students, and professional social work educators who discussed the need for improved social work education programs in the Baltic states and Poland. Social work students were purposely invited to the conference to encourage faculty-student collegiality, and their participation in the conference was instrumental in the direction taken by the conference. Results indicated that the newly developed social work programs in the Baltic states and Poland were further along toward their goals of professional awareness, collegiality, and theory-practice interface than was evident before the conference.

When Will the Needs Assessment Be Carried Out?

Two main choices exist about the timing of the data collection. The assessment may be cross-sectional or longitudinal.

With a **cross-sectional design,** a survey is carried out at one point in time. For example, parents are asked about their need for a respite care program. Although it may take a few months to collect the data, whether through a questionnaire or interview, data are collected from each parent just once. This is the most common type of design for a needs assessment.

A Cross-Sectional Study

Nicholson (1997) conducted a cross-sectional survey of 447 Southeast Asian refugees to determine the influence of preemigration and postemigration stressors on mental health. Results showed that 40% of participants suffered from depression, 35% from anxiety, and 14% from posttraumatic stress disorder. Mental health outcomes were affected by one preemigration factor, experienced trauma, and two postemigration factors, the degree of current stress and perceived health. The author suggested that social workers implement programs that decrease current stressors and rebuild indigenous social supports.

A **longitudinal design** might sometimes be necessary. Longitudinal studies are surveys conducted on multiple occasions over an extended period of time. There are three types of longitudinal studies: trend surveys, cohort surveys, and panel surveys.

A Trend Study

Caputo (1995) compared various measures of African-American and white family income inequality and poverty for the periods 1969–1980 and 1981–1992.

Trend studies require multiple samplings from the same population over months or years to monitor changes or trends. For example, a trend study might examine how the characteristics of clients, or their problems that are served by a program, change over time, with the goal of changing the focus of the program to meet any changing needs.

Cohort studies examine specific subgroups as they change over time. These subgroups have specific characteristics in common; often this characteristic is age. For example, a cohort study may study the changing needs of families over time. In 1985 a group of families with parents in their early twenties were interviewed; in 1990 a different group in their late twenties; and in 1995 families with parents in their early thirties. An analysis of changing needs could then be made. Cohort studies differ from trend studies in that they examine changes over time of a *specific subgroup*, whereas trend studies look at changes in a *population* over time.

Panel studies, unlike trend and cohort studies, study the *same set of people* over time. For example, graduates of a B.S.W. program might be asked about their further education needs two, four, and six years after graduation. In the cohort sample above, it would also be possible that the same families could be studied over a period of ten years.

A Panel Study

Robertson (1997) used data from the National Longitudinal Survey of Youth (NLSY) to compare the earnings and work efforts of young nonresidential fathers, residential fathers, and men without children. The NLSY was a panel study of 12,686 people, 6,403 men and 6,283 women, ages 14 to 21 in 1979. In 1990 there were 5,112 respondents. These were the subjects in the Robertson study. The study found that nonresidential fathers earned less and worked fewer hours than the other groups, generally as a result of lower levels of education and job training.

What Type of Understanding of the Need Is Required?

As with other types of research strategies, the decision about whether a positivist or interpretist approach is appropriate needs to be made.

Generally needs assessments adopt primarily a positivist approach. The goal after all is to provide documentation of need that will withstand the critical review of a funding organization or other monitoring body. As such, needs assessments usually involve either collecting new data through questionnaires (either mailed or face-to-face) or using secondary or already existing data, whether from government or nongovernment sources. (See Chapter 9 for a discussion of these data collection methods.)

Sometimes, however, a more in-depth understanding of a need is required. In such a case it may be necessary to use an interpretive approach or at least to collect more qualitative data than is usual in a needs assessment. For example, you may be interested in finding out more detail about what parents of mentally retarded children have in mind when they express the need for respite care. What is their definition of respite care? What have been their experiences of respite care in the past?

Qualitative data collection methods often include interviewing key informants, using focus groups, a community forum, and observation, all of which are discussed in detail in Chapter 9. These types of needs assessments are less dependent on probability sampling because of the different type of understanding sought.

A Needs Assessment Using Qualitative Data

Chauncey (1994) collected data through individual interviews and group meetings on the emotional concerns and treatment needs of male partners of female sexual abuse survivors. Concerns included conflicts about expressing needs, frustration with various aspects of their relationships, guilt and shame at having feelings, questions about how to deal with relatives, and sexual issues.

What Level of Description Is Useful?

You need to determine whether it is necessary to go beyond basic description and examine the relationship between certain variables in the study. These types of designs are often used in program evaluations and will be described in the next chapter. However, in some needs assessments (unlike program evaluations, where the program itself is the independent variable and can be changed) the independent variable is fixed and cannot be changed in any way. For example, you might be interested in the relationship between the level of retardation in the child and the expressed need of the parents for respite care. Here the level of retardation cannot be changed as the participants in the study already possess this factor (level of retardation) before the study begins. This type of study is known as **ex post facto design** (meaning simply "after the fact"). Common variables in ex post facto designs include gender, ethnicity, age, living situation, and type of problem.

An Ex Post Facto Needs Assessment

Chassler (1997) administered the Attachment History Questionnaire to 30 female anorectic and bulimic patients and 31 primary female social work students who served as the comparison group. The findings demonstrated that the anorectics and bulimics differed significantly from the comparisons on all four subfactors of the questionnaire: secure attachment base, parental discipline, threats of separation, and peer affectional support. These results were interpreted using John Bowlby's attachment theory.

A number of problems are associated with the ex post facto design, and it is important to note that this is not a form of experimental design. The independent variable is simply an attribute, not an experimental manipulation such as random assignment to a program or to the group that is not in the program. In addition, any difference in the dependent variable could be due to many other factors for which this design does not control. Thus the relationship between the variables is simply an association. Statements about causality cannot be made with ex post facto designs. In other words, although there may be a relationship between parents' requesting respite care less frequently and parents' having less severely retarded children, it cannot be said that being a parent of a less severely retarded child *causes* the need for less frequent respite care.

THE AGENCY AND DESIGNING NEEDS ASSESSMENTS

A needs assessment is the type of research most often carried out by generalist social workers. The designs and variations offered in this chapter offer only a glimpse of what can be accomplished with needs assessments. When you need to carry out this type of research, be creative in your attempt to document need. Instead of just a mailed survey, think about some alternative strategies for collecting the data. Involve the participants as much as possible; remember, they are the ones who will be receiving the services.

ETHICAL ISSUES IN DESIGNING NEEDS ASSESSMENTS

A key ethical issue with needs assessments is ensuring that the needs documented in your report are those expressed by the participants in the research, rather than the needs the agency or administration would like to see met. Agencies do have their own agendas; sometimes there is a temptation to respond more to the source of funding than to the needs of the potential or actual clients. Again, as with ethical issues raised previously in this book, this problem can be avoided by ensuring that clients have input into the research. They must direct and design it as much as possible, with the result that they, rather than the agency, come to own it. This approach not only ensures an appropriate focus for the research but also can empower the participants in the study.

An Empowering (and Participatory) Needs Assessment

Larson, Poswa, and van Rooyen (1997) described how a group of students in Kwa Zulu Natal, South Africa, were placed for their field practicum in a community called Bhambayi. Bhambayi was originally a model community established by Gandhi. Now it is primarily a squatters' settlement, with few formal services and extremely high unemployment. The students, in consultation with the community, wanted to assess the needs of the youth in Bhambayi. After interviewing 60 youths, all of whom were officially unemployed, more than half were found to have never attended high school. One of the questions asked about their skills. The responses included carpentry, needlework, shoemaking, and mechanics. It was also disclosed that many held informal jobs. The students and the community built on these skills by developing income-generating projects such as food production, concrete block making, and mechanical repairs. The research itself gave motivation and a sense of hope to the residents of Bhambayi as many commented that until asked about their skills, they had felt they did not possess skills that could result in income.

HUMAN DIVERSITY ISSUES IN DESIGNING NEEDS ASSESSMENTS

The primary purpose of a needs assessment is to identify "deficits" or problems so that they can be addressed through new programs or modifications to existing programs. Identifying needs, while obviously a necessary step, can lead to certain groups' being stigmatized as consistently being associated with certain problems. For example, inner-city African-American youths may be associated with crime, adolescent parents with inadequate parenting skills, refugee groups with acculturation problems, and so on. It is important to remember that needs as-

A "Strengths" Needs Assessment

Marin and Vacha (1994) examined self-help strategies and resources among people at risk for homelessness. They studied the practice of doubling up with friends and relatives and examined the relationships with those who housed them. Recommendations were made to enhance the living conditions among doubled-up households so they can continue to serve as a foundation in the prevention of homelessness.

sessments can also assess the strengths of the participants in the research and often should do this in addition to presenting the needs.

SUMMARY

Designing needs assessments is a central research activity for generalist social workers. There are five reasons for carrying out needs assessments: to determine whether services exist; to determine whether there are enough clients to justify a program; to assess who uses the existing services; to assess the barriers that prevent clients from accessing existing services; and to document the existence of an ongoing social problem. The type of design adopted depends on the reason for conducting the needs assessment; whose need is being assessed; who will have input into the design (that is, whether a participatory design will be used); when will the assessment be carried out (that is, whether it will be a longitudinal or cross-sectional study); what type of understanding is needed (interpretive or positivist); and what type of description is required. Ethical issues include ensuring that participants have maximum input into the design of the needs assessment. Human diversity issues include the importance of addressing strengths as well as deficits in the documentation of needs.

STUDY/EXERCISE QUESTIONS

1. Find an article in a social work journal and identify
   a. limitations in the methodology
   b. how you would have designed it differently
2. Talk with your fellow students about a service/program need that seems to exist at your university. Design a needs assessment for this issue.
   a. Design one using the positivist approach.
   b. Design one using the interpretist approach.

INFOTRAC COLLEGE EDITION

1. Search for a *needs assessment* and describe whose need was assessed, who had input, when was it carried out, what type of understanding was required, and what level of description occurred.
2. In the needs assessment found as a result of the above search, what recommendations for services or programs were made as a result of the research?

REFERENCES

Barnes, C. L., Given, B. A., & Given, C. W. (1995). Parent caregivers: A comparison of employed and not employed daughters. *Social Work, 40* (3), 375–381.

Caputo, R. K. (1995). Income inequality and family poverty. *Families in Society, 76* (10), 604–614.

Chassler, L. (1997). Understanding anorexia nervosa and bulimia nervosa from an attachment perspective. *Clinical Social Work Journal, 25* (4), 407–423.

Chauncey, S. (1994). Emotional concerns and treatment of male partners of female sexual abuse survivors. *Social Work, 39* (6), 669–676.

Marin, M. V., & Vacha, E. F. (1994). Self help strategies and resources among people at risk of homelessness: Empirical findings and social service policy. *Social Work, 39* (6), 649–657.

Nicholson, B. L. (1997). The influence of preemigration and postemigration stressors on mental health: A study of Southeast Asian refugees. *Social Work Research, 21* (1), 19–31.

Ranson, B. K., Poswa, T., & van Rooyen, C. (1997). Youth unemployment— a study in an informal settlement in Kwa-Zulu-Natal. *Social Work, 33* (2), 165–177.

Rittner, B., & Kirk, A. B. (1995). Health care and public transportation use by poor and frail elderly people. *Social Work, 40* (3), 365–373.

Robertson, J. G. (1997). Young nonresidential fathers have lower earnings: Implications for child support enforcement. *Social Work Research, 21* (4), 211–223.

Royse, D., & Thyer, B. A. (1996). *Program evaluation* (2nd ed.). Chicago: Nelson Hall.

Rycraft, J. R. (1994). The party isn't over: The agency role in the retention of public child welfare caseworkers. *Social Work, 31* (9), 75–80.

Singer, M., Bussey, J., Song, L., & Lunghofer, L. (1995). *Social Work, 40* (1), 103–113.

Strober, S. B. (1994). Social work interventions to alleviate Cambodian refugee psychological distress. *International Social Work, 37* (1), 23–35.

Watt, J. W. (1998). Social work education in the Baltic states and Poland: Students assess their programs. *International Social Work, 41,* 103–113.

Designing Program Evaluations

■

here are two different types of program evaluations: formative and summative. These were discussed briefly in Chapter 3. A formative program evaluation focuses on description rather than on causality. For these types of evaluations, the interpretive approach is often more appropriate. A summative program evaluation is used in determining the extent to which the goals of the program were met—in other words, assessing the extent to which the program caused a specific outcome. Usually a positivist approach is adopted with this type of research. Causality demands that three basic conditions be met, as set out in Chapter 1. First, the cause precedes the effect in time. Second, the cause and the effect are related to one another. Third, this relationship cannot be accounted for by other factors. These three conditions are established by aspects of the summative research design, which includes the timing of the data collection and the formation of comparison groups. Different group designs can be used to establish causality. These are designs that help you assess the relationship of the program to a group of client systems rather than one client system as in evaluating individual practice (a topic that will be discussed in Chapter 7).

Both formative and summative program evaluations are critical to assessing programs. A summative program evaluation, however, is usually required by a funding source, and the establishment of causality presents a major challenge. Consequently, the focus in this chapter will be upon these summative evaluations and their associated group designs.

As with other steps of the research process, you may not be directly involved in designing the research for a program evaluation. At some point, however, your agency will undertake such an evaluation, and it is important that you understand the implications of selecting one type of design over another. In some cases, you may find yourself with the responsibility of initiating an evaluation.

Throughout this chapter a case example will be used to demonstrate the pros and cons of different designs. Assume you are employed by a program that offers high-risk adolescents a series of six birth control classes to increase knowledge of birth control practices. You are asked to evaluate the effectiveness of the program. During this process you will need to consider different types of designs.

This chapter will discuss the following:

- formative program evaluations
- summative program evaluations
- types of summative program evaluation designs
- the agency and program evaluation design
- ethical issues in program evaluation design
- human diversity issues in program evaluation design

FORMATIVE PROGRAM EVALUATIONS

Formative evaluations are generally very descriptive and provide detail about a program's strengths and weaknesses. Interpretive approaches using qualitative data are particularly useful with these types of evaluations.

A Formative Program Evaluation

Weissman and LaRue (1998) explored a program that serves students whose parents are incarcerated. The authors looked at the outreach and programmatic approaches that were implemented to address the special needs of the population being served by the program. They found that the holistic, multifaceted, and open approach that the program used to identify, assess, and meet the needs of the students was beneficial.

In the adolescent birth control program, a formative evaluation would be undertaken if you were interested in finding out how the adolescents experienced the program: What did they perceive as its limitations and strengths? Alternatively a formative evaluation might examine how the parenting classes were being conducted, how the syllabus was developed, and whether the syllabus was being followed.

Formative evaluations make no attempt to establish any type of causality—in other words, no claim is made that the program resulted in specific outcomes. Also, no attempt is made to generalize the findings. Consequently, there are no dependent and independent variables and the sampling is generally purposive, rather than random. The focus is on in-depth description and analysis as a means of improving and strengthening the program. Thus much of the emphasis in a formative program evaluation is in assessing quality.

In understanding the adolescents' experiences with the birth control classes, in-depth interviews might be conducted to try to elicit the youths' reactions to the program. The classes could be observed and the facilitator interviewed in an attempt to understand how the classes were being implemented and to identify areas in need of development.

Often, formative evaluations can be strengthened by comparing various factors, such as males and females, ethnic groups, socioeconomic groups, and so on.

Formative evaluations are extremely useful in the first year or so of a program's implementation, since findings from such a study can provide immediate feedback for improvement and growth. Thorough formative evaluations can lay the groundwork for later summative evaluations.

SUMMATIVE PROGRAM EVALUATIONS

Summative program evaluations and their associated group designs are primarily concerned with causality. As such, validity is a central issue. When considering the validity of a research design, two different validity issues are considered: internal validity and external validity.

Internal validity is the extent to which the changes in the dependent variable(s) are a result of the introduction of the independent variable(s) and not some other factor(s). For example, was the knowledge of birth control a result of the adolescents' participation in the birth control classes, or were other factors responsible for this increase in knowledge? This is an attempt to establish causality. In order to ensure internal validity in the birth control question, the three aspects of causality described in the previous section need to be addressed.

The first two conditions—that the cause precedes the effect and that there is a relationship between cause and effect—can be met by one aspect of the research design: the data collection time. With the adolescents, you can measure their level of knowledge about birth control before and after the classes. If you find that their knowledge level is low prior to the classes and high after the classes, this establishes that the classes preceded the increase in knowledge level.

The two measures also allow you to assess the extent of the relationship between a change in knowledge levels and participation in the classes. For example, 80% of those in the classes had a high level of knowledge after their participation. To decide whether this is a significant or important relationship, statistical tests are used (these will be discussed in Chapter 13). Even if you do determine that the relationship is significant, however, you still cannot say the classes caused a change in knowledge level, because the relationship could be explained by other factors. For example, the adolescents may have received some instruction at school on birth control at the same time as you were collecting data, which contributed to the change in knowledge level. This is where the second aspect of research design, comparison groups, as it relates to causality becomes so important. **Comparison groups** either go through another type of program or else receive no type of bona fide intervention. These comparison groups can help strengthen causality claims. If the increase in knowledge level is greater among those who attended the classes than among those who were in the comparison group, you can begin to narrow down the factors responsible for that change to the classes. See Figure 6.1 for an illustration of internal validity.

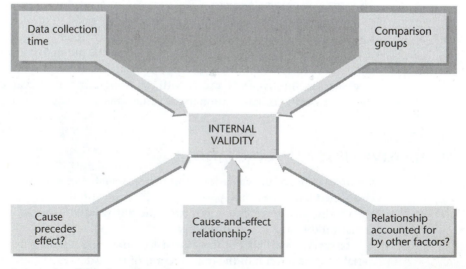

Figure 6.1   ***Internal validity in group design***

It is important that the comparison groups be otherwise equivalent to the group involved in the program being studied. The most reliable way of ensuring equivalence of the groups is to use random assignment of subjects into an **experimental group** (the group that receives the intervention being evaluated) and a **control group** (the group that does not receive the intervention being evaluated). **Random assignment** means that every subject has an equal chance of being assigned to either group. Equivalency of the groups is important because without it you cannot determine whether the disparity in outcome between the two groups is due to the treatment or to the difference between the two groups. Later in this chapter some problems associated with random assignment and some alternative strategies for setting up comparison groups will be discussed.

Do not confuse random assignment with random sampling. Random sampling involves creating a sample from a population, not assigning the experimental and control group, and will be discussed in Chapter 8. Random sampling and random assignment may or may not be used in the same study. They are independent procedures and have different implications for the findings. Random sampling is concerned with the generalizability of the findings and the representativeness of the sample. Random assignment is concerned with the equivalence of the experimental and control groups and with establishing causality. You will see in our next discussion, however, that equivalency of the groups can *also* have an effect on the generalizability of the findings.

External validity is the other type of validity of concern in group design; it refers to the extent to which the research results are generalizable to the wider population. (See Chapter 1 for a discussion of generalizability.) External validity relates to the effectiveness of the treatment with other, similar client systems. As will be discussed in Chapter 8, generalizability is influenced by the sampling approach. In addition, however, generalizability depends on two other conditions: first, ensuring the equivalency of the groups, and second, ensuring that nothing happens during the course of the evaluation to jeopardize the equivalence of the groups or the representativeness of the sample.

The first condition for external validity is to ensure the *equivalency of the groups* being compared. You may decide that randomly assigning the comparison group is not feasible and that the comparison group should be made up of adolescents who are not eligible for the classes. This type of comparison group is problematic, however, because individuals in the comparison group might possess different characteristics from those who entered group therapy. Consequently, not only would any outcome showing differences between the two groups have a lower internal validity than it might otherwise (that is, the causality would be questionable), but in addition the population to which the results could be generalized would be limited. The results could only be generalized to those eligible for the classes.

The second condition influenced by the research design and that affects external validity is ensuring that *no interference* occurs during the course of the evaluation that may decrease the distinction between the experimental and control group. Interference of this kind is sometimes called **treatment diffusion.** It can occur in three different ways. First, the adolescents may discuss the class with their peers, some of whom may be in the comparison group. Then comparison between the two groups becomes problematic. Second, when the program is not clearly defined, the distinction between the program group and the comparison group can be difficult. (This often points to the need for a formative evaluation in order to define the program components more clearly.) Finally, treatment diffusion can result from reactivity effects. Changes occur when people are aware they are participants in a study that blurs the distinction between the program group and the comparison group. Treatment diffusion leads to problems in generalizing the initial results to the wider population. See Figure 6.2 for an illustration of external validity.

TYPES OF SUMMATIVE PROGRAM EVALUATION DESIGNS

In this section, different types of research designs, with their relative validity problems or threats, will be examined.

Preexperimental Designs

A preexperimental design is a group design that often is the only feasible design to adopt. It uses comparison groups rather than control groups or no type of comparison or control group and thus has limited internal and external validity.

One-Group Posttest-Only Design

The **one-group posttest-only design** consists of one group (so that there is no comparison group) with one point of data collection (after the intervention). Figure 6.3 shows how this design might be visualized. Sometimes this design is

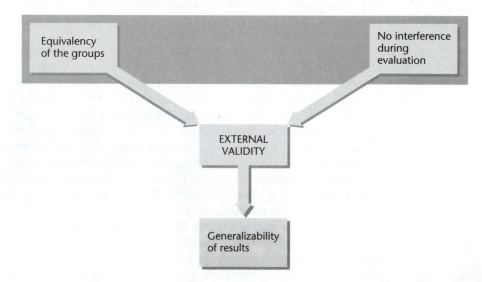

Figure 6.2 **External validity in group design**

Figure 6.3   ***One-group posttest-only design***

referred to as a one-shot case study. Note that although the term *test* is used in the name of this design, this is simply a way of talking about the point at which data collection occurs. The data collection method may be any of the types discussed in Chapter 9, such as observing a behavior or administering a questionnaire.

The one-group posttest-only design can be useful in gathering information about how a program is functioning. This design can answer several questions: For example, how well are participants functioning at the end of the program? Are minimum standards for outcomes being achieved? This type of design is often used for **client satisfaction surveys,** in which clients are asked about how they experienced or perceived the program.

The one-group posttest-only design is very limited in its ability to explain or make statements about whether a program caused particular outcomes for clients and whether the results can be generalized to other client populations. Consequently, this design is viewed as having numerous threats to its validity— both internal and external.

A One-Group Posttest-Only Design

Denby, Rindfleisch, and Bean (1999) studied predictors of foster parents' satisfaction and intent to continue to foster. A sample of 539 foster parents in a specific state completed a questionnaire on the factors that influence the satisfaction of foster parents and the factors that influence the intent of foster parents to continue to foster. The researchers found that efforts to increase the supply of foster homes through recruitment is insufficient and that foster parents need greater support, training, and professional regard after they have begun fostering.

Threats to Internal Validity

Remember that internal validity refers to whether it can be determined if the program caused a particular outcome. With the case example, we need to ask whether it was, in fact, the provision of birth control information that led to any increase in the knowledge.

Using the one-group posttest-only design results in the following threats to internal validity.

Selection.   The kinds of people selected for one group may differ from the kinds selected for another. It may be that the clients who enrolled in the program were already highly motivated to learn about birth control. There was no pretest to measure this potential predisposition of the clients, so this possibility of **selection** threatens internal validity.

History.   **History** involves those events—other than the program—that could affect the outcome. Participants' high levels of knowledge about birth control may result from classes held in school or from some other factor. Without a comparison group, this possibility cannot be assessed.

Mortality.   Subjects may drop out of the groups so that the resulting groups are no longer equivalent; this possibility is called **mortality.** Some adolescents may have attended one class on birth control and then dropped out; however, they are still considered to be members of the experimental group. As a result, the group that ultimately receives the posttest is biased and perhaps shows a higher success rate than would be the case if the success rates of those who dropped out were also monitored. Consequently, the outcome of *all* participants must be assessed, which cannot be done without some type of pretest.

Note that mortality and selection are a little like mirror images. Selection is the bias involved when people initially choose to participate in the program. Mortality is the bias introduced by those who drop out of the program once they have begun.

As for our case example, because the data collection only occurs once (after the intervention) and because of the lack of a comparison group, the extent to which it can be stated that the program caused a change in birth control knowledge is limited with the one-group posttest-only design.

Threats to External Validity

The one-group posttest-only design poses some threats to external validity and generalizability of results. Possible problems include the following.

Selection-treatment interaction.   **Selection-treatment interaction** occurs when the ability to generalize is limited because the sample is not randomly selected or there is no pretest, so you cannot determine how typical the clients are. In our example, the adolescents may all be highly motivated to learn about birth control prior to enrolling in the program so that whether they complete the classes is irrelevant.

History-treatment interaction.   **History-treatment interaction** occurs when other factors may be contributing to the outcome and so might affect the generalizability of the results (for example, if the positive outcomes resulted from a massive media campaign on pregnancy prevention rather than from the program). The program might have a negative outcome if the evaluation were carried out at a different point in time.

One-Group Pretest/Posttest Design

Another preexperimental design, the **one-group pretest/posttest design** (Figure 6.4), is similar to the preceding design except that a pretest is added. In the case example, the pretest might consist of a questionnaire given to all clients

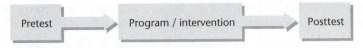

Figure 6.4   ***One-group pretest/posttest design***

that asks about their knowledge of birth control prior to attending the classes. This design helps answer several questions: not only how well participants are functioning at the end of the program, and whether minimum standards of outcome are being achieved, but also how much participants change during their participation in the program. This is a useful design, and certainly one that is often used in program evaluations. It is also a useful design to use when no comparison group is feasible (as, for example, in the Cushman, Kalmuss, and Namerow [1993] study of birth mothers placing their infants for adoption).

Some additional information can be gained from this type of design that can enhance statements of causality. The pretest allows selection to be ruled out as an alternative explanation, because any preexisting information on birth control would be identified. In the long run, however, this design often poses even more threats to validity than the one-group posttest-only design.

A One-Group Pretest/Posttest Design

Hurd (1998) studied strengths-based teaching in social work. To determine what changes had occurred in students' perceptions of their professional strengths, a pretest was administered by the instructor on the first day of class, and a posttest was administered on the last day of class. Results showed that the students viewed themselves as more competent at the end of the course and that these results were statistically significant.

Threats to Internal Validity

The one-group pretest/posttest design poses the following threats to internal validity.

History.   Because there is no comparison group, there is no way to tell whether other events may have affected the outcome.

Maturation.   Even though a change may be detected between the pretest and the posttest, this change may be due not to the subjects' participation in the program, but rather to **maturation.** Subjects may change over the course of time due to lifelong learning rather than program effects. With adolescents, especially, the possibility of maturation is a potentially serious threat to internal validity.

In the case example, the adolescents' level of knowledge would have changed regardless of the program. Maturation is a particularly strong threat if the participants are young, or if there is a long time between the pretest and the posttest. A comparison group helps control for maturation effects.

Testing.   The **testing** threat to validity may occur any time the subjects are exposed to a measuring instrument more than once. If the pretest gave the adolescents information that could increase their knowledge of birth control, this effect cannot be separated from the effect of the classes. A comparison group can help control for these testing effects because if they do exist, they exist for both groups; if the knowledge of the clients in the experimental group changed more than those in the comparison group, the researcher would be much more comfortable in concluding that the intervention was responsible for this change, rather than the pretest.

Instrumentation.   The way in which the variables are measured, known as **instrumentation,** may change during the course of the evaluation. For example, a questionnaire may change between its first and second administration. Sometimes, these changes are difficult to avoid. For example, the context in which the questionnaire is administered may change, as may the person administering it. This change, rather than the intervention, may account for any difference in the results.

Regression to the mean.   In the example, if eligibility for the birth control classes was determined by a test on birth control knowledge (those with low knowledge levels would be eligible), then a posttest after the classes could exhibit a regression to the mean. This may occur because most people tend to perform close to their averages, but on some days they may score particularly high or low. When they take the test again, they will tend to regress to the mean or be closer to their average score. Thus any change in score between the pretest and the posttest would not necessarily reflect the influence of the program but could simply be **regression to the mean.**

Interaction of selection and other threats.   Even if none of these previously discussed threats to internal validity is applicable to the general population, the threats may be relevant for those subjects selected to participate in the study. To take maturation as an example, it may not be the case that women in general become more knowledgeable about birth control as they mature. Adolescents who express a desire to receive more information through counseling, however, may also be more likely to become more knowledgeable just as a function of their age. This represents the interaction of selection and other threats—in this case, maturation.

Threats to External Validity

History-treatment interaction.   History-treatment interaction may be a problem with the one-group pretest/posttest design.

Reactive effects.   **Reactive effects** can occur when subjects change their behavior because they know they are participating in the study. The resulting outcomes may be distorted and cannot be generalized to a wider population. These reactive effects are difficult to overcome in any design because you cannot ethically engage in research without gaining the subject's consent. Consent will be discussed later in this chapter.

Static-Group Comparison Design

The **static-group comparison design** is a third type of preexperimental design. An extension of the posttest-only design, it includes a comparison group that also has a posttest (Figure 6.5). In this design, the groups are nonequivalent in that the comparison group was not randomly assigned, and there is no way of knowing how the groups are different or similar.

Several strategies can be adopted to achieve some equivalency for the comparison group even if random assignment does not occur. These strategies include baseline comparison, matching, cohort groups, and overflow comparison.

A Static-Group Comparison Design

Itzhaky (1995) compared two types of community organizations in Israel. One community center was a project supervised by an interdisciplinary committee and a community social worker; the focus was on the participation of clients. In the other center, decisions were made by the staff and management with no social worker involvement. The experiences of the clients from each center were compared.

Baseline Comparison

Baseline comparison occurs when the comparison group is composed of cases handled prior to the introduction to the program. The problem with this approach is that it is difficult to determine whether cases identified as eligible in the absence of a program actually would have been referred to the program.

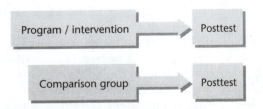

Figure 6.5   ***Static-group comparison design***

Matching

Matching involves selecting certain characteristics that are thought to have an important impact on outcomes—for example, gender or ethnicity—and ensuring that these characteristics are equally represented in each group. In the example, because of previous research and our own experience, you may think that ethnicity—for instance, being Hispanic—is an important factor in determining the effectiveness of the program. Consequently, you make sure the program group has the same proportion of Hispanic adolescents as the comparison group. In a sense, matching is equivalent to quota sampling. Matching can also be combined with random assignment. When combined in this way, it is the equivalent of stratified random sampling. Needless to say, matching has the same problems as stratified or quota sampling. You need to ensure that the variables considered are, in fact, key variables. Often, it is difficult to determine the critical variables because of the lack of previous research or other sources of information to guide these decisions.

Matching

Manion, Firestone, Cloutier, Ligezinska, McIntyre, and Ensom (1998) matched case families with comparison families on the sex and age of the child (within 6 months) and, where possible, the family constellation (single-/two-parent family) to evaluate the emotional and behavioral adjustments of parents and children within three months and one year after the discovery of child extrafamilial sexual abuse. The children in the comparison families had never experienced any form of sexual abuse as reported by the parents and/or the child. The study showed that both parents and children of case families experienced significant effects both initially and one year after the disclosure. For the children, self-blame and guilt for the abuse and the extent of traumatization predicted their symptomology three months and one year postdisclosure. Child age and gender also contributed to the prediction of child outcome measures. For mothers, satisfaction in the parenting role, perceived support, and intrusive symptoms predicted their initial emotional functioning, while longer-term predictors of emotional functioning was predicted by avoidant symptoms, child's internalizing behavior, and mother's initial emotional functioning.

Cohort Groups

Cohort groups provide another strategy for compiling comparison groups. A variation on matching, cohort groups are composed of individuals who move through an organization at the same time as those in the program being evaluated do, but who do not receive the services of the program.

For example, you compare adolescents in the same class at school. Some are enrolled in the program—that is, the birth control class—and others are not; or one entire class is enrolled, and another class is not. Cohort groups can also be combined with matching.

Overflow Comparison

Sometimes people are referred to a program, but because the slots are filled, a waiting list is created. The **overflow comparison group** made up of people on the waiting list can then serve as a comparison group. However the comparison groups are formed in the static-group comparison design, they are all non-equivalent—that is, not randomly assigned. This design offers one advantage over single-group designs: The threat from history is eliminated, because external events that may have an effect on the outcome will be occurring in both groups. The static-group comparison design still has other threats to internal and external validity, however.

Threats to Internal Validity

Selection.   The major threat to the static-group comparison design's internal validity is selection, which results from not randomly assigning the groups and having no pretest. Consequently, it is not possible to determine how similar the two groups are to each other. Any difference that occurs in the outcome between the two groups may not be due to the presence or absence of the intervention, but to other differences between the groups.

For example, if the experimental group is made up of adolescents who elected to enroll in the birth control classes and the comparison group is made up of adolescents who did not want to attend the classes, the comparison group may be very different from the experimental group. The experimental group may later have greater birth control knowledge than the comparison group, but this may be less a function of the classes than a function of the experimental group's greater motivation to learn about birth control. The equivalency of the groups is not assured because of the absence of random assignment and the lack of a pretest.

Mortality.   Because of the absence of a pretest and the absence of a randomly assigned comparison group, mortality is also still a problem with the static-group comparison design.

Threats to External Validity

Selection-treatment interaction.   Selection-treatment interaction is a problem with this design.

Reactive effects.   Reactive effects threaten the external validity of this design.

Quasi-Experimental Designs

These types of designs eliminate more of the threats to internal validity and external validity than preexperimental designs, and use comparison groups rather than control groups and thus will have limited internal and external validity.

Time Series Design

A **time series design** overcomes some of the problems of the designs discussed previously, measuring several times before the intervention and then several times after the intervention (Figure 6.6). For example, the adolescents might be tested on their knowledge of birth control several times over the course of several months prior to the classes. Then the same test is given several times after the classes. The test might also be given during the time of the classes.

The advantage of the time series design is its ability to detect trends in the data before and after the intervention. In effect, this discounts the problems of maturation, testing, and instrumentation associated with the single pretest/posttest design because any trends in these effects could be detected. For example, if maturation is having an effect on the adolescents' knowledge of birth control, that effect will be detected in a difference between the pretest scores.

Time Series

Nugent, Bruley, and Allen (1999) tested the effectiveness of Aggression Replacement Training (ART) on male and female antisocial behavior at a runaway shelter. The case records of 522 adolescent participants who stayed in a runaway shelter were assessed using measures of antisocial behavior for a 310-day period before the implementation of the program and then for a 209-day period after the program. The results suggested that the ART may be useful along with other approaches in reducing juvenile antisocial behavior in a short-term residential setting.

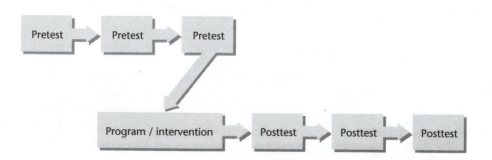

Figure 6.6   ***Time series design***

Threats to Internal Validity

History.   Because of the absence of any type of comparison group, history is a major threat to internal validity in the time series design. Events external to the evaluation would have to be fairly powerful, however, in order to confound the effect of the classes.

Threats to External Validity

History-treatment interaction.   A potential threat to external validity is history-treatment interaction, as history interacts with the classes. An intervention that appears to work under some circumstances may not under others.

Reactive effects.   With repeated testing, reactive effects are also a problem.

Pretest/Posttest Comparison-Group Design

The **pretest/posttest comparison-group design** is a combination of the static-group comparison and the one-group pretest/posttest design (see Figure 6.7). The comparison group is still not randomly assigned, although this

A Pretest/Posttest Comparison-Group Design

Kramer (1998) compared social work students enrolled in a "Grief, Death, Loss, and Life" course to those who were enrolled in other electives in order to determine students' level of death acceptance and sense of preparedness to respond to personal and professional losses. The author administered a pretest on the first day of class to both groups of students and the posttest on the last day of class. The findings suggested that students who enrolled in the grief course perceived greater competence in their knowledge, skills, and sense of preparation for working with grieving clients. Students enrolled in the grief course also demonstrated increased cognitive and affective dimensions of death acceptance.

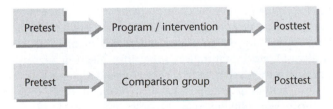

Figure 6.7   **Pretest/posttest comparison-group design**

design can adopt any of the various methods used to set up comparison groups that are mentioned for the static-group comparison design. By combining features of both the static-group comparison and the one-group pretest/posttest design, this design becomes less problematic than either of them. History is controlled due to the comparison group, and the pretest identifies, to a certain extent, differences or similarities between the groups.

Threats to Internal Validity

Selection and maturation interaction.   In the example, the pretest may indicate that the group that received classes had more knowledge about birth control than the comparison group prior to the intervention. If the posttest also indicates this difference between the groups, maturation may have been the cause of the treatment group's having even greater knowledge over time, whether or not they received the classes. This potential problem with internal validity depends a great deal on how the comparison group is selected and what the results indicate.

Threats to External Validity

Selection-treatment interaction.   A potential problem is selection-treatment interaction, which can affect generalizability of the results.

Maturation-treatment interaction.   Another potential problem is maturation-treatment interaction.

Reactive effects.   Also a problem with the pretest/posttest comparison-group design are reactive effects.

Experimental Designs

These designs result in findings that can make the strongest claim for causality.

Pretest/Posttest Control-Group Design

The difference between the **pretest/posttest control-group design** and the previous design is that the comparison group and experimental groups are randomly assigned. When this occurs, the comparison group is referred to as a control group (see Figure 6.8). In the example, random assignment to either the control or experimental group might be made from high-risk students in a high school class. As a result of a randomly assigned control group, the threats to internal validity of history, maturation, mortality, selection, regression to the mean testing, and instrumentation are virtually eliminated.

Only one potential external validity problem with the pretest/posttest control-group design remains. This involves the possible reactive effect of the pretest.

Despite the strength of this design, there are some difficulties in its implementation. Some of these problems are similar to those encountered in setting

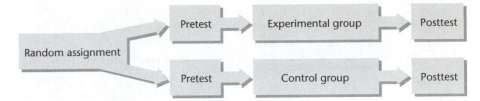

Figure 6.8   ***Pretest/posttest control-group design***

A Pretest/Posttest Control-Group Design

Children with learning disabilities are at risk for poor peer relationships even in mainstreamed classrooms. The program to be evaluated was designed to work with fifth-grade learning disabled (LD) children to improve their acceptance by their nonlearning disabled (NLD) fifth-grade peers. The intervention was a cognitive behavioral program. Hepler (1997) compared pretest and posttest scores of both LD and NLD children who had been randomly assigned to a program group and to a no-treatment (control) group. Results provided positive feedback for the implementation of programs that help LD children increase their social skills and acceptance by their peers.

up nonrandomly assigned comparison groups, including treatment diffusion and nonavailability of a list or pool of clients from which random assignment can occur. Some ethical issues with this design will be discussed later in this chapter.

Posttest-Only Control-Group Design

One way of eliminating the threat to external validity posed by the previous design is simply to eliminate the pretest. In the **posttest-only control-group design** (see Figure 6.9), the two groups are again randomly assigned and consequently should be equivalent, and there should be no need for the pretests. Some

A Posttest-Only Control-Group Design

Reid and Bailey-Dempsey (1995) examined the effect of monetary incentives on school performance. Teenage girls at risk of school failure were randomly assigned to a control group or to one of two experimental groups: one experimental group offering monetary incentives and the other a case management program. Posttest measures included GPAs and absences.

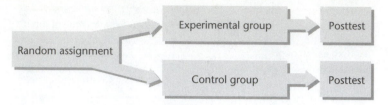

Figure 6.9 **Posttest-only control-group design**

researchers, however, are reluctant to eliminate what is essentially a safety measure to ensure the groups' equivalency.

The Solomon Four-Group Design

The **Solomon four-group design** is a combination of the previous two designs and as a result is extremely valid (see Figure 6.10). It is rarely used in social work research, however. It is usually difficult to find enough subjects to assign

A Solomon Four-Group Design

Kalafat and Elias (1994) used a questionnaire in a Solomon four-group design to assess the effectiveness of suicide intervention classes among tenth-grade students. A prestest was given only to two of the four groups, one to those receiving the intervention and one to those not receiving the intervention. Two comparable groups did not receive a pretest. All four groups received a posttest. The results indicated that those who participated in the classes, compared to the control group, showed gains in knowledge about suicidal peers and more positive attitudes toward seeking help and intervening with their troubled peers.

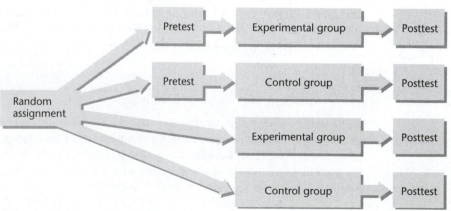

Figure 6.10 **Solomon four-group design**

Table 6.1   **Group research designs—threats to internal and external validity**

Type of design	Threats to internal validity	Threats to external validity
One-group posttest-only	Selection, history, mortality	Selection-treatment interaction, history-treatment interaction
One-group pretest/posttest	History, maturation, testing, instrumentation, regression to mean, interaction of selection, and other threats	History-treatment interaction, reactive effects
Static-group comparison	Selection and mortality	Selection-treatment interaction
Time series	History	History-treatment interaction, reactive effects
Pretest/posttest comparison	Selection and maturation	Selection-treatment interaction, maturation-treatment interaction, reactive effects
Pretest/posttest control group	None	Reactive effects
Posttest-only control group	None	None
Solomon four-group	None	None

randomly between two groups, and the cost of the design exceeds the budgets of most social work program evaluations.

Table 6.1 summarizes each of the summative group designs and their threats to internal and external validity as discussed in this chapter.

THE AGENCY AND PROGRAM EVALUATION DESIGN

It should be clear from this chapter that experimental designs with randomly assigned control groups are preferable to use if you are interested in establishing whether a program or intervention, and not some other factor or factors, was responsible for a specific outcome. As generalist social workers, however, you may find that the textbook research examples are not practical, nor are they necessarily preferred. Don't be discouraged if you can't use a Solomon four-group design or, for that matter, random assignment; it may be that one of the other designs will give you the kind of information you need.

The challenge is to develop designs that are *feasible and appropriate for the research question,* and that is why this chapter includes some practical ideas on, for example, alternative ways of setting up comparison groups. Not only are these alternative strategies compatible with agency practice, but if the comparison groups received services or treatments (including simply part of the intervention being provided to the experimental group), many of these strategies become even more feasible and attractive to agencies. This approach is particularly useful with crisis-oriented or court-ordered services.

Another strategy that may result in the greater participation of agencies involves the use of unbalanced designs with fewer subjects assigned to the comparison or control group. Consequently, clients referred to the agency are more likely to receive services.

Finally, do not overlook the importance of formative program evaluations. They have an important role to play in the development of programs and should be the evaluation of choice for new programs.

Most important is to acknowledge your design's drawbacks and address them in the reporting of the evaluation. If research is conducted in this practical and responsible way, knowledge building in social work can progress with a solid agency-based foundation.

ETHICAL ISSUES IN PROGRAM EVALUATION DESIGN

Two major ethical issues are related to group design, both of them associated with control or comparison groups. First is the issue of whether establishing a comparison or control group involves denying services to clients. Second is the question of whether the subjects' informed consent should be obtained so that a comparison group can be established.

Assignment to the Comparison or Control Group

The NASW Code of Ethics (1997) states that social workers should take appropriate steps to ensure that participants in evaluation and research have access to appropriate supportive services. Participants in the research should always be assured of some services. Whether they will be is an issue when participants are assigned to comparison or control groups.

This research strategy could be viewed as a denial of services, justified in the name of science; it poses an ethical dilemma that can have implications for administration of the evaluation. The personnel may see the creation of comparison or control groups as a way of manipulating clients that could consequently influence the evaluation. For example, in a situation where the comparison group is receiving a variation of the intervention to be evaluated, the staff—if they disagree with the creation of the comparison group—may not adhere to the guidelines governing this variation in an attempt to bring legitimate services to the subjects in the comparison group. In addition, clients simply may not be referred to the project.

Two arguments that use of comparison or control groups does not always pose a serious ethical problem can be made, however. First, the decision about who receives services in an agency is often arbitrary and political. Program services may run on demand, and the deprivation of services is not uncommon. Second, by suggesting that clients are being denied valuable treatment, we are assuming that the intervention being evaluated is effective. Often, though, that assumption has no empirical basis. In fact, if it did, there would be little reason for carrying out the research in the first place. As in practice, however, the situation in research is often not this clear-cut. Usually some evidence—perhaps a combination of practice wisdom and research findings—indicates that the treatment is helpful to some extent. The purpose of the evaluation is then to determine how helpful it is. Consequently, our concern that we are violating subjects' rights by possibly denying them beneficial treatment involves other factors, such as individual judgments and values about how detrimental the denial could be. This is another example of the important role that values play in the scientific process.

Decisions relating to the establishment of control or comparison groups are probably governed by the seriousness of the problem. Under most circumstances, it would be hard to justify establishing a control group of emotionally disturbed children involved in self-destructive behaviors. In addition, the use of waiting lists and cohort groups, baseline comparison groups, and assignment to other types of interventions or programs can help ameliorate some of the potential ill effects of being assigned to the comparison or control group.

Informed Consent

Informed consent involves informing potential subjects fully of their role and the consequences of their participation in the research and seeking their permission. The NASW Code of Ethics (1997) states:

- Social workers engaged in evaluation or research should obtain voluntary and written informed consent from participants, when appropriate, without any implied or actual deprivation or penalty for refusal to participate; without undue inducement to participate; and with due regard for participants' well-being, privacy, and dignity. Informed consent should include information about the nature, extent, and duration of the participation requested and disclosure of the risks and benefits of participation in the research.

- When evaluation or research participants are incapable of giving informed consent, social workers should provide an appropriate explanation to the participants, obtain the participants' assent to the extent they are able, and obtain written consent from an appropriate proxy.

- Social workers should inform participants of their right to withdraw from evaluation and research at any time without penalty.

Informed consent is an issue, first of all, because of the difficulty of forming comparison groups. In seeking a comparison group, you may be reluctant to fully inform potential participants that they will not be receiving a service. In attempting to ensure their participation, you may justify your failure to inform them on the ground that their consent is not necessary if they are not receiving the service. Informed consent is less of a problem with control groups, in which participants will be randomly assigned to the control and experimental groups and therefore can be told that they may or may not be receiving the service. *Consent must be gained at all times for any participation, however*—whether in the experimental group or the comparison or control group.

As discussed in the previous section, the effects of being in the control group can be improved somewhat by adopting alternative strategies—waiting lists, alternative programs, and so forth. These strategies can also help with the consent issue. In other words, the researcher will not be so tempted to avoid seeking informed consent in anticipation of the potential subject's refusing to participate, because ultimately the client will receive some type of intervention. The second issue relating to informed consent is the possibility that informing the subjects of the details of the evaluation will jeopardize the validity of the findings. For example, if the experimental group knows they are the experimental group and the control or comparison group knows that they are the control or comparison group, expectations can be set up that can affect outcomes. The experimental group may expect to change and, regardless of the actual impact of the intervention itself, may show improvement. This threat to validity was discussed earlier in the chapter as a reactive effect. Given the possibility of this threat, it is tempting to avoid giving subjects all the details of their participation. Informed consent should still be obtained, however. One way of dealing with the reactive problem is to inform the subjects that they will either be placed in a control or comparison or in an experimental group, but they will not be told which one in order to protect the validity of the findings. Of course, this is only an option if the control or comparison group is receiving at least some type of intervention, whether it is a variation of the one being evaluated or another intervention completely. If such intervention is not feasible, the researcher needs to acknowledge possible reactive effects rather than not inform the subjects.

HUMAN DIVERSITY ISSUES IN PROGRAM EVALUATION DESIGN

When developing a program evaluation and making decisions about the research design, the major issue relating to human diversity is ensuring that certain groups are not being exploited for the purpose of establishing comparison groups. Sometimes such exploitation can occur unintentionally. In social science research, the tendency is to assign members of disadvantaged groups, such as the poor, minorities, women, and others, to comparison groups. (This is not an issue for control groups when subjects are randomly assigned.)

Parlee (1981) argued that in psychology research (and this argument can be extended to social science research in general), the choice of particular comparison groups demonstrates the scientist's "implicit theoretical framework." She suggested that many of these frameworks are biased against women and that this bias becomes a real problem when we engage in matching. "Knowing" what variables to include entails biases that can favor certain groups over others. The choice of the comparison group defines the perspective that will dominate the research and in turn influence the findings.

Parlee (1981) cited a study in which a matched comparison group of women was sought for a 20-year-old men-only study of aging. One alternative was to match the women according to intelligence, education, and occupation. Another might argue for matching according to physiological similarities, by, for example, including the men's sisters. The former represented the social scientists' perspective while the latter reflected that of biomedical scientists. Clearly, these two alternatives involved two different perspectives on the causality underlying aging and would probably result in very different conclusions being drawn from the study.

It is critical to recognize this potential bias in comparison group selection. To counterbalance this problem, we should involve diverse people in conceptualizing the research, particularly if the program evaluation will have impacts on diverse populations. In this way, alternative viewpoints and perspectives can be fully incorporated into the group design.

SUMMARY

There are two main types of program evaluations: formative and summative. Formative evaluations are primarily descriptive, whereas summative evaluations focus on causality. When designing summative program evaluations, it is necessary to select a group design. Each design poses various threats to internal and external validity. Internal validity is the extent to which the changes in the dependent variable are a result of the independent variable. External validity refers to the generalizability of the research findings to a wider population. Research designs may have to be modified in agency settings. A design's drawbacks should be acknowledged in reporting the evaluation.

Ethical issues relating to group design include potentially denying services to clients when establishing comparison or control groups and obtaining informed consent from clients. Human diversity issues include not exploiting certain groups for use as comparison groups.

STUDY/EXERCISE QUESTIONS

1. The family service agency in which you are employed is planning to conduct an evaluation of its services. As the leader of a support group of parents of developmentally disabled children, you are asked to design an evaluation of this service.
    a. What design could you develop that would be feasible and would maximize the validity of your findings?
    b. Under what circumstances would a formative evaluation be appropriate and how would you carry this out?

2. Review an issue of *Social Work Research and Abstracts* and select an article that used one of the research designs described in this chapter.
   a. What are the threats to internal and external validity?
   b. Were these threats explicitly discussed?
   c. Propose an alternative design that would be feasible.

INFOTRAC COLLEGE EDITION

1. Search for a *client satisfaction survey* and describe the limitations of the findings.
2. Search for three *program evaluations* and compare the research designs used. Did the authors comment on the limitations of the designs used?

REFERENCES

Denby, R., Rindfleisch, N., & Bean, G. (1999). Predictors of foster parents' satisfaction and intent to continue to foster. *Child Abuse & Neglect, 23* (3), 287–303.

Hepler, J. B. (1997). Evaluating a social skills program for children with learning disabilities. *Social Work with Groups, 20* (3), 21–36.

Hurd, E. P. (1998). Strengths-based teaching in social work. *The Journal of Baccalaureate Social Work, 3* (2), 51–65.

Itzhaky, H. (1995). Can social work intervention increase organizational effectiveness? *International Social Work, 38,* 277–286.

Kalafat, J., & Elias, M. (1994). An evaluation of a school-based suicide awareness intervention. *Suicide & Life, 24* (3), 224.

Kramer, B. J. (1998). Preparing social workers for the inevitable: A preliminary investigation of a course on grief, death, and loss. *Journal of Social Work Education, 34* (2), 211–227.

Manion, I., Firestone, P., Cloutier, P., Ligezinski, M., McIntyre, J., & Ensom, R. (1998). Child extrafamilial sexual abuse: Predicting parent and child functioning. *Child Abuse & Neglect, 22* (12), 1285–1304.

National Association of Social Workers. (1997). NASW Code of Ethics. *NASW News, 25,* 24–25.

Nugent, W. R., Bruley, C., & Allen, P. (1999). The effects of aggression replacement training on male and female antisocial behavior in a runaway shelter. *Research on Social Work Practice, 9* (4), 466–482.

Parlee, M. B. (1981). Appropriate control groups in feminist research. *Psychology of Women Quarterly, 5,* 637–644.

Reid, W. J., & Bailey-Dempsey, C. (1995). The effects of monetary incentives on school performance. *Families in Society, 76* (6), 331–340.

Weissman, M., & LaRue, C. M. (1998). Earning trust from youths with none to spare. *Child Welfare, LXXVII* (5), 579–594.

Designing the Evaluation
of Practice

■

D uring the last 20 years, social workers have experienced increased pressure to evaluate their own practice. In part, this pressure stems from studies done in the 1960s and early 1970s, which suggested that social work practice was not as effective as many had expected (Fischer, 1973). On closer examination, the research studies themselves were found to have major methodological problems, raising questions about whether the findings from the studies should be viewed seriously and as an accurate reflection of the state of social work practice. First, the research studies often used no type of comparison group, which led to questions about the internal and external validity of the results. Second, because group designs used in program evaluations pooled the results from both successful and unsuccessful programs to determine average results, they were not able to determine what actually worked with whom and with what kinds of problems. Consequently, the results were often of little use to the practitioner. Third, the group designs generally relied on only two measures—one before the intervention and one after the intervention. There was no way of knowing what happened between these two measurement points. For example, a posttest may indicate that the target problem has not decreased in severity. It is possible, however, that at some point after the intervention but before the posttest, some decrease did occur. It could not be determined whether and why such an effect had occurred because of the way many of these studies were designed.

In addition to these methodological problems, other problems relating to ethical and social issues characterized these early studies. First, it was and is often difficult to get the support of agency personnel in assigning clients to control or comparison groups because of the ethical issues discussed in Chapter 6. Second, it was and is also often difficult to impossible for agencies to come up with the funds for a full-scale evaluation of even a moderate-sized program.

As a consequence of these problems and the continuing demand for accountability of the social services, social workers were increasingly required to evaluate their own practice. Different ways of implementing these evaluations emerged. At first, emphasis was on an approach adopted from psychology, a technology known as **single-system** or **single-subject designs** or **studies.** These types of studies tried to assess the impact of interventions on client systems. Single-system designs relied heavily on the collection of empirical behavioral data and were grounded in the positivist tradition. They grew in popularity as they produced results identifying how specific interventions were effective with specific clients with specific types of problems. An examination of the full range of single-system designs can be found in works such as Bloom, Fischer, and Orme (1995).

Later, after single-system designs were taught in departments and schools of social work, it was disclosed that many graduates tended not to use the single-system technology in their practice (Siegel, 1985). Reasons included the single-system design's perceived limited applicability to different interventions and target behaviors and its lack of congruence with the realities of social work practice (Kagle, 1982). Alternative approaches to evaluating practice began to emerge. Instead of the single-system design approach of assessing the impact of interventions on client systems (that is, explanatory designs), descriptive methods were developed to monitor client progress and to monitor the intervention. Many of these methods used interpretive and qualitative approaches, differing significantly from the positivist approaches associated with single-system studies. In addition, program administrators began to use a group of single-system studies as a means of evaluating entire programs.

These new ways of evaluating practice give the social worker choices about which approach to use. As stressed in Chapter 1 and throughout this book, the choice in part depends upon the question being asked. Practice evaluation involves three major questions. First, how can the intervention be described? Second, how can the client's progress be monitored? Third, how effective is the intervention in bringing about client change? The first two questions are primarily descriptive, whereas the third is explanatory. Different types of descriptive and explanatory designs will be presented in this chapter.

This chapter will discuss the following:

- descriptive designs for practice evaluation
- explanatory designs for practice evaluation
- the agency and practice evaluation
- ethical issues in practice evaluation
- human diversity issues in practice evaluation

DESCRIPTIVE DESIGNS FOR PRACTICE EVALUATION

As just discussed, two types of questions in practice evaluation require descriptive designs: questions that focus on the nature of the intervention and questions that focus on monitoring any client change. Each of these will be presented in this section.

Monitoring Interventions

Often it is important to examine and reflect on the intervention being used; this is referred to as **monitoring interventions.** Evaluation then becomes a process of discovery rather than an experiment (as with a formative as opposed to a summative program evaluation). As a student social worker, you may be asked to evaluate how you are applying an intervention and to describe your activities to your supervisor. You can use various strategies to evaluate an intervention. Three methods can be used to monitor interventions: process recordings, practice logs, and case studies.

Process Recordings

Process recordings are written records based on notes or on a transcription of a recording (audio or video) of interactions between the worker and clients. These qualitative data then become an important source of information for improving practice.

Suppose you are just beginning your employment with Child Protective Services, and your supervisor has given you the go-ahead to visit a family alone. You are still unsure about whether you are conducting the interview appropriately, however. Consequently, immediately after the home visit you sit down and record the major interactions that occurred. You later share this process recording with your supervisor. This process can help identify the strengths and weaknesses in your interviewing skills; if you continue this type of monitoring for several cases, you may see patterns emerging.

Practice Logs

A variation on the process recording is an ongoing **practice log,** using self-reflection and analysis to understand how you and the client worked together in resolving issues raised. Papell and Skolnick (1992) discuss how practitioners' self-reflection can add to their understanding of practice. Practice logs go beyond a process recording in that the writer self-reflects and comments on his or her use

---

Reflecting on Practice

McCormick (1999) reflected on her practice with residents in a halfway-like house for people recently released from jail and/or prison:

Tonight was our second parenting group. About seven of the original members attended with about three new members. I began by having them pair off—one person acting as the parent and the other as the child. I gave the children two pieces of clay and instructed them to go ask their "parent" to play with them. The dads played for a timed ten-minute period. During this time, I went around the room, modeling how to praise, encouraging creativity and interaction. All except two members participated, and they all were very creative and interested. After the ten minutes were up, I talked about "special time" with children and how play benefits children. I encouraged them to spend ten minutes per day with each child doing special time and to make time in their visits with their children for play. Together, the group and I brainstormed ways to play with children. I encouraged storytelling—both with books and orally. I tried to focus on the strengths of their ideas.

I noticed at one point that everyone was talking at once. I asked them to take turns, but it was too late. Next time, I will begin by addressing this issue and asking for agreement. I will ask them to whisper quietly if they need to talk to each other during the group. I may make a talking stick and bring it to the next group. I think kinetic materials work well with this group.

Many of the parents brought up discipline during our discussion, so I think I'll focus on that next time—maybe the next two times. I think they're ready for that now. Otherwise, I'll put their suggestions (from the list they constructed during the first group) back on the board and have them choose which they want to focus on next.

Overall, I think it went well. On the sign-in sheet, some made comments that were positive. I'd like to develop a form that reflects what they feel they got out of the group for each session.

of the intervention and the experience of practice. Practice logs are often required of students in their field practica. As a form of data collection, these will be discussed in Chapter 9.

For example, say you are involved in trying to organize a community center for youths but have never tackled anything like this before. Consequently, you carefully record all your activities, impressions, and thoughts connected with this endeavor, and you share this information with a more experienced community organizer whom you met at a NASW chapter conference the previous year. In this situation, rather than having to rely on anecdotes and your memory, your practice log gives you a systematic record of what occurred. This record can provide potential data for a more explanatory design you might want to attempt at a later date, in which you try to determine whether your strategy actually had the anticipated outcomes.

These types of evaluations are rarely published, since they are used primarily by individual workers and within agencies in order to enhance practice.

Case Studies

Case studies involve a more complete description of the application of the intervention, and tend to be more "objective" and less self-reflecting than the process recordings or practice log approaches. Detailed case studies of unusual cases, successful cases, or unsuccessful cases can yield some vital information. The type of information generated may either support existing practice

A Case Study: Support of Practice Principles

Burman and Allen-Meares (1994) presented a case study of two children who witnessed their mother being murdered by their father. The authors described how theories of psychosocial development and social learning guided the assessment and intervention phases. Behavioral and family intervention practices are also described. There is further discussion about the potential intergenerational cycle of violence and a sociocultural perspective on family violence within an ecological framework.

Multiple Case Studies: Suggestions for Innovations in Practice

Pandey (1998) reported on multiple case studies done in various regions of Nepal where women are involved in community forestry programs. The article discussed the factors that inhibited the participation of the rural poor in these programs, including their fear of exploitation and the inaccessibility of resources. To promote sustainable development, the author suggested that social workers advocate for the participation of the poor.

principles or suggest new approaches and principles. Single or multiple case studies can be used.

One major advantage of monitoring interventions using any one of the three approaches described here is that it provides a means for practitioners to reflect on and study their own practice. The reflective method "would encourage practitioners to examine professional activity and the knowledge reflected in that activity against empirically based theory as well as against their practice wisdom and tacit knowledge, using a range of methodologies" (Millstein, 1993, p. 257).

Monitoring Client Progress

Not only can you monitor an intervention, but also the client's progress. Information is gathered on the client while the intervention is taking place. As a result, decisions can be made as to whether the intervention should be continued, modified, or stopped. These data can be either qualitative, in the form of notes and narrative, or quantitative, in the form of behavioral observations or the different rapid assessment instruments described in Chapter 9, including target problem scales. Whichever data collection method is used, client goals must be clearly specified (Blythe, Topodi, & Boras 1994).

For example, in working with a group of adolescent mothers you may decide to monitor the clients' progress both during the months when the groups are held and after they stop. The change goal was to learn parenting skills, the maintenance goal was to practice those skills, and the prevention goal was to avoid future reporting for child abuse or neglect. The goals were monitored monthly for two years.

This type of practice evaluation is rarely published, although it is an extremely important strategy for evaluating practice as an ongoing activity. Often, the information gained from descriptive evaluations of individual practice can help to formulate hypotheses for future evaluations of our own practice. Consequently, descriptive studies can be viewed as an inductive mode of knowledge building (as discussed in Chapter 1).

EXPLANATORY DESIGNS FOR PRACTICE EVALUATION

Explanatory designs examine the impact of the intervention on the target behavior. These designs are now also called single-system designs or single-system studies. They involve three elements that help establish causality: a baseline, clear identification of the intervention, and target behaviors that can be operationalized and repeatedly measured.

Baseline

Rather than depending on control or comparison groups in their search for causality, single-system designs rely on the target behavior's being measured time and time again. In effect, the client system serves as its own control. A similar principle is in effect here as that used in the time series designs discussed in

Chapter 6; with that group design, however, a group of client systems is monitored, whereas the single-system study monitors only one client system. The repeated measurement prior to the intervention is known as the **baseline.** The baseline allows you to compare target behavior rates before and after the intervention, thus allowing you to assess the impact of the intervention on the target behavior. Figure 7.1 demonstrates how results from explanatory single-system designs are usually displayed. The X axis records the incidents of the target behavior, and the Y axis shows the time interval over which the behavior is recorded. The vertical line represents the point at which the intervention was introduced.

For the assessment to have some validity, a stable baseline is needed prior to the implementation of the intervention. This consists of an observable pattern between the data points. Fluctuations may occur, but as long as they occur with some regularity this should constitute a stable baseline. An unstable baseline makes it difficult to interpret the study's results. A problem with interpreting the findings also occurs when the baseline is stable but is moving in the direction of the desired outcome prior to the intervention's implementation (see Figure 7.2).

Clearly Defined Intervention

Explanatory designs also require a clearly defined intervention, and the point at which it is introduced must be clearly presented.

Operationalization and Repeated Measure of Target Behavior

Explanatory designs also require that the target behaviors that are the focus of the intervention be clearly defined. For example, rather than a target behavior's being defined as a child's inattentiveness, a clearer definition would be the number of times a question is repeated to a child before he or she answers. In addition to being clearly defined, data about the target behavior need to be collected repeatedly.

Different types of explanatory designs will now be presented.

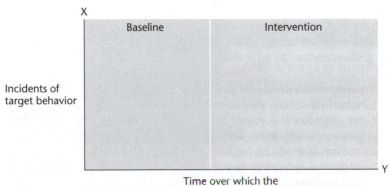

Figure 7.1   ***Displaying the results from explanatory single-system designs***

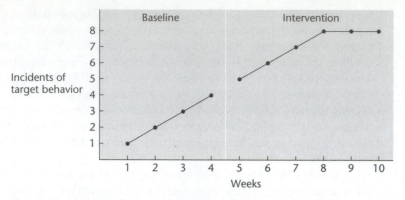

Figure 7.2   ***Example of a baseline moving in the direction of the desired outcome***

AB Design

The **AB design** is the simplest of the single-system designs. Data are collected on the target behavior prior to the intervention, and this constitutes the baseline, or phase A of the design. The B phase consists of measurements of the target behavior after the intervention has been introduced. The effectiveness of the intervention is determined by comparing the A measure of the target behavior to the B measure.

Let's look at a case in which the problem is a family's low attendance at a parenting class. The goal or target behavior of the intervention is to increase attendance. The A phase would be the number of times the family attends the class prior to the intervention. The class is held twice a week, and data are already available on the family's attendance over the previous three weeks. These data can be used as a baseline.

The point at which the intervention is introduced marks the beginning of the B phase. The intervention in this case might be to arrange for another family to help with transportation to the class. The frequency of the target behavior is then recorded for several weeks after intervention. An illustration

An AB Design

Slonim-Nevo and Vosler (1991) used an AB design to discuss the use of single-system designs with brief problem-solving systemic therapy. The case involved a woman who was experiencing constant jealousy over the relationship her husband had with his first wife. The authors developed a scale to measure the intensity of this obsession. After three weeks of baseline, an intervention was implemented using brief problem-solving therapy. An AB design was used in evaluating the impact of the intervention.

of how these data might look if charted is given in Figure 7.3. The results can be analyzed by simply viewing the chart. An increase in attendance is clearly evident.

One of the advantages of the AB design is its simplicity. In addition, the design can easily be integrated into the practice process, giving important information about those interventions that appear to work with particular client systems.

Some problems are associated with this design, however. The major problem is that you do not have any control over extraneous factors or the history threat to internal validity. In our example, it was possible that the classes suddenly became more interesting to the family or that the mother had convinced the father, who was exhibiting the most resistance to attending, of the benefits of the class. Or the results might have been due to a multitude of other factors. Thus the AB design is restricted in the information it can give about causality.

ABC Design

The **ABC design** is also known as the **successive intervention design** because the C phase represents the introduction of another intervention. Others can also be added on as D or E phases. The ABC design is simply the AB design with the addition of another intervention. With this design, the target behavior continues to be measured after the introduction of each intervention.

The ABC design can be convenient in that it often reflects the reality of practice. We introduce one intervention, and if it seems ineffective, we implement another intervention. The ABC design adds an empirical element to this common practice.

To continue with the example we have been using, transportation assistance did not increase attendance for another family. After further assessment it was found that the parents—although English-speaking—were native Spanish speakers and were having difficulty following the class. Consequently, a second intervention was the organization of a Spanish-speaking class for a number of Spanish-speaking families in the community. The families' attendance was

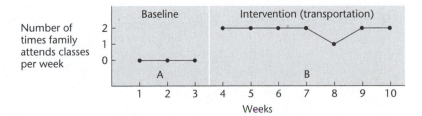

Figure 7.3   ***Example of an AB design***

An ABC Design

Kazi and Wilson (1996) presented several examples of single-case evaluations from a project in Great Britain to train and encourage social workers to apply this type of evaluation to their practice.

One is a modification of the ABC design. The A B BC C design collected data on a 15-year-old's school attendance and the mother's feelings about her relationship with her daughter. Intervention B was weekly counseling sessions with the grandmother, the mother, the 15-year-old, and her boyfriend. These sessions did not improve school attendance although the mother's feelings about the relationship did improve. When intervention C was added to B (positive encouragement from teachers) both dependent variables improved and remained stable for the C phase.

monitored following this intervention and showed an increase. See Figure 7.4 for an illustration of how these results would be displayed.

Although the ABC design nicely reflects the reality of practice, this design has the same types of problems associated with the AB design. You have no way of knowing whether the intervention or some other factor accounted for any change in the target behavior. This validity issue is complicated in the ABC design by not knowing whether it was the C intervention that resulted in the final outcome or a combination of the B and C interventions. Although you may not know specifically which intervention influenced the outcome, you do know about the effect of some combination of the interventions—a finding that in itself can enhance your practice and service to clients.

ABAB Design

The **ABAB design** is also known as the **reversal design** or the **withdrawal design;** it consists of implementing the AB design and then reversing—withdrawing the intervention and collecting baseline data again before implement-

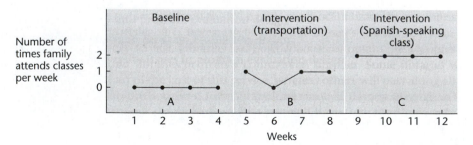

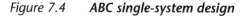

Figure 7.4 **ABC single-system design**

An ABAB Reversal Design

Dugan, Kamps, Leonard, Watkins, Rheinberger, and Stackhaus (1995) investigated the use of cooperative learning groups as a strategy for integrating two students with autism into a fourth-grade class.

The baseline was 40 minutes of teacher-led sessions including lecture, questions and discussion, and the use of maps. The intervention was 10 minutes of the teacher's introducing the material followed by cooperative learning groups that included tutoring on key words and facts, a team activity, and wrap-up and review with the entire class.

The ABAB design showed increases for target students and peers in their scores on weekly pretests and posttests, academic engagement during sessions, and student interaction during the intervention.

ing the intervention a second time. Suppose a school social worker works constantly with the problem of absenteeism. In the past, she has made regular home visits to the families involved, and she has a sense that this is working. She decides to test the intervention, starting with one case, that of a 12-year-old boy. The social worker monitors his attendance at school over a three-week period and then starts the home visits, which include counseling, information, and referral, twice a week. She collects data on attendance for another three weeks and then stops the visits, again monitoring attendance, for another three weeks. Finally, she once again introduces the intervention. The results, displayed in Figure 7.5, indicate that the intervention appears to have some impact on the student's school attendance.

The great advantage of the ABAB design is its ability to tell us about the impact of the intervention versus the impact of other possible factors; in other words, its ability to explain and imply causality is greater than the AB or the ABC designs.

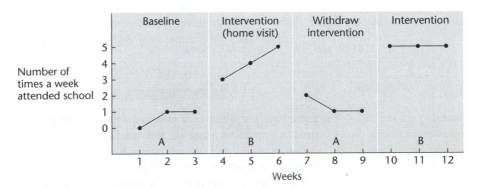

Figure 7.5   ***ABAB—reversal single-system design***

The ABAB design does have a few problems, though. First, it cannot be applied to all target behaviors and all types of interventions. Some interventions cannot be reversed, particularly those that involve teaching a new behavior. For example, suppose you identify the target behavior as a second grader's tardiness, and you assess the problem as resulting from the mother's not being assertive with the child about getting ready for school. The intervention consists of the social worker's teaching the parent how to be assertive with the child. This would be a difficult intervention to reverse, since the mother's learned behavior could not be reversed.

Even if the intervention seemingly could be reversed, some residues of the intervention might remain. In the example of the 12-year-old boy's absenteeism, the home visits might have resulted in some carryover effects even after they were halted; in fact, this seems to have been the case. The interpretation of the results, as well as the precise impact of the intervention, then becomes more difficult.

With any explanatory single-system study, and particularly with the reversal design, you must spell out the details and possible consequences for the clients before the intervention is instituted. This procedure is similar to obtaining clients' informed consent prior to engaging in a group study.

Multiple Baseline Designs

A **multiple baseline design** involves replicating the AB design by applying the same intervention to two or more target behaviors, to two or more clients, or in two or more settings at different points in time. For example, a child is exhibiting problems at school; the target problem is identified as the teacher's concern that the child is not verbally participating in class. After assessment, it becomes apparent that this behavior is associated with the child's Navajo cultural background, which discourages speaking out. Intervention consists of discussion with the teacher about cross-cultural issues, including suggesting that she use some Navajo examples in teaching. This intervention could be tested *across client systems* by using the intervention with three different Navajo children. Alternatively, the intervention could be used *across target problems,* in which additional problems such as low grades and low socialization might be identified. These behaviors could be monitored before and after the implementation of the intervention. The intervention could also be tested *across settings* by, for example, looking at changes in one of the target problems in the day care center and at home in addition to the school setting. Figure 7.6 shows how data from a multiple baseline design might be displayed.

The multiple baseline design offers a great deal of potential for examining the effectiveness of particular interventions and can allow us to be more confident in our belief that the intervention was responsible for any measured change. In effect, the multiple baseline design involves the principle of comparison groups in group design, using either another client, another setting, or another target problem as a comparison. For example, if you find that the same

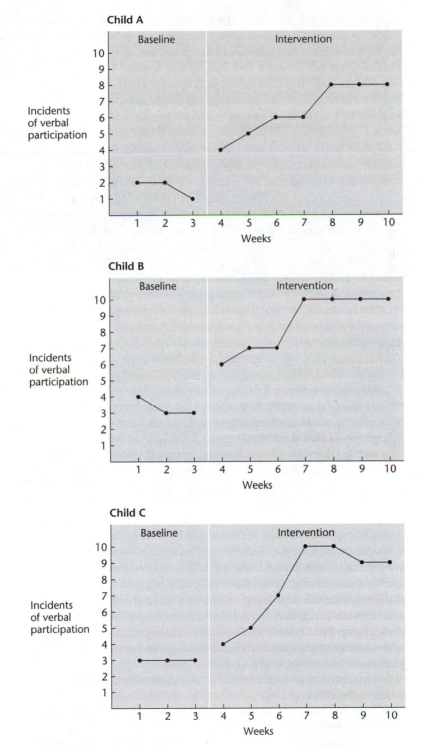

Figure 7.6   ***Multiple baseline design***

intervention for the same target problem for the same setting was effective for two different clients, you would be more certain of the intervention's effectiveness than if you had simply looked at one client.

A Multiple Baseline Design

Reamer, Brady, and Hawkins (1998) used a multiple baseline across families with children who have developmental disabilities to assess the effects of video self-modeling. The intervention combined self-assessment, self-modeling, discrimination training, and behavioral rehearsal on parents' interactions with their children during the childrens' self-care tasks and social play with their siblings. The video intervention was designed to alter parents' assistance patterns and to provide less directive task-related prompts. Results showed increased parental social prompts, altered parental assistance during children's tasks, and an increase in children's social behavior and task completion.

Multiple Baseline and Program Design

Whitfield (1999) evaluated the effectiveness of anger control training with male adolescents. A multiple baseline design across participants was used to assess matched pairs of students (eight experimental and eight control students). The experimental students significantly improved in their anger control, including at a six-month follow up assessment. The author concluded that the cognitive-behavioral approach is more effective at reducing school violence when compared with a nonspecific counseling approach (see Figure 7.7).

Nevertheless, there are some limitations on the extent to which you can hold the intervention responsible for any change in the target problem even with these designs. For example, when applying the multiple baseline design across clients, even if the change in the target problem resulted in a positive outcome for both clients, there is still no guarantee that it was the intervention and the intervention alone that resulted in the specific outcome. In fact, the validity limitations are similar to those associated with many of the nonexperimental designs discussed in Chapter 6.

As mentioned earlier in this chapter, it is the multiple baseline design that can be used to evaluate entire programs. The results of a number of these types of designs can be put together to give an overall assessment of a particular intervention's effectiveness.

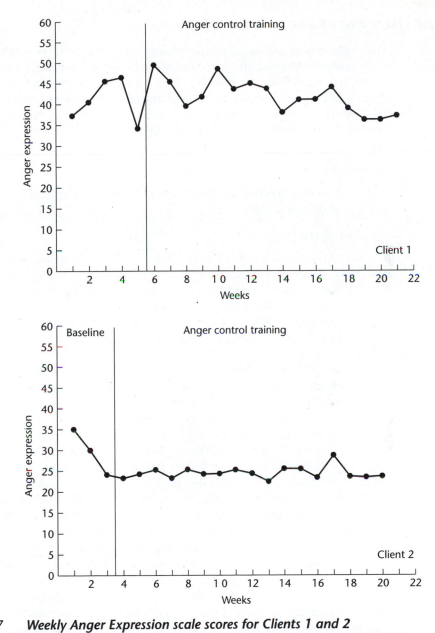

Figure 7.7   ***Weekly Anger Expression scale scores for Clients 1 and 2***

Source: "Validating School Social Work: An Evaluation of a Cognitive-Behavioral Approach to Reduce School Violence," from G. W. Whitfield, 1999, *Research on Social Work Practice, 9* (4), 399–426.

THE AGENCY AND PRACTICE EVALUATION

The evaluation of individual practice should, of course, be extremely compatible with agency settings, although there seems to be some disagreement on this point. Much has been written about the relative strengths and limitations of practice evaluations and specific designs and about their applicability to practice and agency settings. A good overview is presented in an article by Corcoran (1993). These strengths and limitations follow.

Strengths

Strengths include feedback to the client, knowledge building for practice, and low cost and time factors.

Feedback to the Client

One benefit of practice evaluation is that feedback can be provided to the client. The intervention-monitoring and client-monitoring designs provide consistent feedback, and with single-system designs the client is provided with some tangible evidence that the intervention does or does not appear to have an impact on behavior. Feedback can result in longer-term effects and the clients' adopting self-help measures, avoiding further social work intervention.

Knowledge Building for Practice

The activity of monitoring interventions or client progress can enhance workers' knowledge of their practice by allowing workers to critically examine the values and assumptions underlying the use of theories and their associated interventions in practice. Questions that are critical in developing a knowledge of practice include these (Millstern, 1993): Am I doing what I think I'm doing? If not, what am I doing? What does my work tell me about how I make meaning of practice? What ways of knowing do I use?

The single-system explanatory studies offer information about the efficacy of specific interventions. Further information can be obtained by replicating or repeating the single-system studies—testing interventions with other clients, on other target behaviors, and in other settings. Replication increases internal validity (it is the intervention and not something else that is affecting the outcome) and external validity (the results are generalizable to a wider population).

As mentioned earlier in this chapter, knowledge can be built through single-system studies by integrating single-system and group approaches in evaluating program effectiveness. Berbenishty (1989) provided an example:

> The basic building blocks of the advocated methodology are single-case evaluation, intentionally designed, selected, and combined to form an assessment on the agency level. For each intervention, data on the characteristics of treatment, therapist, problem, and client are collected. These data from each single-case study are then aggregated to access the overall ef-

fectiveness of the group of cases. Further, in order to assess differential effectiveness, subgroups were identified and compared (as to their relative improvement), or certain background or treatment characteristics were correlated with outcome measures. (p. 33)

Time and Cost

Unlike group studies, which often require additional funds, evaluation of individual practice can be easily incorporated into practice with no extra expense or excessive time commitment.

Limitations

Evaluation of individual practice, then, offers some advantages in agency settings, but some arguments are also made against use of such evaluations in agencies. They do possess some limitations, including limited application, limited validity, and limited data analysis.

Limited Application

Historically, single-system explanatory designs were used almost exclusively for testing the effectiveness of behavioral intervention techniques. In part, their application was limited because of the emphasis in behavior theory on being able to define behaviors clearly so that any changes in the behaviors can be easily recorded. Many social workers, including generalist social workers, are deterred from using single-system studies because they have assumed the design is appropriate only for behavioral intervention and clearly observable and recordable behaviors. Designs that monitor intervention and client progress, however, can be used with a variety of different interventions and target behaviors.

In addition, some designs such as the withdrawal and multiple baseline designs, are often simply not practical. It is rarely possible to withdraw an intervention. Finally, often it is difficult to select a design when just beginning to work with a client; instead, designs are determined as practice evolves. This is less of a problem with the monitoring designs described in this chapter, which are sensitive to the process of practice.

Limited Validity

Internal and external validity are a problem with the explanatory single-system designs, even when results are replicated. Single-system studies simply are not as valid as well-designed group designs used in program evaluations. As discussed in Chapter 6, however, well-designed group studies are rare. More often, less satisfactory designs (in terms of causality) are used, resulting again in internal and external validity problems. Consequently, in many instances single-system studies can be thought of as no worse in terms of validity than many group designs and are certainly better than no design at all.

Another validity issue is the extent to which the use of self-report instruments, designed to measure subjective aspects of the client's problems, actually result in therapeutic reactive effects. Some claim that these effects are minimal (Applegate, 1992).

Analysis of Results

Another potential drawback of evaluating practice in agencies is that the analysis of findings is largely a matter of judgment, so that their applicability is limited. Some statistical analyses can be carried out for single-system designs, and these will be discussed in Chapters 12 and 13.

ETHICAL ISSUES IN PRACTICE EVALUATION

Issues relevant to other types of social work practice are obviously applicable here, such as issues about confidentiality and informed consent, but two other ethical issues specifically relate to practice evaluation: the use of the reversal design and the issue of the interference with practice.

Reversal Design

One could argue that withdrawing an apparently effective intervention, as we discussed in the reversal design section, is unethical. The counterargument is that withdrawal of the intervention will allow us to determine whether the intervention is responsible for any change in the target problem. This determination not only enhances the worker's knowledge of the intervention's effectiveness but also demonstrates its effectiveness to the client. As a result, the intervention may have a longer effect; parent training is a good example.

Interference with Practice

The second issue—the idea that practice evaluation procedures interfere with practice—has been raised consistently over the years. One response to this position is that practice evaluation studies can enhance practice and help direct and inform social workers in their day-to-day contact with client systems. For example, determining the data collection method may offer opportunities for other insights and further exploration with the clients regarding the target problem. In addition, the client's involvement in the research, particularly in the data collection, can result in the client's being engaged in the change process to a greater extent, simultaneously limiting the problem with confidentiality and informed consent. This effect constitutes not so much an interference as an enhancement of practice.

In conclusion, because of the joint participation of worker and client in several of the methods used in this chapter, ethical violations are far less likely than in group designs for program evaluations.

HUMAN DIVERSITY ISSUES IN PRACTICE EVALUATION

Throughout the process of evaluating individual practice, you need to pay attention to human diversity issues. This effort includes carrying out more studies on diverse clients, recognizing that what may be effective for one type of client is not necessarily effective for another. In fact, practice evaluations provide an excellent opportunity for exploring the richness of human diversity.

SUMMARY

There are two major approaches to evaluating practice: descriptive and explanatory. Descriptive methods include monitoring interventions and monitoring client progress. Explanatory approaches, or single-system designs, include the AB design, the ABC design, the ABAB design (reversal), and the multiple baseline design. The evaluation of individual practice in agency settings is advantageous because of the opportunity for direct client feedback, knowledge building for practice, and time and cost factors. Some problems are also associated with the evaluations, however, including limited analysis, limited validity, and limited application. Because of the partnership required between client and worker, ethical violations are less likely than with group design. Evaluations of individual practice offer many opportunities for exploring the great diversity among different groups.

STUDY/EXERCISE QUESTIONS

1. You are working with a family with an adolescent who is not attending school regularly. You want to evaluate your intervention with the adolescent and will collect data on her school attendance. What would be the advantages and disadvantages of the following designs for this evaluation?
    a. AB design
    b. ABC design
    c. ABAB design
    What would be the ethical issues in this case?

2. You would like to evaluate your practice as a generalist social worker in a hospital, but your supervisor objects, saying it would be too time-consuming. Support your request and address her concerns.

3. Find an article in a social work journal that examines practice evaluation. Summarize the main points.

4. You have been facilitating a support group for teenage parents. The goal is for the group to continue without a facilitator. You will be monitoring attendance at the group as an indicator of its effectiveness. How would you do this?

5. Your supervisor asks you to monitor your practice focusing on the interventions you use. How would you do this?

INFOTRAC COLLEGE EDITION

1. Search for a *case study* and discuss how this research contributes to our knowledge of social work practice.
2. Search for a *single-system design* or *single-subject study*. What type of design was used?

REFERENCES

Applegate, J. S. (1992). The impact of subjective measures on nonbehavioral practice research: Outcome vs. process. *Families in Society, 73* (2), 100–108.

Berbenishty, R. (1989). Combining the single-system and group approaches to evaluate treatment effectiveness on the agency level. *Journal of Social Service Research, 12*, 31–48.

Bloom, M., Fischer, J., & Orme, J. (1995). *Evaluating practice: Guidelines for the accountable professional* (2nd ed.). Englewood Cliffs, NJ: Prentice Hall.

Blythe, B., Topodi, T., & Boras, S. (1994). *Direct practice research in human service agencies*. New York: Columbia University Press.

Burman, S., & Allen-Meares, P. (1994). Neglected victims of murder: Children's witness to parental homicide. *Social Work, 39* (1), 28–34.

Corcoran, K. J. (1993). Practice evaluation: Problems and promises of single-system designs in clinical practice. *Journal of Social Service Research, 18* (1/2), 147–159.

Dugan, E., Kamps, D., Leonard, B., Watkins, N., Rheinberger, A., & Stackhaus, J. (1995). Effects of cooperative learning groups during social studies for students with autism and fourth-grade peers. *Journal of Applied Behavior Analysis, 28*, 175–188.

Fischer, J. (1973). Is casework effective? A review. *Social Work, 18*, 5–20.

Kagle, J. D. (1982). Using single subject measures in practice decisions: Systematic documentation or distortion. *Aretê, 7* (2), 1–9.

Kazi, M. A., & Wilson, A. F. (1996). Applying single-case evaluation methodology in a British social work agency. *Research on Social Work Practice, 6* (1), 5–26.

McCormick, J. (1999). Notes from an MSW student fieldwork journal. New Mexico State University School of Social Work.

Millstein, K. H. (1993). Building knowledge from the study of cases: A reflective model for practitioner self-evaluation. *Journal of Teaching, 8* (1/2), 255–277.

Pandey, J. (1998). Women, environment, and sustainable development. *International Social Work, 41* (3), 339–355.

Papell, C. P., & Skolnick, L. (1992). The reflective practitioner: A contemporary paradigm's relevance for social work education. *Journal of Social Work Education, 28* (1), 18–26.

Reamer, R. B., Brady, M. P., & Hawkins, J. (1998). The effects of video self-modeling on parents' interactions with children with developmental disabilities. *Education and Training in Mental Retardation and Developmental Disabilities, 33* (2), 131–143.

Siegel, D. (1985). Defining empirically based practice. *Social Work, 29,* 325–331.

Slonim-Nevo, V., & Vosler, N. (1991). The use of single-system design with systemic brief problem-solving therapy. *Families in Society, 72,* 38–44.

Whitfield, G. W. (1999). Validating school social work: An evaluation of a cognitive-behavioral approach to reduce school violence. *Research on Social Work Practice, 9* (4), 399–426.

Selecting the Participants in the Research

■

Now that you've decided on your research question and the type of design you will be using, who are going to be the participants in your research? In social work research, **sampling** involves determining who will be the participants in the study. Sampling is necessary because you usually cannot include everyone in the study, just as in practice you cannot interview or meet with all those involved. For example, you may be interested in determining the need for an afterschool program in your community, and you must identify and get opinions from all the families in the city who have school-age children 12 and under. Even in a small-sized city, this could be a large number of families, and you have a limited budget and only two months in which to complete the project. Consequently, you need to select a smaller group of participants, or **sample,** from this large group, or **population,** that is made up of all possible cases that you are ultimately interested in studying (see Figure 8.1).

Sampling should be a familiar concept to you as generalist social workers. You often need to collect information relating to a target problem from a large number of people. When, due to time and other constraints, you cannot contact all of the relevant people, you select a sample. In research, there are specific ways to select a sample; the particular method we use depends on the nature and accessibility of the population and the type and purpose of the study we are undertaking.

Again, as with the steps of the research process already discussed, you may not be directly involved in sampling decisions. Knowledge of the process is essential, however, for two reasons: First, sometimes you will be involved in the sampling decision; second, you need to understand how sampling can affect use of the research findings in your practice.

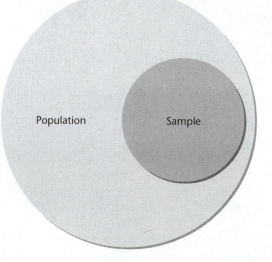

Figure 8.1   *Population and sample*

This chapter will discuss the following:

- key concepts in sampling
- types of sampling methods
- sample size
- the agency and sampling
- ethical issues in sampling
- human diversity issues in sampling

KEY CONCEPTS IN SAMPLING

One of the key concepts of sampling is the extent to which the sample is representative of the population. A **representative sample** means that the sample has the same distribution of characteristics as the population from which it is selected. For example, in assessing the city's need for an afterschool program, you are interested in making statements applicable to the entire city, so your sample needs to be representative. Thus in this case it is important that the sample not be biased in any way. One way bias occurs is if only one neighborhood is selected. Neighborhoods tend to have specific socioeconomic and ethnic characteristics—for example, upper-middle-class suburbs, Hispanic barrios, retirement communities. As a result, they are not usually representative of the entire city population, at least not in terms of socioeconomic and ethnic structure. Neighborhood is only one example of possible bias. Other groupings, such as schools and churches, also may not be representative of the larger community.

If your sample is representative of the population, then you can generalize the findings from your sample to that population. When you generalize, you claim that the findings from studying the sample can be applied to the population. If you discover in your representative sample of families from your city that 70 percent express an urgent need for an afterschool program, you then generalize that 70 percent of the families in your city (that is, your population) will also express this need. In needs assessment studies such as this, it is critical that you are able to generalize your findings. Thus a positivist approach, which emphasizes generalizability of the findings, is taken when conducting many needs assessments.

In other studies, however, generalizability and representativeness are not such important issues. For example, rather than looking at the extent of need for an afterschool program, you instead might be concerned with exploring the experiences of families with children who spend part of the day unsupervised. Here you might use an interpretive approach, where the concern is less with the representativeness of the sample and the generalizability of the findings. In an interpretive study, the key concept is that the sample is **information rich;** that is, the sample consists of cases from which you can learn about issues central to the research question.

Before describing different sampling strategies, you need to become familiar with two other general sampling concepts. First, an **element** in sampling refers to the item under study in the population and sample. In generalist social work research, these items or elements may be the different client systems with which we work—individuals, families, groups, organizations, or communities. The element depends upon the unit of analysis. Elements may be more specific than these basic systems. In our example, families with school-age children 12 and under are a more specific element than simply families.

The second concept is the **sampling frame:** a list of all the elements in the population from which the sample is selected. In the above example, the sampling frame would consist of a list of families in the city with school-age children 12 and under.

As you confront the realities of compiling a sampling frame, you may need to redefine the population. For example, you might have decided on families with children 12 and under as your element because the state in which you are conducting the study legally mandates that children of this age cannot be left without adult supervision. When you begin to compile a sampling frame, however, you run into problems because you find it very difficult to identify families with children of this age and younger. Instead, you discover that through the school system, you can more easily identify families with children in the first through the seventh grade. You may end up with a few 13-year-olds, but this isn't a problem if you redefine your population as families with children in the first through the seventh grades.

TYPES OF SAMPLING METHODS

The sample can be selected in two major ways: probability and nonprobability sampling. **Probability sampling** allows you to select a sample where each element in the population has a known chance of being selected for the sample. This type of sampling increases the representativeness of the sample and should be strived for when using the positivist approach.

Instead of a probability sampling method, you may choose a **nonprobability sampling** or purposive sampling method. **Purposive sampling** allows the researcher to handpick the sample according to the nature of the research problem and the phenomenon under study. As a sampling method, purposive sampling is limited in terms of representativeness, in that the probability of each element of the population being included in the sample is unknown. It is, however, the sampling method of choice in interpretive studies, where generalizability of results is less important.

Probability and nonprobability sampling approaches will be presented in the following sections.

Probability Sampling

Probability sampling occurs when every element in the population has a known chance of being selected; thus, its representativeness is assured. In addition, no subject can be selected more than once in a single sample. There are four major

Table 8.1   **Probability sampling methods and generalization of findings**

Sampling method	Generalizability
Simple random	Can generalize; limitations minimal
Systematic random	Can generalize; limitations minimal—note how the elements are listed in the sampling frame
Stratified random	Can generalize; limitations minimal—make sure the strata involved are reflected in the analysis of the data
Cluster	Can generalize, but some limitations possible—note the characteristics of the elements because there is a possibility of sampling error with this type of probability sampling

types of probability sampling: (1) simple random sampling; (2) systematic random sampling; (3) stratified random sampling; and (4) cluster sampling. Table 8.1 includes each of the probability sampling methods along with their associated potential generalizability.

Simple Random Sampling

Simple random sampling is the easiest of the sampling methods, where the population is treated as a whole unit and each element has an equal probability of being selected in the sample. Because the sampling is random, each element has the same chance of being selected. When you toss a coin, there is an equal chance of its being heads or tails. In the afterschool program needs assessment example, a simple random sample would involve assigning identification numbers to all the elements (families with children in first through seventh grades) and then using a table of random numbers that can be generated by a computer. Most software packages for the social sciences have the ability to generate random number tables. If you did not have the random numbers table, you could literally put all the identification numbers of each element in a container and pick your sample from this.

Simple random sampling is the most straightforward probability sampling method to use. It has some problems, though, which will become apparent as the other types of probability sampling are discussed.

Simple Random Sampling

Tam and Yeung (1994) studied community perceptions of social welfare in Hong Kong. They were interested in a representative sample and so used simple random sampling. Their sample consisted of 2,326 households randomly selected from census information. Questionnaires were mailed to each of these households.

Systematic Random Sampling

Systematic random sampling involves taking the list of elements and choosing every *n*th element on the list. The size of *n* depends upon the size of the sampling frame and the intended size of the sample. For example, if you had 400 elements in your sampling frame and you needed a sample of 100, every fourth element would be selected for the sample. If you needed a sample of 200, every second element would be selected.

Systematic Random Sampling

Johnson, Renaud, Schmidt, and Stanek (1998) studied social workers' views of parents of children with mental and emotional disabilities. A systematic random sample (*n* = 570) was taken of the total membership (12,750) from the National Association of Social Workers (NASW) Register of Clinical Social Workers. The authors found that the most prevalent problematic area reported by the social workers was parent-blaming beliefs.

Generally, systematic random sampling is as random as simple random sampling. One potential problem with systematic random sampling arises, however, when the ordering of elements in the list being sampled from follows a particular pattern. A distortion of the sample may result. In the afterschool program example, students from the school district may be arranged into class lists of approximately 30 students, and all students who moved to the community within the last six months may be placed at the end of each of these lists. In some communities, these recent additions may be made up primarily of migrant workers. Consequently, if you were to select every 10th, 20th, and 30th element in each class list, your resulting sample would be made up of a disproportionate number of migrant workers, because even though each class has only three or four such students, they are more likely to be the 30th element in a class list.

Problems with the ordering of elements can usually be identified quite easily, and precautions can be taken. When lists are available, systematic random sampling may be easier than simple random sampling because it avoids the step of assigning identification numbers.

Stratified Random Sampling

Stratified random sampling is a modification of the previous two methods; in it the population is divided into strata, and subsamples are randomly selected from each of the strata. Sometimes you need to ensure that a certain proportion of the elements is represented, and stratified random sampling provides a greater chance of meeting this goal than either systematic or simple random sampling.

In the afterschool program study, you may be concerned about representation of the different ethnic groups of the families with children in first through the seventh grade. You identify 10 percent of the families as Native Americans. With a simple or systematic random sample, your sample should, if it is truly representative, include 10 percent Native American families. Unfortunately, due to the workings of probability theory, this is not always the result. At this point, we cannot delve into the depths of probability theory, but if we toss a coin 20 times, we might expect to end up with 10 heads and 10 tails. Often, however, results actually vary. We might end up with 12 heads and 8 tails.

To ensure that Native American families are representatively included in the sample, you can use stratified random sampling. Stratified random sampling requires two preconditions. First, you must be sure that membership in the group whose representation you are concerned about actually has an impact on the phenomenon you are studying. In our example, do you think that Native American families' viewpoints on afterschool programs will differ from those of other families? If not, their adequate representation in the sample may not be that important. Second, you need to know the proportion of this group relative to the rest of the population. In our example, 10 percent are Native American.

Stratified random sampling involves dividing the population into the groups or strata of interest; in this example, you would divide the population into Native Americans and non–Native Americans. (Note that you can create more than two strata if necessary. For example, you might also be concerned that Hispanic families be assured adequate representation in the sample. Knowing they make up 40 percent of the population, you would then create three strata: Native Americans, Hispanics, and others.) After creating the strata, simple or systematic random sampling is then carried out from each stratum in proportion to the stratum's representation in the population. In our example, to end up with a sample of 20, you would randomly select 2 from the Native American stratum, 8 from the Hispanic stratum, and 10 from the other stratum (see Figure 8.2).

Although under some circumstances stratified random sampling may be an improvement over simple random sampling, the disadvantages are the two

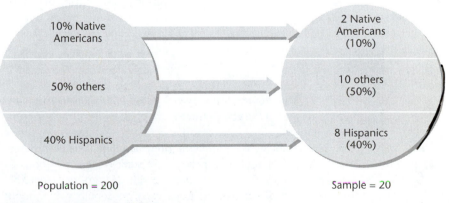

Population = 200　　　　　　　　　　　　　　　　　Sample = 20

Figure 8.2　　**Stratified random sampling**

preconditions described earlier—that is, the certainty that the characteristics with which you are concerned will impact the outcome and that you know the proportions of these characteristics in the population prior to the sampling.

Stratified Random Sampling

Hardina and Carley (1997) investigated the impact of increased allowable work hours on two-parent families receiving welfare. Participants were drawn from residents in central San Joaquin Valley counties who were receiving AFDC-UP during a given time frame. The random sample was stratified by ethnicity and respondents were randomly selected from each of the four ethnic categories: Latino, African American, Hmong, and white people.

Cluster Sampling

Cluster sampling involves randomly sampling a larger unit containing the elements of interest, and then sampling from these larger units the elements to be included in the final sample. Cluster sampling is often done in social work research because it can be used when it is difficult to get a sampling frame, and yet it is still a form of probability sampling. In the afterschool program example, suppose you are required to obtain the lists of students from each school rather than from the school district office. This could present a lengthy undertaking in a large school district with many schools. Or the lists may not be available either from the school or from the school district. In these cases, cluster sampling might provide a feasible solution.

In cluster sampling, a random sample of a larger unit is taken; in this case, the schools in which first through seventh graders are enrolled. This random sampling can be either simple, systematic, or stratified. In the afterschool program example, you use simple random sampling to select four schools. Then a random sample (again, either simple, systematic, or stratified) of the first

Cluster Sampling

Tice (1994) studied a community's response to supported employment—employment for wages in the competitive marketplace with some supports for individuals with severe disabilities or challenges. The sampling frame was the census tract of a rural Ohio county. Using simple random sampling, one community was selected. The study's test population included all adult residents of households in the selected community. A listing of adult individuals from the selected households was compiled, and one individual from each household was randomly selected to serve as a study participant.

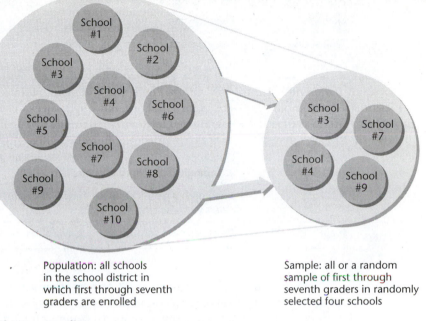

Population: all schools
in the school district in
which first through seventh
graders are enrolled

Sample: all or a random
sample of first through
seventh graders in randomly
selected four schools

Figure 8.3   **Cluster sampling**

through seventh grades in these four schools would be selected (Figure 8.3). Alternatively, if a student list is not available, all first through seventh graders in the four schools would be included in the final sample.

Cluster sampling can be useful in an agency setting, for example, when an agency serves a large number of clients over a yearly period (for example, 8,000 clients are referred). Instead of randomly selecting from this large sampling frame, three months (every fourth month) may be systematically randomly sampled from the year, and the clients referred during those three months included in the sample. Each month represents a cluster.

Cluster sampling has one potential problem. When a small number of units is sampled (for example, four schools), there is greater probability of sampling error. The four schools may consist of three white middle-class schools, whereas the students' population (in ten schools) is a 50-50 mix socioeconomically. Consequently, the sample would be biased in favor of white middle-class students, and other groups would be underrepresented.

Nonprobability or Purposive Sampling

Purposive sampling allows the researcher to intentionally select those elements that are information rich, which makes the sampling method of choice in interpretive studies. In the afterschool program example, you may decide you are more interested in learning about the problems and experiences of families who need afterschool care rather than finding out the proportion of families who are in need of afterschool services.

Table 8.2   **Purposive or nonprobability sampling methods**

Method	Characteristics
Typical cases	Those with "typical" characteristics
Criterion	Participants selected according to some eligibility criteria
Focus groups	Those with an interest in the research topic
Key informants	Those with expertise on the research topic
Community forum	Open to a community; some can be purposively invited
Quota	Certain proportions of participants from different groups selected according to specific characteristics
Snowball	Some participants identified; these participants then identify others with certain characteristics
Availability	Those selected because they are available

There are a number of different types of purposive sampling methods. Described here are eight of the most commonly used in social work: typical case, criterion sampling, focus groups, key informants, community forum, quota, snowball, and availability.

See Table 8.2 for the different types of purposive sampling methods.

Typical Cases

Typical case sampling is the most often used method for purposive sampling. Typical cases are sought using the literature, previous research, or consultation with relevant groups. For the afterschool program example, families who appear typical in their need for services would be contacted through a local agency or the schools.

 A Typical Case

Wagner's (1994) study of the homeless in a New England city purposively selected a large group of homeless people. The resulting cohort "resembled the national demographic profile of the homeless population in terms of age, gender, education, marital status, rates of mental illness, substance abuse and place of birth; race was the sole exception" (p. 720).

Criterion Sampling

Criterion sampling involves picking all cases that meet some criterion—for example, including all families in an agency who meet eligibility criteria to receive services from that agency.

Criterion Sampling

Hughes (1997) studied young adult black and Latino males who had been previously involved in crimes, but who were more recently making positive behavioral changes. The author wanted to know what factors facilitated their decisions to make the positive changes. The criteria applied to the sample included: (1) male between the ages of 18 and 28; (2) history of destructive behavior; (3) evidence of effort(s) to make positive life changes; and (4) evidence of positive involvement in the community. Twenty young adult inner city males made up the sample of this exploratory study. Findings indicated that fatherhood was a primary factor in facilitating positive behavioral changes among the young men.

Focus Groups

Focus groups were discussed in Chapter 3 as a means of helping to formulate a question and will be discussed further in Chapter 9 as a source of data collection. Focus groups are picked purposefully—those invited have some type of interest or expertise in the topic under study. Focus groups are also an excellent way of ensuring maximum participation and involvement by the community and by those on whom the research will have the most impact.

Focus Groups

Freedman, Litchfield, and Warfield (1995) studied the balancing of work and family responsibilities of parents of children with developmental disabilities. Four focus groups were convened to obtain the parents' perspectives.

Key Informant Sampling

Key informant sampling relies on people in the community identified as experts in the field of interest.

Key Informants

Artz (1998) used six key informants in her research on violence among teenage girls. All of the informants, identified as both victims and perpetrators of violence, wanted "to do something about violence." The girls' presentations of themselves revealed that they have negative notions of the self and that they believe that women achieve their greatest importance by commanding the attention of men.

Community Forum

The **community forum** involves publicizing a meeting or series of meetings at which individuals are briefed on the issues and then asked for input. Community members can be purposively invited.

A Community Forum

Delgado (1997) reports on the use of a community forum among Puerto Rican elderly to help interpret results of a survey. After responding to a survey examining how ethnicity and social class impact on the disability level and receipt of care among elderly Puerto Ricans in Springfield, a community forum was held. The forum addressed five questions that emerged from the surveys and a specific format was utilized in addressing the questions. The format included four parts: (1) a statement of the question posed to elders attending the forum, (2) presentation of the rationale for each question, (3) elder responses at the forum, and (4) consideration of these responses in relation to insights derived from focus groups and key informant interviews. Researchers found the community forum to be invaluable in interpreting the quantitative survey data. The forum participants' responses served as recommendations to develop culturally based constructs for practice with other Latino groups.

Quota Sampling

Quota sampling involves a certain proportion of elements with specific characteristics to be purposively included in the sample. In some respects, quota sampling is similar to stratified random sampling, except that no randomness is involved in selecting the elements. When examining the experiences of families

Quota Sampling

Bentelspacher, Chiltran, and Rahman (1994) studied coping and adaptation patterns among Chinese, Indian, and Malay families caring for a mentally ill relative in Singapore. The sample was selected through case records in a psychiatric hospital of those diagnosed with schizophrenia, who were living with a family member, and admitted during one year. Out of the resulting 281 that met these criteria, the cases were stratified according to the three main ethnic groups in Singapore—Chinese, Indian, and Malay—with the objective of interviewing 10 caregivers from each group. On telephone contact, 7 (28%) of the 25 total Indian caregivers, 12 (29%) of the 41 total Malay caregivers, and 11 (27%) of the first 41 Chinese caregivers to be contacted agreed to participate.

with unattended school-age children in an interpretive study, you might be interested in ensuring that you interviewed families from all ethnic groups in the community. Like stratified random sampling, quota sampling requires that you know the proportion of these ethnic groups in the population. The problems associated with this form of sampling, as with stratified random sampling, are that the researcher needs to be sure that the categories or variables selected are important ones and that the proportions of these variables are known in the population. It may be that ethnicity is not a key variable that needs to be included.

Snowball Sampling

Snowball sampling involves identifying some members of the population and then having those individuals contact others in the population. This is a very useful strategy to adopt with less accessible populations—for example, the homeless—although it could also be used with the example of families with children who are unsupervised after school. You might identify and contact a few families and then ask those families to contact others they think are having problems.

Snowball Sampling

George and Ramkissoon (1998) used a snowball sampling method to study the challenges of South Asian women as well as the barriers to social services they experienced in their immigration to Canada. Initially, posters in various languages advertised the study and provided the name of a contact person. Women who responded were briefly interviewed to assess whether they fit the study criteria and were then asked if they could recommend other women who might be interested in participating in the study. Through this method, 47 women were chosen.

Availability Sampling

Availability or **convenience sampling** is used extensively in social work research and involves including available or convenient elements in the sample. Sometimes availability sampling is confused with random sampling, because superficially it appears random. A typical example of availability sampling is interviewing people in a shopping mall in an attempt to get a sample of the community. Alternatively, in an agency you are asked to conduct a program evaluation. The funds for the evaluation are available now, and you have two months to collect the data. Consequently, you decide to include in your sample clients referred to the program during the next 30 days. The population under study is all those referred to the program.

Research findings from availability samples cannot be generalized to the population under study. In the shopping mall example, you are going to be able to include in your sample only people who shop at the mall—maybe a small and not very representative sample of the community as a whole. In the program evaluation example, the clients referred to the agency in the month of the sampling may be different from clients referred at other times of the year; December may not be a very representative month of the entire year. Consequently, the sample is biased, making it difficult to generalize results to the entire community. Availability sampling is also problematic in that it does not possess the advantages of a purposive sampling method. The elements are not picked for their information richness, but selected on the basis of convenience. Availability samples, however, often present the only feasible way of sampling.

Availability Sampling

Lindsey (1998) mailed surveys to directors of 165 homeless and domestic violence shelters in two southern states. The response rate was 54 percent. The author wanted to know the directors' perceptions about what helped or hindered homeless, mother-headed families to emerge from homelessness. Respondents believed that mothers' attitudes and motivation were the most important factors in helping their emergence from homelessness, while lack of social supports and relationship difficulties were those problems that hindered emergence the most. Scarce housing within the community was also identified as a factor that hindered the families emerging from homelessness.

Availability sampling is often the sampling method to use when evaluating your own practice. One case or more is selected and the effectiveness of the intervention assessed. This type of research was discussed in more detail in Chapter 7.

Studying Complete Populations

Sometimes, particularly when conducting program evaluations, it is possible to study the entire population rather than a sample. For example, you could define the population in such a way that you can include all the elements in that popu-

Studying an Entire Population

Levin and Herbert (1995) studied the different work assignments of B.S.W. and M.S.W. social workers in hospitals in four Canadian provinces. They sent a questionnaire to the directors of social work departments in all 89 hospitals in the four provinces.

lation in your study. If the program is relatively small, all the clients served during a certain period (say, six months) could be defined as the population, and all could be studied. (Remember, the definition of the population is in part up to you.) Or if the program is new, it might be quite feasible to study the entire population—namely, all who have been served since the program's inception. It is also possible to study the entire population if the population is quite specific—for example, children with Down's syndrome in a medium-sized city.

SAMPLE SIZE

Statisticians devote a considerable amount of energy to determining how large or small samples should be. Some of the kinds of research that generalist social workers usually conduct, such as program or practice evaluations, do not require you to make a decision about sample size because the sample is fixed—namely, a small program or your own practice.

The size of the sample in part depends on its homogeneity, or the similarity among different elements. If you can be assured that the characteristics of the sample elements are similar on the dimensions you are interested in studying, then the sample can be smaller. In the example of unsupervised children, if all the children are similar in the characteristics in which you are interested—ethnicity, socioeconomic status, and family configuration—then the sample size can be small. If, however, you are interested in comparing the afterschool program needs of different types of families—for example, across family configuration, income, and so on—then you would probably need a larger sample to ensure that you have enough subjects in each category. As we saw in Chapter 3, a minimal number of cases is required in each category to allow certain statistical analyses to occur.

The size of the sample also depends on the research approach used. In positivist studies using probability samples, sample sizes usually need to be quite large, whereas in interpretive studies the sample size is small, and it is the information-richness of the cases that is important. In interpretive studies the size of the sample is no larger than that needed to gather the information of interest. Redundancy is to be avoided.

Also important to consider when deciding on sample size is the issue of sampling error. **Sampling error** is the extent to which the values of the sample differ from those of the population. The margin of error refers to the precision needed by the researcher. A margin of error of 5% means the actual findings could vary in either direction by as much as 5%. For example, a client satisfaction survey that finds 55% of clients were "very satisfied" could have actual results anywhere from 50% to 60%. If the sample is large enough, the sampling error and margin of error can be reduced. With 100 tosses of a coin, you are more likely to end up with 50% heads and 50% tails than you are with 20 tosses. In reporting the results of large-scale surveys, it is important to report the extent of sampling error.

A number of quite complicated formulas can assist in determining sample size. If you have concerns about the size of your sample, consult with a statistician or refer to a good statistics text (see Chapters 12 and 13 for some references).

Table 8.3 gives different sample sizes and their associated **margin of error.** The margin of error reported in this table is 5%. This means the actual findings could vary as much as 5% either positively or negatively. Another way to view this is to state that the findings, using the sample sizes in the table, have a 95% **confidence level,** which expresses how often you would expect similar results

Table 8.3   **Size of sample required at 5% confidence interval**

Population size	Sample size
50	44
75	63
100	80
150	108
200	132
250	152
300	169
400	196
500	217
750	254
1,000	278
2,000	322
4,000	351
5,000	357
10,000	370
15,000	375
20,000	377
25,000	378
50,000	381
100,000	384
1,000,000	384

Source: From *Educational and Psychological Measurement,* by R. V. Krejcie and D. W. Morgan, pp. 607–610. Copyright © 1970 Sage Publications, Inc. Reprinted by permission of Sage Publications, Inc.

if the research were repeated. For example, in a sample with a 95% confidence level and a 5% margin of error, the findings could be expected to miss the actual values in the population by more than 5% only five times in 100 surveys. Use the table as a guide and not as a strict formula for sample size determination.

THE AGENCY AND SAMPLING

As generalist social workers engaging in research, you may need to use sampling methods that are not textbook examples. Two cases of these modifications are discussed in this section: limited probability sampling and combined sampling methods.

Often, an integral part of a needs assessment is the ability to generalize the findings to an entire community, county, or larger area. Unfortunately, it is often not possible to obtain representative samples due to most agencies' time and money constraints. Sometimes, however, it is possible to obtain a **limited probability sample**—for example, from a neighborhood or agency—and then compare the characteristics of this sample with the characteristics of a sample drawn from a larger population. In this way, some tentative generalizations of the findings can be made. Sometimes similarities are not found between the smaller and larger samples. For example, in Schilit and colleagues' (1991) study on lesbian violence, discussed earlier, the authors found that when they compared the ethnicity, income, and education of their subjects to these characteristics in the population of Tucson, there were large differences, thus limiting any generalizations.

This method of expanding generalizations suffers from some problems similar to those of stratified random sampling: the assumption that we know what the important characteristics are when comparing a smaller sample with a larger sample. Consequently, this method should be used with caution.

Another often-needed modification of sampling is to combine sampling methods. Sometimes practical constraints do not allow you to proceed with the type of sampling planned; it may be possible to sample one group using a planned method but not another group.

A Limited Probability Sample

Smith and Kronauge (1990), in their study of who is involved in decision making about abortion, drew a random sample from women who received abortions through one agency in St. Louis, Missouri. The researchers then compared two characteristics of this sample—marital status and age—with a national sample. The similarity they found allowed them to tentatively generalize the findings from their sample to the wider population.

Combined Sampling Methods

Kruk (1994) studied disengaged noncustodial fathers in the United States, Canada, and Great Britain. He managed to secure court records in Canada in order to select a probability sample. In Great Britain, however, he did not have access to these records and had to use an availability sampling method, placing advertisements in newspapers and seeking referrals from legal and social work practitioners.

ETHICAL ISSUES IN SAMPLING

Two ethical issues relate to sampling: first, responsible reporting of the sampling method and, second, obtaining the subject's consent to the research.

Reporting the Sampling Method

It is the researcher's responsibility when reporting research findings—whether in a journal article, a report, or a presentation—to ensure that the research methods used in the study are described as accurately as possible. Details of reporting will be described in Chapter 14. Some discussion is necessary here, however, because inaccuracies and ambiguities in research reports often concern the sampling method.

Sometimes authors write about supposedly random methods of sampling that are really availability or some other form of nonprobability sampling. When reading reports and articles, look for an explicit description of the sampling method along with a frank description of the generalization limitations, particularly if a nonprobability sampling method is used. It is unethical to claim even implicitly that the results of a nonprobability sample are generalizable to a wider population. Such a claim is misleading and can have some serious negative implications. As discussed earlier in this chapter, nonprobability and probability sampling methods have very different purposes.

Informed Consent

Whenever any type of social work research is undertaken, it is critical that no coercion is exerted and that the subject voluntarily agrees to participate. The subjects or participants must always be told about the purpose and goals of the research. As discussed in Chapter 6, voluntary, informed consent should always be obtained from the participants. Figure 8.4 is an example of a consent form.

Many ethical guidelines present dilemmas. You may feel that by disclosing information about the research project to the participant, you will jeopardize the research results. For example, if you are using observation to collect data about a specific behavior and if participants know they are being observed, their behav-

CONSENT TO PARTICIPATE IN RESEARCH

The purpose of this research is to learn more about the needs of families who are in the process of reuniting with their children. I would also like to learn about the services that were provided to you and your family and the meaning each has for you. I would like to hear about how you have coped with your experiences and what you believe would help other families who may one day experience a similar situation.

I am a graduate student social worker and am working independently on this research project, however, with the permission and knowledge of my field placement agency (Department of Children, Youth and Families) and the School of Social Work at New Mexico State University. I will protect your identity by using fictitious names and disguising incidents. I plan to share the results of this study with other helping professionals through presentations and possible publication.

*   *   *   *   *   *   *   *   *   *   *

I hereby acknowledge that I am 18 years or older and agree to participate in this research project. I acknowledge that the information obtained in the interview will be used to prepare a research project and that every precaution will be taken to protect my identity and assure confidentiality. I acknowledge my participation as voluntary and know that I may withdraw my participation at any time.

RESPONDENT _____   RESEARCHER _____

DATE _____   DATE _____

Figure 8.4   ***A form for obtaining participants' informed consent***

ior might change considerably. Another problem arises when you inform participants that their involvement in the research is voluntary: A certain number may choose not to participate. The researcher then does not know whether the results from the participants who agreed to participate are different from those who refused.

Sometimes—and these times are *not* frequent—the voluntary participation ethical standard may need to be modified. If this is necessary, you must clearly understand and explain the reasons. In particular, you must be careful that researchers do not use their power or authority to exploit the subjects. Suppose a professor who is carrying out research on students' experiences of sexual harassment requests that all the students in her class complete a questionnaire that she estimates will take about 15 minutes. She states that participation is voluntary, but those who choose not to participate will be required to write a five-page research paper. This is clearly a form of coercion, with the professor using her authority to force participation. A similar situation can be envisioned with a social work researcher requiring the participation of individuals who are dependent upon the social worker for services. The decision to forgo the participant's consent must be very carefully considered to ensure that no blatant coercion is occurring.

Another way of viewing the issue of the subject's consent is to modify our perspective on the distinction between researcher and participant. The relationship between researcher and participant can be seen as egalitarian, rather than viewed, as it has been traditionally, as a relationship in which researchers wield power and authority over subjects. When an even footing is adopted, the question of the participant's consent becomes a nonissue. Instead, researchers make their research skills accessible to participants, participants become active contributors in the research, and each gains from being involved. Emphasizing the egalitarian relationship between researcher and participant is one way of incorporating this connectedness into research methodology. This type of relationship can be created by using sampling methods such as the key informant, the focus group, and the community forum, in all of which community members have an opportunity to serve both as participants and as contributors. An egalitarian relationship between researcher and participant is a characteristic of participatory research, as discussed in previous chapters.

When evaluating individual practice, the way the research is presented to the client is important and can affect the researcher-participant relationship. If you present the research as something special, different, or separate from practice, then the client will see it that way and often resist being involved (or used) in a research project. But if you stress the integration between research and practice and point out how the client will benefit from feedback on the relative effectiveness of the intervention, then you will be more accurately depicting the whole idea of evaluating practice. In addition, you will be engaging in a true partnership with the client, benefiting all involved.

Breaking down the distinction between researcher and participant has other advantages apart from the issue of the participant's consent. First, it addresses the concern that research is not always responsive to the needs of oppressed groups. When a partnership between researcher and participant is created, responsiveness is more assured. Second, the validity of the research may be enhanced. The more traditional relationship between researcher and participant, which emphasizes separateness, may result in a greater likelihood of the participant's giving invalid responses out of a lack of understanding of the researcher's intent. This problem is avoided by building the partnership. Third, this approach seems to be particularly compatible to social work practice, where emphasis is placed on establishing a relationship with the client.

Creating an egalitarian relationship between subject and researcher thus seems a reasonable approach to adopt and one that offers several advantages. As a final note, however, we should add that in practice an egalitarian relationship can sometimes be difficult to achieve. Srinivasan and Davis (1991) commented on this in an article reporting on the organization of a women's shelter. This study, incidentally, is a good example of the application of feminist research principles. In the article Davis states:

Although my intent was to establish egalitarian relationships with all participants in the study, I was not always successful in this regard. The staff read-
ily accepted and treated me as another volunteer, but the residents had
more difficulty accepting me as an equal. The residents were skeptical about
why I was there. (p. 41)

HUMAN DIVERSITY ISSUES IN SAMPLING

Unfortunately, the social science literature prior to the early 1970s does not provide many examples of studies with heterogeneous samples. For example,
Holmes and Jorgensen (1971) found that subjects were males twice as often as
females, a ratio even higher than the ratio of college student subjects to non–
college student subjects. Not only were the samples homogeneous, but also the
findings from these samples were generalized to the population as a whole—
populations that included non–college graduates, women, and minorities. These
generalizations should never be made because the samples were simply not representative of the populations.

A classic example of this problem is presented by Kohlberg's study of the development of morality. In his initial study, he selected a sample of Harvard male
graduates (1969). Based on this study, Kohlberg developed a model and theory of
moral development that he used as a template to assess the moral development
of *all* individuals. Moreover, as a result of applying this model to women, he
concluded that women often did not reach the higher level of moral development and were, therefore, deficient morally. Later, Gilligan (1977) challenged
these conclusions and studied moral development in a sample of women. She
proposed alternative moral developmental stages for women, concluding that
women were not deviant or deficient in their moral development but simply followed a different course.

Similar assumptions and erroneous generalizations have been made relating
to minority populations. White middle-class samples have been studied, and the
findings have been generalized and presented as the norm by which to evaluate
minorities. Such improper generalizations are not always made explicitly by the
researchers themselves, but often by others who draw assumptions from the
findings and apply them to other groups.

Historically, such generalizations have been made about the effectiveness of
social programs. If a program is demonstrated to be ineffective with a minority
urban sample, it may be concluded that consequently the program would be
ineffective with all minorities. It is critical that we recognize diversity within
minority groups. Program ineffectiveness with some urban minorities does not
mean program ineffectiveness with other minorities or with rural minorities.

The danger of improper generalizations can in part be avoided if research
consumers enhance their knowledge. This includes you! Researchers, as discussed in the previous section, can also help by being explicit about the limitations of their sampling method. It is often easier, however, to be critical of

existing studies than to avoid such pitfalls in our own research. The erroneous assumptions that Kohlberg made seem almost obvious now, but that is because we have an increased sensitivity to gender issues. Additionally, there is an increasing awareness of ethnic and racial diversity when applying research methods. Be cautioned that other dimensions of diversity are less evident. For example, ageism and homophobia are still pervasive in our culture, even among social workers. Sometimes we are not even aware of all the dimensions of diversity. The issue goes beyond consciously excluding a particular group.

Gender in Sampling

Carpenter and Platt (1997) studied the impacts of the changing health care delivery system on the professional identity of clinical social workers, specifically, the fit between personal and professional values. Acknowledging past research, which has used predominantly female samples, the authors in this study obtained a sample with equal numbers of male and female social workers. The findings clarified that there were no gender differences in the description of values. The sense of strain between values varied according to workplace setting.

SUMMARY

Key concepts in sampling are representativeness, generalizability, and information richness. The two different types of sampling strategies are probability and purposive methods. Probability sampling includes simple random sampling, systematic random sampling, stratified random sampling, and cluster sampling. Purposive sampling includes typical case, criterion sampling, focus groups, key informants, community forum, quota sampling, snowball sampling, and availability sampling.

When conducting sampling in an agency, sampling methods may need to be modified. Ethical issues include accurate reporting of the sampling method and the subject's consent. Human diversity issues relate to whether the sampling represents diverse populations adequately.

STUDY/EXERCISE QUESTIONS

1. A local agency has asked you to help them conduct a survey to determine whether the city needs an elder day care facility. The population of the city is 65,000. About 20% of the city's population lives below the poverty level. All persons over the age of 60 would be eligible for the center.
    a. Define the population.
    b. Will probability sampling be possible? If not, why not? If so, what method would you use?

    c. Discuss the pros and cons of each of the following suggestions made by various members of the board of the agency:

        (i) Interview elders who frequent the local shopping mall early in the morning for exercise.

        (ii) Mail questionnaires to members of the local branch of the American Association of Retired Persons (AARP).

        (iii) Conduct a telephone interview using the telephone directory as a sampling frame.

2. Review an issue of *Social Work,* and answer these questions about the research articles.

    a. What was the sampling method used?

    b. What are the limitations with each of the sampling methods?

    c. Were these limitations made explicit in the articles?

INFOTRAC COLLEGE EDITION

1. Search for a research study on gays and lesbians and describe the sampling approach used. Was there any discussion in the study about the consent of the participants?
2. Search for *random sampling.* According to these articles, what are some of the difficulties of implementing random sampling?

REFERENCES

Artz, S. (1998). Where have all the school girls gone? Violent girls in the school yard. *Child & Youth Care Forum, 27* (2), 77–109.

Bentelspacher, C. E., Chiltran, S., & Rahman M. (1994). Coping and adaptation patterns among Chinese, Indian, and Malay families caring for a mentally ill relative. *Families in Society: The Journal of Contemporary Human Service,* 287–294.

Carpenter, M. C., & Platt, S. (1997). Professional identity for clinical social workers: Impact of changes in health care delivery systems. *Clinical Social Work Journal, 25* (3), 337–350.

Delgado, M. (1997). Interpretation of Puerto Rican elder research findings: A community forum of research respondents. *Journal of Applied Gerontology, 16* (3), 317–332.

Freedman, R. L., Litchfield, L. C., & Warfield, M. E. (1995). Balancing work and family: Perspectives of parents of children with developmental disabilities. *Families in Society, 76* (8), 507–514.

George, U., & Ramkissoon, S. (1998). Race, gender, and class: Interlocking oppressions in the lives of South Asian women in Canada. *Affilia, 13* (1), 102–119.

Gilligan, C. (1977). In a different voice: Women's conceptions of self and of morality. *Harvard Educational Review, 47,* 481–512.

Hardina, D., & Carley, M. (1997). The impact of increased allowable work hours on two-parent families receiving welfare. *Social Work Research, 21* (2), 101–109.

Holmes, D. S., & Jorgensen, B. W. (1971). The personality and social psychologists study men more than women. *Representative Research in Social Psychology, 2,* 71–76.

Hughes, M. J. (1997). An exploratory study of young adult black and Latino males and the factors facilitating their decisions to make positive behavioral changes. *Smith College Studies in Social Work, 67* (3), 401–414.

Johnson, H. C., Renaud, E. F., Schmidt, D. T., & Stanek, E. J. (1998). Social workers' views of parents of children with mental and emotional disabilities. *Families in Society, 79* (2), 173–187.

Kohlberg, L. (1969). *Stages in the development of moral thought and action.* New York: Holt, Rinehart & Winston.

Krejcie, R. V., & Morgan, D. W. (1970). Determining sample size for research activities. *Educational & Psychological Measurement, 30,* 607–610.

Kruk, E. (1994). The disengaged noncustodial father: Implications for social work practice with the divorced family. *Social Work, 39,* 15–24.

Levin, R., & Herbert, M. (1995). Differential work assignments of social work practitioners in hospitals. *Health & Social Work, 20,* 21–30.

Lindsey, E. W. (1998). Service providers' perception of factors that help or hinder homeless families. *Familes in Society, 79* (2), 160–172.

Smith, H. W., & Kronauge, C. (1990). The politics of abortion: Husband notification legislation, self-disclosure, and marital bargaining. *The Sociological Quarterly, 31* (4), 585–598.

Srinivasan, M., & Davis, L. V. (1991). A shelter: An organization like any other. *Affilia, 6* (1), 38–57.

Tam, T. S. K., & Yeung, S. (1994). Community perception of social welfare and its relations to familism, political alienation, and individual rights: The case of Hong Kong. *International Social Work, 37* (1), 47–60.

Tice, C. (1994). A community's response to supported employment: Implications for social work practice. *Social Work, 39* (6), 728–735.

Wagner, D. (1994). Beyond the pathologizing of network: Alternative activities in a street community. *Social Work, 39* (6), 718–726.

Collecting the Data

ow that you have decided on the research design and the way participants will be selected, you need to decide how you will gather the information or data. Do you go out and interview people directly? Do you use forms and questionnaires to collect information, or do you need to observe?

In generalist practice, you must also decide how information will be collected, after defining and conceptualizing the problem. This information is referred to in both practice and research as **data** (singular **datum**), and they are collected using a **measuring instrument,** or data collection method. These methods include questionnaires, observation, logs and journals, interviews, scales, and secondary data. All these will be described in this chapter.

As a generalist social worker, you may or may not actually collect the data. The plan and perhaps even the data collection may have already been implemented. Even if you don't direct the collection of the data, and certainly if you are responsible for collecting data, you will need to know what instruments are used under what circumstances.

This chapter will include a discussion of the following topics:

- quantitative and qualitative data
- ways of collecting data
- who collects the data
- combining data collection methods
- determining reliability and validity
- the agency and data collection
- ethical issues in collecting data
- human diversity issues in collecting data

QUANTITATIVE AND QUALITATIVE DATA

As discussed in Chapter 1, the positivist and interpretist approaches tend to involve the collection of different types of data. The former emphasizes the collection of quantitative data, and with the latter the emphasis is on qualitative data. Sometimes the terms *qualitative research* and *quantitative research* are used synonymously with *interpretist research* and *positivist research,* respectively. Strictly speaking, though, *quantitative* and *qualitative* refer to the type of data rather than an entire research approach. Sometimes studies using the positivist approach will collect partly or completely qualitative data, and sometimes interpretive studies will involve the collection of some quantitative data. So using the data collection type to describe the entire research approach can be misleading.

WAYS OF COLLECTING DATA

Six major methods of collecting data, or measuring instruments, will be described in this section (see Figure 9.1): interviews, questionnaires, observation techniques, logs and journals, scales, and secondary data. All these methods can

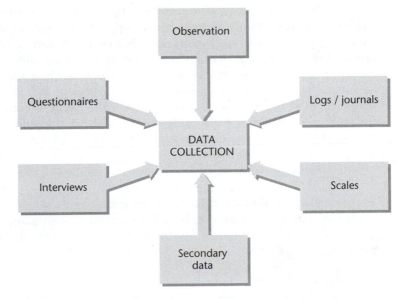

Figure 9.1   ***Methods of data collection***

include both qualitative and quantitative data, except logs and journals, which are generally qualitative, and scales which are quantitative.

At this point, note that you can either construct your own data collection instrument using one or more of the methods listed here, or else use an already existing measure. Whenever possible, use an existing measure, particularly if it is standardized. A standardized instrument is uniform throughout. It includes items uniformly administered and scored according to an agreed-upon procedure. This type of instrument not only is convenient to use but also has established reliability and validity, two measurement concepts discussed at the end of this chapter.

As they are described, each of the six methods will be assessed for both **neutrality** and **applicability.** Patton (1990) proposed the term *neutrality* as an alternative to either *objectivity* or *subjectivity.* Objectivity is one of the central premises of the positivist approach. As discussed in Chapter 1, however, objectivity is virtually impossible to achieve, and even the positivist admits it is a problematic term. Interpretism is more concerned with the subjective experiences of the subjects in the study. *Subjective,* however, is also a problematic term, with negative connotations implying bias and relevance only to specific subjects. *Neutrality* appears to be a more useful term and is defined by Patton as characterizing research in which "the researcher does not seek out to prove a particular perspective or manipulate the data to arrive at predisposed truths" (p. 55).

Patton suggests adopting the term *empathetic neutrality* for the interpretive approach (which he calls the qualitative approach). Here, though, we maintain that *neutrality* is a useful term for both the positivist and interpretist perspectives.

Apart from neutrality, the other criterion by which the data collection methods will be discussed in the next section is applicability. The applicability of a measuring instrument is whether or not it is appropriate and suitable for a particular type of problem. For example, observation would typically not be a useful method to employ if we were collecting information on child abuse, but would be suitable for collecting information on child behavior problems. Each data collection method will be described, along with a discussion of both its strengths and weaknesses in terms of neutrality and its relative applicability for the kinds of research questions we encounter as generalist social workers.

Interviews

As a generalist social work student, you are already quite skilled at conducting interviews. Interviews are structured, semistructured, or unstructured. Often, the questions may be very similar, but the interviews are distinguished based on how they are conducted.

Structured Interviews

In a **structured interview,** the interviewer knows in advance the questions to ask and in many cases is simply administering a verbal questionnaire. Often this questionnaire is already developed by the agency workers.

A Structured Interview

First, Rife, and Toomey (1994) studied the rural homeless. During the 6-month data collection period, 919 homeless adults were interviewed in 21 counties. To ensure standardized use of the instruments, training sessions were held for all the interviewers.

Semistructured Interviews

In a **semistructured interview,** the interviewer has more freedom to pursue hunches and can improvise with the questions. Semistructured interviews often use interview schedules consisting of the general types of questions to ask, but they are not in a questionnaire format. Sometimes semistructured interviews are referred to as open-ended interviews.

A Semistructured Interview

Johnson (1995) examined the nature of the relationship between elders and their caregivers by comparing their attitudes toward the definition, criminalization, and treatment of elder abuse. She collected the data using face-to-face semi-structured interviews designed to gather both qualitative and quantitative data. Results suggested the perceptions of the two groups were similar.

Unstructured Interviews

Completely **unstructured interviews** can also be used. This type of interview is similar to a conversation except that the interviewer and interviewee know that an interview is being conducted and that the interviewee is privy to information of interest to the interviewer.

Neutrality

Although structured and semistructured interviews are more neutral than unstructured interviews—because asking specific questions minimizes some bias—in general, the neutrality of interviewing is limited. We know that we respond differently to different people depending on how we are approached. The answer to an interviewer's question will be influenced by several factors: the interviewer's age, gender, ethnicity, and dress; the context in which the interviewer approaches the interviewee; the manner in which the interviewer speaks; and so forth. In addition, these characteristics will not have a constant effect on all the interviewees. Instead, each interviewee will respond differently to these characteristics depending on previous experiences, and there is no way of knowing exactly how these responses differ. This is referred to as the *reactive effect:* the interviewer influences the interviewee, and the interviewee responds in a particular way, which will then have a feedback effect on the interviewer. With the positivist approach, the reactive effect can be a serious limitation and can jeopardize the data collection method's objectivity, which as you will remember is important in the positivist approach.

If you are using the interpretive approach, reactivity is not necessarily a problem, since the approach involves a recognition that the relationship between the researcher and the subject exists and not only enhances the quality of the data but also can itself create the data. Using the interpretive approach, the researcher and subject explore the topic together, each contributing to the process and each working in different ways.

Thus, when using the interpretive approach, you must acknowledge that objectivity will be lost. Neutrality is still important, however. In fact, interpretist researchers often state "up front" the type of relationship they strive for with their subjects. Gregg (1994) in her study of pregnancy stated:

> I continued (quite consciously) to refrain from developing friendships with the women during the course of the study, even though this sometimes seemed artificial and contrived. I did not want them to feel they had to continue with the study or to feel that they were obliged to reveal things to me out of loyalty or friendship. . . . When I ran into someone I had interviewed, we would say hello, I would ask her how she was, and we would go on. These encounters were awkward for me. (p. 55)

Some of the problems undermining the neutrality of interviews can be overcome by training the interviewers. They can be given an explicit protocol or format that they are required to follow. As a generalist social worker, you may be required to conduct interviews of this type. Also, audio recordings allow the interviews to be reviewed. Recordings can sometimes inhibit the interviewees, however, resulting in a distortion of their responses.

The advantage of interviews is that they allow ambiguous questions to be clarified. This opportunity does not exist when questionnaires are administered, particularly by mail. Then respondents interpret the question in their own way, which may be very different from the intention of the researchers when they developed the questions.

Interviewing also has a positive effect on the **response rate,** the proportion of people who respond to the questions in either a questionnaire or interview. We have all been asked to participate in research—on the telephone, on the street, or through the mail. Sometimes we agree, and sometimes we refuse to participate. For researchers, a problem arises when many people refuse to participate, because these people might turn out to be very different from those who do. For example, if you send out 100 questionnaires asking about people's experiences of childhood sexual abuse, but only 25 people respond—all of whom state they were not abused as children—you have no way of knowing whether the nonrespondents were all abused and were reluctant to disclose this on their questionnaire, or were not abused and decided not to respond, or were distributed between abused and not abused. Because you do not know, you have to be cautious and assume that the results may well be biased. Interviews, however, generally obtain a high response rate. This is particularly true for face-to-face interviews, less so for telephone interviews.

Nevertheless, the high response rate of even face-to-face interviews is not always assured. The response rate does not just depend on the method of data collection; other factors include the characteristics of the subjects, the purpose and nature of the research question or project, and the characteristics and training of those applying the data collection instruments.

One form of interviewing involves focus groups. These were described in Chapter 3 as a means of helping to develop the research question and in Chapter 8 as a sampling method; they can also be used as a way of collecting data.

Applicability

Interviewing may be preferred to other techniques in the following circumstances:

- You are interested in a high response rate.

- You want to gather in-depth information. Interviewing is one of the main methods for collecting qualitative data and is a key data collection method in many interpretive studies, where the focus is on collecting information that discloses the richness of the subject's experience.

- Anonymity is not of primary importance. If your research involves a sensitive issue—such as the incidence of spousal abuse in a community—and the community is relatively small, anonymity may be important, and interviewing would not be an appropriate data collection method. People are less reluctant to share such sensitive information with strangers.

- Time and money are of no great object. Interviews are time-consuming, particularly if you are interested in getting responses from a large geographic area. In addition, interviewers often need to be trained. Consequently, this data collection method is expensive. If the budget is low and the sample large, interviewing would not be the data collection method of choice.

- The respondent is not comfortable with writing or is illiterate.

Questionnaires

In general, questionnaires have many advantages that interviews do not have; at the same time, they lack the strengths of interviews. There are several types of questionnaires.

Mailed Questionnaires

Mailing questionnaires is a popular method of distributing questionnaires. Agencies often use this method to survey their clients as part of a program evaluation or needs assessment.

A Mailed Questionnaire

Fogel and Ellison (1998) mailed surveys to a random sample of 230 directors of field education at accredited social work programs to determine the prevalence of sexual harassment for B.S.W. students in their field settings. Reminder postcards were also sent to those who did not respond within the previously requested three weeks. Eighty-eight surveys were returned, and responses indicated that sexual harassment in B.S.W. field settings is relatively common.

Face-to-Face Questionnaires

Face-to-face questionnaires may be administered much as structured interviews are. Structured interviews can be thought of as verbally administered questionnaires.

Group Questionnaires

These questionnaires are administered to groups. For example, if you are interested in getting feedback on a foster parent training session, you might administer questionnaires to the entire group at one time.

Bilingual Questionnaires

In many communities and with certain populations, bilingual questionnaires are essential.

A Face-to-Face Questionnaire

Hines and Graves (1998) examined the behaviors related to AIDS protection and contraception among African-American, Hispanic, and white women. Trained interviewers collected the data through face-to-face interviews that took place in the respondents' homes. The respondents had the option of having the interview conducted in Spanish and were asked questions on AIDS-related behaviors and attitudes. The results indicated that during their most recent sexual encounter, a significant number of all the women and their partners did not use any form of protection.

A Group Questionnaire

Greene, Causby, and Miller (1999) studied fusion in lesbian relationships. They collected data from lesbians who attended a March on Washington for Lesbians and Gays. Surveys were distributed the morning of the march, and the researchers waited for the participants to complete them. A comparison group of heterosexual women from an introductory communication class completed the surveys outside of class in lieu of a short written assignment. The study showed no differences between lesbian and heterosexual women's levels of fusion, and it revealed that fusion was strongly related to satisfaction and dependence.

A Bilingual Questionnaire

Marx (1999) examined motivational characteristics associated with volunteering in the health and human services field. A face-to-face questionnaire was administered in English and, when necessary, in Spanish. The sample was derived from a representative national sample of 2,719 adult Americans. Marx found that volunteers in health and human services, as compared to other fields, volunteered to "gain a new perspective on things" and were more likely to be motivated by altruistic reasons. The author advises managers in social work to educate their volunteers about the broader significance of their assignments.

Neutrality

Questionnaires are relatively neutral. Interviewer bias is absent, and the responses are clear and usually unambiguous. The neutrality of the responses, however, depends a great deal on the care with which the questionnaire has been constructed. Ambiguities can be minimized by stating questions as clearly and simply as possible. For example, avoid questions containing double negatives, such as "Do you disapprove with the refusal to build a day care center in your neighborhood?" Also avoid double-barreled questions or two questions in one, such as "How many children under the age of 12 do you have, and do you have problems with child care?"

In addition, avoid leading and biased questions that indicate to the respondent the way in which you want the question answered. For example, "There is a great deal of community support for the new youth center; are you in favor of it?" Also, ask only questions respondents are capable of answering, so that they have some knowledge of the issue being researched. Try not to ask questions about future intentions, instead focus on the present. Finally, in an effort to maintain maximum neutrality, avoid response sets—in other words, don't phrase a series of questions in such a way that the answers will probably all be the same (for example, all yes's or all no's), since people tend to become set in a certain way of responding.

Just as interviews generally have high response rates, questionnaires—particularly those that are mailed—have low response rates. You can take some precautions to help improve the response rate, though. Such precautions include taking care with the questionnaire's length, the structure of the questions, the content of the questions, the format of the questionnaire, the cover letter, and follow-up.

Length.   Make the questionnaire as short as possible and eliminate unnecessary questions. When constructing a questionnaire, for each question ask yourself, "How is this question relevant to my research question?" If you cannot come up with a good answer, drop the question.

Structure of the questions.   Questions can be structured in two ways: closed-ended and open-ended. A **closed-ended question** gives the respondent a limited number of categories to use as answers. For example:

Name those who help you with child care:

_____ parents

_____ older children

_____ other relatives

_____ day care center

_____ family day care

_____ unrelated babysitter

_____ other

These are easy for the researcher to understand once the questionnaire is returned, but it is important to ensure that all possible categories are included for the respondent. Closed-ended questions result in quantitative data.

An **open-ended question** leaves it up to the respondent to create a response. No alternatives are given. For example:

What kinds of improvements would you suggest the day care center make in this next year? _____

Open-ended questions can be intimidating to respondents and they may be put off by them, but this type of question ensures that respondents can answer in ways that accurately reflect their views—that is, they are not forced to respond using the researcher's categories. Open-ended questions are particularly useful when you do not know a great deal about the subject that you are investigating. They also provide a way of collecting qualitative data.

The content of the questions.   One strategy for increasing the response rate is to limit sensitive questions, or if they have to be included, to embed them within the questionnaire. The same holds true for many demographic questions such as gender and educational level. Instead of starting the questionnaire with these questions, place them at the end. Most respondents are not interested in these questions and can be discouraged if they are the first questions.

Format of the questionnaire.   The response rate can also be enhanced by the overall packaging of the questionnaire. Make sure it is free of typographical and spelling errors. Ensure that the layout is clear and uncluttered.

New Mexico State University
School of Social Work
3SW, PO Box 30001
Las Cruces, NM 88003-8001

I would like to ask you to take about 10 minutes to complete this questionnaire. This is part of a study on women and employment. Your answers will help in the planning of services and programs to assist working women like yourself.

Please do not write your name on the questionnaire.

This questionnaire will be picked up tomorrow, or you can mail it to the above address.

If you have any questions about the study, please ask the person who is distributing the questionnaire, or call me at 555-2143.

Also, if you are interested in the results of this study or would be willing to be interviewed, complete and mail the attached postcard to me.

Christine Marlow, Ph.D.
Professor of Social Work

Figure 9.2   ***Example of a cover letter***

Cover letter.   If you are mailing the questionnaire, include a **cover letter** that very briefly describes the purpose of the study and encourages the person to respond. It also should include how confidentiality will be maintained (confidentiality is discussed later in this chapter). You may want to include a small incentive, such as a quarter, coupons, or a pen. Of course, the person should never be coerced to respond. Also, emphasize in the cover letter that responses will be kept confidential. An example of a cover letter is shown in Figure 9.2.

Follow-ups.   Second mailings can enhance the response ratio of mailed questionnaires by about 10%, but of course they add to the cost of the project.

A checklist for constructing a questionnaire or an interview schedule is given in Table 9.1.

Even with a carefully designed and administered questionnaire, response rates can still suffer. As we discussed in relation to interviews, other facts can influence the response rate besides the structure of the instrument or the way it is administered. These factors include the topics and variables included in the research itself.

Applicability

Questionnaires can be used in preference to other data collection techniques when

- a high response rate is not a top priority
- anonymity is important
- budgets are limited, although extensive mailings of questionnaires can also be expensive
- the respondents are literate

Observation Techniques

Not all phenomena can be measured by interviews or questionnaires. Examples of these types of phenomena include illegal behaviors or children's behavior. If we are interested in a child's behavior in the classroom, interviewing or administering a questionnaire to the child would probably not elicit objective responses. As a social work student, you probably realize that observation is an integral part

Observation

Soloman (1994) used observation as one of several data collection methods in her study of welfare workers' responses to homeless welfare applicants. She observed 25 interviews between welfare recipients and their caseworkers. She spent 100 hours at the welfare office watching the exchanges. She also noted her impressions of the workplace physical facilities, two staff meetings, and two in-service training sessions.

Table 9.1   *Checklist for constructing questionnaire and interview questions*

_____ The questions are short.

_____ There are no double-barreled questions.

_____ The questions are clear and focused.

_____ There are no sensitive questions.

_____ There are no leading questions.

_____ The respondents are capable of answering the questions.

_____ The questions are focused on the present.

_____ There are no questions containing double negatives.

_____ The response categories are balanced.

_____ The questions are in a language that can be understood by the respondent.

_____ Consent has been given to answer the questions.

_____ Anonymity and confidentiality have been assured.

If mailed:

_____ A cover letter is attached.

_____ The questionnaire is clearly formatted.

_____ The questionnaire is short.

_____ There are mostly closed-ended questions.

_____ There is a return date.

_____ A stamped, addressed envelope is included.

of social work practice, and you have already learned to be a good observer. Observation can be structured or unstructured.

Structured Observation

When behaviors are known and categorized prior to the observation, and the intention is to collect quantitative data, **structured observation** is the method of choice. In this method, behaviors are categorized prior to the observation according to their characteristics, including their frequency, direction, and magnitude. These categories can then be quantified.

Take the example of trying to measure a child's inattention in the classroom. First, inattention needs to be clearly defined, perhaps as talking with other children without the teacher's permission. Frequency would be the number of occasions, during a specified period of time (for example, one hour), that the child talked with other children without permission. Duration would be the length of time the child talked. Magnitude would be how loudly the child talked within a specified period of time. Clearly, selection of the method of observation depends on what behavior is being measured, how the behavior is defined, and how often it occurs.

Unstructured Observation

When little is known about the behaviors being observed, or when an interpretive approach is adopted and the goal is to focus primarily on collecting qualitative data, **unstructured observation** is used. This method is used extensively in anthropology for studying unfamiliar cultures.

The observer interacts to varying degrees with those being observed. When the observer fully submerges him- or herself to become one of the observed group, this is known as **participant observation.** A classic example of participant observation in social work is the observer's becoming a member of a gang in order to observe gang behavior.

Participant Observation

Sands (1995) studied the parenting experiences of low-income single women with serious mental disorders. Several methods of data collection were used; one of these was participant observation by the researcher and her assistant at the "social rehab" program. Each observer spent four to five hours a day on separate occasions for eleven days over a period of four months observing the children, teachers, and mothers. At times the observers assisted the teachers with the children.

Neutrality

Observation varies in its neutrality. The degree of neutrality depends a great deal on the type of observation, the level of training, and the control for reactivity.

Type of observation.   Generally, structured observation is more neutral than unstructured observation, because in structured observation, the behaviors are defined beforehand. With unstructured observation, behaviors are not so clearly defined. In addition, in unstructured observation, the observer's involvement in the behavior can further bias the observation.

The level of training.   The more training the observers receive regarding the procedures to be followed for the observation, the greater the neutrality. Often, particularly in structured observation, the categories are not immediately apparent, no matter how much care was taken in their development. Observers may need to be instructed in what is meant by, for example, asking for the participant's opinion.

Control for reactivity.   **Reactivity,** or the reactive effect, is the problem of subjects changing their behavior in some way as a result of the observer's observing them. (This effect was discussed earlier in regard to interviewing.) Reactivity can be partly controlled by using one or more of the following four strategies:

videotapes, one-way mirrors, time with observer, and participant observation. A videotape recorder can be used to record behavior, but this may further inhibit the subject.

Second, sometimes one-way mirrors can be used, although we must be sure to obtain consent from those being observed. A third method for controlling reactivity is for the observer to spend some time with the subject so that the subject can become more comfortable with the observation. For example, if you want to observe classroom behavior, sit in the classroom for some time before you actually make the observation. Finally, we can overcome some reactivity effects with participant observation.

One further comment regarding neutrality is that observation need not always be visual. Sometimes enough information can be gained by listening to audio recordings. Maybe you have already used this method of observation as a means of improving your practice. Remember that since you are then without the nonverbal part of the interaction, neutrality can decrease from possible misinterpretation of the communication.

Applicability

Observation can be used in preference to other data collection techniques when behaviors are difficult to measure using other techniques, and observers and funds are available for training.

Logs and Journals

Sometimes logs, journals, or diaries can be used to collect data. These could be considered forms of self-observation but really warrant a separate discussion from observation. Logs, journals, or diaries—like observation—can be structured or unstructured.

The client may record his or her own behavior, or the social worker may record the client's behavior. Social workers also use logs and journals to record their own behavior. In Figure 9.3, the social worker is assessing her feelings and reactions to a home visit by recording in a journal. This log is unstructured and can allow for a stream of consciousness type of data collection; often these types of data are very valuable in an interpretive study. Logs can also be used to collect

A Log

Burack-Weiss (1995) examined the memoirs and journals of people who have cared for severely ill and disabled parents, mates, and children. She concluded that the experiences have multiple meanings, many of them positive and life enhancing.

SOCIAL WORKER'S JOURNAL RECORD OF A HOME VISIT TO A CLIENT
Thursday, February 15

Tonight I visited Art A. again. The house looked dark when I pulled up, and I felt kind of uneasy. I went through all the safety precautions I had learned previously and then went to the door and knocked. My stomach felt jittery. Finally, after several minutes, I heard footsteps inside and Art opened the door. He looked kind of disheveled and I sensed that he was upset about something, but he asked me very politely to come in and sit down. The house was so dark! I asked him to turn on some lights, and I sat near the door, just in case. Something just didn't feel right. Then it hit me—his dog Spike hadn't barked when I knocked and that dog was his constant companion. I didn't want to ask him about Spike because I was sure it was bad. I felt a lump forming in my throat. What a great social worker I am! I'm supposed to be calm, cool, and collected! I guess if I didn't empathize though, I wouldn't have been there in the first place. Sure enough, Spike was dead—he'd been run over by a car.

CLIENT'S LOG OF DRINKING BEHAVIOR
Monday

10:00 I took my break at work and had a couple of sips of George's beer (he brings it in his lunch pail).

12:00 Drank 2 beers with lunch.

5:00   Stopped after work at Charlie's Grill and had 3 beers and 2 or 3 shots of whiskey, which my friends bought for me.

7:00   Jack Daniels before dinner (on the rocks).

8:00   3–4 beers watching the Broncos whip the Cowboys.

11:00 Went to buy cigs and stopped at Fred's bar, had a couple of beers.

1:00   Had a shot of whiskey before bed to help me get to sleep.

Figure 9.3   ***Examples of journal and log recordings***

quantitative data. Service logs are of this type, where the entries involve checking or noting numbers next to categories.

Neutrality

Neutrality of logs and journals can be fairly limited, particularly if they are not structured or guided in some way. Neutrality can be enhanced by the use of more structured journals and logs so that the client or worker responds to specific questions. It is also helpful to encourage the client to record behaviors as soon as they occur rather than to rely too much on retrospective information.

Applicability

Logs and journals can be used in preference to other data collection techniques when detailed personal experiences are required from subjects, and subjects are literate.

Scales

Most variables are not clear-cut and cannot be contained in one question or item; instead, they are composed of a number of different dimensions or factors. Level of functioning, marital satisfaction, and community attitudes are all of this complex type. Composite measures consisting of a number of items are called **scales.** Scales can be used in interviews and questionnaires—sometimes even in structured observation—and they are important when you need to collect quantitative data.

Standardized scales are a type of scale that is uniform and tested extensively. Usually, published scales are accompanied by information about what they are intended to measure and with what type of population.

Scales are composed of several questions or observations "that have a logical or empirical structure to them" (Ruben & Babbie, 1997, p. G8). The most common form for social science research is the **Likert scale.** The respondent is shown a series of statements and is then asked to respond using one of five response alternatives, for example, "strongly agree," "agree," "no opinion," "disagree," "strongly disagree," or some variant of these. An example of a standardized scale including Likert measures is given in Figure 9.4. This is the F-COPES scale (McCubbin & Thomson, 1991) used to measure family coping.

Sometimes you may need a scale to measure a specific variable—for example, child well-being or aggression. Whenever possible, as with other types of data collection methods, try to use existing scales; they can eliminate considerable work. There are some drawbacks to using existing scales, though: They may not be designed to measure the variables in your study. For example, a family coping scale would not be appropriate for measuring family cohesion. The other problem is the temptation to design research around a standardized instrument—for example, changing your study to look at family coping rather than family cohesion.

Three specific types of scaling are commonly used in social work research, particularly in practice evaluations: target problem scales, goal attainment scales, and rapid assessment instruments.

Target Problem Scales

Target problem scales are a means to track changes in a client's target behavior. This type of scale is particularly useful when actual outcomes are difficult to identify. The scale involves identifying a problem, applying an intervention, and then repeatedly rating the extent to which the target problem has changed. One

Purpose:

The Family-Crisis Oriented Personal Evaluation Scale is designed to record effective problem-solving attitudes and behavior which families develop to respond to problems or difficulties.

Directions:

First, read the list of response choices one at a time.

Second, decide how well each statement describes your attitudes and behavior in response to problems or difficulties. If the statement describes your response very well, then circle the number 5 indicating that you STRONGLY AGREE; if the statement does not describe your response at all, then circle the number 1 indicating that you STRONGLY DISAGREE; if the statement describes your response to some degree, then select a number 2, 3, or 4 to indicate how much you agree or disagree with the statement about your response.

WHEN WE FACE PROBLEMS OR DIFFICULTIES IN OUR FAMILY, WE RESPOND BY:	Strongly disagree	Moderately disagree	Neither agree nor disagree	Moderately agree	Strongly agree
1. Sharing our difficulties with relatives	1	2	3	4	5
2. Seeking encouragement and support from friends	1	2	3	4	5
3. Knowing we have the power to solve major problems	1	2	3	4	5
4. Seeking information and advice from persons in other families who have faced the same or similar problems	1	2	3	4	5
5. Seeking advice from relatives (grandparents, etc.)	1	2	3	4	5
6. Seeking assistance from community agencies and programs designed to help families in our situation	1	2	3	4	5
7. Knowing that we have the strength within our own family to solve our problems	1	2	3	4	5

(*continued on next page*)

Figure 9.4   ***Family-Crisis Oriented Personal Evaluation Scale (F-COPES)***

Source: From "F-COPES: Family-Crisis Oriented Personal Evaluation Scales," by H. McCubbin, D. Olson, & A. Larsen. In H. I. McCubbin, A. I. Thomson, & M. A. McCubbin (Eds.), *Family Assessment: Resiliency, Coping, and Adaptation: Inventories for Research and Practice.* Copyright © 1996 University of Wisconsin System. Reprinted with permission.

WHEN WE FACE PROBLEMS OR DIFFICULTIES IN OUR FAMILY, WE RESPOND BY:	Strongly disagree	Moderately disagree	Neither agree nor disagree	Moderately agree	Strongly agree
8. Receiving gifts and favors from neighbors (e.g., food, taking in mail, etc.)	1	2	3	4	5
9. Seeking information and advice from the family doctor	1	2	3	4	5
10. Asking neighbors for favors and assistance	1	2	3	4	5
11. Facing the problems "head-on" and trying to get solutions right away	1	2	3	4	5
12. Watching television	1	2	3	4	5
13. Showing that we are strong	1	2	3	4	5
14. Attending church services	1	2	3	4	5
15. Accepting stressful events as a fact of life	1	2	3	4	5
16. Sharing concerns with close friends	1	2	3	4	5
17. Knowing luck plays a big part in how well we are able to solve family problems	1	2	3	4	5
18. Exercising with friends to stay fit and reduce tension	1	2	3	4	5
19. Accepting that difficulties occur unexpectedly	1	2	3	4	5
20. Doing things with relatives (get-togethers, dinners, etc.)	1	2	3	4	5
21. Seeking professional counseling and help for family difficulties	1	2	3	4	5
22. Believing we can handle our own problems	1	2	3	4	5
23. Participating in church activities	1	2	3	4	5

(continued on next page)

Figure 9.4   Continued

WHEN WE FACE PROBLEMS OR DIFFICULTIES IN OUR FAMILY, WE RESPOND BY:	Strongly disagree	Moderately disagree	Neither agree nor disagree	Moderately agree	Strongly agree
24. Defining the family problem in a more positive way so that we do not become too discouraged	1	2	3	4	5
25. Asking relatives how they feel about problems we face	1	2	3	4	5
26. Feeling that no matter what we do to prepare, we will have difficulty handling problems	1	2	3	4	5
27. Seeking advice from a minister	1	2	3	4	5
28. Believing if we wait long enough, the problem will go away	1	2	3	4	5
29. Sharing problems with neighbors	1	2	3	4	5
30. Having faith in God	1	2	3	4	5

Figure 9.4   Continued

such target problem scale is shown in Figure 9.5. This example includes a global improvement scale that summarizes the amount of change that actually took place in the target problem.

Goal Attainment Scales

Goal attainment scales (GAS) reflect the achievement of outcomes and are used both to set client goals and to assess whether goals have been met. Goal attainment scaling involves four steps:

1. identifying the problem
2. specifying the areas where change is desired
3. making specific predictions for a series of outcome levels for each area
4. by a set date, scoring the outcomes as they are achieved (five possible outcomes are designated, from least to most favorable).

Goal attainment scales can be used for a wide variety of problem situations. Figure 9.6 shows a modification of a goal attainment scale used by the New Mexico Human Services Department. In identifying the problem, positive

TARGET PROBLEM (rated by client)	TARGET PROBLEM RATING					GLOBAL IMPROVEMENT
	Degree of Severity				Degree of Change	
	Session #					
	1	2	3	4	Month	
Difficulty in talking about feelings	ES	ES	S	S	S	3
Getting to work on time	ES	S	S	NVS	NP	5
Fear of leaving house in daytime	ES	S	S	NVS	NP	5
			TOTAL		13 / 3 = 4.3	
						Somewhat to a lot better

Severity Scale			Improvement Scale		
NP	=	No problem	1	=	Worse
NVS	=	Not very severe	2	=	No change
S	=	Severe	3	=	A little better
VS	=	Very severe	4	=	Somewhat better
ES	=	Extremely severe	5	=	A lot better

The global improvement rating is obtained by totaling the change scores and dividing by the number of target problems. This yields a number that reflects the client's overall improvement on all problems.

Figure 9.5   ***Example of a target problem and global improvement scale for one client***

terms should be used, as in this example. Instead of stating that the client lacks parenting skills, it is stated that she would like to learn new methods or techniques for parenting. The 0 level is the expected outcome for this goal, with two less successful (−2, −1) and two more successful (+1, +2) possible outcomes, with their respective criteria for attainment. At the initial time of scoring, this client was scored at a −2, or the most unfavorable outcome, but at a later date, the score was +2, indicating the client had achieved the best anticipated successful outcome for this goal. The GAS is an excellent way for both social worker and client to monitor progress and to determine the desirability of specific outcomes.

Rapid Assessment Instruments

A **rapid assessment instrument (RAI)** is a standardized series of structured questions or statements administered to the client to collect data in practice evaluations. Rapid assessment instruments are short, easy to administer, and

Family Name: Vin Social Worker Name: Remington/Drake

Goal Number: 1 Goal: To increase knowledge of parenting skills to reduce the family's need for the services of the Human Services Department.

Statement of problem: The client is requesting new methods or techniques to help parent her children.

Date Goal Scaled: During first week Date when scored: Weekly

Rating of Client when goal was first scaled: −2

Rating of Client when goal was last scored: +2

Whose goal?: Client and Family Preservation Services team

Outcome Categories	Client's Attainment Criteria
Most unfavorable outcome thought likely* (−2)	The client totally disregards her parenting skills or tools when interacting with her children.
Less than expected success (−1)	The client listens to and understands new parenting skills and techniques presented but does not follow through with applying them.
Expected level of success (0)	The client learns a new parenting skill or technique suggested by Family Preservation Services.
More than expected success (+1)	The client applies one new skill or technique suggested by Family Preservation Services.
Best anticipated success* (+2)	The client applies two new skills or techniques suggested by Family Preservation Services.

*Unlikely, but still plausible.

Figure 9.6 **Example of a goal attainment scale**

Source: From "Goals and Attainment Scaling in the Context of Rural Child Welfare," by W. C. Horner and J. L. Pippard. Copyright © 1982 Child Welfare League of America. Used with permission. This article was originally published in *Child Welfare, 61* (7), 1982, p. 419.

easy to complete. The Multi-Problem Screening Inventory (MPSI) (Hudson, 1990) is an example. The MPSI can be used in conjunction with practice to collect data on several variables, including generalized contentment and marital satisfaction. These scales are computerized.

Neutrality

Scales are designed to be as neutral as possible, particularly those that are standardized.

Applicability

Scales are useful in studies where the emphasis is on collecting quantitative data. They are also useful for measuring multifaceted concepts. Scales are helpful when there is not a great deal of time available for data collection.

Secondary Data

Secondary data are data collected for purposes other than the present research. They may be data collected for another research project or data that were not collected with research in mind at all. With computers, secondary data have become more accessible even to the most humble of researchers. We use sec-

Secondary Data Use

Caputo (1995) studied the relationship between gender and race with regard to economic conditions and employment opportunities between 1969 and 1991. The study used data contained in the *Economic Report of the President* and the U.S. Department of Commerce's *Money Income of Household, Families and Persons in the United States* to examine annual mean differences in black and white, male and female employment opportunity and median income in the 1970s and 1980s.

Using Case Records as Data

Lewis, Giovannoni, and Leake (1997) assessed placement outcomes two years after prenatally drug-exposed children had been placed in foster care. The authors compared the data with the two-year outcomes of nonprenatally drug-exposed children who had also been placed out of the home. Retired social workers of the Department of Children and Families reviewed the agency records on each infant enrolled in the study. Findings indicated that two-thirds of the drug-exposed children and more than half of the nondrug-exposed children were still in care at two years.

ondary data all the time in generalist practice—by consulting case records written by others and by referring to agency statistics when writing up reports. In fact, case records provide an important secondary data source for agency-based social worker research. Other sources of secondary data include U.S. census data and the numerous reports generated by state and federal government.

Agencies—both private and public—are creating data banks in increasing numbers and storing information about their operations, including the number of clients served, types of target problems, outcomes, staffing patterns, and budgets. Additionally, information can be obtained on crime rates, child abuse and neglect rates, and so forth.

These types of data are particularly useful when conducting a needs assessment. Two strategies can be adopted using secondary data in a needs assessment: rates under treatment and social indicators. The **rates under treatment** approach uses existing data from agencies to determine the needs of a community. The problem with this approach is that use of existing services may not, in fact, reflect unmet needs.

Rates Under Treatment

Benbenishty and Oyserman (1995) examined the present state of children in foster care in Israel in order to design future programs and develop policy. Data for the study consisted of existing information generated from the clinical information system set up for Israel's foster care service in 1988–1989. Under the system, each worker is expected to gather information about each of the children in his or her care on a series of standardized forms. The study was based on workers' annual reports on each child's situation and on plans for that child's immediate and long-term future.

The **social indicators** approach selects demographic data from existing public records to predict a community's needs. Existing statistics relating to people's spatial arrangement and facilities in a community, housing patterns,

Social Indicators

Ozawa (1995) investigated the economic status of vulnerable older women. She used a number of existing data sources that provided various economic indicators for older women. Data included surveys carried out by the Social Security Administration.

crime patterns, and so on, can help us determine where, for example, to place a community center.

It is also possible to use **vignettes** in collecting data. These are hypothetical situations either drawn from a source or developed by the researcher (in which case the vignettes are not strictly secondary data) for the purpose of eliciting certain responses from the participants in the study.

Using Vignettes to Collect Data

Savaya (1998) utilized vignettes to collect data examining the effects of economic need and self-esteem on the attitudes and use of professional services by Arab women. The vignettes simulated potential help-seeking situations and at the end of each one, a hypothetical professional family counseling service was presented. Each woman in the study was asked to respond to one vignette. Findings indicated that self-esteem was associated with the women's help-seeking behavior, but not their attitudes, and only when economic need was not taken into account. When economic need was accounted for, the effect on self-esteem disappeared. These findings suggest that more attention needs to be focused on economic need and less on a "threat to self-esteem" model to explain underutilization of professional services.

Indirect Sources

Indirect sources refer to information that can be used for research but that was initially collected for some other purpose. Indirect sources include case records, newspapers, and other media reports. For example, we may be interested in studying an agency's attitudes toward the developmentally disabled, so we consult case records on this topic. The most common way of dealing with indirect sources is to subject it to content analysis. **Content analysis** is a method of coding communication to a systematic quantifiable form. It will be discussed further in Chapters 10 and 11.

Neutrality

When using secondary data, we need to be aware that sometimes these data have limited neutrality. Indirect sources can often be particularly biased because they were not initially collected for research purposes. For example, there may be gaps in a record that we are using. In addition, because records were made for a purpose other than ours, information relating to our research question may be missing. For example, if we were gathering information on agency attitudes toward the developmentally disabled, that information may be missing from case records.

Direct sources are more neutral, but the researcher needs to verify the exact form of the questions that were initially asked. The form of questions asked later by the secondary researcher may be different; we need to know what this difference is. For example, you may be interested in the number of juveniles who had a previous record of substance abuse seen by the local juvenile probation office. You may be interested primarily in alcohol use, whereas the data collected did not distinguish between alcohol and other types of substance abuse. When using secondary data, you cannot assume that the first researcher's questions are similar to your own.

Colby (1982) discussed some of these problems in her article on secondary analysis. She also pointed out that secondary analysis is especially valuable for the study of women because theories about women, and women themselves, have undergone substantial change. Consequently, it is important to reanalyze data to determine the extent to which different results are due to a different interpretation or in fact due to changes that have occurred over time.

Applicability

Secondary data can be used when the data are available (this is not always the case). Secondary data also can be applied when the definition of the secondary data variables and the form of the questions are the same (or similar) to yours; if not, you must at least be aware of the differences. Secondary data can be helpful when a needs assessment is required, and the budget is limited. Secondary data can yield much information when you are interested in conducting a historical study—for example, the history of an agency or of the way a particular problem has been addressed in the past.

WHO COLLECTS THE DATA

As with the other decisions to be made concerning data collection, the decision about who should collect the data depends greatly on the type of research question asked. We tend to think of the researcher as the only person who should collect the data, as when interviewing or administering a questionnaire.

Apart from the researcher, the client or subject can also collect the data. Journals or diaries can be used in this way. Questionnaires can be self-administered; mailed questionnaires are the obvious example. Clients can also observe and record their own behavior using scales or checklists. Engaging the client in the data collection process is particularly valuable in conducting single-system studies, and as we saw in Chapter 7, can provide opportunities for feedback on changes in the client's behavior.

Earlier reactivity effects were discussed. This reactivity effect can also be a problem when the client collects data on his or her own behavior or uses **self-monitoring.** This reactivity can be quite strong, resulting in self-monitoring being used as an intervention device. Kopp (1988) presented an interesting review of the literature on how self-monitoring has been used both as a research and as a practice tool in social work.

COMBINING DATA COLLECTION METHODS

Methods and instruments can and should be used in conjunction with one another. As mentioned earlier in the chapter, both qualitative and quantitative data can be collected. In addition, a number of different methods can be used in the same study (see Table 9.2).

Using Multiple Measures

Dore and Doris (1997) studied a placement prevention program designed to help substance-abusing mothers who had been reported for child maltreatment get treatment for their addiction. The researchers used several measures in their study: the Beck Depression Inventory, the Adult-Adolescent Parenting Inventory, the Behavior Checklist for Infants and Children, and the Denver Developmental Screening Test. Results indicated that almost half of the participants were able to complete the program and achieve sobriety. Those who had used the program's child care were three times more likely to complete treatment.

Combining measures can enrich your study and help ensure that you are tapping a maximum number of dimensions of the phenomenon under study. Using a number of data collection methods is sometimes called **triangulation.** Other forms of triangulation include using a number of different theories, researchers, or research methods—for example, a mix of interpretive and positivist approaches. Triangulation, particularly in interpretive studies, can help enhance the validity of findings.

DETERMINING RELIABILITY AND VALIDITY

Before a measuring instrument is used in the research process, it is important to assess its reliability and validity. This is important regardless of whether an interpretive or positivistic approach is used, although the way in which they are assessed does vary according to the approach and according to whether the data are qualitative or quantitative. Quantitative data collection instruments—particularly scales and highly standard interview, questionnaire, and observation schedules—lend themselves most easily to the tests for reliability and validity presented here. Standardized scales are always accompanied by the results of validity and reliability tests. Open-ended, qualitative instruments, however, are

Table 9.2   **Characteristics of data collection methods**

	Unstructured interviews	Mailed question-naire	Participant observation	Standardized observation	Logs	Face-to-face administered standardized scales
High response rate	yes	no	n/a	yes	maybe	yes
Anonymity assured	no	yes	no	no	no	no
Low reactivity effects	no	yes	maybe	maybe	yes	yes
Illiterate subjects	yes	no	yes	yes	no	no
Semilegal or illegal behavior	no	maybe	maybe	no	no	no
Large sample or limited funds	no	yes	no	no	no	yes
In-depth, "thick description"	yes	no	yes	no	yes	no

more difficult to assess for reliability and validity. The principles presented here, if not the specific tests themselves, can still be used as guidelines with open-ended instruments to improve their validity and reliability.

Reliability

Reliability indicates the extent to which a measure reveals actual differences in the phenomenon measured, rather than differences inherent in the measuring instrument itself. Reliability refers to the consistency of a measure. To illustrate, a wooden ruler is a reliable measure for a table. If the ruler were made of elastic, however, it would not provide a reliable measure, because repeated measures of the same table would differ due to the ruler's expanding and contracting. If a client is chronically depressed and you measure the degree of depression at two points in time, the instrument is reliable if you get close to the same score each time, provided the level of depression has not in fact changed. Clearly you need to establish the instrument's reliability before you can determine true changes in the phenomena under study.

As generalist social workers, you need to assess the extent to which the data collection instrument is reliable. There are two major ways to assess the instrument's reliability: assessing sources of error and assessing the degree to which the instrument's reliability has actually been tested. Each of these will be discussed in turn.

Sources of Error

When assessing the reliability of an instrument, you need to determine whether there is evidence of certain sources of error. The following are four major types of error: unclear definition of variables, use of retrospective information, variations in the conditions for collecting the data, and structure of the instrument.

Unclear Definitions of Variables

As we saw in Chapter 4, variables can be difficult to define because many social work terms tend to be vague. If a variable is not clearly operationalized and defined, its measurement lacks reliability: The possible outcome can be interpreted differently by different social workers. The wording of questions in questionnaires often creates problems with unclear definitions of variables. A question might be phrased in such a way that two individuals interpret it differently and provide two different answers, even though the actual behavior they are reporting is the same. For example, people might be asked, "Do you often use public transportation in the city?" In responding, people may interpret *often* in different ways. Interpretive studies where the variables are not necessarily clearly defined and operationalized clearly pose a particular challenge. Extensive use of interviews in these types of studies overcomes some of the problems, because the unstructured data collection method allows exploration of the concepts to take place. If the variable described by the respondent is unclear, the respondent can be asked to elaborate and define. The definition comes from the subjects, rather than from the researcher.

Use of Retrospective Information

Retrospective information is gathered through subject recall, either by a questionnaire or an interview. These data are almost inevitably distorted. Moreover, sometimes subject recall is hampered because of the nature of the topic under study—as you might expect if you were investigating an adult's experience of childhood sexual abuse, for example. Case records are one form of retrospective data collection, and they are consequently subject to considerable error. Case records usually reflect the idiosyncratic recording practices of the individual social worker. The worker will select out certain aspects of the case for recording, resulting in impaired reliability.

Variations in Conditions for Collecting the Data

When interviews are used to collect data, interview conditions can also affect reliability. The subject may respond differently depending on whether the interviewer is male or female. (This is the reactive effect we discussed earlier.) Similar problems may arise due to the ethnicity and age of the interviewer. Where the interview is conducted may also cause disparities in responses. Even with questionnaires (for example, mailed questionnaires), lack of control over the conditions under which they are administered can result in low reliability.

Structure of the Instrument

Certain aspects of the data collection method itself may enhance or decrease reliability. An open-ended questionnaire that requires that responses be categorized and coded can present reliability problems.

Testing Reliability

In addition to identifying the sources of error in an instrument, we can also assess the extent to which the instrument's reliability has been tested. As generalist social workers, you will need to be able to understand what reliability tests, if any, others have conducted. In addition, you may be able to use these tests on some of the instruments you develop.

Reliability is determined by obtaining two or more measures of the same thing and seeing how closely they agree. Four methods are used to establish the reliability of an instrument: test-retest, alternate form, split half, and observer reliability.

Test-Retest

Test-retest involves repeatedly administering the instrument to the same set of people on separate occasions. These people should not be subjects in the actual study. The results of the repeated administrations are then compared. If the results are similar, reliability of the instrument is high. A problem associated with this method of testing reliability is that the first testing has influenced the second. For example, during the second testing the individuals may be less anxious, less motivated, or less interested, or they may simply remember their answers from the first test and repeat them. In addition, they may have learned from the first testing, particularly with attitude questions. To avoid these problems, measuring instruments that are strongly affected by memory or repetition should not be tested for reliability using this method.

Alternate Form

With **alternate form** tests, different but equivalent forms of the same test are administered to the same group of individuals—usually close in time—and then compared. The major problem with this approach is in the development of the equivalent tests, which can be time consuming. In addition, this approach can still involve some of the problems associated with the test-retest method.

Split Half

With the **split half method,** items on the instrument are divided into comparable halves. For example, a scale could be divided so the first half should have the same score as the second half. This testing method looks at the internal consistency of the measure. The test is administered and the two halves compared. If the score is the same, the instrument is probably reliable. A major problem with this approach is ensuring that the two halves are equivalent. Equivalency is problematic with instruments other than scales.

Observer Reliability

Observer reliability involves comparing administrations of an instrument done by different observers or interviewers. To use this method effectively, the observers need to be thoroughly trained; at least two people will code the content of the responses according to certain criteria.

Each of these methods of testing for reliability involves comparing two or more results. Usually, this comparison uses some kind of **correlation coefficient.** This is a statistic that measures the extent to which the comparisons are similar or not similar—that is, the extent to which they are related or correlated. The concept of correlation will be discussed in more detail in Chapters 12 and 13. For our purposes now in assessing reliability, the correlation coefficient can range from 0.0 to 1.0, the latter number reflecting a perfect correlation, or the highest level of reliability possible. Generally, a coefficient of .80 suggests the instrument is reasonably reliable. Table 9.3 summarizes the criteria that can be used to assess an instrument's reliability.

Table 9.3   **Criteria for assessing the reliability of measuring instruments**

1	Is the variable clearly defined?
2	Is retrospective information avoided?
3	Are there controlled conditions under which the data are collected?
4	Is the question format closed?
5	Are reliability tests used? Is so, is the correlation coefficient greater than 0.5?

If the answer is yes to most of these questions, then the instrument is probably reliable.

Instruments with High Reliability

The scales included in the Multi-Problem Screening Inventory developed by Hudson (1990) all have a test-retest and split half reliability correlation coefficients of at least .90. The scales were developed for a variety of behaviors, including child problems, guilt, work problems, and alcohol abuse.

Reporting Reliability

Teare, Peterson, Authier, Schroeder, and Daly (1998) investigated maternal family satisfaction following youths' return home from an emergency-crisis shelter. The study utilized several instruments and reported their reliability. The Inventory of Parent and Peer Attachment, for example, had a three-week test-retest reliability coefficient of .93 for the parent attachment measure. Results of the study indicated that higher ratings of family satisfaction were related to greater maternal problem solving skills and less conflict within the family.

Validity

The **validity of a measuring instrument** reflects the extent to which you are measuring what you think you are measuring. This is a different idea than reliability. To take the example used previously, if a wooden ruler is used to measure the dimensions of a table, it is a reliable and valid instrument. If you use the ruler to measure ethnicity, however, the instrument maintains its reliability, but it is no longer valid. You would not be measuring ethnicity but some other variable (for example, height), which has no relationship to ethnicity as far as we know.

Validity is not as straightforward as reliability because there are different types of validity, and each one is tested in a different way. The three main types of validity are criterion validity, content validity, and construct validity. Each type of validity relates to different aspects of the overall validity of the instrument, and each addresses different dimensions of the problem of ensuring that what is being measured is what was intended to be measured. These types of validity will be discussed along with the ways in which each can be tested.

Validity testing can be quite complex, and sometimes entire articles in the social work literature are devoted to testing the validity of specific instruments. For example, Guttmann and Brenna (1990) assessed the validity of the Personal Experience Inventory (PEI), an instrument for assessing the level and nature of substance abuse in adolescents. Gupta (1999) examined the reliability and validity of the Caregiver Burden Scale. As generalist social workers, you will need to understand what type of validity testing has been carried out and in some cases test instruments you have developed.

Criterion Validity

Criterion validity describes the extent to which a correlation exists between the measuring instrument and another standard. To validate an instrument developed to assess a program that helps pregnant teenagers succeed in high school, a criterion such as SAT scores might be used as a comparison. Similarities in scores would indicate that criterion validity had been established.

Content validity

Content validity is concerned with the representativeness of the content of the instrument. The content included in the instrument needs to be relevant to the concept we are trying to measure. For example, the content validity of an instrument developed to measure knowledge of parenting skills could be obtained by consulting with various experts on parenting skills—perhaps social workers who run parenting groups and a professor at the department of social work. They could then point out areas in which the instrument may be deficient. Clearly, content validity is partly a matter of judgment and is dependent upon the knowledge of the experts who are available to you.

Construct validity

Construct validity describes the extent to which an instrument measures a theoretical construct. A measure may have criterion and content validity but still not measure what it is intended to measure. Construct validity is the most difficult to establish, because as we mentioned earlier, many research variables are difficult to define and theoretically vague. Constructs used in social work include aggression, sociability, and self-esteem, to name just a few. With construct validity, we are looking not only at the instrument but also at the theory underlying it. The instrument must reflect this theory.

For example, in testing the construct validity of an instrument to measure aggression in preschoolers, the associated theoretical expectations need to be examined by referring to the literature and research on the topic. One explanation that may be found is that the highly aggressive children will not be achieving well in the classroom. If the instrument does not reflect this dimension of the topic, the instrument probably does not have construct validity. IQ tests provide an example of a measure with low construct validity. IQ tests were created to measure intelligence. Since their development, however, it has become apparent that they measure only one dimension of intelligence—the potential to achieve in a white middle-class academic system. Other dimensions of intelligence remain untapped by IQ tests, resulting in their limited validity for measuring intelligence.

One way of more fully ensuring construct validity is to define the construct using small, concrete, observable behaviors (Duncan & Fiske, 1977). Such definition helps avoid some of the wishy-washiness associated with many constructs used in social work practice. For example, if both the verbal and nonverbal behaviors of preschoolers are recorded, and certain patterns of these behaviors become apparent in those children previously labeled aggressive, you can be more fully assured that your label does in fact have construct validity.

Once you are familiar with this information on validity and the ways it can be tested, you are then in a position as a generalist social worker to assess the validity of the measuring instruments you read about or that you propose to use. Table 9.4 presents a checklist that can be used to assess the validity of instruments.

Table 9.4   ***Criteria for assessing the validity of quantitative measuring instruments***

1   Was the instrument tested for criterion validity?
2   Was the instrument tested for content validity?
3   Was the instrument tested for construct validity?
4   Is the variable defined as clearly and concretely as possible?

If the answer is yes to most of these questions, then the instrument is probably valid (that is, if the findings from the tests support the validity of the instrument).

Feedback

Feedback is an important way of testing the validity of quantitative data collected from interpretive studies. In this type of research, the concepts under study may not be clearly defined at the outset. Moreover, the intent of the research may well be to define and elaborate on these concepts. However, data must be understandable and relevant to the participants in the research. The participants should be allowed to verify the data. This feedback can be carried out both formally (for example, through focus groups or community meetings) or informally (for example, through meetings and informal gatherings with the participants).

Note that often in the collection of qualitative data, responsibility for validating the data lies directly with the researcher rather than being assured through the use of prescribed methods, such as a criterion validity check. Therefore it is even more important for the researcher to act responsibly and ethically.

THE AGENCY AND DATA COLLECTION

As generalist social workers, you often do not have much of a choice when it comes to selecting a data collection method. You may be asked to help develop a questionnaire for a needs assessment, in which case the decision about the data collection has already been made.

Because of time and money constraints, some of the more complicated and time-consuming data collection techniques—such as lengthy questionnaire and scale construction, participant observation, and extensive interviews—cannot be considered by the generalist social worker engaged in research. Instead, consider using rapid assessment instruments, case records, and self-observation (by the client) as much as possible.

It should not be forgotten, however, that generalist social workers can be key players in the data collection process. After all, it is they who have access to critical data, both directly from the clients and indirectly from the agency records. Thus the challenge for generalist social workers becomes to explore the opportunities offered in the agencies for data collection and research by either undertaking research themselves or by encouraging their agencies to explore research possibilities.

ETHICAL ISSUES IN COLLECTING DATA

When collecting data for a research study, we need to be concerned about three ethical issues: potential harm to the subjects, anonymity and confidentiality, and justification of the research.

Harm to the Participants

Clearly, we need to avoid harming the participants in any way. The NASW Code of Ethics (1997) states:

- Social workers engaged in evaluation or research should carefully consider possible consequences and should follow guidelines developed for the protection of evaluation and research participants. Appropriate institutional review boards should be consulted.

- Social workers engaged in evaluation or research should protect participants from unwarranted physical or mental distress, harm, danger, or deprivation.

As simplistic as these mandates may seem, on closer examination these things are easier said than done. When asking questions in whatever form—whether interviewing or using a questionnaire—you are often requiring participants to examine and assess their own behavior. Questions relating to childhood abuse may be painful for the respondent. Other questions that are difficult to answer concern income and the ability to pay for a proposed service.

Consequently, assessing the extent of discomfort for the participant can be difficult. Some projects—for example, federally funded research and research conducted at universities—require the proposed research to be reviewed by **human subjects committees** or **institutional review boards.** During the review process, the researcher must answer specific questions regarding potential harm to participants. Even when an outside review is not required, we need to be sensitive to the impact of our data collection method on participants.

Anonymity and Confidentiality

Both anonymity and confidentiality help participants avoid harm. Again, the NASW Code of Ethics (1997) states:

- Social workers engaged in evaluation or research should ensure the anonymity or confidentiality of participants and of the data obtained from them. Social workers should inform participants of any limits of confidentiality and when any records containing research data will be destroyed.

Anonymity means that the researcher cannot identify a given response with a given respondent. It was mentioned previously that an interview can never be anonymous, and when identification numbers are put on questionnaires to facilitate follow-up and increase the response rate, anonymity is also jeopardized. Ensuring anonymity not only reassures the subjects but can also enhance the objectivity of the responses. For example, if you are asking questions about deviant behavior, the respondent is more likely to give a response that accurately reflects the behavior if anonymity can be assured.

Confidentiality means that the researcher knows the identity of the respondents and their associated responses but ensures not to disclose this information. Obviously, confidentiality becomes particularly critical when conducting interviews, for which anonymity is impossible to ensure. The principle of confidentiality should be explained to respondents either verbally or in a cover letter accompanying the questionnaires. Do not confuse confidentiality and anonymity; they are different and are both extremely important.

Justification of the Research

The NASW Code of Ethics (1997) states:

- Social workers should never design or conduct evaluation or research that does not use consent procedures, such as certain forms of naturalistic observation and archival research, unless rigorous and responsible review of the research has found it to be justified because of its prospective scientific, educational, or applied value and unless equally effective alternative procedures that do not involve waiver of consent are not feasible.

Informed consent was discussed in Chapter 6. Using data that is not collected directly from the participants (such as client records and other secondary data) does not exempt the researchers from another ethical responsibility: ensuring that the research is needed and justified.

HUMAN DIVERSITY ISSUES IN COLLECTING THE DATA

Awareness and knowledge of human diversity issues during the data collection stage of the research process is very important. Some of the central issues to which we need to pay attention are the selection of the data collection method for diverse populations; the relevance to diverse populations of the content of the data collection method; and the application of the data collection method to diverse populations.

Selection of Data Collection Methods for Diverse Populations

The extent to which data collection methods may or may not be applicable to certain groups within a population needs to be considered. Some groups may be uncomfortable with the notion of being administered a questionnaire or being

Methodological Issues in Conducting Research with Diverse Groups

Gibbs and Bankhead-Greene (1997) described the methodological issues involved in conducting research with inner-city African-American youth. The study investigated the impact of the verdict and the subsequent civil disturbances in the Rodney King police brutality case. A number of civic, religious, and professional leaders in an African-American community in Los Angeles were contacted for suggestions on how to process with the study. The researchers collected both qualitative and quantitative data using focus groups and face-to-face interviews with both community leaders and youth. The authors discussed throughout the article the importance of carefully considering the research methods used in this type of study.

interviewed; you need to be sensitive to the ways in which different cultural groups might regard different methods.

Gilligan's (1982) analysis of the development of men's and women's resolutions of moral conflicts concluded that women develop a mode of thinking that is "contextual and narrative" and their understanding is based on the individual in the context of their relationship with others. This way of thinking is contrasted with men's, which is seen as focusing on autonomy and separation from others. Some authors (such as Davis, 1986) have suggested that women's different ways of thinking require different approaches to research—particularly different data collection techniques. Male research methodology—the traditional approach—emphasizes the abstract and formal and lends itself to quantification and the use of the positivist approach, whereas the female approach, with its emphasis on connection, lends itself more easily to an interpretive approach and its associated qualitative data.

Relevance to Diverse Populations of the Content of the Data Collection Method

In addition to the appropriateness of a particular data collection instrument, taking account of human diversity requires considering the content of that instrument and its appropriateness to the group under study.

Certain words or phrases—whether in interview or questionnaire form, whether conducted under the auspices of a feminist or traditional research approach—may be interpreted by the respondent in a different way from that intended by the researcher. In many cases, this divergence of interpretations may be due simply to the researcher's lack of understanding or insensitivity to the cultural group that is being studied. For example, some groups may interpret questions about mothers as including mothers-in-law. Serious validity problems can result, since the researcher is thinking of *mother* in one sense, and the subject is defining *mother* very differently. Reliability problems also arise.

Another perhaps less obvious problem might occur when conducting, for example, a research project concerned with methods and problems of disciplining children. You would need to acknowledge the methods and problems experienced by gay and lesbian parents (unless we purposefully *intend* to exclude them) in addition to those of heterosexual parents, because some of the problems gay and lesbian parents encounter might be different. Consequently, you would need to include questions relevant to this group so as not to exclude problems such parents might be experiencing and thus jeopardize the validity of your findings.

Earlier, we discussed the usefulness of rapid assessment instruments and other instruments that have already been developed. Check to see whether the instruments you use have been used with diverse populations and whether their reliability and validity have been tested with these groups.

Many of these issues are an extension of the discussion in Chapter 3 about the need to include relevant variables in the study. You must not only account for all the relevant variables but also be aware of human diversity issues in phrasing or constructing the data collection instrument.

Validating an Instrument with Diverse Populations

Briggs, Tovar, and Corcoran (1996) assessed the validity and reliability of the Children's Action Tendency Scale with Latino youth. They concluded that it may be usefully employed with Latino sixth and seventh graders.

Application of the Data Collection Method to Diverse Populations

Even if the data collection method and the structure and content of this method are sensitive to the needs of diverse populations, the way in which the instrument is administered still may not be.

For example, you may be carrying out a needs assessment for socially isolated, recently immigrated Asian women. To obtain valid and reliable information, you would need not only to include questions relevant to this population, but also to ensure that the interviews are conducted so that they elicit the required information. This necessitates the use of people who are sensitive to the population under study as interviewers, administrators of questionnaires, and observers. For example, with the Asian women, an interviewer would need to be familiar with this group's language, gender role, and intergenerational role expectations in order to engage the subject in the interview and obtain valid and reliable data.

SUMMARY

Quantitative approaches create categories of the phenomenon under study and assign numbers to these categories. Qualitative approaches examine the phenomenon in more detail. Data collection methods include interviews, questionnaires, observation, logs and journals, and secondary data. Scales can measure complex variables. There are several techniques for checking the reliability and validity of data collection methods.

When collecting data in an agency, data collection methods that are compatible to the practice need to be used. Ethical issues include considering potential harm to the subjects and the issues of confidentiality and anonymity. When considering human diversity issues, the selection, relevance, and application of the data collection method need to be considered.

STUDY/EXERCISE QUESTIONS

1. Develop a questionnaire to assess the campus needs (such as parking, day care, and so on) of students in your class. Include both open-ended and closed-ended questions.
   a. How do you decide what questions to include?
   b. How would you administer the questionnaire?

2. Have another student in the class critique your questionnaire and comment on its reliability and validity.

3. Search for a suitable instrument to measure adolescents' self-esteem.
   a. Report on its validity and reliability.
   b. Are there any groups for which the instrument may not be reliable or valid?

4. Your agency has asked you to participate in planning a program for adults with a history of childhood sexual abuse.
   a. How would you collect data that would demonstrate the need for such a program?
   b. How would you ensure confidentiality?

5. Design a structured interview to assess the satisfaction of clients who have just finished receiving services from a family service agency.
   a. Conduct this interview with a classmate.
   b. Would other methods of data collection be more reliable or valid in this case?

6. Design a way of observing a Head Start student who is reported to be disruptive in the classroom.
   a. How would you check the validity and reliability of this method?

INFOTRAC COLLEGE EDITION

1. Search for *"participant observation."* Could another data collection method have been used in this study?
2. Search for *"secondary data"* and examine two of the articles that used secondary data as their primary source of data. What limitations about the data were cited by the authors?
3. Search for *institutional review boards* and review three of the concerns/issues raised by the authors in how institutional review boards can both help and hinder research.

REFERENCES

Benbenishty, R., & Oyserman, D. (1995). Children in foster care: Their present situation and plans for their future. *International Social Work, 38* (2), 117–131.

Briggs, H., Tovar, D., & Corcoran, K. (1996). The CATS: Is it reliable and valid with Latino youngsters? *Research in Social Work Practice, 6* (2), 229–235.

Burack-Weiss, A. (1995). The caregiver's memoir: A new look at family support. *Social Work, 40* (3), 391–396.

Caputo, R. (1995). Gender and race: Employment opportunity and the American economy, 1969–1991. *Families in Society, 76* (4), 239–247.

Colby, A. (1982). The use of secondary analysis in the study of women and social change. *Journal of Social Issues, 38* (1), 119–123.

Davis, L. V. (1986). A feminist approach to social work research. *Affilia, 1,* 32–47.

Dore, M. M., & Doris, J. M. (1997). Preventing child placement in substance-abusing families: Research-informed practice. *Child Welfare, 77* (4), 407–426.

Duncan, S., & Fiske, D. (1977). *Face-to-Face Interaction.* Hillsdale, NJ: Erlbaum.

First, R. J., Rife, J. C., & Toomey, B. G. (1994). Homelessness in rural areas: Causes, patterns, and trends. *Social Work, 39* (1), 97–107.

Fogel, S. J., & Ellison, M. L. (1998). Sexual harassment of BSW field placement students: Is it a problem? *The Journal of Baccalaureate Social Work, 3* (2), 17–29.

Gibbs, J. T., & Bankhead-Greene, T. (1997). Issues of conducting qualitative research in an inner-city community: A case study of black youth in post-Rodney King Los Angeles. *Journal of Multicultural Social Work, 6, 1* (2), 41–57.

Gilligan, C. (1982). *In a different voice.* Cambridge, MA: Harvard University Press.

Greene, K., Causby, V., & Miller, D. H. (1999). The nature and function of fusion in the dynamics of lesbian relationships. *Affilia, 14* (1), 78–97.

Gregg, R. (1994). Explorations of pregnancy and choice in a high-tech age. In C. Riessman (Ed.), *Qualitative studies in social work research.* Newbury Park, CA: Sage.

Gupta, R. (1999). The revised caregiver burden scale: A preliminary evaluation. *Research on Social Work Practice, 9* (4), 508–520.

Guttman, D. R., & Brenna, D. C. (1990). The personal experience inventory: An assessment of the instrument's validity among a delinquent population in Washington State. *Journal of Adolescent Chemical Dependency 1* (2), 6–10.

Hines, A. M., & Graves, K. L. (1998). AIDS protection and contraception among African American, Hispanic and white women. *Health and Social Work, 23* (3), 186–194.

Hudson, W. (1990). *The multi-problem screening inventory.* Tempe, AZ: Walmyr Publishing.

Johnson, I. (1995). Family members' perceptions of and attitudes toward elder abuse. *Families in Society, 76* (4), 220–229.

Kopp, J. (1988). Self-monitoring: A literature review of research and practice. *Social Work, 24* (4), 8–21.

Lewis, M. A., Giovannoni, J. M., & Leake, B. (1997). Two-year placement outcomes of childrens removed at birth from drug-using and non-drug-using mothers in Los Angeles. *Social Work Research, 21* (2), 81–90.

Marx, J. D. (1999). Motivational characteristics associated with health and human service volunteers. *Administration in Social Work, 23* (1), 51–66.

McCubbin, J. L., & Thomson, A. I. (Eds.). (1991). *Family assessment inventories for research and practice.* Madison: University of Wisconsin.

National Association of Social Workers. (1997). NASW Code of Ethics. *NASW News, 25,* 25.

Ozawa, M. (1995). The economic status of vulnerable older women. *Social Work, 40* (3), 323–331.

Patton, M. (1990). *Qualitative evaluation and research methods.* Newbury Park, CA: Sage.

Ruben, A., & Babbie, E. (1989). *Research methods for social work.* Belmont, CA: Wadsworth.

Sands, R. (1995). The parenting experience of low income single women with serious mental disorders. *Families in Society, 76* (2), 86–96.

Savaya, R. (1998). Associations among economic need, self-esteem, and Israeli Arab women's attitudes toward and use of professional services. *Social Work, 43* (5), 445–454.

Solomon, C. (1994). Welfare workers' response to homeless welfare applicants. In C. Riessman (Ed.), *Qualitative studies in social work research.* Newbury Park, CA: Sage.

Teare, J. F., Peterson, R. W., Authier, K., Schroeder, L., & Daly, D. L. (1998). Maternal satisfaction following post-shelter family reunification. *Child & Youth Care Forum, 27* (2), 125–138.

Organizing the Data

■

S ometimes you get so caught up in designing the project and in planning the data collection that once the data are in hand, you may wonder what to do with it all. The three types of research discussed in this book—practice evaluation, program evaluation, and needs assessment—all have the potential to overwhelm you with data.

This chapter is concerned with organizing the data once they are collected. This stage bridges the gap between data collection and data analysis. In generalist practice, data organization and data analysis are equivalent to the analyzing resource capabilities in practice.

How the data are analyzed depends to a great extent on whether the data are qualitative or quantitative. As discussed in Chapter 1, quantitative data are the result of fitting diverse phenomena into predetermined categories. These categories are then analyzed using statistical techniques. Qualitative data, on the other hand, produce a mass of detailed information in the form of words rather than numbers. Such data must be subjected to forms of analysis that will help make sense out of these words.

These different data also require different strategies for their organization before they can be analyzed.

This chapter includes the following topics:

- organizing quantitative data
- organizing qualitative data
- the agency and organizing the data
- ethical issues in organizing the data
- human diversity issues in organizing the data

ORGANIZING QUANTITATIVE DATA

You work for a public agency that provides assistance to foster care families. Your supervisor has just asked you to develop a questionnaire to mail to all foster families in the area served by the agency to identify their unmet needs. There are 300 foster families in your area. You send out a two-page questionnaire to all 300 families and receive 150 back. These questionnaires contain a considerable amount of valuable data for your agency. These data are in raw form, however, and as such are not very useful to you. Imagine trying to tally answers to 30 questions for 150 questionnaires by hand—a very time-consuming and tedious process. This mass of quantitative data can be analyzed using statistical procedures, which can be further facilitated through the use of the computer.

You need to be thinking about how the data will be organized as early in the research process as possible. This is especially important when you use a questionnaire to collect data because the way questions are structured can influence the way data can ultimately be organized. Organizing quantitative data involves coding the data and using statistical software in preparation for analysis.

Coding the Data

Referring to the foster family questionnaire, the first step to transferring the information from the questionnaire to the computer is to code it. **Coding** involves organizing the collected information so that it can be entered into the computer. Coding is accomplished in three steps: (1) converting the responses to numerical codes; (2) assigning names to the variables; and (3) developing a code book.

Converting the Responses to Numerical Codes

In the foster care example, one question on the questionnaire is: "How many times in the last month were you contacted by a worker in the agency?" The response to this type of question is very straightforward; it simply entails entering the number reported into the computer. Note that this response is at the ratio level of measurement and reflects the absolute magnitude of the value (see Chapter 3). The level of measurement determines the type of statistical analysis that we can perform. With ratio data, you have a great deal of latitude in that responses can be manipulated in a variety of ways: They can be added, subtracted, multiplied, and divided. They represent real numbers and are not strictly codes.

When you look at the other types of questions and their responses, however, often the number that is assigned to the response is a code, and there is a certain amount of arbitrariness in its assignment. This is the case with data at the nominal and ordinal level of measurement. For example, the questionnaire might read: "How would you gauge your overall level of satisfaction with the services our agency provides? (Circle the most applicable response.)

very satisfied   satisfied   somewhat satisfied   not satisfied

This information can be entered more easily if you assign numeral codes to each of the possible responses—for example:

very satisfied	1
satisfied	2
somewhat satisfied	3
not satisfied	4

Note that the level of measurement of this variable is ordinal. The numbers are ranked, but the distance between the numbers is not necessarily equal. Thus our use of these numbers in statistical analysis will be more limited than it was for those in the previous question. Note that this satisfaction question constitutes one variable with four different possible responses or values, coded 1 to 4.

Another question on the questionnaire is this: "Specifically, which services could be expanded to meet any of your needs more to your satisfaction? Please check all that apply."

_____   Individual counseling
_____   Family counseling
_____   Training—preparation for foster child
_____   Other, please specify: _____

For this question, more than one response could be checked. The easiest way to deal with this type of question is to divide it into three subquestions or three variables, rather than one. The three would consist of individual counseling, family counseling, and training. A number would be assigned (1 or 2) according to whether the respondent checked or did not check each item. Note that here we are dealing with variables that are at the nominal level of measurement. The numbers have been assigned arbitrarily to the responses, and they are not ranked in any way.

		numerical code
individual counseling	checked (yes)	1
	not checked (no)	2
family counseling	checked (yes)	1
	not checked (no)	2
training	checked (yes)	1
	not checked (no)	2

Another characteristic of this question that demands special attention is the "other" item, which directs respondents to write in an answer. One solution is to categorize the response to this subquestion or variable into finite (countable) groups (for example, individual services, group services, information and referral, and so on) and then assign numbers to each of these groups. Alternatively, the data can be fitted into existing categories. We need to be careful not to lose the meaning intended by the respondent. An alternative strategy is to treat this item as qualitative data. After all, this is essentially a qualitative mode of collecting data, in that it is attempting to seek information from the subject's perspective rather than imposing previously constructed categories on the subject's behaviors. Organization of qualitative data will be discussed later in this chapter.

Whatever type of question you are coding, two guidelines need to be followed: The coding categories should be mutually exclusive and exhaustive. When categories are mutually exclusive, a given response can be coded in one way only for each variable. That is why in the last example the question needed to be treated as several variables to accommodate the fact that more than one yes response was possible.

The codes should also be exhaustive; in other words, all the data need to be coded in some way. Coding is a tedious task in research. Do not omit coding some responses because you think you will not need them in the analysis. (If this is the case, the questions should not have been asked.) Moreover, it is very difficult to perform coding later and to add to the data set once data analysis has begun. So, although it can be tiresome, coding must be done with care. Any mistakes lead to a misrepresentation of the results.

Assigning Names to the Variables

It is too cumbersome to enter the entire question into the computer. Also, the computer cannot read questions in this way. Consequently, the variables themselves need to be coded or named so that they can be understood by the computer. This means translating the questions into words that are of a certain length—for example, usually no more than seven characters. Generally, the first character has to be a letter; it cannot be a numeral. It is useful to pick a variable name that relates to the question. Say the question was this: "How would you gauge your overall level of satisfaction with the services our agency provides?" A possible variable name could be SATISFY. For the question that asked about individual counseling, family counseling, and training services, these three variables could be denoted SERVICE1, SERVICE2, and SERVICE3.

Developing a Code Book

The code book is used to record how responses are coded and how each variable is named. The code book provides a reference for you and other researchers who would need to know or remember to what the codes originally referred. Sometimes, particularly on smaller projects, a code book may not be needed because the codes can be included on the questionnaire. When designing the questionnaire, bear this in mind; it can save work later. In the last example, you would need to note in the code book that the code for a yes response to the question about expanding individual counseling, family counseling, and/or training services is 1; for a no response, the code is 2.

The next step is to enter the information into the computer. In order to do this, you need to select a statistical software package.

Using Statistical Software

Statistical software can be used to make data analysis a simple and efficient task. Data are collected and then organized to be entered into the computer and analyzed by the statistical software, producing statistical results.

Many statistical programming packages are available, such as SPSS for Windows, SYSTAT, MINITAB, and MICROCASE.

Many of the programming principles are similar, whatever particular software you use. Some software is more user-friendly than others. For all of them, the following general steps are followed:

1. Data are usually entered in rows (although some statistical packages do not require this). Columns are assigned to variables. The first few columns are usually assigned to the ID number of the questionnaire or interview schedule. In the previous example, if 150 questionnaires were returned, three columns will be needed for the ID number in order to cover the ID numbers 001 to 150. The next variable, SATISFY, needs only one column since the codes range only from 1 to 4.

2. Names can be given to each of the variables. There are usually restrictions on the form and length of these variable names.

3. The program is run choosing from the menu of commands. Each command refers to a specific statistical test. You can also use the commands to recode the data—for example, to convert ratio level data into categories at the nominal level, or to give instructions concerning what to do about missing data.

4. You will receive **output** from running the program. The output will appear on the screen, or you can produce hard copy that contains the results of the statistical analysis.

To gain familiarity and confidence with this software, check out university computer centers. They usually provide workshops and instruction in the use of specific software packages. If you plan to do statistical analysis using a computer, these workshops, which are usually free to students, can be very helpful.

ORGANIZING QUALITATIVE DATA

Organizing qualitative data can be even more overwhelming than organizing quantitative data simply because of the nature of this type of information. Quantitative data by definition are pieces of information that fit into certain categories, which in most cases have been previously defined. Consequently, organizing the data is a matter of ensuring that the data are correctly assigned to the categories and are in a form that the computer can read. On the other hand, qualitative data, once collected, are usually completely uncategorized in order to capture as much in-depth information as possible. Analysis becomes a much more complex process.

Use of the computer is not confined to quantitative data, but is equally useful for organizing and analyzing qualitative data. A word processor is very helpful for recording field notes. Word processing programs such as WordStar, Word-Perfect, and MacWrite allow you to move text around easily. Different types of files can also be maintained and cross-referenced with minimal effort.

In addition, software packages are designed specifically for analyzing qualitative data, such as ETHNOGRAPH and NUDIST. Weitzman and Miles (1995) have compiled a good listing of qualitative software.

Before you start collecting data, it is a good idea to decide what role the computer is going to play in your project and what software you will be using. Then you will be able to organize your field notes and codes accordingly.

Four different elements involved in the organization of qualitative data will be described: note keeping, organizing files, coding notes, and identifying gaps in the data.

Note Keeping

As discussed in Chapter 9, the primary mode of collecting qualitative data is through observation or interviewing. Much note keeping is involved. Sometimes, particularly in the case of participant observation or informal interviewing, these notes are haphazard. Consequently, one of the first steps is to organize and rewrite these field notes as soon as possible after you have taken them. Rewriting the notes will help jog your memory, and the result will be more detailed, comprehensive notes than you could have produced in the field. Bernard (1994), an anthropologist, suggested five basic rules in the mechanics of note taking and managing field notes:

1. Don't put your notes in one long commentary; use plenty of paper and keep many shorter notes.

2. Separate your note taking into physically separate sets of writing.

   ■ Field jottings—notes actually taken in the field. These provide the basis of field notes.

   ■ Field notes—write-ups from your jottings.

   ■ Field diary—a personal record of your experience in the field, chronicling how you feel and how you perceive your relations with others in the field.

   ■ Field log—a running account of how you plan to spend your time, how you actually spend it, and how much money you spend.

3. Take field jottings all the time; don't rely on your memory.

4. Don't be afraid of offending people when you are taking field jottings. (Bernard made an interesting point about this: Being a participant observer does not mean that you *become* a fully accepted member of the group, but rather you *experience* the life of your informants to the extent possible.) Ask permission to take notes; usually it will be given. You can also offer to share your notes with those being interviewed.

5. Set aside some time each day to write up your field notes.

Field Notes

Skucas (1996) examined the reactions of informal support networks of five women who had been assaulted. She used field notes while audio recording semi-structured interviews. When the recordings were transcribed, the subject's emphases were not captured in the transcriptions; the field notes were used to assist in identifying emerging themes.

When collecting qualitative data, you can **transcribe** interviews, or write down verbatim a recording of the interview. Transcriptions are extremely time-consuming. It takes six to eight hours to transcribe a one-hour interview. Sometimes, in the case of process recordings (discussed in Chapter 7), you can complete a shorthand transcription, writing down the main interactions in sequence.

Using a Transcription

Depoorter (1996) transcribed five interviews she conducted with social workers when investigating how they understood the concept of success in therapy. Although time-consuming, transcription allowed her to identify more clearly the elements of this concept.

This results in something more than field notes but less detailed than a full transcription.

Of course, there may be occasions when the transcription is necessary and central to the study. For example, Marlow (1983) transcribed from a videotape a behavior therapy interview to look at the relationship between nonverbal and verbal behaviors. The transcription included very small behaviors—for example, intonation and slight movements of the hands and facial features. Descriptions can give some important, detailed information that can enrich our understanding of client and worker experiences.

Organizing Files

Your rewritten field notes will form your basic or master file. Always keep backup copies of these notes as a precautionary measure. As you proceed with the data collection, you will need different types of files or sets of notes. Generally, at a minimum you will need five types of files: descriptive files, methodological files, biographical files, bibliographical files, and analytical files.

The descriptive file includes information on the topic being studied. In the case of a program evaluation, this file would include information on the program itself, its history, its development, and so forth. Initially, this file will contain most of your notes.

The methodological file or set of notes deals with the techniques of collecting data. It gives you the opportunity to record what you think has improved or damaged your interviewing and observation techniques.

The biographical file includes information on individuals interviewed or included in the study. For example, it might include information about clients, the director, and so on.

The bibliographical file contains references for material you have read related to the study. This file is very similar to the type of file you might keep when completing a research term paper.

Finally, the analytical file provides the beginnings of the analysis proper. It contains notes on the kinds of patterns you see emerging from the data. For example, when interviewing the clients from a family service agency, you may have detected the relationship between their perceptions about the benefits of the program and the specific type of problem they brought to the agency. Consequently, you may start a file labeled "Benefit-Problem." Your analytical set of notes will initially be the smallest file.

Do not forget to cross-reference your files. Some materials in the "Benefit-Problem" file pertaining to a particular client may need to be cross-referenced with a specific biographical client file. A note in each will suffice. This preparation and organization will help the analysis later on.

Coding Notes

In addition to cross-referencing the five main types of notes, additional coding will help when you come to the analysis stage. As you write up the field notes, use codes for categorizing the notes. These codes can be recorded at the top of each page of notes or in the margin and can be either numbers or letters. Don't forget, though, to keep a code book just as you would for quantitative data.

Obviously, these codes will vary in their precision and form depending on the purpose of the study. In a program evaluation, the codes may refer to the different channels of authority within the organization, the different types of clients served, or any other aspect of the program that is of concern in the evaluation. In a practice evaluation where you may be monitoring the application of an intervention, codes can be used to categorize the content of the interview or meeting. A description of how this coding is carried out is included in Chapter 11.

Identifying Gaps in the Data

Throughout the organization of the data, you need to keep notes on gaps in the data or missing information. Keeping track of gaps is not so necessary in a quantitative study when decisions pertaining to data collection are made early in the study. With a qualitative study, however, you often do not know what data need to be collected until well into the project, when new insights and ideas relating to the study become apparent.

THE AGENCY AND ORGANIZING THE DATA

The central message of this section is to make optimal use of computers.

If your agency does not have easy computer access, lobby for it. Fairly inexpensive computers and software are available. Not only are computers essential to organize and analyze data, but they can be used for many aspects of practice and research, including literature reviews, writing reports, clinical assessment, and Internet and World Wide Web access.

ETHICAL ISSUES IN ORGANIZING THE DATA

Two ethical issues are involved in data organization—one for each type of data, quantitative and qualitative. For quantitative data, ethical issues are minimized because most decisions about how to handle the data have been made prior to this stage. The major problem is how to deal with the "other" responses.

As mentioned before, you can create categories for these responses, or they can be fitted into existing categories. In adopting the latter approach, you need to be careful that we preserve the integrity of the data and that you do not try to put the data into categories that are inappropriate or that simply reflect your preferences.

Ethical issues relating to the organization of qualitative data are more pervasive. At each stage you must be careful that your biases do not overtly interfere. For example, when compiling field notes from your field jottings, ensure that the field notes reflect as closely as possible your observations in the field and are not molded to fit your existing or developing hypothesis. This is a difficult process because one of the underlying principles governing the interpretive approach (which usually involves qualitative data) is that objectivity is not the overriding principle driving the research. Instead, the researcher recognizes the role of subjectivity and that the nature of the data is in part a product of the relationship between the researcher and the participant.

When coding the notes, be aware of the same issue. If you doubt your objectivity, you may want to consult with someone who can examine part of your notes or your coding scheme and give you some feedback. What you are doing here is conducting a reliability check, which in itself can serve the purpose of ensuring that the research is being conducted in an ethical manner.

HUMAN DIVERSITY ISSUES IN ORGANIZING THE DATA

The primary human diversity issue parallels the ethical issues concerning quantitative data that were just discussed. When ambiguous data are categorized, such as responses to "other" questions, attention needs to be paid to ensuring that the categorization adequately accounts for the various human diversity issues that may be involved in the responses.

Human diversity issues arise in different stages in the organization of qualitative data. Field notes need to reflect any human diversity elements, although this depends on from whom you are getting your information. The coding also needs to tap this dimension. And you may wish to pay particular attention to whether or not human diversity issues were addressed when trying to determine whether gaps exist in your data. For example, in collecting data on clients' perceptions of the services they are receiving from a family service agency, it may be important to ask clients about how significant their social worker's ethnicity is to them or about whether clients feel that their social worker and the agency are sensitive to cultural differences.

SUMMARY

Organizing quantitative data includes coding the data and identifying statistical software packages. Organizing qualitative data also involves identifying appropriate software, in addition to note keeping, organizing the files, coding the notes, and identifying gaps in the data. Ethical and human diversity issues include ensuring that the integrity of the data is preserved.

STUDY/EXERCISE QUESTIONS

1. The agency in which you are employed has no computers available to the social workers. As a means of lobbying for computers, draw up a list of the ways in which the computer could be used for research and practice in the agency.

2. Construct a questionnaire of about five items to find out students' attitudes on combining research with practice. Administer the questionnaire to five students in the class.
    a. Create a code book.
    b. Enter the data in a computer using statistical software.

3. Interview five students in the research class about their attitudes on combining research with practice. How would you organize these data?

INFOTRAC COLLEGE EDITION

1. Search for *transcription*. Describe a study that transcribed the data.

REFERENCES

Bernard, H. R. (1994). *Research methods in cultural anthropology.* Newbury Park, CA: Sage.

Depoorter, A. (1996). *How practitioners define success.* Unpublished master's research project, New Mexico State University, Las Cruces.

Marlow, C. R. (1983). *The organization of interaction in a behavior therapy interview.* Unpublished doctoral dissertation, University of Chicago, Chicago.

Skucas, L. (1996). *Female sexual assault victims and their informal support networks: Family preservation's potential.* Unpublished master's thesis, New Mexico State University, Las Cruces.

Weitzman, E. A. & Miles, M. B. (1995). *Computer programs for qualitative data analysis.* Newbury Park, CA: Sage.

Analysis of Qualitative Data

With Colin Collett van Rooyen, M.Soc.Sc.

W orking with qualitative data can initially appear overwhelming! For the new qualitative researcher, Mason (1996) suggests that the almost reflexive "impulse to impose some form of organization and order to your data" (p. 8) simply adds to the feeling of being overwhelmed. No matter how you collect qualitative data—through interviews, open-ended questionnaires, or personal logs—the amount of data and its apparent lack of order can become an unnecessary stressor. However, this need not be so, because there are systems for organizing and managing the data in ways that allow the producer and consumer of the data to interact with it in a meaningful way.

This chapter describes ways that qualitative data can be analyzed. The primary focus of this chapter will be on analyzing data in interpretive studies, in which the data are usually qualitative. Although interpretive studies will be the focus, some of the techniques and approaches discussed can also be used to analyze the qualitative data collected as part of positivist studies.

This chapter discusses the following topics:

- Approaches to analyzing qualitative data
- The agency and qualitative analysis
- Ethical issues in qualitative analysis
- Human diversity issues in qualitative analysis

APPROACHES TO ANALYZING QUALITATIVE DATA

Analysis of qualitative data and analysis of quantitative data differ in a number of important ways. Neuman (1997) suggests that the nature of the data, and what is defined as data, are important sources of difference. Following are a few points that further illustrate the differences.

First, the distinctions among data collection, data organization, and data analysis are much more difficult to define when the data are qualitative. For example, data analysis can often begin before data collection is completed. This is at times referred to as *interim analysis* (Huberman & Miles, 1994). This process allows for the exposure of "layers of the setting" for the researcher, which in turn influences further data collection.

Second, the methods of analysis are much less structured than they are with quantitative data. As a result, qualitative data analysis is much more challenging and at times very difficult to complete successfully. Many decisions are left to the researcher's discretion.

Third, the primary mission in the analysis of qualitative data is to look for patterns in the data, noting similarities and differences. Various techniques can be used to identify these patterns, and they will be discussed in the next session of this chapter.

Fourth, it is important to keep the data in context to avoid the temptation to present emerging data patterns as independent conclusions that will stand on their own. In qualitative research "the context is critical" (Neuman, 1997,

p. 331). Understanding the context within which an action took place and through which meaning was developed is central to the qualitative research process. Information interpreted or presented devoid of contextual content is thus seen as information that is lacking in ability to convey meaning and may present an event or situation in a distorted manner. Contextual analysis is thus central to interpretist research. Data must always be presented in context by referring to the specific situations, time periods, and persons around which the identified pattern occurred.

Fifth, qualitative data analysis tends to be inductive rather than deductive. Careful observation leads to the description of connections and patterns in the data that can in turn enable us to form hypotheses and then ultimately develop them into theoretical constructs and theories. These theories evolve as the data are collected and as the process of interim analysis takes place. In this way, and given the cognizance afforded to contextual issues, the findings are grounded in real life patterns—hence the term *grounded theory* is also used to refer to qualitative data analysis (Glaser & Strauss, 1967).

Five dimensions will be presented as guidelines for the analysis of qualitative data. In this context dimensions refer to activities of process that are engaged in with the data by the researcher. The researcher may choose to use all these dimensions, or just one or two, depending on the purpose of the study. These dimensions include presenting the data as descriptive accounts; constructing categories or themes; carrying out logical analysis; proposing hypotheses; and validating the data. (see Figure 11.1.)

Figure 11.1   ***Dimensions of qualitative analysis***

Descriptive Accounts

The basis of qualitative analysis often consists of a description. Descriptive accounts are, in their simplest form, just what the name denotes—rich descriptions of the study's unit of analysis. This description, or narrative, includes all the materials you have collected: observations, interviews, data from case records, or impressions of others. These accounts are also called case studies.

Case studies have extreme value in qualitative research. A "case" around which study is focused may be an event, an individual, an institution, a group, or any other particular phenomenon that is identifiable in itself, allowing itself some common definition or generally recognizable characteristic. For example, a quantitative study may provide a profile of 250 women living with HIV (human immunodeficiency virus), the virus that eventually leads to AIDS (acquired immune deficiency syndrome). In this hypothetical example the results may suggest that these women are, on average, 26 years old, have one child each, and live in extended families. A qualitative study may involve far fewer women (participants) in the study, perhaps five. Through the construction of case studies, a richer and fuller understanding of their situation may develop. For example, the case study approach may allow the researcher to understand why women in this age category are particularly vulnerable to HIV (remembering the importance of context), and may provide cultural insights into their understandings of the im-

A Case Study for Evaluation of Practice

Cooper and Lesser (1997) explored how race affects the helping process in their description of a cross-racial therapy session between a white female worker and an African-American woman. The authors describe approaches taken by the worker as well as proposing what she could have done differently. They examine issues of biculturalism, identity development, and the effects of cross-racial counseling through the case material.

Case Study for Needs Assessment

Goldberg-Glen, Sands, Cole, and Cristofalo (1998) studied three families in which grandparents were raising the grandchildren without the parents present. The families are described through genograms, structure, interactional processes, and links with prior generations. Examination of these families revealed the strengths and vulnerabilities, as well as the diversity, of grandparent-headed families. The authors argued that grandparent-headed families have unique multigenerational patterns and family structures that are important for service providers to identify.

A Case Study for Program Evaluation

Mwansa, Mufune, and Osei-Hwedie (1994) examined, using a case study approach, youth policies and programs in the countries of Botswana, Swaziland, and Zambia. These youth programs are designed to deal with three challenges faced by the youths: work and employment, education and skills training, and social life. The authors concluded, first, that a formally constituted governmental base is integral to the success of youth development and, second, that more research in these countries is called for to determine needs from the youths themselves.

plications of having HIV, and may provide insight into the nature of extended family support. It may help the researcher show and share with the research consumer the emotional aspects of dealing with a potentially terminal illness while having a young child to care for.

Patton (1990) suggested three steps for constructing a case study. Using the hypothetical study mentioned earlier we will review each of these steps.

First, the raw case data are assembled. These data consist of all the information collected for the case study. This may be audio recordings of interviews with the research participants, journals kept by the participants, health/medical records provided to the researcher by the participants, family maps drawn by the researcher or participants, or even photographs of the participants and the contexts within which they live.

The second step is constructing a case record; the case data are organized, classified, and edited into an accessible package. Here the researcher may begin to categorize information—for example, transcribe audio tapes and sift out pieces of data that are considered relevant to the aims of the study. Data related to similar issues or themes, for example, health and medical data may be organized as one set of data and stored together. Data relating to the financial status of the participant (e.g. salary, grants, other benefits) or their family structures may also be set aside in common "clusters" for easy recognition and retrieval. This allows for the development of themes around the case and begins to form a skeleton framework for the presentation of the case, i.e. the narrative. An alternative in data organization may be the clustering or organization of data along a time line, chronologically arranging information and perhaps using important events (by the participant's definition preferably) as markers in time.

The third step is writing the case study narrative. The narrative can be chronological or thematic (or both). For example, our hypothetical case study may take the form of an account that describes the life of the participant since the day on which she heard of her HIV positive test result—touching on important events since this day. This would constitute a chronological narrative. A thematic narrative would use the themes that emerged through the organization of the data as the framework for presentation. What is important is that the narrative be a holistic portrayal of a person, program, event, or case.

As we have seen, the case study can take the form of any of the research types we have considered in this book: a practice evaluation, a description of the problem for a needs assessment, or a description of a program for a formative program evaluation. What should also become clear is that the case study approach is not foreign to social workers who often gather complex and detailed data in order to better understand their client's contexts and to plan interventions that are holistic and appropriate.

One particular type of case study is ethnography. As described in Chapter 9, ethnography is a description of a culture. Ethnography is also regarded as a specific approach to interpretive research (see Patton, 1990, for a presentation of the different approaches to qualitative or interpretive research). Historically, ethnography was the domain of anthropology. Anthropologists rely on participant observation to produce ethnographic studies or monographs of exotic cultures. Social workers have recognized the value of this approach in describing the different cultures with which they are involved—for example, the culture of homelessness or of gangs. In anthropology, ethnographies are often long and detailed, but social work researchers have produced mini-ethnographies. Note that ethnographies (both full-length and short ones) can also be a useful resource for social workers and can help acquaint them with the cultures with which they work.

Ethnography in Social Work

Rojiani (1994) used an ethnographic approach to describe the experiences of a patient who had received community-based long-term care, services, and planning. Rojiani described the formal care provided by professionals as a distinct culture from the care provided by friends and families.

Constructing Categories

As mentioned earlier, interpretive studies and analyses of qualitative data generally use an inductive rather than a deductive approach. Patterns, themes, and categories emerge from the data rather than being developed prior to collection. Our hypothetical example used in the section earlier showed how this process emerges as well as its use in case studies.

There are two main strategies for identifying categories once the data have been collected: indigenous categories and researcher-constructed categories.

Indigenous Categories

Indigenous categories, which use the **emic** approach, identify the categories used by those observed or adopt the natives' point of view. In many ways, this approach is very compatible to the practice skills of building rapport and developing empathy so that the worker can see the world from the client's point of view. These indigenous categories are often referred to as themes or recurring patterns in the data.

Indigenous categories are constructed from data collected using the **frame elicitation** technique. Frame elicitation involves asking or posing questions in such a way that you find out from the research participants what they include in a particular topic or category. An approach that works well for community needs or strengths assessments is to ask subjects what kinds of strengths community members already have that will help resolve identified community challenges. For example, if you are interested in finding ways in which the community can better deal with its physically challenged citizens, you can ask: "What kinds of services for the hearing impaired can community members offer?" Categories of responses are then elicited from the respondents rather than by the researcher. To identify overlapping areas of different responses, the researcher can ask whether one category of response is the same as or part of another category. Using our example, the question would be framed thus: "Is afterschool care the same as respite care?" Such questions elicit data with which you can construct a taxonomy of the respondent's perception of services that are important to the physically challenged.

Another example of this process was one used by Main (1998), who studied a group of South African health workers' understandings of community participation. Main went to great lengths to ensure that the research participants defined the categories of their responses.

Through a group process participants were able to identify common responses and develop their own categorizations of "community participation." Through the use of frame elicitation, questions were posed by Main that helped clarify the participant's explanations rather than through a "once removed" researcher imposing his or her own categories.

You need to be aware of a number of issues when constructing taxonomies or categories in this way. First, inter-informant variation is common, that is, different informants may use different words to refer to the same category of things. Second, category labels may be fairly complex, consisting of a phrase or two rather than simply a word or two. Third, for some categories, informants may have no label at all. Fourth, the categories overlap.

Where possible, the use of group processes for data gathering may allow for clarity and identification of different terminology for similar concepts. Groups, however, are not always ideal because group dynamics themselves can impact on the process. Once these issues have been considered, however, indigenous categories can be useful to the generalist social worker. You can be assured that the case is being presented from the client's perspective and is not being interpreted inappropriately by the researcher. This allows for a level of integrity in the results that creates a sense of trustworthiness and credibility, important components in qualitative research.

The use of indigenous categories is essential to the specific interpretive approach called *phenomenology*. The details of this approach (see Patton, 1990) will not be discussed here except to note that it is concerned with answering the question: "What is the experience of this phenomena for these people?" To capture this experience, the researcher should use indigenous categories or identify themes.

Using Indigenous Categories or Themes

Krumer-Nevo (1998) listened to the stories of three mothers from multi-problem families regarding their perceptions of their stressful situations and methods of assistance available to them. After recording their responses, the author derived categories, based on the language they used, which accurately portrayed their experiences. "The way distress and obtaining help are experienced are keys to understanding the central conflicts of the speaker, her central sensitivities, and the code of her interpretative system."

Researcher-Constructed Categories

Researcher-constructed categories are categories that researchers apply to the data. These categories may be relatively meaningless to the people under study, but the categories do provide a good overall picture of the phenomenon being investigated. Studies using researcher-constructed categories can be considered interpretive or qualitative as long as the study follows the major principle of interpretive research—namely, that data are considered in context rather than through rigidly imposed categories.

Using Researcher-Constructed Categories

Dunbar, Mueller, Medina, and Wolf (1998) explored the psychological and spiritual growth of women living with HIV. Based on the interviews with the women, the authors constructed a model with categories that reflected the descriptions the women made regarding the positive aspects of living with HIV. Five categories were found to be important in the womens' psychological and spiritual growth: reckoning with death, life affirmation, creation of meaning, self-affirmation, and redefining relationships.

Central to the concept of researcher-constructed categories is the process of coding. Codes represent categories that are familiar to the researcher who created them; they are a kind of shorthand that makes it possible to categorize large amounts of data.

The researcher makes informed decisions, based on her or his knowledge of the field of study and about the types of responses that may emerge. The specific aims and objectives of the study will also influence the process of category construction and thus of coding.

An example of such a process could be a study of guidance, advice, and predictions made by a Zulu *isangoma* in South Africa. The *isangoma* is, in general terms, a respected person among the Zulu nation who is a traditional healer and medium to the ancestors, and is often incorrectly referred to from within a western framework as a witch doctor. In this hypothetical study the researcher may have obtained permission to record the words of the *isangoma* as he or she consults with clientele. Based upon the researcher's prior knowledge of the traditions, she or he may have developed categories within which to place some of the content so that it becomes more organized and easier to deal with when attempting to connect it to the aims and objectives of the study. For example, the researcher may have developed the following categories and related codes to simplify the process:

- Predictions of good health (code P-GH)
- Predictions of wealth (code P-WE)
- Positive message from ancestors (code M-PO)
- Negative message from ancestors (code M-NE)
- Prescription of herbal remedy (code R-HE)
- Prescription of remedy of animal origin (code R-AN)

The development of these categories is subjective, although based upon the researchers prior knowledge. The use of the codes allows for quicker, more efficient management of the material. In this way, lengthy statements may be reduced to manageable data segments. For example, the following lengthy statement

> "You have been working hard for many years, and although you are not wealthy now, this does not mean things will always be the same. There is a choice that if you continue to work at the company that now employs you, then you will become wealthy and be able to afford a new car and a larger house that will make your family happy and allow you to retire in comfort."

could be reduced to the code P-WE. Often researchers find it helpful then to create tables, which set out the broad category, the relevant code allocated to the category, and possibly "typical" examples of statements allocated this code. Data on the number of occurrences of such statements may also be tabulated. This then reduces a high volume of data into a manageable structure.

Berg (1998, p. 238) suggests the use of what he calls "coding frames." Here he refers to a process by which codes may start out representing relatively broad categories, this being the initial frame; then within these broader categories, more specific codes may be developed. Using the earlier example, an initial coding frame may consist quite simply of positive responses and negative responses. These two categories may then be broken down within the positive-negative frame to the categories and codes used in the example. Further frame development may still be possible.

One approach to researcher-constructed categories that involves coding is content analysis. Content analysis involves written coding and oral communications and then making inferences based on the incidence of these codes. This approach was first mentioned in Chapter 9 when discussing the use of secondary data. Content analysis can be performed on transcribed recorded interviews, process recordings on a case, published articles in newspapers or journals, and so forth.

Alter and Evens (1990) suggested six steps for content analysis:

1. Select the constructs of interest and define them clearly.

2. Select a unit of analysis (word, sentence, phrase, theme, and so on) to be coded.

3. Define the categories. They should be mutually exclusive and should be fairly narrow.

4. Test this classification scheme on a document/recording.

5. Revise if reliability is low and test again until an acceptance level of reliability is achieved.

6. Code the text of interest and do a category count.

Allen-Meares (1984) discussed the important role content analysis can have in social work research. An early example of content analysis is provided by Hollis (1972), who used coding typology. Hollis was interested in describing and understanding the communications that take place in social casework interviews. Interviews were transcribed and coded line by line using the following codes:

U—unclassified
A—sustainment
B—direct influence
C—exploration, description, ventilation
D—person-situation reflection
E—pattern-dynamic reflection
F—developmental reflection

Interviews could then be understood depending upon the frequency of the different types of communication. These codes were developed specifically for casework practice; thus, different categories would need to be developed to do content analysis on generalist practice interviews.

Although content analysis is often used in social work research it has a number of problems. First, the validity of codes, like any other researcher-constructed category, may be an issue. Second, the coding of the text can be unreliable if it is done by only one coder. Intercoder reliability should be established, which often means training the coder. Third, the coding almost inevitably involves lifting concepts out of context, which essentially negates much of the value of qualitative research.

Content Analysis

Petr and Barney (1993) reported the results of a content analysis of focus group interviews of parents of children with developmental disabilities, emotional disorders, and technology-supported needs. Categories included special needs (2,241 statements); reasonable efforts in crisis situations (92); parent-professional relationships (278); and definition of reasonable efforts (82). Each of these categories also had four or five subcategories.

Logical Analysis

Logical analysis involves looking at the relationships between variables and concepts. This is similar to the quantitative processes of correlation and cross-tabulation, described in Chapter 12, which extend the one-dimensional picture of the data.

In qualitative analysis, a similar process, called **cross-classification,** is used to look at these relationships. Patton (1990) described cross-classification as

> creating potential categories by crossing one dimension or typology with another, then working back and forth between the data and one's logical constructions, filling in the resulting matrix. This logical system will create a new typology, all parts of which may or may not actually be represented by the data. (p. 155)

An important aspect of examining the data this way is to display the data in a table or matrix. If we use the earlier example of the Zulu *isangoma* and his or her interactions with the client, we may develop a table or matrix that could look something like the table presented in Table 11.1.

This table allows the researcher to organize data in a way that they are easily accessible, have some structure, and allow the identification of relationships. In our hypothetical example, the system that the researcher has used allows easy access to positive, negative, and neutral responses and also helps attempts to link clients to types of responses.

Proposing Hypotheses

Interpretive research is primarily concerned with developing hypotheses, rather than testing them. Part of qualitative and interpretive analysis, however, does involve speculation about causality and linkages. One way of representing and presenting causality is to construct **causal flowcharts.** These are visual representations of ideas that emerge from studying the data, seeing patterns, and seeing possible causes for phenomena. We have been using causal flowcharts in this text

Table 11.1   *Matrix of client questions and isangoma responses*

Client questions	Positive response	Negative response	Neutral response
"Will I be wealthy one day?"	Client A: "Yes, you have worked hard and you will be rewarded."	Client C: "How can you ask me this? It is clear that you will be wealthy, the ancestors say this." Client B: "You will continue to struggle in this life."	Client D: "Wealth is not important to you so you will never be rich, but you will be happy." Client E: "Wealth is not important, what is more important is that you and your family are healthy."	Client F: "This is not something that I can speak about—maybe you need to consult a bank manager on this."
"Can you cure me of HIV?"	Client A: "I can make medicine from herbs that can cure you of any illness." Client B: "You may struggle with wealth but you will be cured of this illness."	Client C: "No, there is no cure of that disease—but you will have money to make your life good." Client E: "There is nothing that I can do to stop you from getting ill."	Client D: "Often people ask me that question, but I do not know the true answer as they do not return to me to tell me how the herbs have worked."	Client F: "This I cannot answer—it depends on many things that are beyond my work."

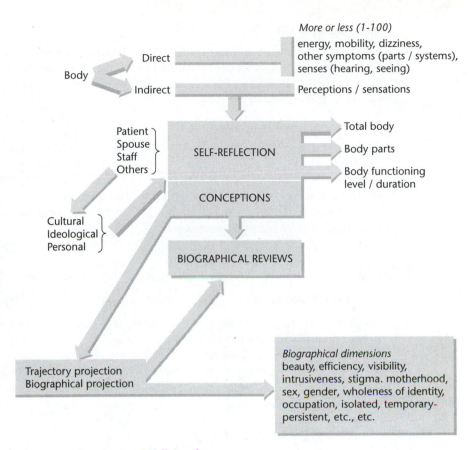

Figure 11.2 **An example of a causal flow chart**

Source: From *Basics of qualitative research,* by A. Strauss and J. Corbin, Thousand Oaks, CA: Sage Publishers, p. 240. Reprinted by permission of Sage Publications, Inc.

to illustrate some of the research methods. Often, causal flowcharts consist of a set of boxes connected by arrows. The boxes contain descriptions of states (attitudes, perceptions, ages, and so on), and the arrows tell how one state leads to another. See Figure 11.2 for an example of a causal flowchart.

The development of hypotheses and causal statements should be firmly rooted in the data and not imposed on the data or overly influenced by the researcher's theoretical biases. If a researcher uses a category previously defined theoretically, the qualitative nature of the research can be ensured by the nature of the data collection methods and the manner in which those data are used either to support or to refute the categories. The context of the data must be taken into full consideration. The research should try to avoid the linear thinking associated with quantitative analysis. One strength of qualitative analysis is its potential for revealing contextual interrelationships among factors and their circular and interdependent natures.

Validating Data

Validation of qualitative data requires rather different processes than validation of quantitative data. Processes for validation of qualitative data include consideration of rival or alternative hypotheses, negative cases, triangulation, and preservation of the context of the data.

Rival or Alternative Hypotheses

After a hypothesis has been developed and proposed, **rival or alternative hypotheses** need to be explored and compared to the proposed hypothesis. Rival hypotheses can emerge from the literature or from the data. The rival hypotheses and the proposed hypothesis are both tested by looking at the data and considering which hypothesis appears to most closely reflect the data. In some cases, both hypotheses appear to be supported.

Rival Hypotheses

Gregg (1994) stated: "When initiating the study, I planned to explore how women make choices about genetic information and prenatal diagnosis: Do they use a rational, cost benefits model . . . ? My research was able to answer the original question: For the most part women did use a rational, cost benefits approach. But the research also provides additional, unanticipated answers" (p. 63). Gregg found that women experienced pregnancy as a risk-laden path and also experienced a state defined as "a little bit pregnant"—two outcomes or rival hypotheses that Gregg did not anticipate.

Negative Cases

Patterns in data emerge when researchers look at what occurs most often. Almost always, however, there are exceptions, or **negative cases,** that do not fit the patterns. These need to be examined and explained. When you encounter a case

A Negative Case

Depoorter (1996) studied practitioners' views of success and found one negative case. This worker, rather than suggesting that lack of success was due to some difficulty in establishing reachable goals with the client, tended to blame the client for not cooperating. This case led Depoorter to speculate that some characteristic of the worker could explain this perspective. The negative case gave Depoorter some directions for future research—for example, comparing male and female views of success.

that does not fit your theory, ask yourself whether it is the result of (1) normal social variation, (2) your lack of knowledge about the range of appropriate behavior, or (3) a genuinely unusual case. Force yourself to think creatively on this issue. As Bernard (1994) stated:

> If the cases won't fit, don't be too quick to throw them out. It is always easier to throw out cases than it is to reexamine one's ideas, and the easy way out is hardly ever the right way in research. (p. 321)

Triangulation

Triangulation involves the use of different research approaches to study the same research question. One way to use triangulation is to collect different kinds of data, such as interviews and observations, which may include both qualitative and quantitative data. Another approach is to have different people collect and analyze the data or to use different theories to interpret the data. Finally, data from different sources can be compared, such as examining consistent and

Triangulation Using Multiple Data Interpreters

Gutiérrez , DeLois, and GlenMaye (1995) examined the concept of empowerment through the perspectives of human service workers. They stated:

> The data were independently analyzed by three readers. . . . The three readers then met to discuss their findings and to work toward a common understanding. Areas of agreement and disagreement were noted during each meeting and became the focus for discussion. When the readers were satisfied that all themes from an interview had been identified they moved on to the next transcript. After all transcripts were completed, notes from the analytic meetings were used to identify common themes across interviews. These themes then became the central findings of the study. (p. 516)

Triangulation Using Different Data Sources

Soloman (1994) used six different data collection methods in her study of welfare workers and homeless welfare applicants. By comparing the results of these six methods she was able to partly validate her findings. The six methods included: (1) discussions with eight key informants; (2) observations in a welfare office; (3) observations of 47 application interviews; (4) observation of 25 interviews between welfare recipients and their caseworkers; (5) individual interviews with four welfare application intake workers; and (6) interviews with 15 homeless applicants.

inconsistent information from different sources and consistent and inconsistent information from different informants.

Using triangulation may result in what appears to be conflicting information. Such conflicts do not automatically invalidate the proposed hypothesis. Instead, such conflicts may simply indicate that new and different information has been acquired, adding another dimension to our understanding of the phenomenon being studied.

Preserving the Context of the Data

One central purpose of interpretive research and qualitative data analysis is that the data are kept in context. This contextualization provides a greater level of assurance that the findings are not distorted. The context of each response needs to be considered. Additionally, it is important to recognize the limitations of the sampling method used, for these limitations can affect the external validity of the findings. Generally, sampling methods are purposive in interpretive studies. The context of the findings is limited; to put it another way, the findings have limited generalizability.

The Limited Context of the Findings

Pettys and Balgopal (1998) studied the multigenerational conflicts that Indo-American immigrants experience. Interviews with 30 Indo-American families, some including grandparents, revealed the natures of the major conflicts, the role of grandparents, and the coping strategies these families used. The authors identified several areas in which this study is limited: the small sample size, the economic profile of the families interviewed (i.e., middle and upper-middle classes), the non-Brahman identity of the families (vs. Brahman identities, which are different), and the fact that all of the families were from South India, which tends to be more conservative than other regions of India.

THE AGENCY AND QUALITATIVE ANALYSIS

Qualitative data and its subsequent analysis can be invaluable to the generalist social worker. By its nature, it is very compatible with practice. We interview as part of our practice, and we keep logs as part of our practice. Both are important sources of qualitative data.

One preconception about qualitative analysis is that it is not as complex as quantitative analysis and that it does not require as sophisticated skills as does quantitative analysis. One goal of conducting qualitative research in an agency setting is to dispel this notion, both to enhance the credibility of qualitative studies and to earn the time and support necessary to conduct qualitative data analysis, thereby producing reports that can make a meaningful contribution to the agency.

ETHICAL ISSUES IN QUALITATIVE ANALYSIS

There are ethical issues in the analysis of qualitative data that you don't encounter in the analysis of quantitative data. Quantitative analysis is protected by the nature of statistical analysis and the rules that govern whether findings are statistically significant. Without this kind of objective guide, the interpretation and analysis of qualitative data depend a great deal more on judgment; thus, the possibility that ethical standards might be violated increases.

Personal, intellectual, and professional biases are more likely to interfere with qualitative data analysis, despite the existence of validation controls. For example, we discussed earlier the use of negative cases as a method of validation. Sometimes it can be tempting to ignore negative cases, implying that there is more agreement than actually exists among the findings in order to make the proposed hypothesis or argument appear stronger. For example, a negative case may not have been examined because the researcher did not see it as an exception but in fact interpreted it as supporting the proposed hypothesis.

On the other hand, qualitative analysis can sometimes expose distortions in previous research. Consequently, qualitative studies can make an important ethical contribution to our knowledge. Srinivasan and Davis (1991) conducted research on the organization of shelters for battered women. They stated that these shelters have tended to be idealized as collectivist organizations that empower both residents and staff. Their qualitative research at one shelter indicated that despite an implicit philosophy of empowerment, a shelter is an organization like any other. An egalitarian, collectivist structure existed for relationships among staff members, and a hierarchial structure existed for relationships among staff and residents. The authors recommended that feminist social workers continuously assess how ideology affects the organizational environment in which services are delivered.

HUMAN DIVERSITY ISSUES IN QUALITATIVE ANALYSIS

As with ethical issues, analysis of qualitative data provides more opportunities to ignore human diversity issues than does the analysis of quantitative data. Data can be analyzed and hypotheses generated that directly reflect the researcher's biases, which may reflect negatively on certain groups. Although such biases can also appear in quantitative research, they are more likely in qualitative research, and additional precautions need to be taken. Researchers conducting qualitative analysis should constantly use self-examination to determine whether they are perpetuating stereotypical or negative images of the participants in their studies. The purpose of the validation procedure is partly to ensure that stereotyping and other forms of bias do not occur.

Qualitative analysis can also be a great asset in ensuring that human diversity issues are recognized. The qualitative approach can provide a richer and fuller picture of the complexity of how certain groups are viewed and treated in the research.

Overcoming biases can be a difficult task, even through the use of careful qualitative strategies. Sometimes it is very hard for us to identify these biases in our thinking; even the definition of a bias can be problematic. As social workers we know that the environment and society in which we live profoundly affect the way we think, including the way we think about different groups. Our upbringing and social environment may result in our unconscious exclusion of certain groups. This effect provides the foundation for discourse analysis.

Discourse analysis focuses on ways in which all analyses are embedded in the researcher's biographical and historical location (Warren, 1988). A great deal of emphasis in discourse analysis has been placed on how women have been marginalized (Keller, 1985):

> "Our laws of nature" are more than simple expressions of the results of objective inquiry or of political and social pressures; they must also be read for their personal—and by tradition, masculine—content. (p. 10)

This perspective relates to the discussion in Chapter 1 concerning the difficulty of achieving true objectivity and the impact of values on how science is conducted.

SUMMARY

The primary mission in qualitative data analysis is to look for patterns in the data while maintaining a focus on the importance of the study's context. Approaches to qualitative analysis include descriptive accounts (case studies), constructing categories (indigenous categories and researcher-constructed categories), logical analysis (cross-classification), proposing hypotheses (using causal flowcharts), and techniques of validation (using rival hypotheses, negative cases, triangulation, and contextualization).

Although qualitative data analysis is naturally compatible with social work practice, the myth persists that it is unduly time-consuming, unsophisticated, and nonproductive. Researchers in agency settings have the responsibility of dispelling this myth. Indeed, most of them are, at times unknowingly, gathering and analyzing qualitative data and are thus well placed for dispelling the myths that exist. Because qualitative data are less structured than quantitative data, It is important to ensure that personal, intellectual, and professional biases do not interfere with the process or that steps are taken to minimize the extent to which they might interfere. It is also important that diverse and minority groups are recognized at this stage of the research process and, indeed, throughout the process.

STUDY/EXERCISE QUESTIONS

1. Conduct an interview with a fellow student, gathering information on what he or she considers to be his or her family's culture.
   a. Use the indigenous category approach discussed in this chapter.
   b. Compare your findings with others in the class.

c.   Is it possible to propose a hypothesis based on these findings?

d.   How would you validate your findings?

2.   Carry out a content analysis on ethics and research using issues of a social work journal. Note that you will need to define *ethics* and *research,* and specify the number and type of journal. What conclusions can you draw from your findings?

INFOTRAC COLLEGE EDITION

1.   Search for *content analysis* and for two articles describe the codes that were used to analyze the data.

2.   Search for *ethnography.* Selecting one article, present a rationale for using this approach for the phenomena under study. Would another research approach have yielded a greater understanding?

REFERENCES

Allen-Meares, P. (1984). Content analysis: It does have a place in social work research. *Journal of Social Science Research 7,* 51–68.

Alter, C., & Evens, W. (1990). *Evaluating your practice.* New York: Springer.

Berg, B. L. (1998). *Qualitative research methods of the social sciences* (3rd ed.). Boston: Allyn and Bacon.

Bernard, H R. (1994). *Research methods in cultural anthropology.* Newbury Park, CA: Sage.

Cooper, M., & Lesser, J. (1997). How race affects the helping process: A case of cross racial therapy. *Clinical Social Work Journal, 25* (3), 323–335.

Depoorter, A. (1996). What factors contribute to a therapist's decision to rate a client as successful? Unpublished research project. School of Social Work, New Mexico State University, Las Cruces.

Dunbar, H. T., Mueller, C. W., Medina, C., & Wolf, T. (1998). Psychological and spiritual growth in women living with HIV. *Social Work, 43* (2), 144–154.

Glaser, B. G., & Strauss, A. L. (1967). *The discovery of grounded theory strategies for qualitative research.* New York: Aldine de Gruyter.

Goldberg-Glen, R., Sands, R. G., Cole, R. D., & Cristofalo, C. (1998). Multigenerational patterns and internal structures in families in which grandparents raise grandchildren. *Families in Society, 79* (5), 477–489.

Gregg, R. (1994). Explorations of pregnancy and choices in a high-tech age. In C. K. Reissman (Ed.), *Qualitative studies in social work research.* Newbury Park, CA: Sage.

Gutiérrez, L. M., DeLois, K. A., & GlenMaye, L. (1995). Understanding empowerment practice: Building on practitioner based knowledge. *Families in Society, 76* (9), 534–542.

Hollis, F. (1972). Casework: A psychosocial therapy. New York: Random House.

Huberman, A. M., & Miles, M. B. (1994). Data management and analysis methods. In N. K. Denzin & Y. S. Lincoln (Eds). *Handbook of qualitative research.* Thousand Oaks: Sage.

Keller, G. F. (1985). *Reflections on gender and science.* New Haven, CT: Yale University Press.

Krumer-Nevo, M. (1998). What's your story? Listening to the stories of mothers from multi-problem families. *Clinical Social Work Journal, 26* (2), 177–194.

Main, M. P. (1998). Community participation: A study of health workers' perceptions. Unpublished Masters Dissertation. University of Natal: Durban, South Africa.

Mason, J. (1996). *Qualitative researching.* London: Sage Publications.

Mwansa, L. K., Mufune, P., Osei-Hwedie, K. (1994). Youth policy and programmes in the SADC countries of Botswana, Swaziland and Zambia: A comparative assessment. *International Social Work, 37,* 329–263.

Neuman, W. L. (1997). *Social research methods: Qualitative and quantitative approaches.* Boston: Allyn and Bacon.

Patton, M. Q. (1990). *Qualitative evaluation and research methods.* Newbury Park, CA: Sage.

Petr, C. G., & Barney, D. D. (1993). Reasonable efforts for children with disabilities: The parents' perspective. *Social Work, 38* (3), 247–254.

Pettys, G. L., & Balgopal, P. R. (1998). Multigenerational conflicts and new immigrants: An Indo-American experience. *Families in Society,* July–August, 410–432.

Rojiani, R. H. (1994). Disparities in the social construction of long-term care. In C. K. Reissman (Ed.), *Qualitative studies in social work research.* Newbury Park, CA: Sage.

Soloman, C. (1994). Welfare workers' response to homeless welfare applicants. In C. K. Reissman (Ed.), *Qualitative studies in social work research,* Newbury Park, CA: Sage.

Srinivasan, M., & Davis, L. V. (1991). A shelter: An organization like no other. *Affilia, 6* (1), 38–57.

Strauss, A., & Corbin, J. (1998). *Basics of qualitative research: Techniques and procedures for developing grounded theory,* 2nd ed. Thousand Oaks, CA: Sage.

Warren, C. (1988). *Gender issues in field research.* Newbury Park, CA: Sage.

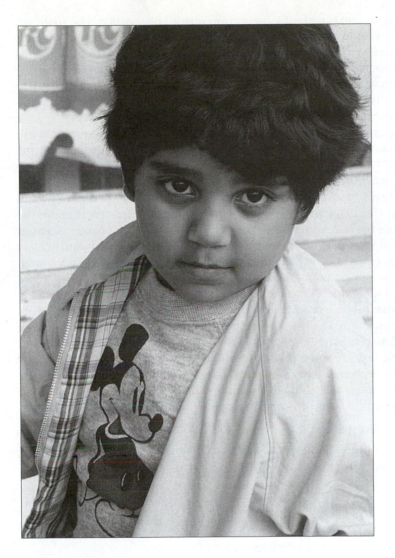

Analysis of Quantitative Data: Descriptive Statistics

T his chapter and Chapter 13 discuss how quantitative data can be analyzed. As discussed in Chapter 1, these are data that can be counted or quantified. The analysis stage of the research process makes some sense out of the information collected. This research stage compares to the analyzing resource capabilities in practice. This stage in research often elicits considerable anxiety in students. This text attempts to describe and explain statistics in as straightforward a manner as possible.

Meaning can be derived from quantitative data in two ways. One is through the use of **descriptive statistics,** which summarize the characteristics of the sample or the relationship among the variables. During this process, you want to get as full a picture as possible of the data. A number of different statistical techniques allow you to do this. You can also use **inferential statistics,** which are techniques for determining whether generalizations or inferences about the population can be made using the data from your sample. This chapter discusses descriptive statistics, whereas the next chapter discusses inferential statistics.

The focus of these two chapters is twofold. First, they focus on understanding which statistics are useful for which purpose. Some statistics are simply not appropriate and are meaningless when used with certain types of data. This approach to statistical understanding prepares you to become an informed and observant consumer of research—a critical role for the generalist social worker. Part of using findings for practice involves understanding and interpreting statistical analysis of the data in various studies. A second focus of these chapters is on how to run different statistical tests using statistical software. Many different statistical software packages are available, which all use similar procedures and commands.

This chapter discusses the following topics:

- frequency distributions
- measures of central tendency
- measures of variability or dispersion
- measures of association
- descriptive statistics and practice evaluation
- the agency in descriptive statistics
- ethical issues in descriptive statistics
- human diversity issues in descriptive statistics

FREQUENCY DISTRIBUTIONS

As discussed in Chapter 4, each variable possesses values. The variables' names, along with their values, are entered into the computer as described in Chapter 10. One of the first things you need to do in statistical analysis is to get an idea about how these values are distributed for each variable. In order to do so, you use **frequency distributions.** These are descriptions of the number of times values of a variable occur in a sample.

For example, say you have collected data on the need for a day care center on a local university campus. Let's assume that 25 students with preschool children were interviewed. Each of these students represents one **observation,** or case; this is equivalent to a unit of analysis. The variables included number of preschool children, ethnicity, expressed need for day care on campus, and miles from campus. The ethnic groups are represented by codes: 1 for white non-Hispanic; 2 for Hispanic; and 3 for African American. Expressed need for day care on campus is coded on a 4-point scale, with the number 4 representing greatest need, and 1 the least need. The number of preschool children in a family and miles from campus are represented by the actual numbers of children and miles. We could present the data as in Table 12.1.

Table 12.1 **Data on four variables by each observation**

Observation number	Number of children	Ethnicity	Need for day care	Miles from campus
1	2	1	3	2
2	1	1	4	1
3	1	3	4	10
4	1	1	4	23
5	1	2	3	4
6	1	1	3	2
7	2	2	4	1
8	2	1	3	1
9	1	2	2	6
10	3	1	4	40
11	2	1	3	2
12	1	2	1	1
13	1	1	2	3
14	2	1	4	7
15	2	1	4	8
16	1	3	4	9
17	1	1	3	15
18	2	1	4	12
19	1	2	1	23
20	2	1	1	1
21	2	1	4	2
22	1	2	4	1
23	2	1	4	3
24	1	1	4	1
25	2	1	3	6

Simply reviewing this table does not make it easy to understand what the data really look like. Several frequency distributions can be constructed for the previous example: one for the variable ethnicity (see Table 12.2), one for expressed need for day care (see Table 12.3), and one for number of preschool children (see Table 12.4). One can also be constructed for miles from campus (see Table 12.5); rather than list each distance separately, however, you can categorize values to make data more readable. Try to use categories that make some intuitive or theoretical sense. You also need to ensure that categories are of same size. For example, you might use categories such as "less than 5 miles," "5–9 miles," "10–14 miles," and "15 miles and over." By grouping data points into categories in this way, of course, some information is inevitably lost.

An example of a frequency distribution table that resulted from the use of a statistical software package is presented in Figure 12.1. This table shows

Table 12.2   **Frequency distribution of ethnicity**

Label	Value	Frequency	%
non-Hispanic white	1	17	68
Hispanic	2	6	24
African American	3	2	8
	Total	25	100

Table 12.3   **Frequency distribution of need for day care**

Label	Value	Frequency	%
No need	1	3	12
A little need	2	2	8
Some need	3	7	28
Great need	4	13	52
	Total	25	100

Table 12.4   **Frequency distribution of number of preschool children in the household**

Value	Frequency	%
1	13	52
2	11	44
3	1	4
Total	25	100

Table 12.5   **Frequency distribution of miles from campus**

Value	Frequency	%
Less than 5 miles	14	56
5–9 miles	5	20
10–14 miles	2	8
15 miles and over	4	16
Total	25	100

```
AGEGR     AGE AT GRADUATION

VALUE LABEL            VALUE         FREQUENCY        PERCENT

                        20              1               1.0
                        21             16              16.2
                        22             23              23.2
                        23             15              15.3
                        24             10              10.1
                        25              5               5.1
                        26              1               1.0
                        27              1               1.0
                        28              1               1.0
                        29              1               1.0
                        30              1               1.0
                        31              2               2.0
                        32              6               6.1
                        33              1               1.0
                        35              1               1.0
                        37              2               2.0
                        40              1               1.0
                        41              1               1.0
                        44              1               1.0
                        45              1               1.0
                        46              1               1.0
                        48              2               2.0
                        49              1               1.0
                        50              1               1.0
                        51              1               1.0
                        62              1               1.0
                         •              1               1.0
                                      ____            _____
                        Total          99             100.0
```

Figure 12.1   **An example of a frequency distribution table**

Table 12.6   **Abuse in backgrounds of abused women and abusers**

Type of abuse	n	%	n	%
Childhood abuse	96	.55	96	.62
Adult sexual abuse	92	.48	–	–
Childhood sexual abuse	93	.42	93	.15
Alcohol abuse	92	.24	95	.84
Drug abuse	91	.23	92	.59
Abuse in family of origin	73	.62	68	.62
Parental substance abuse	70	.53	67	.64

Notes: n = number out of 100 sheltered women reporting abuse in their own backgrounds and those of their abusers.

Source: From "Association between substance abuse and child maltreatment in the context of woman abuse," by M. J. Markward, C. D. Dozier, and C. Colquitt, 1998, *Aretê, 22* (2), 1–11. Reprinted by permission of the publisher.

distribution of ages of B.S.W. graduates over a period of two years. In this example, again, the data could have been grouped to make frequency distribution easier to read, this time according to the age of graduates.

Note that one respondent did not respond to the question about age. The missing response is represented by a dot at the bottom of the value column. These incomplete data are referred to as **missing values.**

Sometimes frequency distributions can be displayed as graphs or charts. Chapter 14 discusses how to do so. An example of a frequency distribution from a published article is displayed in Table 12.6. This table presents some of the results of a study carried out by Markward, Dozier, and Colquitt (1998) who studied the substance abuse-child abuse association seen in abused women. The authors found a significant association between child abuse and substance abuse by parents of abusers. Note that both raw numbers (n) and percentages (%) of the backgrounds of the abused women and their abusers are presented.

MEASURES OF CENTRAL TENDENCY

Another important perspective on data is the location of the middle of the distribution, or the average value. There are three different types of averages, each determined in a slightly different way. These three types are mode, median, and mean.

Mode

The **mode** is the value possessed by the greatest number of observations. In Table 12.2, non-Hispanic white is the mode for ethnicity because this category or value occurred most often. In Table 12.3, "great need" is the mode for expressed need for day care, and in Table 12.5, "less than 5 miles" for distance from campus. The mode can be used regardless of the level of measurement. It can be used for ethnicity (a nominal level of measurement), expressed need for day care (an ordinal level of measurement), and for miles from campus (a ratio level of measurement). In contrast, other measures of central tendency and other statistics discussed in this chapter (measures of variability and measures of association) are restricted in terms of levels of measurement that they can use.

Median

The median, another type of average, can be used only with ordinal, interval, and ratio level data. **Median** is that value at which 50% of observations lie above it and 50% of observations lie below it. The median is thus the value that divides the distribution in half.

The median cannot be used for nominal levels of measurement because it has meaning only with ranked data. Nominal data cannot be ranked, and consequently it cannot be determined whether cases lie above or below a particular nominal value. Numbers are often assigned to nominal data, but these numbers do not have any inherent meaning. We cannot rank, say, the values of ethnicity in any order from highest to lowest, and thus we cannot determine the middle or median value. The median is a popular measure of central tendency primarily because it is not influenced by extreme values that can be a problem with the mean (see the following section). In addition, the median is more stable than the mode, although less stable than the mean. Salaries are often described using the median. (See Appendix B for the formula for the median.)

Mean

The mean, the third type of measure of central tendency, is even more restrictive in the level of measurement that can be used. It can be computed only from interval and ratio levels of measurement (although some will argue that it can also be used with ordinal level data). The **mean** is a result of summing the values of observations and then dividing by the total number of observations. The mean miles from campus for our participants in the needs assessment (Table 12.1) is 7.36 miles. (See Appendix B for the formula for the mean.)

The major strength of the mean is that it takes into consideration each value for each observation. Extreme values, however, either high or low, can distort the mean, particularly if sample size is relatively small. Let's look at the example of miles from campus again but substitute one high value (60 miles) for a middle-range value (6 miles). The mean now becomes 9.52 (238/25 = 9.52), a two-mile difference in the mean as a result of one observation. The mean is the most stable measure of central tendency, however, and in addition is the prerequisite for computation of other statistics.

In summary, to determine which measure of central tendency to apply, you need to consider how you are going to use the information. For example, means

A Study Using The Mean

Cook, Selig, Wedge, and Gohn-Baube (1999) explored social, environmental, and psychological barriers that interfere with early and regular use of prenatal health services. The researchers developed a 24-item Access Barriers to Care Index (ABCI) and interviewed low-income adult women who were hospitalized on the postpartum unit of a large medical center. The women were asked to rate each barrier from 2 to 5, 2 being slightly difficult and 5 being extremely difficult. The researchers reported the means and standard deviations among the answers for each item, or barrier, of the ABCI. Results showed that barriers involving family and friends significantly increased the odds of receiving inadequate care. Other important barriers were those related to the health care system and intrapersonal issues.

are appropriate when you are interested in totals. If you know the national average is 2.3 children per family, then you can guess that a town of 100 families should have about 230 children. If you know that the mode is 1 child per family, then any family you choose at random will probably have 1 child. The reason the average household income is often reported as the median rather than the mean is that often we are interested in an individual comparison of our own financial situation to other normal-range incomes. The mean is inflated by the few unusual persons who make millions. Mean income, however, is more useful in comparing different countries' gross national product (GNP).

Visual Distribution of Data

Data can sometimes be presented as a **normal distribution,** or a bell-shaped curve. Properties of a normal distribution are as follows:

1. The mean, median, and mode have the same score value.
2. It is symmetrical: The right half of the distribution is the mirror image of the left half.
3. Most scores are concentrated near the center.

If distributions have most scores concentrated at one end of distribution rather than at the middle, this is referred to as a **skewed distribution** (see Figure 12.2). The assumption that a distribution is normally distributed underlies many inferential statistical tests, which will be discussed in the next chapter.

MEASURES OF VARIABILITY OR DISPERSION

Another dimension for describing data is the extent to which scores vary or are dispersed in distribution. Figure 12.3 depicts three distributions. They have the same measure of central tendency, but they differ in the extent to which they are spread out, or in their variability.

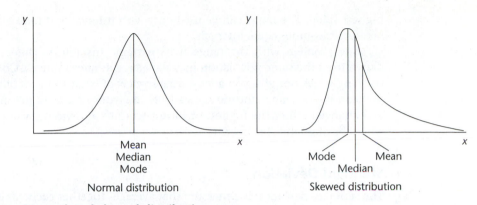

Figure 12.2   ***Normal and skewed distributions***

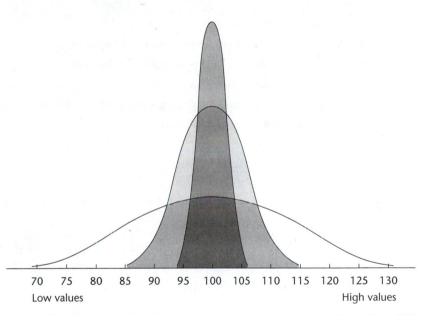

Figure 12.3   ***Three distributions with the same measure of central tendency but different variabilities or dispersions***

Like measures of central tendency, measures of variability differ, with each one more appropriate in some situations than in others. Two types of measures of variability are discussed here: the range and the standard deviation.

Range

The **range** is the easiest measure of variability to compute and to understand: It is simply the distance between the largest or maximum value and the smallest or minimum value. The range is computed by subtracting the lowest value from the highest value. The range can be used only with interval and ratio levels of data because it assumes equal intervals.

The problem with the range is its extreme instability. Different samples drawn from the same population may have very different ranges. Consequently, the range does not give you a very reliable view of what the variability is in the population. The range for the age variable in Figure 12.1 is 42 (62 minus 20). If you changed either the highest or lowest score to an extreme value, the range would be dramatically affected.

Standard Deviation

The standard deviation is a measure that averages together each value's distance from the mean. Calculating the **standard deviation** involves the following steps:

1. Calculate the mean.
2. Measure the distance of each score from the mean.
3. Square these distances (to eliminate negative values).
4. Add the squared differences from the mean.
5. Divide by the n, thus calculating a mean of the differences from the mean.
6. Take the square root of the result.

(See Appendix C for the formula for the standard deviation.)

Because the standard deviation uses the mean and is similar to the mean in many respects, it can be used only with interval and ratio level data. The standard deviation is the most stable of the measures of variability, although it too, because it uses the mean, can be affected by extreme scores.

Table 12.7 displays the results of a study by Jackson and colleagues (1999) that examined factors that place parents at risk of abusing their children by predicting parents' use of discipline practices and attitudes that may bias parents to

Table 12.7   **Descriptive statistics for each discipline variable**

Discipline items	Never happened		M	SD	Mdn	Range
	N(%)					
Explained	55	(6)	4.84	1.68	6.00	0–6
Time out	187	(19)	3.34	2.17	4.00	0–6
Shook child	846	(85)	.28	.77	.00	0–6
Hit child on bottom with a hard object	705	(71)	.72	1.33	.00	0–6
Gave child something else to do	164	(16)	3.36	2.11	4.00	0–6

Table 12.7   *(continued)*

Discipline items	N(%) Never happened		M	SD	Mdn	Range
Shouted, yelled at child	133	(13)	3.70	1.98	4.00	0–6
Hit child with fist or kicked	986*	(99)	.02	.19	.00	0–4
Spanked child on bare bottom with hand	364	(36)	1.78	1.82	1.00	0–1
Grabbed child around neck and choked	993*	(99)	.01	.08	.00	0–6
Swore, cursed at child	738	(74)	.79	1.51	.00	0–6
Hit child as hard as could over and over	994*	(99)	.01	.12	.00	0–2
Threatened to send child away/kick out	933*	(93)	.16	.68	.00	0–6
Burned or scalded child on purpose	999*	(100)	.001	.03	.00	0–1
Threatened to spank or hit child	381	(38)	2.20	2.18	2.00	0–6
Hit child with a hard object	950*	(95)	.13	.63	.00	0–6
Slapped child on hand, arm, or leg	487	(49)	1.40	1.75	1.00	0–6
Grounded/removed privileges	215	(22)	3.10	2.07	3.00	0–6
Pinched child	939*	(94)	.15	.71	.00	0–6
Threatened child with a knife or gun	999*	(100)	.001	.03	.00	0–6
Threw or knocked child down	992*	(99)	.01	.16	.00	0–4
Called child dumb or lazy	822	(82)	.52	1.24	.00	0–6
Slapped child on face, head, or ears	936*	(94)	.13	.58	.00	0–6

Note: N = 1,000 per variable. Items in the table are listed in the order in which they appear in the survey.

*Variable with less than 10% endorsement by participants, therefore the variable was dropped from further analysis.

Source: From "Predicting abuse-prone parental attitudes and discipline practices in a nationally representative sample," by S. Jackson, R. A. Thomson, E. H. Christiansen, R. A. Coleman, J. Wyatt, C. W. Buckendahl, B. L. Wilcox, R. Peterson, 1999, *Child Abuse and Neglect, 23* (1), 15–29. Reprinted by permission of Elsevier Science.

"abuse proneness." The means, standard deviations, ranges, and medians of the variables are displayed.

MEASURES OF ASSOCIATION

Up to this point we have been looking only at **univariate measures,** which measure one variable at a time, and we have been trying to develop a picture of how that one variable is distributed in a sample. Often, though, we want to measure the relationship between two or more variables; such measures are, respectively, **bivariate** and **multivariate measures.**

Often, when carrying out a program evaluation, you are interested in the relationship between two or more variables. For example, you may want to study the effect of a special program for high school students on their self-esteem. You would need to look at the relationship between the independent variable (the special program) on the dependent variable (self-esteem). Or you may wish to compare the dependent variables of an experimental and control group—that is, outcomes from two different programs. To do so, you need to use bivariate statistics.

Similarly, in needs assessments, sometimes you are interested in examining the relationship among variables. For example, in investigating a community's need for a YMCA/YWCA, you want to know not only how many people express this need but also the characteristics of these individuals—ages of their children and so forth. Here the two variables are expressed need and ages of children.

Multivariate analysis involves examining the relationships among more than two variables. This text does not discuss this type of analysis, but you should be able to find plenty of statistics texts and courses on this topic.

Two bivariate measures of association are discussed in this section: cross-tabulation and correlation.

Cross-Tabulation

Cross-tabulation is probably the most widely used bivariate statistic, because it is simple to use and extremely versatile. Cross-tabulations are also known as **contingency tables.** Cross-tabulations may be used with any level of measurement. If interval and ratio (and sometimes ordinal) levels of measurement are used, however, they must be collapsed into a smaller number of categories (the meaning of *smaller* here is discussed a little later).

An example of a cross-tabulation, shown in Figure 12.4, is from a study that examined the workplace service needs of women employees. This particular contingency table looks at the relationship between how the women perceived their husband's participation in household chores (CHORE) and their need for flexible work hours (FLEX).

Generally, the dependent variable (in this case, the need for flexible work hours) is displayed in columns, and the independent variable (husband's participation in chores) is displayed in the rows. The row totals plus percentages and column totals plus percentages are written at the end of each row and column respectively. CHORE has three values (low, medium, and high participation), and FLEX has two values (yes, a need; no, no need). Consequently, we have what is called a 3 by 2 (3 values by 2 values) contingency table, with 6 cells or boxes. If the variables had more values, the table would be larger. You need to be careful that the table is not too large; we also cannot let the number of cases in any of the cells get too low (5 or fewer) because then there are problems in the use of inferential statistics. (Inferential statistics will be discussed in Chapter 13.) Sometimes several values need to be combined to reduce the number of values and so reduce the size of the table. As a result, the number of cases in each cell increases.

Let's continue reading the table. The top number in each cell refers to the number of cases. In the top left-hand cell in Figure 12.4, the number of cases is 75. The second number is the row percentages—that is, for the percentage of women who stated their husbands were low participants in household chores, 83.3% requested flexible work hours. The third number in the cell is the column percentage: In our example, this represents the percentage of women who requested flexible work hours—65.8% reported low participation of their husbands in household chores. The bottom number in the cell is the total percentage. In other words, the number of cases in the cell, 75, is 53.6% of the total number of cases. The total number of cases can be found in the lower right-hand corner. In Figure 12.4, this number is 140 and, as is recorded immediately below

CHORE		Count Row % Column % Total %	FLEX Yes	FLEX No	Row total
Low participation	1		75 83.3 65.8 53.6	15 16.7 57.7 10.7	90 64.3
Medium participation	2		15 83.3 13.2 10.7	3 16.7 11.5 2.1	18 12.9
High participation	3		24 75.0 21.1 17.1	8 25.0 30.8 5.7	32 22.8
Column total			114 81.4	26 18.6	140 100.0

Figure 12.4   **Cross-tabulation of two variables: FLEX and CHORE**

140 in the cell, represents 100% of cases. You can go through and read each of the cells in this manner. To the extreme right are the row totals and percentages, and at the bottom of the table, the column totals and percentages. Note that the labels on the table help guide your interpretation.

The availability of percentages allows you to compare groups of unequal size. A sense of association can be gained by comparing these percentages. For example, a slightly lower proportion of those reporting high participation of their husbands in household chores requested flexible work hours (75%) than those who reported medium and low participation (83.3% for both). Is this difference big enough to signify a relationship between the variables, or is it simply due to change? This question is answered in the next chapter when the topic of inferential statistics is discussed.

Correlation

Correlation is another common way of looking at the relationship between variables, which can be used only with interval and ratio level data. In our example of a study investigating the impact of a program directed at increasing the adolescent participants' self-esteem, it was hypothesized that the number of sessions adolescents attended would have an impact on their level of self-esteem measured on an equal interval scale. Ten adolescents were tested on their level of self-esteem before and after the program (see Table 12.8).

These data can then be plotted on a chart called a **scattergram** (Figure 12.5). The horizontal axis (X) represents the client's length of time in the program, and the vertical axis (Y) represents the difference in the client's level of self-esteem before and after participation in the program.

In Figure 12.5, the line connecting the dots is perfectly straight. In this case, there is a **perfect correlation** between the two variables: When one variable increases or decreases, the other does so at the same rate. A perfect correlation very rarely occurs; usually you find that the dots do not perfectly follow the line but are scattered around it. The direction of the relationship can vary. Figure 12.5 demonstrates a **positive correlation** between the number of sessions attended and the level of self-esteem. As the number of sessions attended increased, so did the level of self-esteem. A **negative correlation** can also occur; this is depicted in Figure 12.6. Here the high values of one of the variables, self-esteem, are associated with the low values of the other variable, the number of sessions attended.

The extent to which data points are scattered gives us an indication about the strength of the relationship between the two variables. There is a formula to precisely measure the strength of this relationship; again, it involves inferential statistics and will be discussed in the next chapter.

The line passing through the dots is used to predict certain values. This prediction involves **regression analysis,** which will be discussed briefly in the next chapter.

Table 12.8   **Self-esteem scores and number of weeks in the program (n = 10)**

Client ID	Self-esteem score	Number of weeks in program
1	8	1
2	10	2
3	12	3
4	14	4
5	16	5
6	18	6
7	20	7
8	22	8
9	24	9
10	26	10

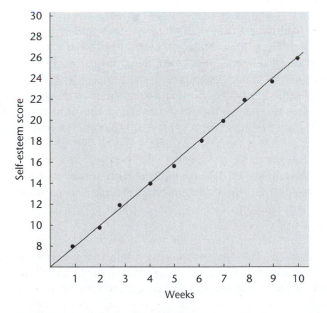

Figure 12.5   **Scattergram of relationship between self-esteem score and time in program (a perfect positive correlation)**

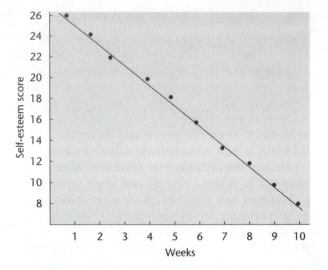

Figure 12.6   ***Scattergram of relationship between self-esteem score and time in program (a perfect negative correlation)***

DESCRIPTIVE STATISTICS AND PRACTICE EVALUATION

Descriptive statistics are not necessarily limited in their application to group studies. They can also be used in single-system studies when quantitative data are collected. Many measures of central tendency and of variability can be used in single-system designs. For example, mean measures during baseline and intervention can be calculated. Calculating mean measures, however, does involve losing much data through aggregation—something that single-system studies are in fact designed to avoid. Consequently, the most effective way to describe the results of single-system studies is to display the results visually. You can think of data charts as possessing certain properties (Bloom, Fischer, & Orme, 1995), as follows.

Level.   The magnitude of data is the level. Differences in levels can occur between the baseline and the intervention. A change in level is called a **discontinuity** (see Figure 12.7).

Stability.   Where there is clear predictability from a prior period to a later one, the data are stable. Stability occurs if the data can be easily represented by a mean line. Data lines can still be stable even if they change in magnitude. See Figure 12.8 for two examples of stability of data between baseline and intervention periods.

Trends.   Where the data tend in one direction—whether the pattern is increasing or decreasing—a trend is present. Trends are called **slopes** when they occur

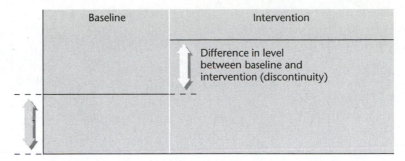

Figure 12.7   **Levels of data**

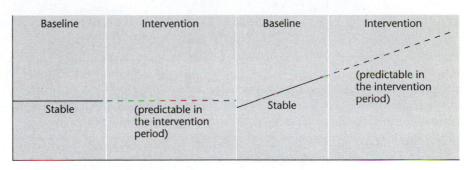

Figure 12.8   **Stability of data between baseline and intervention**

within a given phase and **drifts** when they occur across phases. See Figure 12.9 for variations of trends.

Improvement or deterioration.   Specific comparisons between the baseline and intervention periods can show improvement or deterioration in the target behavior. Of course, a determination of what is improvement and what is deterioration depends on whether greater or lesser magnitudes of the behavior are desired. Figure 12.10 illustrates this idea.

Other factors that need to be considered when describing findings from the charts include the following:

The timing of the effects.   Sometimes effects occur immediately after the baseline and sometimes they are delayed (Figure 12.11).

The stability of the effects.   The effect of the intervention may wear off. If so, implementation of a different intervention is indicated (Figure 12.12).

Variability in the data.   This often happens but needs to be treated cautiously, particularly when the variability occurs during the baseline period. In both ex-

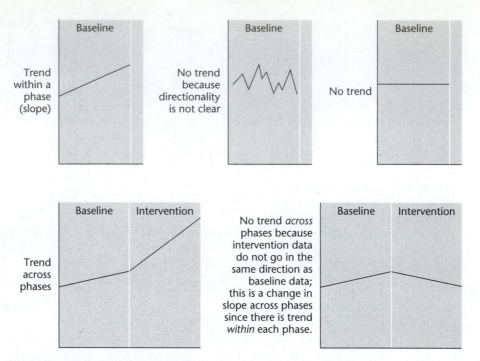

Figure 12.9 **Trends within and across phases**

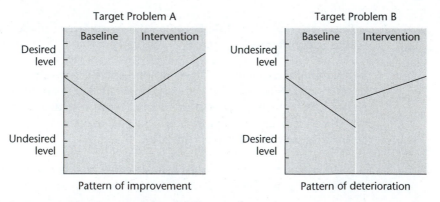

Figure 12.10 **Patterns of improvement and deterioration**

amples in Figure 12.13, it is difficult to interpret the effects due to variability in the baseline data.

The next chapter will discuss how data from single-system studies can be analyzed using specifically designed statistical techniques. These techniques then give you an indication of the data's statistical significance. This is particularly useful when the data are variable, as in Figure 12.13.

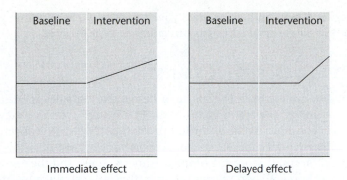

Figure 12.11 **Immediate and delayed effects**

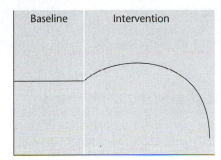

Figure 12.12 **Unstable effects**

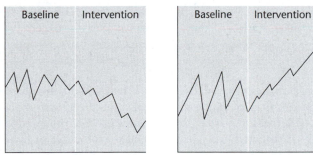

Figure 12.13 **Variability in data**

THE AGENCY IN DESCRIPTIVE STATISTICS

Descriptive statistics can be easily generated in agency settings for needs assessments and program evaluations. Obviously, using a computer enhances the generation of such statistics. Discuss the analysis of single-system data with your colleagues. They can help validate your conclusions. In addition, you can show them how single-system designs can enhance their practice.

ETHICAL ISSUES IN DESCRIPTIVE STATISTICS

One major ethical issue in the use of descriptive statistics is ensuring that the correct—that is, the appropriate—statistic is being used to portray the data. In addition, you must avoid distorting the data to fit any preconceived ideas. Beware of leaving out data that do not support your hypothesis—this is completely unethical. Accurate reporting of the methods you use and the results you obtain is the backbone of good science. Only in this way can we replicate studies and add to the knowledge base of social work. The NASW Code of Ethics (1997) states:

- Social workers should report evaluation and research findings accurately. They should not fabricate or falsify results and should take steps to correct any errors later found in published data using standard publication methods.

HUMAN DIVERSITY ISSUES IN DESCRIPTIVE STATISTICS

In categorizing values—for the purpose of constructing frequency distribution tables or for cross-tabulations—care must be taken that differences between groups of individuals are respected. Often, the number of subjects in some minority groups is small, and there is a temptation to collapse these groups into one. In doing so, however, we may lose critical information about human diversity. Consequently, it is important to devise a means to retain this information. One strategy would be to add a qualitative or interpretive dimension to your study.

SUMMARY

Descriptive statistics summarize the characteristics of a sample. Frequency distributions are descriptions of the number of times the values of a variable occur in a sample. The measures of central tendency are the mode, median, and mean. Data can be distributed in a normal or bell-shaped curve or in a skewed pattern. Measures of variability are the range and standard deviation. The measures of association are cross-tabulation and correlation. One of the most effective ways to use descriptive statistics with single-system studies is to present the results visually, although statistical analyses can also be conducted.

STUDY/EXERCISE QUESTIONS

1. Look for articles in social work journals that use
   a. the mean/median or mode
   b. the standard deviation

    c.   correlation

    d.   cross-tabulations

2.   One of the Study/Exercise Questions in Chapter 10 asked you to develop a questionnaire for measuring student attitudes on combining research and practice, to administer the questionnaire, and to construct a code book. Construct a frequency distribution table for two of the variables included in this questionnaire.

3.   Find an article in a social work journal that uses a single-system design. Are the data presented visually? Are the results clear as a result of this visual presentation?

INFOTRAC COLLEGE EDITION

a.   Search for *standard deviation* and examine how this is used to describe the data in at least three articles.

b.   Search for *correlation* and examine how this is used to describe the data in at least three articles.

REFERENCES

Bloom, M., Fischer, J., & Orme, J. (1995). *Evaluating practice: Guidelines for the accountable professional* (2nd ed.). Boston: Allyn and Bacon.

Cook, C. A. L., Selig, K. L., Wedge, B. J., & Gohn-Baube, E. A. (1999). Access barriers and the use of prenatal care by low-income, inner-city women. *Social Work, 44* (2), 129–139.

Jackson, S., Thomson, R. A., Christiansen, E. H., Coleman, R. A., Wyatt, J., Buckendahl, C. W., Wilcox, B. L., & Peterson, R. (1999). Predicting abuse-prone parental attitudes and discipline practices in a nationally representative sample. *Child Abuse & Neglect, 23* (1), 15–29.

Markward, M. J., Dozier, C. D., & Colquitt, C. (1998). Association between substance abuse and child maltreatment in the context of woman abuse. *Aretê, 22* (2), 1–11.

Analysis of Quantitative Data:
Inferential Statistics

■

ow that you have an understanding of how to describe quantitative data, when you are evaluating a program or your own practice you might ask: How important is a difference in outcome between those who received the intervention and those who did not? Can we generalize these findings to a wider population? These questions can be answered with inferential statistics. Inferential statistics allow us to determine whether an observed relationship is due to chance or whether it reflects a relationship between factors, and they allow us to generalize the findings to the wider population.

Chapter 12 was concerned with describing the profile of the sample or population. In this chapter, quantitative analysis is taken one step further, and hypotheses are tested using statistical procedures or tests. This type of analysis is critical in assessing the effectiveness of programs and practice. Hypotheses, as discussed in Chapter 3, are specific ways of structuring and stating research questions as "if-then" statements. In the case of a program evaluation, the hypothesis might be something like this: "If pregnant adolescents complete the prenatal classes provided by program A, then they will be less likely to give birth to low birth-weight babies than those adolescents who do not complete the program."

It is important to know whether this type of hypothesis can be supported by data. Descriptive statistics can be used to present the characteristics of the sample—for example, their ages, marital status, other children, and other demographic information. In order to test hypotheses, however, inferential statistics are needed.

As generalist social workers, you are not necessarily involved in direct analysis of data. Thus the emphasis of this chapter, as in the last, is not on computing statistics but rather on understanding which statistics are useful for which purpose.

This chapter will discuss the following:

- sources of error and the role of inferential statistics
- types of hypotheses
- significance levels
- statistical power
- steps in the computation of statistical tests
- types of statistical tests
- inferential statistics and practice evaluations
- the agency and inferential statistics
- ethical issues in inferential statistics
- human diversity issues in inferential statistics

SOURCES OF ERROR AND THE ROLE OF INFERENTIAL STATISTICS

Throughout the research process, there are possibilities for error in our conclusions. Errors can come from three different sources, and each source of error can be addressed by specific strategies.

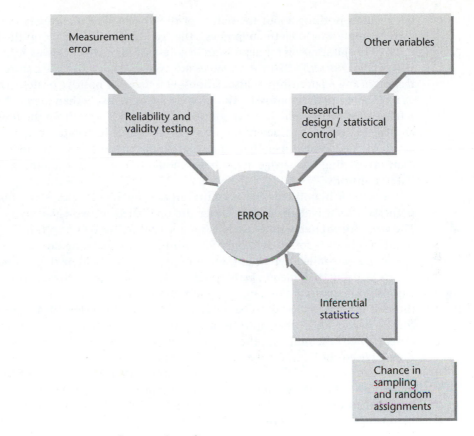

Figure 13.1   ***Sources and corrections for error***

First, a measurement error may affect data collection; this possibility can be assessed by checking the reliability and validity of the data collection instrument (see Chapter 9 for a discussion). Second, other variables might be responsible for the relationship, and they need to be controlled. Variables can be controlled by the research design or, as we discussed in the last chapter, statistically. The third source of error is chance. Chance has to do with sampling variability, as was discussed in Chapter 8. A randomly drawn sample and a population may differ due to chance. The role of chance factors can be assessed through the use of inferential statistics, which relies on probability theory. (The specific statistical tests involved are described later in this chapter.) These three sources of error and the strategies for their assessment are illustrated in Figure 13.1.

TYPES OF HYPOTHESES

A hypothesis suggests that two or more variables are associated in some way. There are two types of hypotheses. First, the **two-tailed** or **nondirectional hypothesis** simply states that there is an association between two or more variables but predicts nothing about the nature of the direction of the association. One such example would be the hypothesis that gender has an impact on the likelihood of hospitalization for depression. A **one-tailed** or **directional hypothesis** specifies not only that the variables are associated but also the nature or direction of the relationship or association—whether it is positive or negative. For example, we might hypothesize that women are more likely than men to be hospitalized for depression. The state of prior knowledge drawn from the literature and theory will in part determine whether one-tailed or two-tailed hypotheses are developed. Remember that when developing hypotheses you do need to draw on existing knowledge; hypotheses should not be based on impulse or initial impressions.

A type of hypothesis that is central in inferential statistics is the null hypothesis, which is derived from either the one-tailed or two-tailed hypothesis. The **null hypothesis** states there is no association between the variables. The null hypothesis is formulated only for testing purposes. Using our previous example of a one-tailed hypothesis, the null hypothesis would be that women are not more likely than men to be hospitalized for depression or that there is no relationship between gender and hospitalization. Statistical analysis then allows the null hypothesis to fail to be rejected. If the null hypothesis is not rejected, then it is concluded that no relationship exists between the variables. On the other hand, if the null hypothesis is rejected, there does appear to be a relationship between the variables that is not a result of chance.

This process may seem unnecessarily complicated. The concept of the null hypothesis is important, however, because it reminds us that statistical tests are intended to determine to what extent a relationship is due to chance, rather than whether or not the hypothesis is true.

SIGNIFICANCE LEVELS

When data are first examined it is not possible to draw clear conclusions based on the findings. For example, in the question relating to gender and hospitalization for depression, the results may disclose that of the people hospitalized for depression, 55% were women versus 45% men. Just looking at these results does not disclose whether this 10% difference between the men and women is simply due to chance or is due to the effect of the program or some other variable. A statistical test must be used for this purpose.

A finding is **statistically significant** when the null hypothesis is rejected and the probability that the result is due to chance in the sample or population falls at or below a certain cutoff point. This cutoff point has been established by statistical convention to be .05. In other words, if a relationship occurs due to chance no more than 5 times out of 100, the null hypothesis is rejected. In this case, it is very unlikely that the relationship is based on chance, and the hypothesis acknowledges that the variables named in it are having an impact on the outcome. Sometimes the significance level is set at lower levels (for example, .01) or, under special circumstances, higher levels (.10). The important thing to remember is that the significance level is set prior to the statistical testing.

The observed level of significance is signified by $p < .05$ (or $p < .01$), and any level below .05 (or .01) is regarded as statistically significant. Establishing statistical significance at the .05 level or less does not mean there is a proven relationship between the variables but rather that there is only a 5% probability that the relationship is a result of chance occurrence. Avoid stating that a hypothesis has been proved. A more accurate statement is that the hypothesis is statistically significant at the .05 level.

STATISTICAL POWER

Sometimes decision errors can be made in either failing to reject or rejecting the null hypothesis. These two errors are referred to as Type I and Type II errors. **Type I error** is the rejection of the null hypothesis and the false conclusion that a relationship exists between the variables when in fact no "real" relationship does exist. **Type II error** is the failure to reject the null hypothesis and so the failure to identify any "real" relationship between the variables (see Figure 13.2). Obviously these errors can present some serious problems.

A statistical test's ability to correctly reject a null hypothesis is referred to as the test's **power.** Generally, the power of the test increases as sample size increases. The test's power is also greater the higher the level of measurement—that is, tests using ratio level data will be more powerful than those using nominal level data.

STEPS IN THE COMPUTATION OF STATISTICAL TESTS

The computation of statistical tests all involve similar steps:

1. Identify the appropriate test and identify its formula.
2. Enter the raw data into the formula and compute the statistical score. (The formulas for the statistical tests can be found in Appendix B.)

		What the "real" relationship is between the variables.	
		True	False
Researcher decision about the relationship between the variables	Fail to reject null hypothesis	Correct decision	Type II error
	Reject null hypothesis	Type I error	Correct decision

Figure 13.2   ***Type I and Type II errors***

3. Compute the degree of freedom, which is related to the size of the sample and the power of the test.

4. Use the probability tables (see Appendix C) to assess the probability level and statistical significance of the statistics score.

These steps are completed rapidly and accurately by whichever statistical software you may be using. Generally, the statistics score and its statistical significance are reported.

TYPES OF STATISTICAL TESTS

In this section will be described the most common statistical tests encountered in the social work literature and those needed for the analysis of most of your data. Four tests will be discussed: t-tests, analysis of variance (ANOVA), correlational analysis (including regression analysis), and chi-square analysis.

Each test is appropriate only under certain conditions. When selecting a test, you need to consider four factors: first, the structure of the null hypothesis; second, the need to use certain tests only with certain levels of measurement; third, the size of the sample; fourth, the distribution of the responses—whether or not the distribution is normal. A summary table of the tests and their conditions for use is presented in Table 13.1.

Table 13.1   ***Types of statistical tests and some conditions for use of correlational analysis***

	T-test	ANOVA	Correlation coefficient	Chi-square analysis
Comparing means of two populations	Yes	No	No	No
Comparing means of more than two populations	No	Yes	No	No
All variables at interval/ratio level of measurement	No	No	Yes	No
One variable only at interval/ratio level of measurement	Yes	Yes	No	No
All variables at ordinal/nominal level of measurement	No	No	No	Yes

T-Tests

Conditions of Use

The t-test is used under the following conditions:

1. You are interested in testing a null hypothesis to find whether two samples have the same mean.

2. The dependent variable is at the interval level of measurement at least (although some argue that the ordinal level of measurement is acceptable), and the other variable (usually the independent variable) is at the nominal level of measurement.

3. The sample size can be small.

These conditions often occur in social work. Many program evaluation designs include comparison groups. Each group that is compared represents a value at the nominal level of measurement. Program evaluations often measure the outcome or dependent variable (for example, the number of months an individual has held a job, or the score on a standardized test) at the interval or ratio level. The null hypothesis in such a program evaluation could be that the intervention had no effect; in other words, the two groups had similar outcomes or mean scores. Just on the basis of probability, though, outcomes are likely to be different. The t-test discloses whether this difference could be due to chance. Similarly, you would want to use this test when comparing two groups such as males and females, urban and rural residents, or married and unmarried people, and looking at their differing outcome variables. This type of t-test is known as an independent samples t-test or a groupwise comparison t-test.

Another type of t-test is the paired samples or pairwise comparison t-test. Also commonly used in social work research, the paired samples t-test compares two means at different points in time for the same sample. For example, such a test might compare academic and cognitive scores for children at the beginning of a Head Start program with their scores at the end of a year.

The degrees of freedom for the t-test is accomplished by subtracting 2 from the *n* (the total number of participants in both groups).

The Use of T-Tests in the Literature

Saulnier (1997) studied the effectiveness of social group work on the alcohol problems and marginalization of lesbians. Participants chose their own goals and identified personal and environmental factors that contributed to their use of alcohol. Discussion took place within a feminist perspective. A pretest and a posttest measured alcohol consumption and frequency of drunkenness. Using a t-test, the pretest and posttests were compared, and the differences were statistically significant for both of the dependent variables. These findings were supplemented by some qualitative data.

Analysis of Variance (ANOVA)

Conditions of Use

The analysis of variance statistical test (ANOVA) is used under these conditions:

1. You are interested in testing a null hypothesis to find whether or not the means in more than two samples are the same.

2. The dependent variable is at least the interval level of measurement, and the other variable, usually the independent variable, is measured at the nominal level.

3. The sample size can be small.

Sound familiar? The t-test is in fact a special case of ANOVA, and the conditions of the use of ANOVA are consequently very similar to those of the t-test, except that ANOVA is used to compare more than two groups. The ANOVA results in an *F*-test statistic.

ANOVA is useful if, for example, you are comparing the outcomes of three or more programs in different parts of the state and the outcome is being measured at the interval level or above.

The Use of ANOVA

Secret and Green (1998) used analysis of variance (ANOVA) to test their hypothesis that there would be differences in the psychological well-being, social well-being, and husbands' participation in family activities among three groups of mothers: those with full time professional/managerial jobs, those with full-time working class/blue collar jobs, and those who were unemployed. The authors found that women with professional/managerial jobs and women who were unemployed scored higher on all four well-being scales than did women with working class/blue collar jobs; however, time spent by husbands in family activities was found to be greater for women with working class/blue collar jobs than for women with professional/managerial jobs and for unemployed women.

Correlational Analysis

Conditions of Use

The correlation coefficient gives an indication of the strength of the correlation between two variables. It is used under the following conditions:

1. You are interested in testing the null hypothesis to find out whether two variables are not correlated.

2. Both variables are at the interval level of measurement or a higher level.

3. A normal distribution of responses is not required.

Chapter 12 discussed the use of the scattergram to look at the relationship between two variables. This relationship was described as a correlation. The correlation coefficient examines the strength and direction of the relationship between two variables and discloses whether the relationship is statistically significant. The correlation coefficient statistic is represented by r, also referred to as the Pearson r. The coefficient is in the range of -1.0 to $+1.0$. The -1.0 represents a perfect negative correlation, and $+1.0$ represents a perfect positive correlation.

The degrees of freedom for the Pearson r is simply the n. You need to remember that the r statistic is simply looking at the strength and relationship between two variables; under no circumstances is it to be used to imply causation. Level of self-esteem and performance on an aptitude test for social work might be highly correlated but this does not mean that one causes the other; the other conditions of causality also need to be met (see Chapter 3).

Correlational Analysis

Zunz (1998) explored whether protective factors that contribute to resiliency in other populations could be applied to human service managers facing job-related burnout. The study examined several previously identified protective factors, three additional protective factors, and four social support measures as they correlated to burnout measures. Among the findings, for example, protective factors were negatively correlated with emotional exhaustion and depersonalization and positively correlated with personal accomplishment. Because there were several correlations detected, data from the study could be used to provide concrete, proactive suggestions for interventions that might prevent burnout.

Regression Analysis

One of the main strengths of the r statistic is with prediction. Regression analysis is used for this purpose and involves finding the straight line that best fits the data. Such lines show how much change in the dependent variable is produced

Regression Analysis

Erdwins, Casper, and Buffardi (1998) surveyed 1,675 parents of preschool-aged children. They used regression analysis to determine that parents were more satisfied with child care that was provided by relatives or au pairs in the home than either center-based care or home care providers. There was no significant difference found in parental satisfaction of the latter two forms of child care. Regression analysis also allowed the data to reveal that child care satisfaction was a good predictor of work/family balance for both mothers and fathers.

by a given change in an independent variable or several independent variables. Regression produces coefficients that indicate the direction and amount of change in the dependent variable to be expected from a unit change in the independent variable.

Chi-Square Analysis

Conditions of Use

Chi-square analysis is one of the most widely used statistical tests in social work research, in part because it is a test that can be used with the ordinal or nominal levels of measurement.

The chi-square is used under these conditions:

1. You are interested in testing the null hypothesis to find whether there is no relationship between two variables.

2. The variables are both measured at the nominal or ordinal level. Although chi-square can be used with data at any level of measurement, often at the interval or ratio level of measurement the data will need to be collapsed into categories.

In the last chapter, cross-tabulation was discussed, which is a way of describing the relationship between two variables measured at the nominal or ordinal level. With cross-tabulation, we are eyeballing or estimating the relationship. The chi-square statistic can be applied to cross-tabulation to give us a more accurate reflection of the significance of the relationship between two variables.

Chi-Square Analysis

Krahé, Scheinberger-Olwig, Waizenhofer, and Koplin (1999) studied the link between childhood sexual abuse and revictimization in adolescence. A sample of adolescents between the ages of 17 and 20 completed the Sexual Experiences Survey that was used to measure unwanted sexual contacts in adolescence and whether the girls had experienced childhood sexual abuse. Nearly 9% of the respondents indicated childhood sexual abuse, and 8.5% reported uncertainty of childhood sexual abuse. Both of these groups of girls were more likely to report unwanted sexual contacts in adolescence than girls who did not report childhood sexual abuse. Girls who reported childhood sexual abuse also had higher levels of sexual activity, which implies that childhood sexual abuse can be a risk factor of adolescent sexual victimization.

Chi-square analysis assesses the extent to which the frequencies in our cross-tabulation, called the **observed frequencies,** differ from what we might expect to observe if the data were distributed in the cross-tabulation according to

Table 13.2 **Association between child abuse and substance abuse by parent of abusers (n = 100)**

	Child Abuse	
Substance Abuse by Parent of Abusers	*Yes*	*No*
Yes	18	19
No	2	10

Note: n = 49.

$p \leq .05$, $\chi^2 = 3.84$

Source: From "Association between substance abuse and child maltreatment in the context of woman abuse," by M. J. Markward, C. D. Dozier, and C. Colquitt, 1998. *Aretê, 22* (2), 1–11. Reprinted by permission of the publisher.

chance. These chance frequencies are called the **expected frequencies.** The chi-square statistic is represented by χ^2. The degrees of freedom for the chi-square are related to the number of cells rather than to the *n*. They are computed using the following formula:

$$df = (r-1)(c-1)$$
r = number of rows
c = number of columns

Exercise caution when using chi-square analysis. If the sample is too small or if one or more of the cells has an expected value of less than 5, chi-square should not be used.

Table 13.2 displays the results of a chi-square test used in the study described in the last chapter by Markward, Dozier, and Colquitt (1998). A significant relationship was found between child abuse and substance abuse by a parent of abusers.

INFERENTIAL STATISTICS AND PRACTICE EVALUATIONS

Chapter 12 discussed how results from practice evaluations, particularly single-system studies, can lend themselves to the use of descriptive statistics and how various software packages can facilitate this process. It is also possible to use statistical techniques with the results from single-system studies giving some indication about the effectiveness of our interventions.

Before describing some of these techniques, a distinction needs to be made between three types of significance, which can be encountered in the analysis of group data but often are more relevant in single-system studies: These types of significance are practical or clinical, visual, and statistical. **Practical** or **clinical significance** is attained when the specified goal of the intervention has been reached. For example, the goal of an intervention may be to increase a child's school attendance from 50% to 90%. Anything below this goal may not be of practical significance, even though that figure may be higher than what is needed for statistical significance. This distinction between practical and statistical significance is also relevant to the analysis of group data, not just single-system data.

Chapter 12 discussed the importance of visual presentation of the data from single-system studies. If the results look significant, this is known as **visual significance.** As with practical significance, there can be some discrepancy between visual significance and statistical significance. Occasionally, visual significance may not represent statistical significance; we may be looking for even a very slight visual trend.

Some have argued that statistical analysis cannot be conducted on data from single-system studies (Campbell & Stanley, 1966) because of the completely different nature of single-system and group data. Another potential problem with using inferential analysis with single-system data is that often we find that outcome scores are related to one another. This relationship, called **autocorrelation,** occurs when scores are related so that if we know what happened in the past, we can predict what will happen in the future. Autocorrelation can result in misleading findings and can complicate any statistical analysis.

In recent years, however, attempts have been made to accommodate these potential problems involved in analyzing single-system data. For example, Bloom, Fischer, and Orme (1995) described methods to manage and interpret autocorrelation in some detail.

The three following analytical procedures will be discussed: celeration line approach, standard deviation approach, and relative frequency approach.

Celeration Line Approach

This approach for analysis of single-system data was developed by Gingerich and Feyerherm (1979). It involves connecting the midpoints of the two values of baseline data with a line and projecting this line into the intervention period. The line may either accelerate or decelerate depending upon its direction—hence the term **celeration line.** If a certain proportion of the data are on the desired side of the celeration line, then an estimate can be made of the statistical significance using tables. Details of this method can be found in Bloom, Fischer, and Orme (1995).

The celeration line approach has the advantage of not being influenced by autocorrelation, but it is subject to a number of limiting conditions. These include the fact that the number of observations in the baseline and intervention phases should be approximately the same number. Second, celeration lines cannot be used when the baseline is bounded—that is, when the line reaches either the maximum or the minimum. In these cases, the line obviously cannot be extended into the intervention phase. See Figure 13.3 for a visual representation of the celeration line.

Standard Deviation Approach

This approach is based on the standard deviation, which measures the dispersion of scores around the mean (see Chapter 12). With this approach for analyzing data of single-system studies, if the possible intervention mean is more than two

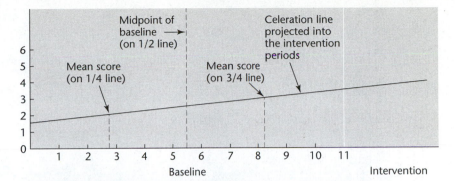

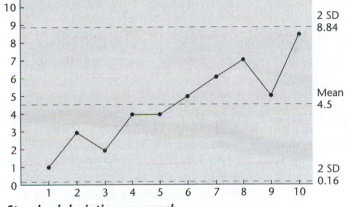

Figure 13.3   **Celeration line approach**

Figure 13.4   **Standard deviation approach**

standard deviations from the baseline mean then there is a statistically significant change. Figure 13.4 illustrates this procedure. See Bloom, Fischer, and Orme (1995) for details of how to compute this approach.

This simple procedure can be used for almost any number of data points. This approach cannot be used with data that are autocorrelated, however, unless the adjustments mentioned earlier are made (see Bloom, Fischer, & Orme, 1995).

Relative Frequency Approach

This approach assumes that typical behavior is represented by the middle two-thirds of the baseline behavior. The proportion of scores that fall outside this range during the intervention period is calculated, and the proportion is located on a probability table. The value from the probability table is the estimate of statistical significance of the change. See Bloom, Fischer, and Orme (1995) for details on the computations involved in this approach. The relative frequency procedure is illustrated in Figure 13.5.

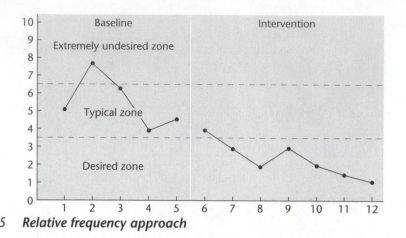

Figure 13.5   **Relative frequency approach**

As with the celeration approach, the number of observations in the baseline and intervention period should be approximately the same. Also, autocorrelation can interfere with interpretation of results using this approach.

THE AGENCY AND INFERENTIAL STATISTICS

Commonly, the outcomes from agency-based research studies are not subject to much in-depth analysis. Often, the report simply contains descriptive statistics. This results from a number of different factors: first, the need to focus on practical over statistical significance; second, the lack of statistical knowledge; and third, the lack of access to computers.

The focus on practical significance is understandable in an agency setting. Often, this practical significance can be thought of as political significance. If an agency is carrying out a program evaluation, the agency may not be concerned with whether the results are statistically significant but rather with whether the goals of the program have been met. Demonstrating statistical significance could enhance practical findings considerably, however, and therefore strengthen the agency's case.

Unfortunately, lack of statistical knowledge in agency settings is all too common. This overview of statistics has given you some basic knowledge that you can build on by enrolling in statistics courses or by exploring the many available statistics texts. If you still feel at a loss when confronted with analysis of your data, seek consultation. Universities often have statistical consultants, or you can look in your community for someone with statistical know-how. If you are writing a grant or research proposal, budget in the cost of a statistical consultant. Whenever possible, bring in the consultant early in the project's planning stage. As we have seen, the type of analysis you carry out is contingent upon other aspects of the research process—the levels of measurement, design, and sample size. Thus, utilizing the consultant from the start will ultimately help the data analysis itself. Statistical consultation groups also exist on the Internet.

Lack of access to computers and software is another potential stumbling block to data analysis in an agency setting. As generalist social workers you need to lobby for their inclusion in the budget.

ETHICAL ISSUES IN INFERENTIAL STATISTICS

Two ethical issues need to be considered in the use of inferential statistics: first, the selection of the most appropriate test; and second, the presentation of statistical significance.

Selection of the Test

Selection of the most powerful test is critical. For example, if a less powerful test is used in place of a more powerful one—assuming conditions allow use of the latter—then there is a smaller likelihood that the null hypothesis will not be rejected when, in fact, it should have been. In other words, a Type II error may be committed. Essentially, a Type II error is a distortion of the results and can be regarded as unethical.

You also must be careful to avoid selecting only tests that support your hypotheses. Watch for this not only in your own research but when you are reading articles.

Presentation of Statistical Significance

It is important to recognize that statistical significance is not a concrete entity or property of a particular set of data. The presence of statistical significance may or may not indicate strong relationships and depends on a number of factors, many of which we have already discussed, including sample size, type of question being asked, and the influence of other factors. Consequently, we need to be careful in how we present results and in how we draw conclusions when referring to statistical significance.

Weinbach (1989) stated: "If practitioners are to make intelligent and informed discussions regarding whether a finding is meaningful for them, they must know more than just whether a relationship between variables is statistically significant" (p. 35). He stressed the importance of responsible reporting of results, including a statement of the sample size and whether this size falls within the usual-size range for which the test is best suited. Such reporting would help the reader assess the appropriateness of the particular test for the research. The strength of the relationship should be presented as clearly as possible—as a percentage difference or an actual correlation. Weinbach concluded: "The ethical researcher who invites replication and feels comfortable in the use of statistical testing should not object to any of these requirements" (p. 35).

HUMAN DIVERSITY ISSUES IN INFERENTIAL STATISTICS

Human diversity issues in inferential statistics relate to your interpretation and understanding of statistical findings, however clearly and responsibly they are reported. Occasionally, findings can seduce us into believing that something is related to something else when actually the findings are partial or otherwise open to question. You must be careful that these results are used responsibly and that they have acknowledged their potential bias against certain groups. As we have discussed throughout this book, the sources of these biases can exist at each stage of the research process.

SUMMARY

One possible source of error in research is chance. The role of chance factors can be assessed with inferential statistics and the use of probability theory. Hypotheses can be two-tailed, one-tailed, or null. A finding is statistically significant when the null hypothesis is rejected and the probability that the finding will occur due to chance falls at or below a certain cutoff point. The ability of a statistical test to correctly reject a null hypothesis is the power of the test.

Four statistical tests are t-tests, ANOVA, correlational analysis, and chi-square analysis. Techniques for analyzing the results from single-system studies include the celeration line approach, the standard deviation approach, and the relative frequency approach. Ethical issues involved in inferential statistics are the selection of the most appropriate test and the notion of statistical significance. We must also ensure that the findings are used responsibly and that they acknowledge potential bias against certain groups.

STUDY/EXERCISE QUESTIONS

1. Look in social work journals and find two articles reporting on program evaluations that used inferential statistics.
    a. What hypotheses were being tested?
    b. What inferential statistics were used?
    c. Did they seem to be appropriate tests?
    d. What was the statistical significance of the findings?
2. Under what circumstances would you need to undertake the statistical analysis of findings from a single-system study?

INFOTRAC COLLEGE EDITION

1. Search for the *t-test* in the article describing the two variables being tested. To what extent were the results statistically significant?
2. Search for *chi-square* and describe the types of variables included in this type of analysis.

REFERENCES

Bloom, M., Fischer, J., & Orme, J. (1995). *Evaluating practice: Guidelines for the accountable professional* (2nd ed.). Boston: Allyn and Bacon.

Campbell, D. T., & Stanley, J. C. (1966). *Experimental and quasi-experimental designs for research.* Chicago: Rand McNally.

Erdwins, C. J., Casper, W. J., & Buffardi, L. C. (1998). Child care satisfaction: The effects of parental gender and type of child care used. *Child & Youth Care Forum, 27* (2), 111–123.

Gingerich, W., & Feyerherm, W. (1979). The celeration line technique for assisting client change. *Journal of Social Service Research, 3,* 99–113.

Krahé, B., Scheinberger-Olwig, R., Waizenhofer, E., & Kolpin, S. (1999). Childhood sexual abuse and revictimization in adolescence. *Child Abuse & Neglect, 23* (4), 383–394.

Markward, M. J., Dozier, C. D., & Colquitt, C. (1998). Association between substance abuse and child maltreatment in the context of woman abuse, *Aretê, 22* (2), 1–11.

Saulnier, C. F. (1997). Alcohol problems and marginalization: Social group work with lesbians. *Social Work with Groups, 20* (3), 37–59.

Secret, M., & Green, R. G. (1998). Occupational status differences among three groups of married mothers. *Affilia, 13* (1), 47–68.

Weinbach, R. W. (1989). When is statistical significance meaningful? A practice perspective. *Journal of Sociology and Social Welfare, 16* (1), 31–37.

Zunz, S. J. (1998). Resiliency and burnout: Protective factors for human service managers. *Administration in Social Work, 22* (3), 39–54.

Research Writing

■

You've analyzed the research results, and in front of you are several computer printouts or, in the case of qualitative data, masses of notes and coded material. Inevitably, there comes a time when you need to write up your research results. Writing the research report is necessary both for yourself—particularly when you are evaluating your own practice—and for others. In fact, for needs assessments and program evaluations, the writing of the report is a critical research stage; as a generalist social worker, you may be more involved in this stage than any other. In addition, you may be asked to assist with developing research proposals, often as part of larger grant proposals. Alternatively, as a student, you will need to write up research reports and, in a graduate program, a thesis or dissertation. Finally, you may decide to submit an article, based on a completed research project, for publication in one of the many professional journals in social work or a related field.

Writing about research is the focus of this chapter. The two basic types of research writing—proposal writing and reporting research results—are analogous to similar steps in practice: first, the writing of an assessment and intervention plan; and second, the reporting of the results of the intervention.

This chapter discusses the following:

- general principles of research writing
- the research proposal
- the research report
- disseminating the report
- the agency and research writing
- ethical issues in research writing
- human diversity issues in research writing

GENERAL PRINCIPLES OF RESEARCH WRITING

Four general principles of research writing are addressed here: knowing your audience; using appropriate citations and references; the structure of the report or proposal; and, finally, the process of writing.

Knowing Your Audience

One of the basic principles of writing, research or otherwise, is to identify your audience. The content and style of the written product should differ according to your intended readers. For example, in writing a research proposal for a needs assessment to establish a date rape prevention program on a university campus, clarify from the outset to whom the proposal is directed—the university administration, a local chapter of NASW, or some other audience. Obviously, audiences are very different. The university administration might need considerable information about the phenomenon of date rape and a discussion of its potential impact on student recruitment, whereas the NASW chapter might require more emphasis on the social and psychological costs of the problem, such as date rape's impact on women's self-esteem.

Your audience influences not only the content of your proposal or report but also the style you adopt. If writing for the university administration, your writing style would be more formal than if you were writing a report for a group of parents in the community.

Referencing Sources of Information

When you are writing any type of report that refers to work by other authors, whether quoting them directly or through indirect reference, it is critical that you appropriately cite your sources of information. Although you can use a number of different referencing styles, the one most widely used in social work literature is the American Psychological Association (APA) referencing method. This is the style used in this book.

The *Publication Manual of the American Psychological Association,* 4th ed. (1994) is the guidebook for the APA style. This book contains a great deal of information; therefore only some examples will follow:

Quotations from a Source

He stated, "A test of discrimination on the grounds of disability is whether a person treats an individual with mental retardation less favorably in identical or similar circumstances than he or she treats or would treat other people" (Tse, 1994, p. 359).

Referencing Citations in the Text

Textor (1995) discussed the changes occurring in the German child welfare system as a result of the passage of the Child and Youth Welfare Law enacted in 1991.

These citations in the text, whether direct quotes or ideas, are then listed in a bibliography. The sources are listed alphabetically by author, using the following format:

Journal articles

1. One author

MacPherson, S. (1996). Social work and economic development in Papua, New Guinea. *International Social Work, 39,* 55–67.

2. Two authors, journal paginated by issue

Ribner, D. S., & Schindler, R. (1996). Ethiopian immigration to Israel: The apparatus of absorption. *Journal of Multicultural Social Work, 4* (1), 75–88.

Books

Midgley, J. (1997). *Social welfare in a global context.* Thousand Oaks, CA: Sage.

Articles or chapters in edited books

Solomon, C. (1994). Welfare workers' response to homeless welfare applicants. In C. K. Riessman (Ed.), *Qualitative studies in social work research* (pp. 153–168). Thousand Oaks, CA: Sage.

Reports

National Institute on Drug Abuse. (1992). *Socioeconomic and demographic correlates of drug and alcohol use* (DHHS Publication No. ADM 92-1906). Washington, D.C.: U.S. Government Printing Office.

Note that lower case is used quite extensively in the APA style. Guffey (1997) presents in her article the different ways in which electronic sources can be cited. The article is full of examples and can be accessed by InfoTrac. Also refer to Szuchman and Thomlison (2000) who specifically discuss APA style and social work.

The Structure of the Proposal or Report

This section outlines some general principles relating to the structure of the report. (The specifics of the content of both the proposal and the report are discussed in the following section.) Again, the APA manual is useful since it not only contains details about referencing sources but also describes each component of the report or proposal.

In general, these conventions should be followed:

- *Title*   Use a clear and concise title.

- *Authorship and sponsorship*   Credits should be inclusive. Don't forget anyone!

- *Abstract*   An overview of the contents of the report or proposal is provided in the form of an abstract to prepare the reader for what follows. Abstracts are often included at the beginning of journal articles.

- *Appendices*   Sometimes the report may include material that is relevant but too bulky to include in the text of the proposal or report. These materials are then included as appendices. Common materials to place in the appendices are the data collection instruments and statistical tables that do not relate directly to the findings.

- *Bibliography and referencing*   As was discussed in the previous section, be sure to cite all your sources appropriately.

Remember that your report or proposal should maintain a consistent style. For instance, if you use the APA style for references, you should also use this manual for instructions in how to structure titles and abstracts.

The Process of Writing

Research reports and proposals should be written as clearly and as concisely as possible. This is not the place for flamboyant writing. Remember that you want others, possibly from very diverse backgrounds, to read and understand the results of your research. A long and convoluted report may not only cloud comprehension of the findings but also discourage some from even trying to read the report. Be as straightforward in your writing as possible. The following suggestions can help you achieve this clarity:

- Keep a research log to facilitate the process of the report or proposal writing as well as the process and development of the research itself. A **research log** is an informal but systematic record of ideas and progress relating to the research. Once the research is completed, it may be difficult to remember exactly why one research strategy was adopted over another or what doubts there were about a particular approach. The research log can help jog the memory.

- Prepare an outline (details will be discussed in the next section). You may not end up following your outline exactly, but that's OK. The idea is to at least have a rough idea in your mind and on paper of how the report or proposal is structured. The outline helps avoid a written product that wanders from one topic to another.

- Write a first draft, then revise and revise and revise, if necessary. Do not expect your first draft to be anything like the final one.

- Ask colleagues, faculty, or students to read early drafts and give their comments. Do not be afraid of criticism at this point. Generally, the more input you receive, the higher the quality of the written product. Have your readers comment on structure, content, style, grammar, and spelling.

- Have someone proof the final copy—primarily for grammar and spelling.

THE RESEARCH PROPOSAL

A **research proposal** is a paper proposing the undertaking of a specific type of research. This is often necessary to obtain permission and funds to conduct the study.

Writing the proposal can also directly assist the researcher in conceptualizing the research. By systematically thinking through each step of the research process, as is required in the research proposal, the researcher can gain new insights and clarifications regarding the research itself.

The format required for a research proposal varies depending upon the specific conditions under which the proposal is being written. These include the following:

- The funding agency may provide application forms that specify the information being requested.

- The funding agency may request a letter of intent, which requires the researcher to describe the proposal briefly. The funding source, based on this letter, may or may not ask the researcher to submit a full-fledged proposal.

- Sometimes, funding agencies send out requests for proposals (RFPs) that specify what they are interested in funding and how proposals should be submitted.

Taking these conditions into consideration, generally a standard outline is used for writing research proposals. The different components include these:

- statement of the research topic
- literature review
- research questions and hypotheses
- research design
- sampling strategy
- data collection
- data analysis
- presentation of the results
- administration and budget
- credentials of the researcher and other relevant personnel

These outlines tend to have a quantitative or positivist bias. Although it could be argued that the outline could also accommodate an interpretive or qualitative study, many funding agencies are, in reality, still primarily interested in more traditional approaches. As discussed in Chapter 1, however, researchers are increasingly adopting a number of different methods of inquiry, which will eventually influence the format and expectations of RFPs.

Each step of the outline has been explained sequentially in this book. A few items should be clarified, though. First, the literature review varies according to what type of research is being proposed (as was also discussed in Chapter 4). In the case of a program evaluation, this section would report why the program is being evaluated and would include findings from the evaluations of similar programs. For a needs assessment, this section would include a description of prior research that has reported on the extent of the social problem to be investigated. Some of this information could be found in the social work literature, but it may also be found in various government document depositions or in agencies' archives. The literature review for a less applied study—for instance, looking at the impact on a child's self-image of one parent being physically challenged (a possible thesis topic)—would be different. Here the literature review would include a discussion of the various theories that have suggested a relationship may occur, in addition to reporting similar research and their findings. This information could be found in the social work and social science literature in university libraries.

In the data collection section, you are generally required only to state the method you will use to collect data. For example, if the data collection requires the development of an instrument—such as an interview schedule or a questionnaire—typically this does not need to be completed for the proposal, but you will need to state what types of variables you will be including. If you plan to use scales or other instruments that have already been developed, then you would include these in an appendix to the proposal.

The data analysis section clearly cannot be discussed in any detail in the proposal except to indicate which statistical tests or other forms of analysis will be used. The presentation of results section should include a discussion of how and to whom the results will be presented. The budget section should itemize all expenses, including supplies, personnel costs, mailing costs, computer costs, and so forth. Finally, you usually need both to summarize your credentials as they relate to the project and to include a curriculum vitae.

THE RESEARCH REPORT

As with the research proposal, the organization of the research report depends in part upon the demands of the agency or the funding source. In general, however, this outline is followed:

- statement of the research topic
- literature review
- research questions and hypotheses
- research design
- sampling strategy
- data collection method(s)
- results
- discussion
- limitations
- recommendations for future research
- implications for practice

These sections apply whether you are reporting on a practice evaluation, needs assessment, or program evaluation study and regardless of whether the study employs a primarily quantitative or qualitative approach.

Obviously, this outline is very similar to the proposal. In fact, if you have a well-structured and well-informed proposal, the research report will be much easier to complete. Some differences do exist between the proposal and the report. The report includes four additional sections: the results of the study, a discussion of the findings, the limitations of the study, and suggestions for future research.

Results Section

Regardless of your audience and the type of research, the focus of your report will be on the results. How results or findings are reported depends on whether the study has adopted a positivist or interpretist approach, and reference will be made to this distinction throughout the following sections. Reporting findings often involves the use of tables, graphs, and pie charts. These visual representations are particularly useful for presenting quantitative data. In the following section, we will describe some forms visual representations can take.

Tables

Statistical tables are the most common form of reporting quantitative findings and are essentially types of frequency distributions. Several principles need to guide the presentation of the data. First, clearly display the data and do not clutter the table with unnecessary details. Second, make the table as complete as possible, usually including both raw numbers and percentages (percentages facilitate comparison). Third, provide a summary of the statistical tests at the bottom of the table when appropriate. Finally, clearly label the table, including footnotes where appropriate. Ziesemer, Marcoux, and Marwell (1994) examined the differences in academic performance, adaptive functioning, and problem behaviors of 145 elementary school children who had experienced homelessness

Table 14.1   **Range of mean scores of self-perception profile for children**

Subscale	Low-SES national norm	Homeless (n = 42)	Matched sample* (n = 41)	Comparison sample (n = 40)
Global self-worth				
M	2.66–3.24	3.17	2.99	3.05
SD	.44–.85	.63	.64	.63
Scholastic				
M	2.61–2.95	2.84	2.81	2.92
SD	.56–.86	.65	.68	.72
Social				
M	2.56–3.00	2.79	2.91	2.79
SD	.47–.92	.67	.69	.65
Athletic				
M	2.47–3.21	2.94	2.81	2.82
SD	.54–.88	.71	.77	.68
Physical appearance				
M	2.62–3.16	3.16	2.84	2.76
SD	.58–.94	.63	.74	.66
Behavior				
M	2.75–3.32	3.00	2.87	3.04
SD	.34–.72	.55	.73	.59

Note: SES = socioeconomic status.

* Students with low SES who were geographically mobile.

Source: From "Homeless Children: Are They Different from Other Low-Income Children?" by C. Ziesemer, L. Marcoux, and B. E. Marwell, 1994, *Social Work, 39* (6). Copyright © 1994 National Association of Social Workers, Inc. Reprinted with permission.

and a matched group of 142 mobile children with low economic status. The authors used tables along with other visual aids to present the results. Table 14.1 indicates the range of mean scores on a self-perception profile for the children in the study.

Graphs

Graphs are an alternative or a supplement to tables that present the data more visually. Similar guidelines apply to graphs as apply to tables. One drawback of graphs is that they lack the detail of tables; but their advantage is that they present a visual image of the data that makes the results apparent at a glance. Graphs are particularly useful in presenting data from practice evaluation studies. Some of the principles of graphing were discussed in Chapter 7.

Various types of graphs can be used. The **line graph** connects various data points with lines. These types of graphs are used extensively for the evaluation of individual practice.

Another type of graph is the **bar graph.** Bar graphs are useful visual means of displaying data at the nominal level of measurement. In a study by Valentine, Edwards, Gohagan, Huff, Peireira, & Wilson (1998) bar graphs were used to display the extent to which doctoral students in social work are prepared for teaching. These bar graphs are displayed in Figure 14.1.

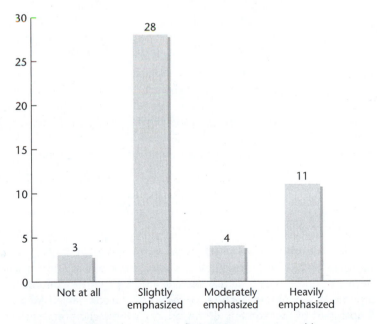

Note: Due to incomplete answers, five responses were unusable.

Figure 14.1 **Emphasis on preparation for teaching in doctoral programs (n = 46)**

Source: From "Preparing social work doctoral students for teaching: Report of a survey," by D. P. Valentine, S. Edwards, D. Gohagan, M. Huff, A. Pereira, & P. Wilson, 1998, *Journal of Social Work Education, 34* (2) 273–282.

Pie Charts

A final type of pictorial or visual presentation of data is the pie chart. **Pie charts** can be used when we want to show the relative contributions of each value to the whole variable. Pie charts are particularly useful for displaying a budget. If too many values need to be included, however, pie charts can look cluttered and be confusing. Figure 14.2 is an example of pie charts used in the Ziesemer, Marcoux, and Marwell (1994) study. The chart shows the proportion of the samples in student functioning risk categories.

Many computer programs can generate graphs and charts, often in different colors. Remember when constructing these visual aids that the goal is to make the data more accessible and clearer to the reader.

Apart from reporting the results using visual aids, the other part of presenting findings is to describe them in writing. This description need not be extensive and can simply consist of translating the findings as straightforwardly as possible. When describing the findings, it is important to avoid interpreting the data; simply report the information and, when necessary, the statistical tests and their results.

Sometimes studies include both qualitative and quantitative results. The quantitative results might be presented followed by a description of the qualitative findings. A discussion section would then integrate the two.

Reporting Results from a Positivist or Quantitative Study

North and Smith (1994) compared homeless white and nonwhite men and women. The Diagnostic Interview Schedule and Homeless Supplement was used in interviewing 900 homeless people. The authors' presentation of the results followed the usual format for reporting the results of a positivist or quantitative study.

First, the authors described the sample demographics using a table:

Table 1 shows selected sociodemographic information. The majority of the subjects (70 percent of men, $n = 418$, and 84 percent of women, $n = 252$) were African American; 3 percent ($n = 18$) of men and 4 percent ($n = 12$) of women were of other ethnicities. . . . (p. 641)

Then the authors presented the results from each set of questions from the interview schedule, including questions about employment and financial resources, history of homelessness, family and childhood, psychiatric disorders, and psychiatric treatment history. Each set of results was accompanied by a table. For example, part of the reporting of the results for the section on history of homelessness reads as follows:

Table 3 shows subjects' histories of homelessness. White men and women reported more episodes of homelessness than nonwhites, and white women had experienced more years of homelessness than nonwhite women. . . . (p. 643)

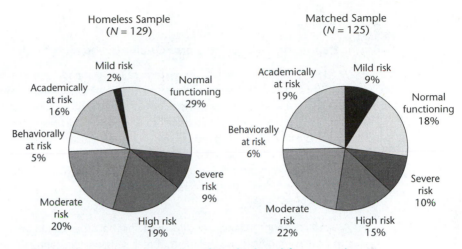

Homeless Sample
(N = 129)

Matched Sample
(N = 125)

Figure 14.2   **Proportion of samples in student functioning risk categories**

Source: From "Homeless Children: Are They Different from Other Low-Income Children?" by C. Ziesemer, L. Marcoux, and B. E. Marwell, 1994, *Social Work, 39* (6). Copyright © 1994 National Association of Social Workers, Inc. Reprinted with permission.

 Reporting Results in an Interpretive or Qualitative Study

Johnson (1999) reports on interviews with 25 women who had previously lived in an emergency shelter. The team of interviewers conducted the interviews using a personal narrative approach so that the women's experiences would be told within the context of their lives. The research disclosed that the onset of homelessness was different for working and nonworking women and that the women obtained different perspectives on their problems from living in the shelter. Homelessness was viewed as part of a process of solving worse problems. Substantive themes emerged such as "Initial Reactions," "New Perspectives on Problems," "Help in Dealing with Problems," and "Leaving Harmful Relationships."

Several quotes were included in the article. The following is one made by Emily, a 31-year-old-Puerto Rican:

> Just specifically being homeless with no place to turn to—nowhere—it's given me something totally different about life. As a woman you have to fight for your rights—for what you believe in. You've got to see the positive things about the bad things that are happening. You got to use that, you know. There's nothing wrong with being in a shelter. It showed me that I will never go back and I will never be in that position. I will never look at the world the same way I looked at it before. Life is not a joke, marriage is not a joke, having children is not a joke. (p. 53)

Reporting Quantitative and Qualitative Results

Lopez (1999) studied a fictive kin system called *compadrazgo* (co-parenthood) among 39 Latinas. The system encourages the sharing of child-rearing responsibilities between the parents and the acquired godparents. Quantitatively, the author reports on the mean and standard deviations among responses to 20 statements on the respondents' experiences with their closest *comadre* (co-mother). Qualitatively, the study included open-ended questions that asked the respondents why they selected nonfamily members to serve as *comadres* and to make additional comments on the *compadrazgo* system itself.

One woman stated:

> We selected our compadres because we know how they would bring our children up if we were not around. Religious, moral, sensitive and caring persons, they are the type of model persons, and we know they would take (the children) in as their own. (p. 37)

Discussion Section

Unlike a research proposal, a research report always contains some kind of discussion section. The discussion section follows and is closely linked to the results section, and it provides an explanation of the results. This section is important

A Discussion Section from a Positivist or Quantitative Study

Slonim-Nevo, Cwikel, Luski, Lankry, and Shraga (1995) examined caregiver burden among three-generation immigrant families in Israel. Data were collected using a face-to-face questionnaire including a Caregiver Strain Index. After presenting the results, the authors proposed that they were best explained by a model including four variables: the health condition of the elderly person, the amount of care provided by the caregivers, the psychological condition of the children in the family, and the length of stay in the new country. This model includes universal components shared by both immigrant and nonimmigrant caregivers as well as elements specific to the immigrant group.

The authors refer to the literature in describing the universal components:

> As shown in other studies, caregiver strain increases when the health condition of the elderly deteriorates and the caregiver has to provide more care (Baruch and Barnett, 1983; Mindel and Wright, 1982). . . . Observing the severe condition of close relatives (usually parents or spouses) often creates feelings of despair, guilt, hopelessness and fear about one's own future (Feinauer et al. 1987). Such feelings are likely to increase caregiver strain. (p. 198)

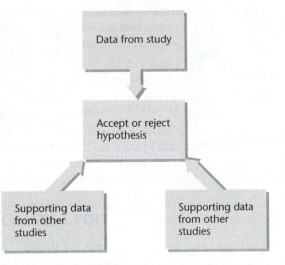

Figure 14.3   **Structure of the discussion section of a research report**

whether you are discussing the results of an evaluation of your own practice, a needs assessment, or a program evaluation. The findings are related to the hypotheses (if there are any) and to the theoretical premise of the study itself. Part of this process involves comparing your research findings to findings from comparable research in the literature and pointing out similarities and differences in the results and conclusions. In this way, you can make connections among various empirical findings, thereby providing collective support and evidence for theories (see Figure 14.3).

In qualitative studies, the distinction between describing the results and discussing the findings can be fuzzy. In part, this fuzziness may result from our attempt to provide an insightful description of the phenomenon under study.

 A Discussion Section from a Qualitative Study

Walzer (1995) presented pregnant daughters' reports about how their mothers influenced their own identities as mothers. In the discussion section Walzer states:

> For the women in this sample, the first pregnancy appears to be a transition during which daughters reflect on their relationships with their mothers while coming to terms with their own notions of motherhood. Most of the women in this sample did not articulate a sense of feeling closer to and more identified to their mothers. The mixed feelings that daughters reported regarding the caretaking they received from their mothers and the role of this ambivalence in their own conceptions of motherhood may partly reflect the unattainable expectations that our culture places on mothers (O'Connor, 1990). (p. 601)

We still need to make a careful distinction between the description and the interpretation.

Limitations Section

By now, it should be very evident that no research is perfect. Flaws and limitations may result from the nature of the question that is being asked, but often—and particularly in social work research—these imperfections simply reflect the social and political context of the studies. For example, random assignment into the experimental and control groups is not always feasible, as discussed in Chapter 6. Sometimes there simply is not time to carry out in-depth interviews with as many people as you would like. In reporting the limitations, go through the research process and point out the drawbacks of the method at each stage. Some common limitations have been discussed in previous chapters, but here is a summary of these problems:

- *Problems associated with the research strategy or approach* The study's approach—descriptive, explanatory, positivist, interpretist—needs to be made explicit, and the approach's drawbacks need to be acknowledged.

- *Limitations of the sampling method* Nonprobability sampling will result in limited generalizability of the findings; but probability sampling may not yield information-rich cases.

- *Limited response rate* A response rate of less than 50% limits generalizations even if probability sampling is used.

- *The reliability and validity of the data collection methods* These need to be specified.

A Limitations Section

Greenberg (1995) examined the role of adult children with severe mental illness as a source of support for their aging parents. The data were collected through face-to-face interviews with 105 mothers aged 55 and older who were living with and caring for an adult child with a serious mental illness. The author discussed in some detail the limitations of the study. Excerpts from this discussion follow:

> There are several limitations to this study. First, this study is based on a nonprobability sample of mothers who volunteered to participate in the study. Thus, caution should be exercised in generalizing the findings. Second, as with all survey studies, the findings are based on self report data and have all the limitations of such data. . . . Third, there is a potential confound between the mother's report of the adult child's assistance and her level of subjective burden. Finally, and most important, the study is cross sectional and therefore cannot establish causal relationships. (p. 421)

- *The problems associated with internal and external validity* Validity problems can occur when the research is explanatory (rather than descriptive) and often result from the lack of a comparison group, particularly one that has been randomly assigned. These problems need to be acknowledged.

- *The problems associated with the interpretation of the results* It is important to point out that interpretations are just that, interpretations; other people may interpret the results rather differently. Interpretive problems may arise whether statistical tests have been used or the data are qualitative.

Obviously, there are other limitations, which will be explored further in the next chapter. The ones presented here provide a general guideline to follow when writing the limitations section of your report, paper, or article.

The extent to which you discuss limitations depends on your audience. You must devote at least a paragraph to addressing these issues. If you are writing up the results of a needs assessment or a program evaluation, the limitations section can be minimal. But if your audience is more knowledgeable about research, you must provide a more extensive limitations section.

Recommendations Section

The next section of the report consists of recommendations for further study and explicitly states the questions that have arisen from the research itself.

Recommendations for Further Research Section

Tracy, Whittaker, Pugh, Kapp, and Overstreet (1994) described network characteristics and support resources from a sample of 40 families receiving family preservation services. In the final section of the article they recommended future research:

> Future research in this area might include experimental studies of social network interventions in combination with family treatment services. Such studies would need to incorporate valid and reliable measures of social support and social networks, longitudinal designs, and adequate control over the implementation of the intervention by different workers and different program models. (p. 489)

Implications for Practice

An implications for practice section is critical to many reports and central when the research is a needs assessment or a program evaluation. After all, these implications are a central purpose of the research.

The order and structure of these last few sections can vary. Often the discussion section includes the implications for practice section, the limitations section, and the suggestions for further research section.

An Implications for Practice Section: Needs Assessment

Loveland Cook, Selig, Wedge and Gohn-Baube (1999) studied the social, environmental, and psychological barriers that interfere with the early and regular use of prenatal services by low-income, inner-city women. The authors suggested the following initial screening of the women to identify those most at risk to target the highest risk group, particularly when resources and staff are in short supply; mailed and telephone reminders of appointments; on site child care; and community outreach, including home visiting.

An Implications for Practice Section: Program Evaluation

Block and Potthast (1998) discuss a program, *Girl Scouts Beyond Bars,* that enhanced regular prison visits between daughters and their prison-residing mothers. The program supported the mother-daughter relationships and eased some of the problems caused by incarceration.

The authors suggest several implications for child welfare professionals based on program results. The professional has responsibilities to help maintain contact between the parent who is incarcerated and her children, to provide resources to the family, to develop permanency plans, and/or to facilitate reunification. The professional can do this by communicating with the mothers, supporting regular visits by the children, and encouraging qualifying children and mothers to become involved in available programs. At the organizational level, child welfare agencies are encouraged to establish linkages with visiting programs such as the Girl Scouts Beyond Bars program, in their communities.

DISSEMINATING THE REPORT

Disseminating or distributing the research report is an essential prerequisite to incorporation of research into practice (see Chapter 15). The dissemination of a report can take several forms: Reports can be orally presented; distributed internally in written form; and published in journals.

Oral Presentation

You may be required to present your research results orally at a community meeting, at a meeting of the agency's board of directors, or to legislators. In the case of practice evaluations, usually the results are discussed more informally with the client and others who might be involved. When presenting orally at a formal meeting, keep the following items in mind:

- Know how much time you have to give the report and stick to this time. Rehearsing your presentation will help.

- Allow time for questions and discussion. Know in advance how much time will be allocated for discussion.

- Use visual aids (overheads, slides, and so on) and handouts (containing a summary of the results and perhaps some charts and scales) when appropriate.

- Try not to become defensive about the research if someone criticizes it during discussion or question time. Simply answer the questions as clearly and as straightforwardly as possible. You should already be aware of the limitations and have thought them through, but you may have missed some.

Distributing Written Reports Internally

The appearance of the report is important even if it is only to be distributed in-house. The term *in-house* can encompass anything from a small agency to a large government department. Be sure that the original report is clear and will reproduce good copies; it can be frustrating to read a report that has been poorly copied. Make sure that everyone who is meant to receive the report actually does.

Publishing the Report

You should strive to publish whenever possible. Publication undoubtedly allows the professional the best access to research findings. Social work journals are making a conscious effort to solicit and publish articles written by practitioners. As a practitioner, you have important contributions to make that can be very different from academicians'.

There are some ways to assess whether or not your report has potential for publication. Consider the following:

- Is it investigating a problem that has received little attention in the past in the research literature? Many journals devote entire issues to research on a newly explored topic.

- Does it have a new slant or perspective on a problem? For example, there may have been many program evaluations on the effectiveness of parent training on reducing the incidence of child abuse and neglect. But if your agency has a program that serves a large number of Puerto Rican clients and you have been involved in evaluating the program, you might have excellent material for publication if none has previously been published on this type of intervention with this particular client group.

■ Is it an innovative research method or combination of methods?

Use participatory principles in disseminating the report. Petersen, Magwaza, and Pillay (1996) used the following methods:

> The participants decided that the results of the epidemiological study needed to be made accessible to the community via pamphlets which could be distributed in the community as well as an audiotape which could be played at the district hospital. On a more regional and national level it was decided that the results needed to be made accessible to other communities experiencing violence via the media such as the national/public radio as well as an article published in a black national Sunday newspaper. The participants agreed to distribute the pamphlets to the parents of the pre-school children. Due to the lack of community resources, the researchers were requested to ensure that the other above-mentioned tasks were carried out. (p. 71)

If you are considering publishing, you should know that different journals are interested in different types of articles. To get a sense of who is interested in what, refer to the *NASW Guide to Social Work Authors.* This gives information on many journals and lists their specific requirements in terms of length of article, reference style, number of copies, and so on.

THE AGENCY AND RESEARCH WRITING

Very often the agency for which you are completing the research will give you specific requirements on how to write the report. Usually, an in-house report on a program evaluation or needs assessment will focus on the results section. A needs assessment may also concentrate on the implications of the findings for practice. If you are writing the report for publication and wider distribution, you may want to emphasize the methods section over the results and devote some attention to a discussion of how the results support or reject previous research. This will enable other researchers to replicate or augment your study.

As a generalist social worker employed in an agency, you will most often write reports on individual cases. These are also research reports if you used some type of evaluation as part of your practice. So start now—combine research and practice and contribute to social work knowledge.

Also, don't forget that another important way in which you can contribute is to give presentations at conferences. For example, your state NASW chapter probably holds conferences every year and strongly encourages practitioners to contribute.

ETHICAL ISSUES IN RESEARCH WRITING

Two major ethical issues arise in research writing. The first issue is appropriately referencing material that is included in a report. The second is confidentiality of results. We will discuss each of these issues in turn.

Referencing Appropriately

Existence of Previous Work

Whenever research is being planned and conducted, it is imperative that you consult other work that has been completed in the target area. For example, you may have been asked by your supervisor to conduct a needs assessment for an afterschool program in your community. You are excited about the opportunity to show off some of your newly acquired research skills. But the next day an ex-classmate calls you from a neighboring city; after you tell her about your assignment, she tells you she has just finished conducting such a study in her community. You are tempted to ignore this piece of information and continue with your own plans because that way you could do your survey alone and collect the credit. Ethically, however, you need to acknowledge your friend's information as useful assistance in the development of your needs assessment; perhaps you may even be forced to recognize that there is no need for this type of study in your community at this time.

Citing References Appropriately

Given that you do decide to use information from your friend's study, it is imperative that you give her credit for her work. This applies to a study published locally as a report, as well as to more widely distributed publications. Recognizing others' contributions can present dilemmas. It would be impossible to credit everyone who has contributed to our intellectual and professional development. In the case of specific research endeavors, however, you must recognize the contributions of others; otherwise, you may be guilty of plagiarism.

Confidentiality of Results

Just as confidentiality needs to be ensured during the data collection phase, you also need to preserve confidentiality when writing and disseminating the report. Subjects' identities should not be disclosed without their permission. Confidentiality may be problematic in qualitative reports with extensive quotes that inadvertently reveal the subject's identity. It is also an issue with practice evaluations. The NASW Code of Ethics (1997) states:

- Social workers engaged in the evaluation of services should discuss collected information only for professional purposes and only with people professionally concerned with this information.

■ Social workers who report evaluation and research results should protect participants' confidentiality by omitting identifying information unless proper consent has been obtained authorizing disclosure.

Another related issue is **copyright.** Copyright law applies not only to published materials but also to in-house reports. Be sure to check on the restrictions that might pertain to distribution and publishing before you disseminate a report more widely.

HUMAN DIVERSITY ISSUES IN RESEARCH WRITING

Three human diversity issues are involved in research writing. First, you must ensure that bias against certain groups is not contained in the report. Second, you should avoid using exclusive language. Third, you must consider to whom the results are being disseminated.

Bias Against Certain Groups

Be careful to exclude biases in the writing that tend to stereotype groups in our society. You are less at risk for this if you paid careful attention to human diversity issues throughout the research process. Then you simply ensure the data are accurately presented and equitably and nonjudgmentally discussed.

Exclusive Language

The issue of exclusive language involves acknowledging our differences and avoiding sexism. Although the predominant use of the male pronoun as a generic pronoun is becoming increasingly less acceptable, we do need to ensure that nonsexist terms are employed consistently. This involves not only the appropriate use of male, female, and plural pronouns, but also the use of terms that are gender neutral, such as *chair* instead of *chairman*.

We also need to ensure that terms do not reflect ethnic or cultural biases or a lack of sensitivity to human diversity. Use a descriptor of a cultural group that is recognized by the group itself. For example, using the term *Mexican American* in New Mexico to refer to Hispanics could be offensive to some individuals who view themselves as Spanish Americans with minimal connections to Mexico. Accuracy often requires that we not lump groups of people together under one label.

Disseminating the Results

The final human diversity issue relating to research writing is the question of who should receive the results. There is a growing argument in favor of giving the findings to the participants included in the research rather than just to the practitioners and other researchers. This is of course critical when conducting participatory or action research.

This does not necessarily entail making the entire research report available to the participants, particularly if it is extensive or excessively technical. Instead, a smaller report can be written specifically for those participating in a needs assessment or program evaluation, in which the results could potentially influence an entire community. One advantage of practice evaluations is that the results are routinely shared with the client (usually verbally).

Advocates of the feminist perspective point out that sharing the results with the participants is another dimension of how "the researcher and subject can work in different ways to explore a 'truth' that they mutually locate and define" (Davis, 1986). This results in a participatory and consensual style attributed to feminist approaches, not only in research but also in administrative style and social work practice (Schwartz, Gottesman, & Perlmutte, 1988).

Giving participants access to findings is also being increasingly viewed as a minority issue. It is being recognized that research results can be empowering to subjects. Historically, minority subjects have often been used by the researcher and have reaped no benefits. Apart from making the results accessible to the participants, researchers need to pay more attention to repaying the participants. Of course, in social work research, the results of needs assessments, program evaluations, and practice evaluations all directly contribute to the development or improvement of interventions designed to assist those who are studied. Sometimes, though, benefits can be extended further—for example, by returning a proportion of the royalties from book sales to the community or by paying participants for the time they spend being interviewed.

SUMMARY

Four general principles of research writing are to know your audience, to use appropriate citations and references, to structure your research report or proposal correctly, and to write the report as clearly and as concisely as possible. The research proposal is a paper proposing a specific type of research. The funding agency may have requests for proposals (RFPs) that list the projects they are interested in funding and how the proposals should be submitted. Like the research proposal, the research report should follow an outline structure: statement of the research topic, theoretical framework, research questions and hypotheses, data collection methods, sampling strategy, research design, results, discussion, limitations, recommendations for future research, and implications for practice. Reports may be presented orally, distributed internally (in-house), or published.

In an agency, generalist social workers are involved in writing not only formal reports and proposals but also case reports. The ethical issues involved in research writing include appropriately referencing material and ensuring confidentiality of the results. Human diversity issues of concern in research writing are eliminating stereotyping of certain groups, avoiding exclusive language, and disseminating results to subjects.

STUDY/EXERCISE QUESTIONS

1. Request sample grant applications from organizations in your city or state that fund research efforts related to social work. Share these in class and discuss their similarities and differences.

2. Select a social work journal article and critique it, using the structure of a research report presented in this chapter as a guide.

3. Select research articles from social work journals that contain tables or charts.
   a. Do they clearly illustrate the results of the research?
   b. What changes would you make to improve them?

REFERENCES

American Psychological Association (1994). *Publication manual of the American Psychological Association* (4th ed.). Washington, DC: Author.

Block, K. J., & Potthast, M. J. (1998). Girl scouts beyond bars: Facilitating parent-child contact in correctional settings. *Child Welfare, LXXVII* (5), 561–578.

Davis, L. V. (1986). A feminist approach to social work research. *Affilia, 1,* 32–47.

Greenberg, J. S. (1995). The other side of caring: Adult children with mental illness as supports to their mothers in later life. *Social Work, 40* (3), 414–423.

Guffey, M. E. (1997). Formats for the citation of electronic sources in business writing. *Business Communication Quarterly, 60* (1), 59.

Johnson, A. K. (1999). Working and nonworking women: Onset of homelessness within the context of their lives. *Affilia, 14* (1), 42–77.

Lopez, R. A. (1999). *Las Comadres* as a social support system. *Affilia, 14* (1), 24–41.

Loveland Cook, C. A., Selig, K. L., Wedge, B. J., Gohn-Baube, E. A. (1999). Access barriers and the use of prenatal care by low-income, inner-city women. *Social Work, 44* (2), 129–139.

Morawski, J. (1997). The science behind feminist research methods. *Journal of Social Issues, 53* (4), 667–682.

National Association of Social Workers. (1997). NASW Code of Ethics. *NASW News, 25,* 24–25.

North, C. S., & Smith, E. M. (1994). Comparison of white and nonwhite homeless men and women. *Social Work, 39* (6), 639–647.

Petersen, I., Magwaza, A. S., & Pillay, Y. G. (1996). The use of participatory research to facilitate a psychological rehabilitation programme for child survivors of violence in a South African community. *Social Work/ Maatskaplike Werk, 32* (1), 67–74.

Schwartz, A. Y., Gottesman, E. W., Perlmutte, F. D. (1988). Balckwell: A case study in feminist administration. *Administration in Social Work, 12* (2), 5–15.

Slonim-Nevo, V., Cwikel, J., Luski, H., Lankry, M., & Shraga, Y. (1995). Caregiver burden among three-generation immigrant families in Israel. *International Social Work, 38* (2), 191–204.

Szuchman, L., Thomlison, B. (2000). *Writing with style: APA style for social work.* Brooks/Cole Publishing.

Tracy, E. M., Whittaker, J. K., Pugh, A., Kapp, S. N., & Overstreet, E. J. (1994). Support networks of primary caregivers receiving family preservation services: An exploratory study. *Families in Society, 75* (8), 481–489.

Valentine, D. P., Edwards, S., Gohagan, D., Huff, M., Pereira, A., & Wilson, P. (1998). Preparing social work doctoral students for teaching: Report of a survey. *Journal of Social Work Education, 34* (2), 273–282.

Walzer, S. (1995) Transition into motherhood: Pregnant daughters' responses to their mothers. *Families in Society, 76* (10), 596–603.

Ziesemer, C., Marcoux, L., & Marwell, B. E. (1994). Homeless children: Are they different from other low-income children? *Social Work, 39* (6), 658–668.

Using Research Findings in Practice and Evaluating Research

With Patricia Sandau-Beckler, M.S.W.

One more stage of research needs to be discussed—the use and evaluation of the research findings. This step's equivalent in practice is both activating resources, creating alliances, and expanding opportunities (implementation), and recognizing issues and integrating gains (evaluation) (see Figure 15.1). As discussed in Chapter 2, practice is enhanced when social workers are producers and consumers of research.

Using the results of research in our practice necessitates evaluating the research itself. Conducting research is not a flawless endeavor, as we have seen throughout this text. An important step in the research process is critically assessing research results to identify their strengths and weaknesses. Remember, too, that although this chapter focuses on research findings that result from using science, remember from Chapter 1 that other sources of understanding can be used in practice: values, intuition, experience, and authority.

The two final tasks of evaluating the research and using the results in practice are linked. By first evaluating the research, you can assess the findings' applicability to your particular practice situation.

Both steps will be discussed in this chapter, along with the other topics listed here:

- using research findings in practice
- evaluating research
- the agency in the use and evaluation of research findings
- ethical issues in the use and evaluation of research findings
- human diversity issues in the use and evaluation of research findings

USING RESEARCH FINDINGS IN PRACTICE

Case Examples

We will consider five cases, each dealing with different client systems: individual, family, group, organization, and community.

- *Individual client system* Sue—an adolescent female who is a substance abuser
- *Family client system* The Kickingbird family—a Native American family in which an incident of a child's physical abuse has been reported
- *Group client system* Parents in community—a number of parents who have expressed concerns about their children who have attention deficit disorder
- *Organization client system* The Children's Center—an agency to plan and develop foster care services for children with AIDS
- *Community client system* STOP—a community task force formed to reduce teen suicide

For cases such as these, research findings can be used during each stage of the generalist social work process. A summary of the stages and the relevance of research findings for each stage follow.

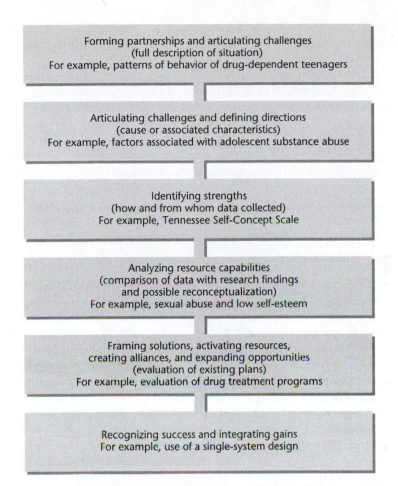

Figure 15.1   **Use of research findings in practice**

Forming partnerships.   The initial step in practice can be helped by consulting the literature and research on different models that can facilitate the forming of partnerships.

Articulating challenges.   Consulting the research, particularly that relating to human behavior; this will bring an understanding of the challenges and difficulties presented by the client system.

Defining directions.   Research may disclose some useful instruments to help define directions to help the client system.

Identifying strengths.   An increasing number of tools are being developed and tested that can help the social worker identify the strengths of the client system.

Analyzing resource capabilities.   Research can be invaluable in understanding and interpreting the information that has been gained throughout the work with the client system.

Framing solutions. The results of program evaluations and other research disclosing the efficacy of different interventions can be important sources of information at this stage of practice.

Activating resources, creating alliances, and expanding opportunities. The research can be consulted to give guidance as to the most effective way of implementing this stage.

Recognizing success and integrating gains. The research literature can be consulted for current information on how practice evaluations can be conducted.

Individual Client System

Client: Sue

Presenting concern: Dependence on drugs

Referral: Sue, a 15-year-old Hispanic adolescent, was referred to a drug treatment program for substance abuse at her local high school. She was suspended from school and cannot return until she completes treatment. At the treatment intake, the worker assessed Sue's drug use pattern and family relationships. A review of her drug use patterns indicated that she had started using drugs only in the past six months. Her use of drugs increased recently, and she admitted that she can not place limits on her behavior or reduce her preoccupation with drug use. She stated that she had many reasons to stop using them but worried that she would lose her friends.

Forming Partnerships

In building a relationship with Sue, the worker used an effective strategy called *Motivational Interviewing* (Miller & Rollnick, 1991). Prochaska, DeClemente, and Norcross (1992) developed the Transtheoretical Model of Change, a stages of change model that includes precontemplation, contemplation, preparation, action, and maintenance. Based on each stage, specific motivational skills are used to engage the individual. These skills are matched with the individual's stage of readiness for change (Prochaska et al., 1992). Skills used to engage and build a relationship with Sue included open-ended questions, reflective listening, affirming, summarizing, and eliciting self-motivational statements (Miller & Rollnick, 1991).

Articulating Challenges

In attempting to clarify the challenges with Sue, the worker used research to determine whether the patterns of behavior were consistent with a drug-dependent individual. The behaviors were found to be similar to those outlined by Jellinek

(1960), who developed a model of alcoholism as a disease that progresses according to certain symptoms and behaviors (Acoca & Barr, 1989). The worker also wondered about the relatively short duration of the substance-abusing behavior. She found that the average time from initiation to addiction is significantly shorter for women than men (National Institute of Alcohol Abuse and Alcoholism, 1990; Ellinwood, Smith, & Vaillant, 1966). She also found that clients make the decision to change based on assessing the pros and cons (Prochaska et al., 1992). Research using the Transtheoretical Model indicates that motivation to change can be increased by helping clients see that more risks exist than benefits if they continue their current substance abuse behavior (Prochaska et al., 1992). Consequently, this research began to provide some basis for understanding the challenges faced by Sue.

Defining Directions

The worker wondered what challenges might be associated with adolescent substance abuse; she found that sexual victimization affects about 75% of women in treatment for substance abuse (Yandow, 1989). Miller, Downs, and Testa (1993) reported rates of 87%. In addition, a study of female adolescents who entered drug treatment showed that sexual abuse victims used drugs more frequently than nonvictims did. Sexual abuse victims also appeared to begin drug use at an earlier age than their peers (Harrison, Hoffman, & Edwall, 1989). Research also suggests that addicted women under 30 are more likely than those 30 and over to have histories that include dropping out of school, unemployment, welfare dependence, and psychophysiological problems (Harrison & Belille, 1987). Substance abuse in women is also often associated with low self-esteem (Beckman, 1978; Beckman, Day, Bardsley, & Seeman, 1980; Cuskey, Berger, & Densen-Gerber, 1977; McLachlan, Walderman, Birchmore, & Marsden, 1979; Sandmaier, 1992). This research then helped the worker understand some of the underlying challenges associated with teen female drug abuse.

The research literature can be consulted to identify assessment tools that can assist in the collection of information on Sue's challenges. For example, the tool used by the Chemical Dependency Adolescent Assessment Project in St. Paul, Minnesota (Nakken, 1989), the Personal Experience Inventory Test (Winters & Henly, 1989), or the Tennessee Self-Concept Scale that has been used for female substance abusers (Wheeler, Biase, & Sullivan, 1986) may be appropriate in this case. Using standardized tools can help us compare clients to other groups of clients experiencing the same or similar issues; this provided a basis for the total assessment of Sue's substance abuse. The worker also found that the URICA, a tool developed by Velicer, DeClemente, Prochaska, and Brandenburg (1985) helps identify both the stage of change for the individual and the person's readiness for change.

From the worker's assessment, which included standardized assessment tools, it was found that Sue had been sexually abused by a neighbor and had low self-esteem. This supports the research findings cited earlier that found an association between substance abuse and sexual victimization and low self-esteem.

Using the stages of change model she concluded that while Sue recognized her worries about her drug use, she was ambivalent about stopping. She found that Sue was in a contemplation stage and was considering the pros and cons of taking action to stop her substance use. The analysis of this information thus laid the foundation for a solution-focused plan.

Identifying Strengths

The worker and Sue together identified individual, family, and community strengths available to Sue in her efforts to reach her dream of having a drug-free life. Using a well-researched brief solution-focused approach (Berg & Miller, 1992), the worker found that asking Sue what her life would be like without the drug in using the miracle question, yielded information that was helpful. This included Sue wanting closer relationships with her family and better school achievement. A family strengths inventory (New Mexico Family-Centered Assessment Tool, 1999) assisted her family in identifying strengths and resources to help Sue with her change process. Tools such as Strength Cards and Strength Cards for Kids (St. Luke's Innovative Resources, 1994) were used to stimulate the family to identify strengths that could help Sue meet her goals.

Analyzing Resource Capabilities

In order to mobilize and utilize the community strengths and resources, the worker conducted an assessment using an Eco-map (Hartman, 1978) to represent the strong and supportive resources available to Sue and her family as she addressed her challenges. A conference was held, coordinated by the worker, where community resources assisted Sue and her family to further explore their hopes and dreams together and to determine what resources and services could best assist Sue in her efforts to reduce her chemical use and gain a better relationship with her family.

Framing Solutions

Sue, her family, the worker, and relevant community resources developed a solution-focused plan. It included information about the risks of continuing the behavior and research-based strategies of motivational interviewing (Miller & Rollnick, 1991) to help Sue move toward taking action. When Sue made the decision to take action, she moved into a preparation stage of change, and the worker assisted her in developing a plan to attend an inpatient drug treatment program specifically for young women. The plan also addressed the challenge of sexual abuse. Research findings indicate that unless women receive treatment for the sexual abuse their risk of relapse increases (Young, 1990). Early research indicated that the success rate for the recovery of female substance abusers is only 20% to 30% (Bowman & Jellinek, 1974; Pattison, 1974), suggesting that traditional programs may need to be redesigned to meet the special needs of women (Doshan & Bursh, 1982; Reed, 1987). Root (1989) discussed how programs are not designed for women who experience posttraumatic stress. The cultural background of the client also needs to be considered. In a discussion of drug abuse treatment for Hispanics, Marin (1991) suggests that many drug treatment programs do not include culturally relevant material. These evaluations needed to be considered when a program was selected for Sue.

Activating Resources: Creating Alliances, and Expanding Opportunities

Sue and her worker addressed the ambivalence of her stopping her use of chemicals by exploring the benefits and costs of staying the same and the benefits and costs of changing her use pattern. Sue attended an outpatient treatment program in her school for substance abuse. It was specifically designed for adolescent Hispanic young women. Issues of self-esteem and sexual abuse were addressed through culturally responsive interventions. Sue and her parents attended family therapy together. The therapist used a brief solution-focused approach with the family focusing on dreams and hopes for the future. Ongoing conferences with Sue, her family, and her resource networks were held regularly to coordinate services and set the stage to monitor progress.

Recognizing Success and Integrating Gains

In this situation, a single-system design was well suited to assess the gains made by Sue and her family. Behaviors such as the reduction or abstinence of substance abuse, family time together, and improved school performance were monitored using a goal attainment scale (Bloom, Fisher, & Orme, 1995). Self-reports may compromise this approach as they depend on Sue, her peers, or her family's reliability for accurate information. However, Sue consistently began using fewer substances and agreed to utilize urine analysis when treatment was completed. The Tennessee Self-Concept scale as administered to Sue at the beginning of the

---

Family Client System

Client: The Kickingbird family

Presenting concern: Report of physical abuse of a child

Referral: The Kickingbird family was referred to a Native-American health and social services agency due to an incident of physical abuse. The family had physically abused their 12-year-old child for leaving the home and not caring for her three younger siblings while the parents were away. One sibling had played with matches and had started a fire in the kitchen. The father spanked the 12-year-old until she was black and blue. The incident was reported to the agency by school officials. The family is described as having few friends and little contact with their extended family.

case, every three months, and at closure. Significant changes occurred that Sue and her family celebrated. The URICA scale assessing the readiness for change showed Sue to be in the action stage at the time of case closing. The family was reminded that the next stage of maintenance relies heavily on a helping relationship (Prochaska et al., 1992). This information helped Sue and her family seek an ongoing group for substance-affected adolescents that used an AA approach for long-term support, thus giving Sue the necessary supports to maintain her sobriety.

Forming Partnerships

In establishing a relationship with the Kickingbird family, the worker sought to understand a cultural model that could assist in development of a healing process. Cross (1998) suggests that a Relational Model that defines four major forces or sets of factors (the context, the mind, the body, and the spirit) provides a framework for understanding the world view of the balance Native Americans feel. These forces become unbalanced when problems or symptoms occur. The effective helper is one who "gains understanding of the complex interdependent nature of life and learns how to use physical, psychological, contextual and spiritual forces to promote harmony (Cross, 1998, p. 147). This approach focuses on the resilience of the family and their strengths. It assists the family in achieving harmony and survival. The helper assists in providing "restorative balance" to the family. Other helpers who form a partnership with the family are the natural helpers that exist in the community.

Articulating Challenges

To identify the challenges in the Kickingbird family, the worker needed to first acknowledge that defining physical abuse of a child is sometimes difficult and can be affected by many factors. One such factor might be cultural variations in its definition. Existing research can be consulted to help understand these various definitions. Long (1986) suggested that physical abuse of children within their own families is "a culture-bound issue" (p. 131). Community standards are different for different cultural groups, and the definition of what constitutes abuse is defined within the context of the group. She also suggested that abuse must be assessed and treated within the cultural context.

To determine the factors associated with the abuse in this family, it was useful for the worker to examine the research that has been conducted on child abuse and neglect, particularly among Native Americans. A multitude of contributing factors have been identified. Mannes (1990b) reported:

> According to the Milwaukee Indian Health Board, Inc. . . . some of the more general problems that Indian families confront are: (1) perpetuating cycles of violence, (2) social isolation, (3) economic deprivation, (4) poor child-rearing skills, (5) personal frustration, (6) guilt, (7) emotional trauma, (8) marital problems, (9) too many children, (10) rigid sex roles, (11) drug and alcohol abuse and consumption, (12) psychoses, and (13) poor health. (p. 11)

These factors are, in fact, similar to the patterns of behavior associated with abuse outlined by the National Institute of Mental Health (Gelles, 1987). Research on the relationship between social supports and child abuse suggests a relationship between parental isolation and physical abuse (Chan, 1994; Corse, Schmid, & Trickett, 1990; Gaudin & Pollaine, 1983). This relationship is more strongly linked in the area of neglect (Seagull, 1988). These studies have not been conducted with Native American families, however.

Defining Directions

The worker selected a risk assessment tool to help determine the areas of family strength and to collect information on the family's service needs. In this way, the worker was able to consistently document the necessary information for the analysis. Risk assessment tools have been developed to assess family risk factors. The Washington Risk Assessment (English, 1989), the Family Risk scales (Magura & Moses, 1986), and the New Mexico Structured Decision Making Tool (Meyers, 1999) are three examples. The Family Risk scales consist of 26 items designed to measure a child's risk for entry into foster care, including child-related, parent-related, and economic risk factors. Other items covered are living conditions, family residence, social support, parental health (including mental health), use of physical punishment, use of verbal discipline, sexual abuse of child, child's health, and school adjustment. The Family Risk scales may need to be used in conjunction with other assessment tools (Fraser, 1990). The New Mexico Structured Decision Making Tool assesses the levels of risk for family members and is used to determine the level of need for services. An advantage of this structured decision making tool is that it has been validated for an area of the country that provides services to Native American families. Many instruments lack complete documentation of their reliability and validity, especially with specific population groups; thus, care is recommended when selecting instruments (Rzepnicki, Schuerman, & Littel, 1991).

In order to balance the information on the family, the worker supplemented the risk assessment tool with a newly developed strengths assessment tool, which is part of the New Mexico Family Centered Assessment Tool (1999). This tool, however, needs to be used with care because it is currently in the process of validation. This research process will include Native American families of the Southwest. The diversity and variation within Native American cultures must also be taken into account for this tool to be effective. Preliminary results suggest that the family strengths inventory combined with the strengths approach of the family preservation and family support projects are helpful for Native American families (Sandau-Beckler, 1999). A social network tool was also selected to assess the family's resources and support systems (Tracy & Whittaker, 1990). Qualitative interviews with Native American families suggest that the tool assisted them in recognizing resources (Sandau-Beckler, 1999).

Using the Relational Model, the four major forces of context, mind, body, and spirit are to be brought into balance (Cross, 1998). Figure 15.2 shows examples of each of the areas.

CONTEXT
    Family
    Culture
    Work
    Community
    History
    Climate / weather

MIND
    Intellect
    Emotion
    Memory
    Judgment
    Experience

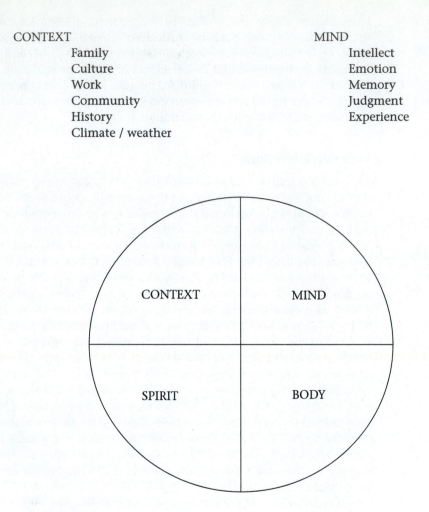

SPIRIT
    Spiritual practices / teach-ings
    Dreams / symbols / stories
    Gifts / intuition
    Grace / protecting forces
    Negative forces

BODY
    Chemistry
    Genetics
    Nutrition
    Substance use / abuse
    Age
    Conditioin

Figure 15.2

The assessment of these areas may be extremely effective in understanding how the forces may be brought back into balance. The research of this model and its effectiveness for assessing Native American families is a challenge to our traditional ways of conducting research. Participatory approaches to help the family and community study the effectiveness of this model may provide opportunities for us to better understand the process of change and design culturally responsive services.

Identifying Strengths

The strengths approach to assessing Native American families relies heavily on looking for and using the characteristics and resources that can support the balance and harmony in relationships. The family and community identify natural helpers and healers from the community that can help with the process of regaining balance (Cross, 1998). Clan systems, elders, and the interrelationships with extended family are some sources of strengths than can be identified. The willingness to enhance these connections for this family was an important strength. The results of the family strengths inventory (New Mexico Family Centered Assessment Tool, 1999) showed that the family had many strengths. The results of the social support network map (Tracy & Whittaker, 1990) indicated that they had good friends and some extended family that they were underutilizing and that the family recognized their potential for support.

Analyzing Resource Capabilities

Existing research on the current needs of high-risk Native American families reviewed by the worker identified Native American families' difficulties in obtaining counseling and transportation to obtain services (English, 1989). Using this information, the worker paid attention to those elements of the risk assessment tool that identified these particular needs. Both of these needs were clearly necessary for the Kickingbird family. The family strengths inventory identified such strengths as the family members' commitment to one another and the beliefs and traditions that connected them. The social network map helped the family and the worker identify extended family support that previously had not been seen as a resource. Knowing that a natural healer in the community would assist the family in grieving and expressing sorrow about the abuse was also helpful to the family in restoring their balance.

Framing Solutions

The family and the worker developed a solution-focused plan for the delivery of in-home family preservation services that would build on the family's strengths. This type of program was designed for families whose children are at imminent or high risk for foster placement. Research carried out on home-based programs indicates an average of 79% effectiveness in families staying together (Nelson,

Landsman, & Deutelbaum, 1990). Barth and Berry (1987) and Magura (1981) stated that evaluations of family preservation services programs concluded that these have only limited success. These tentative findings, however, are partly due to the lack of a precise operationalization of *imminent risk* for out-of-home placement (Stein & Rzepnicki, 1983; Tracy, 1992; Wells & Biegel, 1992). Workers who determine what imminent risk is may be motivated by a variety of influences, such as cost cuts, program waiting lists, worker relationships with the family preservation services program, or worker caseload size. Another problem with evaluating the findings from family preservation programs is the lack of adequate control groups in many of the studies. This makes it difficult to conclude whether the program or some other factor is responsible for outcomes (Rossi, 1992; Wells & Biegel, 1992). Random assignment of cases to different groups and services is the best way of achieving group equivalency and increases the internal and external validity of the findings (Rzepnicki et al., 1991). More recently, a meta-analysis of the effect size in the research results of eight quasi-experimental and experimental designs found a statistically significant outcome representing more positive results in the family preservation program evaluations (Blyth, Salley, & Jayaratne, 1994). None of the programs evaluated was, however, focused on evaluating family preservation services with the Native American population. While seen as a potentially culturally sensitive response, programs designated specifically for Native American families may also vary in their effectiveness (Mannes, 1990a; Mannes, 1993; & Tafoya, 1990). By recognizing these limitations in the family preservation research findings in framing the solutions, the worker may remain flexible to other service options if this one is unsuccessful.

Understanding the tentative nature of the findings from the evaluation of family preservation services, the worker considered a short-term intensive in-home program to be the least restrictive for this family. The plan also included culturally specific parenting skills based on the family's beliefs and traditions as well as extensive work with the Kickingbirds' extended family to increase contact and support for the Kickingbirds. Natural healers from the community also assisted the family in their "restorative" process of gaining balance.

Activating Resources, Creating Alliances, and Expanding Opportunities

A family group conference was used by the worker and the family to augment the in-home services by bringing together the family and their resources to build a family plan. The family group conference approach started with Maori families in New Zealand has been demonstrated to be more effective in plan compliance than services provided without the benefit of such a meeting (Merkel-Holguin, 1998). Used in this country for the past several years, culturally responsive adaptations have been conducted with tribes in the Northwest (Vance & Elofson, 1998). Although the adaptations are made with each specific tribe, this approach was seen as supporting the process of restoring balance for the Kickingbird family. Culturally responsive methods, such as a traditional prayer and a ritual that included song and drumming, opened and closed the meeting. The Kickingbird family and their resource systems were able to develop a solution-focused plan that included in-home services while also using the natural community and family helpers. Special stories were utilized to help discuss the abuse and challenges facing the family.

Recognizing Success and Integrating Gains

While generalizability is low from single-system studies, as seen in the previous case, the use of a single-system design was appropriate here. The worker chose from a variety of single-system designs from Alter and Evens (1990) but settled on one that was descriptive. Although the worker selected the least rigorous design to enable the worker and family to monitor progress, more rigorous designs—including withdrawal and multiple baselines designs—allowed the worker to assess which aspects of services or techniques are most beneficial. However, ethical issues may be encountered with withdrawal of services in high-risk child-abuse situations (Rzepnicki et al., 1991). Goal attainment scaling was used to address the father's increased use of appropriate discipline. Increases in communication with elders regarding traditional responses to children's misbehavior were measured. Scales from the Multi-Problem Screening Inventory (Hudson, 1990) were used to demonstrate changes in parental attitudes. A pretest and posttest using the North Carolina Family Assessment Tool (Kirk, Reed, & Lin, 1996) were also used for evaluating overall changes in the family. The Relative and Friend Support Index was used to assess the changes in social support of the family (McCubbin & Thompson, 1987). As stated by Cross (1998), measurement of balance provides challenges when using a nonlinear, relational framework for change.

Group Client System

Client: Parents in a community

Presenting concern: Concern with children who have attention deficit hyperactivity disorder (ADHD)

Referral: A group of parents from a school district are concerned about services and support for families of children with attention deficit hyperactivity disorder (ADHD). They have asked the school social worker to help them develop a plan to meet their children's needs.

Forming Partnerships

When forming partnerships with a group of parents, several models could be explored. The National Institute of Mental Health, Children and Adolescent Service System Program (CASSP) has defined Child and Adolescent Service System Program values and core principles for interacting with families whose children have mental health issues (Stroul & Friedman, 1994). These are a blueprint for entering partnerships with parents with a spirit of cooperation and collaboration. Research findings indicate that these qualities in a relationship with parents from this population reduce negative affect and foster feelings of hope and positive expectations that are highly correlated with positive outcomes (Greenberg & Pinsof, 1986). Dedmon (1997) suggests that parents are excellent sources of information about their children and are in the best position to explain to the extended family, the school, and the wider public the child's behavior and the issues they experience. Frequently others see the behavior as a result of poor discipline and do not understand the neurobiological issues involved.

Articulating Challenges

The first step for the worker was to clarify the challenge and assess its magnitude. Research findings can be an important resource for problem definition. The fourth edition of *Diagnostic and Statistic Manual of Mental Disorders* (DSM-IV) is a reference manual that lists definitions and research findings on psychological disorders (American Psychiatric Association, 1994). Although the DSM can be a useful resource, workers must acknowledge the potentially negative effects experienced by clients who are so labeled. According to the DSM criteria, ADHD refers to a condition in which developmentally inappropriate degrees of inattention, impulsiveness, and hyperactivity are evident. There symptoms must last over a six-month time period and occur in two or more settings (American Psychiatric Association, 1994). The DSM-IV estimates that 3% to 5% of children have ADHD; other estimates have ranged up to 14.3% and 20% (Gordon & Asher, 1994; Schachar, Rutter, & Smith, 1981). Shapiro and Garfinkel (1986) screened an elementary school population (315 children) and found that 8.9% of the children qualified for a diagnosis of attention deficit disorder or conduct disorder. The DSM-IV suggested ADHD occurs more frequently if a first-degree family member has ADHD or other psychiatric challenges such as mood and anxiety disorders, learning disorders, substance abuse-related disorders, and emotional and personality disorders (American Psychiatric Association, 1994; Frick, Lahey, Christ, Lobber, & Green, 1991; Seidman, Biederman, & Faraone, 1995).

The worker needed to look at the current research to identify the causes of this problem and its associated characteristics. Chess and Thomas (1984) view behavior disorders as a result of difficulty of fit between the capacities of the child and environmental pressures. Others argue for the biological underpinnings of ADHD (Brickman et al., 1985; Dubey, 1976; Rapport & Ferguson, 1981; Tramontana & Sherrets, 1985). Studies on the genetic correlations of ADHD indicate that children have high incidence of ADHD if a family member of either gender is also diagnosed with ADHD (Biediman et al., 1992). In twin studies, in 79% of cases in which one identical twin was diagnosed with ADHD the other was also diagnosed with ADHD. In studies of fraternal twins, if one was diagnosed with ADHD, the other was also diagnosed at a rate of 32%, a rate ten times more than the general population (Gillis, Gilger, Pennington, & Defries, 1992).

Other studies look at the associated characteristics and the effects on the family. In one study, Green (1990) noted that the style of interaction and communication in ADHD families is characterized by the following: lack of clear and consistent rules for rewards and punishment; disciplinary responses based on parental moods; attempts to resolve arguments through increased threats and counterthreats; communication characterized by intensity of physical action and sound, such as gestures and yelling instead of words and logic; compliance demanded through the use of force; and finally, disruption of the orderly flow of ideas in communication due to frequent and sudden topic changes. The worker needed to be cautious about adopting this view of ADHD as a family problem, however, because it can reinforce feelings of guilt and inadequacy by the parents and may harm children by stressing a treatment approach that is ineffective unless balanced with other treatments (Johnson, 1988). The worker needed to be prepared to assist parents who may have unrecognized ADHD and other psychiatric disorders (Kaplan & Shachter, 1991). Multisystemic Family Treatment, a highly successful ecological approach to treating adolescents with an emphasis on working in both the school and the home environment that is built on the CASSP principles, has been shown to be effective with this population (Henggeler et al., 1998; Henggeler et al., 1994; Henggeler et al., 1997).

Defining Directions

Several instruments may be appropriate for obtaining information about children with ADHD. Tools for assessing children who show disruptive behavior include interviews with parents; reports from schools and community agencies; medical history and physical examination; neurological examination; psychological testing; allergy evaluation; laboratory studies; interviews with and observation of the child; behavior rating scales completed by parents, teachers, and significant others in the child's life; and self-report scales (Shekim, 1986). The Connors Scales are often used for assessing hyperactivity and attention deficit disorders (Benton & Sines, 1985; Connors, 1985). The Self-Report Delinquency Scale (Elliott & Ageton, 1980), the Child Behavior Checklist (Achenback, 1991; Curtiss et al., 1983) and the Parent Daily Report (Patterson, Chamberlain, & Reid, 1982) also may be useful in this case.

Identifying Strengths

While little research focusing on formal strength-based inventories for assessing groups has been conducted, the traditional elements of groups lend themselves well to assessing the group's strengths. Group goals, group cohesion, leadership, membership, purpose, recruitment, and group dynamics were used to identify the potential strengths of the group's support of this project. Parent members of this group were highly motivated to develop a program that was responsive to their needs and the needs of others with similar experiences. Other strengths identified were the parent's recognition of their current limitations in child management skills and their forthright ability to express their need for assistance.

Analyzing Resource Capabilities

The parent members organizing this project with the school system had both internal and external resources that were of assistance. Examples of the internal resources were members who had an ability to develop a vision of the group's needs and run the group meetings. Other members had talents and skills such as graphic design and computer skills to design media presentations and flyers for the group. Other members were good at establishing telephone trees to recruit and remind people of the group meetings. The external resources from the school were also mobilized for this project. Meeting space; trained teachers and social workers with expertise in working with children with ADHD; telephones, computers, overheads, VCRs and copying machines; and supportive administration were some of the identified resources. The state department of education also made a commitment to provide funding for transportation, child care, speaker fees, and refreshments for the group.

Framing Solutions

The information that the worker gathered for this case can be compared with existing research findings. Between 1960 and 1975, 2,000 articles were published on children with hyperactivity or minimal brain dysfunction. When the nomenclature was reviewed and ADHD became identified, 7,000 more articles were published (Weiss, 1985). However, the validity of the psychological testing used in many of these research articles is complicated by the possibility of racial and ethnic bias (Cronbach, 1975). These issues need to be considered when comparing findings from individual cases to the findings in the literature.

While several strategies could have been considered, the group of parents requested immediate assistance with learning more skills for managing their children's behaviors at home. Effective reinforcement, home-token economy systems, and alternatives to behavior management can be of help to parents (DuPaul & Stoner, 1994). Therefore, a parent support group offering eight sessions of child management skills was chosen by the parent's group. In a study in one state, parents requested concrete management skills training from professionals (New Mexico Children's Services Subcommittee, 1991).

Activating Resources, Creating Alliances, and Expanding Opportunities

The parents decided to explore a relationship for support from a state organization associated with the Federation for Families for Children's Mental Health. Groups like these have been developed to monitor schools, boards of education, and state agencies to ensure that handicapped children receive services (Johnson, 1988). As a group, parents "can organize and exert political pressure, and they can provide parents with the often desperately needed support that comes through finding out that many have similar problems and that such problems do not always have to be defined in terms of the failure of individual parents and individual children" (Johnson, 1988, p. 354). Parents can provide support, assistance in problem solving, access to useful information, and solutions to social isolation problems (Johnson, 1988). Although the effectiveness of these particular groups for parents has recently been established through only limited research, extensive literature is available on the use of support groups in general (Bennett, DeLuca, & Allen, 1996; Pisterman et al., 1989; Pollard, War, & Barkley, 1983; Toseland & Rivas, 1984). This relationship provided useful support from other parents who have already navigated through the service systems.

Recognizing Success and Integrating Gains

The support group for parents was evaluated with parent satisfaction inventories that they developed using participatory methods. They defined the questions they were interested in evaluating. These included topic relevance, skill acquisition, amounts of group support, and presentation styles. A variety of approaches were used, including reviewing existing inventories that were modified to meet the needs of this particular group and video taping use of the skills (Toseland & Rivas, 1984). Focus groups were held with families to discuss the group's outcomes and on how to modify future groups to enhance their effectiveness.

Organization Client System

Client: The Children's Center

Presenting concern: Need for foster parents for families in which the mother is HIV-infected and some of the children may also be HIV-infected.

Referral: The Children's Center, in a large urban area, has had continued demand for foster care services for HIV-infected babies and their siblings. Large numbers of children have needs for permanency due to their mothers' HIV status. While the rate of HIV-infected women is increasing, the recent drops in perinatal transmission, which has resulted from new medication and HIV testing during pregnancy, has resulted in new considerations for the needs of these families, including support and care for the whole family not only the children. The agency is asking a group of workers, foster parents, and families in which a member is HIV infected to develop strategies for permanency that includes foster care recruitment to support these families.

Forming Partnerships

The Children's Center designed a team of professionals, foster parents, and HIV-infected mothers who are or have received services from the child welfare services program to discuss the needs of families in which one or more members are HIV infected. Permanency for these children and support to the family was defined as the goal of the foster care recruitment project.

Articulating Challenges

According to statistics from the Centers for Disease Control (CDC) in Atlanta, the number of children with HIV infection rapidly increased until 1992 and has been decreasing since that time (Lindergren et al., 1999). Originally, health officials estimated that 80,000 children would be orphaned as a result of AIDS by the year 2000 (Michaels & Levine, 1992), with 25% to 35% of these children requiring substitute care (National Adoption Information Clearinghouse, 1989). "Ninety percent of children with AIDS acquire the infection in the womb from infected mothers who are intravenous drug users or the sexual partners of intravenous drug users" (Child Welfare League of America, 1988, p. 1). The CDC (1992) confirmed similar rates of 85%. Women infected with HIV have a 15% to 40% chance of giving birth to an infected baby or transmitting HIV through breast feeding (Brown, 1990; Husson, Comeau, & Hoff, 1990; Johnson et al., 1989; Mofenson, 1994; Oxtoby, 1994). The discovery of new drugs such as zidovudine have decreased this probability to 8.3% (Connors et al., 1994). Recent changes indicated that there was a 67% decline in perinatal AIDS cases between 1992 and 1997 (Lindergren et al., 1999). HIV testing during pregnancy increased the use of the drug zidovudine from 7% to 91%, drastically reducing the transmission rates (Lindergren et al., 1999). Current estimates of children reported to have AIDS are 7,472, which is markedly smaller than early estimates (*MMWR*, 1996).

Planning foster programs and selecting culturally responsive homes and appropriate services for HIV-infected babies require an understanding of why many of these children are in need of foster care. In New York City, 80% of the infants with AIDS are born of drug-using parents, and 42% are African American and Hispanic. Many of these families live in poverty, and their family systems are chaotic. Support is often unavailable since other family members are not knowledgeable about AIDS (Rowe & Ryan, 1987). Because of this background these children are at high risk for neglect or abuse. There is also the need for permanency as parents may not be able to provide long-term stability. Research findings from interviews with HIV-infected mothers indicated high rates of mother-child separations due to such issues as drug rehabilitation, hospitalizations, or foster care placement (Tompkins, Henker, Whalen, Axelrod, & Comer, 1999). Mothers who were interviewed indicated that their primary concerns were disclosing to their children their HIV status and permanency planning (Tompkins et al., 1999). Foster parents may be a resource to assist in the permanency process.

The worker reviewed a study by Groze, McMillen, & Haines-Simeon (1993) that suggested that those foster parents who chose to provide foster care for HIV-infected children were highly motivated because they had work-related experiences with HIV-infected children. They also scored higher (38%) in the belief that they "had something to offer children" compared to the control groups (20%). They also had higher rates of willingness to again provide care for the foster care system (95%) compared to the control groups (87%). Foster parents have many challenges to face as they prepare to provide care. One challenge is knowing the extensive biopsychosocial needs of these children and their parents and siblings (Landry & Smith, 1998; Ingram & Hutchinson, 1999).

Defining Directions

In this case a useful initial strategy would be to assess the knowledge of AIDS by foster parents. This would assist in the development of an effective recruitment program. The Child Welfare League of America has a tool that assesses knowledge and attitudes toward HIV and AIDS (Annin, 1990). Beckler (1990) adapted this tool for use by foster parents. The agency's survey of foster and potential foster parents indicated that the number of families willing to provide care for HIV-infected children was low. In addition, families' knowledge of the transmission and symptoms of HIV and AIDS was limited. These data corresponded to the research findings cited earlier. The foster families also indicated the need for increased financial assistance for medical costs, transportation, education on hygiene and safety, respite care, and counseling for the stress resulting from caring for such children (Lowenthal, 1997; New Jersey Department of Human Services, 1989).

Identifying Strengths

The strengths of the group were used in identifying strategies for foster parent recruitment. The group's strength was their ability to represent many of the necessary groups who understand the needs for permanency for these children and what were required supports for the family. Another strength of the agency was its recognition of the need and its willingness to take action. A substantive strength was that the agency was given a $10,000 contribution from a local citizens group to support the recruitment effort. The group used a network map to illustrate the connections of a typical HIV parent and her children, who included an HIV-infected child. Using this case approach, they designed the ideal supports for permanency and effective services. This visioning process opened up new avenues for creative connections and service supports within their community.

Analyzing Resource Capabilities

The group did an assessment of the resources for each of the systems involved in the family's life to see what supports could assist with permanency. When assessing the supports in the biological and caregiver support systems, they drew on research on the impact of HIV on the family system (Lesar & Maldonado, 1997). They discovered that the psychological burden of the illness was related to the child's HIV status. There were also financial, social, and family burdens. If the caregiver was HIV infected, the psychological burden was even greater (Lesar & Maldonado, 1997). The group also assessed the resources to support foster parents in the process of providing support for HIV mothers and their children. Model programs exist that use intensive care management for biological parents, recruitment of foster-adoptive parents, and training of foster parents (Ford & Kroll, 1990). Consulting these programs and reviewing other new program innovations such as foster care for the whole family were helpful in assessing their ability to recruit and train foster parents. The flexibility of the Children's Center to entertain a new innovative approach was also seen as an asset.

Framing Solutions

In addition, other model programs—such as the New Jersey Special Home Services Provider Program, which supplies financial support, intensive training, counseling, and in-home support—can give ideas for foster parent recruitment (New Jersey Department of Human Services, 1989). Finally, it has been suggested that the recruitment program should include an educational component in addition to attitude and skills training in caring for HIV-infected children and in providing support to HIV-infected mothers and siblings (Anderson, 1990). This education seems particularly appropriate with the families in this community whose knowledge of HIV and AIDs is limited. New developments in how to assist these families by offering a range of services, from support and respite foster care to fully assisting the mothers with their children's care in the foster home, was explored. Much of the information for the educational component can be drawn from existing research—for example, information on the symptoms of AIDS, such as chronic diarrhea, fatigue, and weight loss, has been the subject of much research (Landry & Smith, 1998; Lockhard & Wodarski, 1989; Oleske, 1987; Rogers, 1985, 1987a, 1987b; Scott, 1987; Shannon & Animann, 1985). The recruitment plan recommendations for this agency largely involved efforts to recruit families in the helping professions that would have experiences with HIV-infected children, including nurses, hospital personnel, clergy, and professional and paraprofessional caregivers. The second strategy was a public media campaign that focused on advertising for foster parents or potential foster parents who felt they had resources to offer both the children and their parents.

Activating Resources, Creating Alliances, and Expanding Opportunities

The recruitment plan developed by the group included recruitment of helping professionals as potential foster parents and service providers. The group obtained assistance from the social work, nursing, and psychology licensing boards to provide workers from these professions information on the needs of this population. Individual letters and stories in professional newsletters were two strategies that were used. The group also partnered with the foster parent organization to ask for recommendations from foster parents for helpers who they felt were sensitive to the needs of clients with HIV. Parents who were receiving services for HIV were also asked to help identify possible candidates.

The group members working on the media campaign enlisted the help of the local AD Council, who helped them develop a low-cost media campaign that was supplemented/funded in part by the AD Council. A local celebrity volunteered time to make educational commercials and to speak at meetings about the needs for parents to support these families.

Recognizing Success and Integrating Gains

Program evaluation techniques were used to evaluate the effectiveness of the training and recruitment program. Models such as those used by Groze, McMillen, and Haines-Simeon (1993) were reviewed. Measures that included knowledge and attitude inventories for the foster parents, a count of the number of HIV-infected children actually placed, and continued commitment to provide foster care for HIV-infected children and to support families were used to evaluate the program. Focus groups of foster parents, HIV-infected mothers, and workers were conducted to determine the impact of the recruitment and the training for the foster parents. This included a follow-up evaluation of the project's success in assisting families. The qualitative interviews, using research strategies based on phenomenology, captured the experiences of both biological and foster families in their efforts to provide permanency for children.

Community Client System

Client: STOP, a community task force

Presenting concern: Teen suicide in a community

Referral: A task force has been developed in a rural community after three suicides were committed in three months. Community leaders, school officials, and interested community members have joined together to develop a comprehensive community plan for assisting their youth.

Forming Partnerships

A task force was developed with concerned parties from the schools, community agencies and groups, and individual interested members in the community. Some parents whose children had attempted or committed suicide and children who had made attempts were invited to participate or serve as spokespersons to the group as they defined the challenges facing them in their efforts to reduce teen suicide in their community.

Articulating Challenges

An overview of the challenges of teen suicide is available in the research findings. The second leading cause of death for 15- to 24-year-olds is suicide (Kerne, Eick, Bechtold, & Manson, 1996). In an interview, Garfinkel stated that in the past 30 years the number of childhood suicides has increased by 300%, and the number of suicide attempts has increased by 350% to 700% (Frymier, 1988). The scope of the problem suggested by Hepworth, Farley, and Griffiths (1986) is that half a million young people attempt suicide each year and of that number approximately 5,000 succeed. Keane and colleagues (1996) report 6% to 8% of American adolescents attempt suicide.

Much research has investigated the causes of suicide and many provide useful information for this case. Factors such as chronic adjustment problems, dislocation, the stress associated with adolescence, and a recent traumatic event seem to interact and contribute to adolescent suicide. Alcohol is a further factor. Grueling and DeBlassie (1980) found that more than 50% of teenagers who had committed suicide had a history of moderate to severe drinking. Prosser and Mc-Ardele (1966) reported that suicide, depression, and substance abuse are increasingly connected. Jones (1997) indicated that the role of drugs and alcohol in suicide attempts is significant. Garfinkel stated that rural youth kill themselves at a higher rate than do urban youth (Frymier, 1988). More recent studies have not found statistically significant differences between rural and urban populations but have suggested further longitudinal studies (Albers & Evans, 1994).

Defining Directions

The community task force to prevent teen suicide would need to gather local statistics on the incidence of suicide in their community. In addition, assessment instruments for individuals, such as the Beck's Depression Inventory, the Suicide Intent Scale, and the Children's Depression Inventory can measure depression and suicidal ideas (Beck et al., 1961; Teri, 1982; Pierce, 1977, 1981; Kovacs, 1980–1981). More recent tools developed, including the Measure of Adolescent Potential for Suicide (MAPS) (Eggert, Thompson, & Herting, 1994) and the Suicidal Ideation Questionnaire (Keane et al., 1996), offer opportunities to assess risk factors. The ability of these instruments to accurately measure depression must be assessed for members of diverse cultural groups. Allen-Meares (1987) noted that the items in these particular instruments were derived from white and African-American psychiatric patients between the ages of 15 and 44. More research is needed with diverse cultural groups.

The community group also assessed factors associated with suicidal behavior. Reviewing the research, they found factors such as depression, substance abuse, offending behavior (Presser & McArdle, 1996), anger expression, socially prescribed perfectionism (Rigby & Slee, 1999), adolescent problem-solving deficits (Lester, 1998), a history of physical or sexual abuse, poor family communication, loss of caregiver, and psychopathology in first-degree relatives (Wagner, 1997) to be associated with adolescent suicidal behavior.

Identifying Strengths

When the group met to discuss factors leading to suicide, it decided to look at protective factors—individual, family, and community—that also supported resilience in adolescents. Using an ecological framework for the analysis of protective factors and risk whose methods have been described by Nash and Fraser

(1997), the community sought to assess the protective factors that their community had in place to reduce the risk factors for teen suicide. The strengths found included trained teachers and an early intervention system for substance abuse that could easily be expanded to the area of suicide.

Analyzing Resource Capabilities

The community determined the extent of the risk factors by conducting a survey of community teens. The survey of community teens indicated high rates of depression. These rates were then compared to the literature. Garfinkel stated that between 6% and 8% of junior and senior high school students have been severely or profoundly depressed (Frymier, 1988). The males were found to consider suicide more indirectly and were more likely to use drugs as a coping mechanism. These findings were comparable to those of Fomboone (1998) and Harlow, Newcomb, and Bentler (1986). The survey results also indicated that most students wanted to learn more about suicide. This was also consistent with the research findings completed with 25,000 high school students (Carson, 1981; Elkind, 1984a, 1984b; Smith, 1976). The community also used a community asset inventory (Carson, 1981; Kretzmann & McNight, 1993) to look at what available community assets could assist in the implementation of a community plan.

Framing solutions

The high rates of suicidal thinking and drug abuse indicated in the survey led the community task force to choose educational strategies. One successful program educated teens to monitor their own depression and helped them to identify coping styles and mechanisms (Frymier, 1988). Peer helpers are resources that can be used in this process. Seventy-five percent of teenagers who are severely depressed or suicidal turn to peers for help, compared to 18% who turn to parents and only 7% who choose to see a mental health professional (Frymier, 1988). Another successful program (Cliffone, 1993) demonstrated shifts in attitudes toward more positive attitudes about suicide prevention, such as seeing suicidal thinking as treatable. Students learned to prepare themselves to assist others by encouraging them to obtain help from professionals. Informational sessions for parents on warning signs, and current research findings on protective factors, also were conducted for parents.

Activating Resources, Creating Alliances, and Expanding Opportunities

Town meetings were designed to bring the public and private sector leaders and community members together to assist in the recognition and awareness of the problem. Discussions were held on how to use the natural community network and resources to heighten awareness and identify students at risk. The school system and several agencies designed to support families expanded the current networks for substance abuse identification to include suicide potential. Additional workshops for teachers, professionals, parents, and interested community resources were held to build a comprehensive system of care.

Recognizing Success and Integrating Gains

The reduction of teen suicide in this community was evaluated through a number of methods including the use of mental health statistics on children at risk for suicide; evaluation of students using the Measure of Adolescent Potential for Suicide (MAPS); evaluation of students' level of understanding of stress symptoms and safety issues, including supporting other students in obtaining professional assistance; and parental and school personnel recognition of the signs of suicide risk. Evaluation of students seeking assistance and referred by peers and others to the school's network for students at risk also helped the community understand the results of intervention methods. Participating evaluations in community workshops and action plans on the support of the community's protective factors also measured increased awareness and supports reducing teen risk of suicide.

LIMITING CONDITIONS

We may find that the extent and manner in which we use research findings depends on a number of factors, many of which are beyond our control. Mullen (1988) referred to four of these limiting conditions: tradition, philosophy, technological skills, and quality of information.

Traditionally, social workers have not relied on information drawn from research, but rather from theory and experience. Incorporating research into practice still seems alien to many social workers. Philosophically, research may seem to be dramatically opposed to the practice of social work. Research can be viewed as mechanistic and devoid of a humanitarian perspective. As research methods in social work become more sophisticated in their ability to tap the intricacies of human interactions, however, this perceived gap between social work practice and social work research will narrow.

Technological skills are another limiting condition. Many social workers simply do not understand the complexities of research methods. This problem will gradually lessen as graduates of social work programs are required by the Council on Social Work Education (CSWE) to have completed at least one course in social work research methods. The knowledge and skills discussed in this text provide more than enough information for the social worker to use research in practice.

The limitation on quality of information refers to the social work research findings themselves. There are both problems with existing research and great gaps in the research literature. Again though, we can optimistically assume that as social workers become more knowledgeable about research through the incorporation of research content into the social work curriculum, so the body of research literature will gradually expand. In the interim, research findings need to be incorporated as much as possible into practice. The limitation of poor quality research is addressed in the next section, in which we discuss how to evaluate research information.

EVALUATING RESEARCH

Although the evaluation of research is discussed here as a separate step in the research process, as is true of steps in the practice process, this step can merge or overlap with other research stages—particularly the step of evaluating the intervention. It is not only the findings per se that are of interest, but also the quality of the research. No research study is completely flawless. One of the researcher's responsibilities in writing up the results of the study is to include a limitations section, to guide readers in their assessment of the research. Often, however, the limitations section is incomplete. Identifying all the limitations in a research study is critical if you are to effectively use research findings in social work practice.

Use the guide in Figure 15.3 to help you evaluate research studies.

THE AGENCY IN THE USE AND EVALUATION OF RESEARCH FINDINGS

To be responsible generalist practitioners we need to take research seriously; this includes using and evaluating research findings. Although there is no denying that time is a factor in agencies, the challenge is to carry out research within your time constraints. Here are some guidelines:

1. Use computer searches as much as possible to locate research on specific topics. You can also use the Internet to identify listservs relevant to your topic, and of course the World Wide Web can yield some good sources. As noted earlier, the Web also contains some not so good sources, so be selective in your search.

2. Be specific in identifying relevant research. There is an enormous amount out there. For example, if you are researching the second case in this chapter (the Kickingbird family), don't look for everything on child abuse, but specifically for physical abuse in Native American families. Being specific will considerably limit the amount of literature you need to review. If you come up with nothing in the specific area, broaden your search.

3. List only those findings that are relevant to the practice issues. Be concise. Next, comment on the quality of the evidence. At this point you can refer to the frameworks described earlier. Don't be too compulsive in their use, though; simply note some of the major problems with the research.

A. Statement of the Situation
1. What is the situation under study?
2. Is the situation clearly stated, identified, and understandable?
3. Is the importance of the situation clearly presented?
4. Is the research question or hypothesis clearly stated?

B. Research Approach
1. Is the research strategy/approach clearly presented?

C. Literature Review
1. Does the literature review include a thorough coverage of the problem?
2. Are the findings and their sources clearly referenced?
3. Does the literature review use current references? If older references are used, are they important links to the history of the problem?
4. Does the literature review provide information on how concepts should be defined and measured?

D. Variables
1. When applicable, are the dependent and independent variables clearly identified?
2. When applicable, are the dependent and independent variables defined and operationalized?

E. Sampling
1. Is the population in the study clearly described?
2. Is the sampling method defined?
3. Is the sampling method appropriate for the research approach?

F. Study Design
1. Is the design of the study clearly presented?
2. Is the design appropriate for the research approach?

G. Data Collection
1. Are the data collection methods clearly specified?
2. Are the data qualitative, quantitative, or both?
3. What procedures were used to ensure reliability and validity of the data?
4. Are there additional sources of data that could have been used?

H. Data Analysis
1. When present, are tables and graphs understandable?
2. Is there an orderly and clear interpretation of research findings?
3. For quantitative data, were appropriate statistical tests used?
4. For qualitative data, is the method of analysis clearly described?
5. Do the conclusions follow logically from the data analysis?
6. Are the data sufficient to warrant the conclusions?

(continued on next page)

Figure 15.3   **Checklist for evaluating research**

Source: From an unpublished outline by Rose Rael (modified).

I. Ethical Issues   Yes No
    1. Are the consequences for human beings considered?   ☐ ☐
    2. Was informed consent obtained from the subjects?   ☐ ☐
    3. Are the participants protected from harm?   ☐ ☐
    4. Is there assurance that the data will be kept confidential?   ☐ ☐
    5. Is appropriate credit given for the research?   ☐ ☐

J. Human Diversity Issues
    1. Is the research question of interest or does it apply to diverse groups?   ☐ ☐
    2. Is the data collection method relevant for the group(s) under study?   ☐ ☐
    3. Is the sample diverse?   ☐ ☐
    4. If there are comparison groups, what is their membership?   ☐ ☐
    5. Is the subject involved in the research project beyond simply
       being a subject?   ☐ ☐
    6. Does the categorization of data maintain diversity?   ☐ ☐
    7. Is the research report written in an exclusive or stereotypical manner?   ☐ ☐
    8. Were the results disseminated?   ☐ ☐
    9. Was there maximum participation from many groups in the research?   ☐ ☐

K. Limitations of the Study
    1. Are the limitations of the study clearly stated?   ☐ ☐

L. Conclusions and Recommendations
    1. Are the conclusions substantiated by the research findings?   ☐ ☐
    2. Are the conclusions significant and relevant to the problem and
       population under study?   ☐ ☐
    3. What are the recommendations for future studies?   ☐ ☐
    4. Does the study identify implications for social work?   ☐ ☐

Figure 15.3   *Continued*

4. Keep this record of the findings, limiting conditions, and quality of the research as brief as possible. Form a data bank for your own use.

ETHICAL ISSUES IN THE USE AND EVALUATION OF RESEARCH FINDINGS

Although social workers can benefit from applying research findings to their practice, research cannot always provide the answers. Sometimes the questions that interest you have not yet been investigated, for any number of reasons. Funding may not have been available, for example. Even if your topic has been researched, this research may have been constrained by a particular theoretical framework or a particular type of research method, limiting the usefulness of the findings.

Due to these gaps in the knowledge, you cannot always use research. You need to explicitly acknowledge this patchiness, recognizing that every stage of the practice process cannot be supported with information derived from research. An intellectual and personal honesty is required in acknowledging where the gaps in your practice knowledge exist. This honesty also provides a means for developing a personal research agenda—program evaluation, needs assessment, evaluating your own practice, or pure research.

HUMAN DIVERSITY ISSUES IN THE USE AND EVALUATION OF RESEARCH FINDINGS

When referring to research studies to enhance your practice, you need to be sure that these studies are themselves sensitive to human diversity issues. You may be able to ascertain this when assessing the quality of the research. For example, in the research studies on physical abuse, you note that none of the samples includes Hispanic families; consequently, any results from these studies would be limited in their ability to be generalized to a wider population. When evaluating research studies, bear in mind the comments relating to human diversity issues made in each chapter regarding each step of the research process.

SUMMARY

Using the results of research in practice necessitates evaluating the research itself. The process of using research in practice is explored with five different client systems: individual, family, group, organization, and community. At each stage of practice, research findings can assist. Four limiting conditions deter the use of research in practice, however: These are tradition, philosophy, technological skills, and quality of information. Several frameworks have been suggested to assist in the evaluation of research.

Agency issues include advocating the importance of using research in practice. As generalist practitioners, we are faced with the challenge of conducting research within the agency's time constraints. Ethical issues involve recognizing the gaps in our research knowledge; we cannot support every stage of the practice process with research. Human diversity issues relate to the existing research. We must be sensitive to human diversity when assessing the quality of research.

STUDY/EXERCISE QUESTIONS

1. Select an article in a social work journal and apply the checklist for the evaluation of research displayed in Figure 15.3.

2. Take a case in which you have been involved either as a volunteer or a practicum student and describe how you would use research findings at each step of the practice process.

REFERENCES

Achenback, T. (1991). *Manual for the Child Behavior Checklist/4–18 and 1991 profile.* Burlington: University of Vermont, Department of Psychiatry.

Acoca, L., & Barr, J. (1989). *Substance abuse: A training manual for working with families.* New York: Edna McConnell Clark Foundation.

Albers, E. & Evans, W. (1994). Suicide ideation among a stratified sample of rural and urban adolescents. *Child and Adolescent Social Work Journal, 11* (5), 379–389.

Allen-Meares, P. (1987). Depression in childhood and adolescence. *Social Work, 32* (6), 512–516.

Alter, C., & Evens, W. (1990). *Evaluating your own practice: A guide to self-assessment.* New York: Springer.

American Psychiatric Association. (1994). *Diagnostic and statistical manual of mental disorders* (4th ed.). Washington, DC: Author.

Anderson, G. R. (1990). Foster parent education: Preparing for informed and compassionate caregiving. In G. R. Anderson (Ed.), *Courage to care: Responding to the crisis of children with AIDS.* Washington, DC: Child Welfare League of America.

Annin, J. B. (1990). Training for HIV infection prevention in child welfare services. In G. R. Anderson (Ed.), *Courage to care: Responding to the crisis of children with AIDS.* Washington, DC: Child Welfare League of America.

Barth, R., & Berry, M. (1987). Outcome of child welfare services under permanency planning. *Social Service Review, 61,* 71–90.

Beck, A., Ward, C., Mendelson, M., Mock, J., & Erbaugh, J. (1961). An inventory for measuring depression. *Archives of General Psychology, 4,* 561–571.

Beckler, P. (1990). Resources for HIV/AIDS education: Cases. In G. R. Anderson (Ed.), *Courage to care: Responding to the crisis of children with AIDS.* Washington, DC: Child Welfare League of America.

Beckman, L. J., Day, T., Bardsley, P., & Seeman, A. (1980). The personality characteristics and family background of women alcoholics. *The International Journal of the Addictions, 15* (1), 147–154.

Bennett, T., DeLuca, D., & Allen, R. (1996). Families of children with disabilities: Positive adaptation across the life cycle. *Social Work in Education, 18* (1), 31–44.

Berg, I. K., & Miller, S. D. (1992). *Working with the Problem Drinker: A Solution-Focused Approach.* New York: W. W. Norton.

Biederman, J., Farsone, S. V., Keenan, K., Benjamin, J., Knifcher, B., Moore, C., Sprich-Buckminster, S., Ugaglia, K., Jellineck, M. S., Steingard, R., Spencer, T., Norman, D., Kolony, R., Kraus, I., Perrin, J., Keller, M. B., & Tsuang, M. T. (1992). Further evidence for family-genetic risk factors in attention deficit hyperactivity disorder: Patterns of comorbidity in probands and relatives in psychiatrically and pediatrically referred samples. *Archives of General Psychiatry, 49,* 728–738.

Benton, A. L., & Sines, J. O. (1985). Psychological testing of children. In H. Kaplan & B. Sadock (Eds.), *Comprehensive textbook of psychiatry* (4th ed., pp. 1625–1634). Baltimore: Williams & Wilkins.

Bloom, M., Fischer, J., & Orme, D. (1995). *Evaluating practice: Guidelines for the accountable professional.* Englewood Cliffs, NJ: Prentice Hall.

Blyth, B., Sally, M., & Jayaratne, S. (1994). A review of intensive family preservation services research. *Social Work, 18* (4), 213–224.

Bowman, K. M., & Jellinek, E. M. (1974). Alcohol addiction and treatment. *Journal of Studies on Alcoholism, 35* (2), 98–176.

Brickman, A. S., et al. (1985). Neuropsychological assessment of seriously delinquent adolescents. *Journal of the American Academy of Child Psychiatry, 23,* 453–457.

Carson, G. A. (1981). The phenomenology of adolescent depression. *Adolescent Psychiatry, 9,* 411–412.

Chan, Y. C. (1994). Parenting stress and social support of mothers who physically abuse their children in Hong Kong. *Child Abuse and Neglect, 18,* 261–269.

Chess, S., & Thomas, A. (1984). *Origins and evolution of behavior disorders.* New York: Brunner/Mazel.

Child Welfare League of America. (1988). Report of the CWLA task force on children and HIV infection: Initial guidelines. Washington, DC: Author.

Cliffone, J. (1993). Suicide prevention: A classroom presentation to adolescents. *Social Work, 38* (2), 197–203.

Conners, C. K. (1985). *The Conners rating scales; Instruments for the assessment of childhood psychopathology.* Unpublished manuscript.

Connor, E., Sperling, R., Gelber, R., Kiselev, P., Scott, G., O'Sullivan, M. J., VanDyke, R., Bey, M., Shearer, W., Jacobson, R., Jimenez, E., O'Neil, E., Bazin, B., Delfraissy, J., Culnane, M., Coombs, R., Elkins, M., Moye, J., Stratton, P., & Balsley, J. (1994). Reduction of maternal-infant transmission of human immunodeficiency virus type 1 with zidovudine treatment. *New England Journal of Medicine, 331,* 1173–1180.

Corse, S., Schmid, K., & Trickett, P. (1990). Social network characteristics of mothers in abusing and nonabusing families and their relationships to parenting beliefs. *Journal of Community Psychology, 18,* 44–59.

Cronbach, L. J. (1975). Five decades of public controversy over mental testing. *American Psychologist, 30,* 1–14.

Cross, T. L. (1998). Understanding family resiliency from a relational world view. In H. McCubbin, E. Thompson, A. Thompson, & J. Fromer (Eds.), *Resiliency in Native American and immigrant families* (pp. 143–157). Thousand Oaks, CA: Sage Publications.

Curtiss, G., et al. (1983). Measuring delinquent behavior in inpatient treatment settings: Revision and validation of the adolescent antisocial behavior checklist. *Journal of the American Academy of Child Psychiatry, 22,* 459–466.

Cuskey, W., Berger, L., & Densen-Gerber, J. (1977). Issues in the treatment of female addiction: A review and critique of the literature. *Contemporary Drug Problems, 6* (3), 307–371.

Dedmon, S. R. (1997). Attention deficiency and hyperactivity. In M. Fraser (Ed.), *Risk and resilience in childhood: An ecological perspective.* Washington, DC: NASW Press.

De Leon, G. (1996). Therapeutic communities: AIDS/HIV risk and harm reduction. *Journal of Substance Abuse Treatment, 13* (5), 411–420.

Doshan, T., & Bursh, C. (1982). Women and substance abuse: Critical issues in treatment design. *Journal of Drug Education, 12* (3), 229–239.

DuPaul, G. J., & Stoner, G. (1994). *ADHD in the schools: Assessment and intervention strategies.* New York: Guilford Press.

Eggert, L. L., Thompson, E. A., & Herting, J. R. (1994). A Measure of Adolescent Potential for Suicide (MAPS): Development and preliminary findings. *Suicide and Life-Threatening Behavior, 24,* 359–381.

Elkind, D. (1984a). *All grown up and no place to go.* Reading, MA: Addison-Wesley.

Elliott, D. S., & Ageton, S. S. (1980). Reconciling race and class differences in self-reported and official estimates of delinquency. *American Sociological Review, 45,* 95–110.

English, D. J. (1989, August). *An analysis of characteristics, problems and services for CPS cases by ethnicity.* Paper presented at the American Public Welfare Association 3rd Roundtable on Risk Assessment, San Francisco.

Family Centered Assessment Tool. (1999). Santa Fe, NM: Children, Youth and Families Department.

Fombonne, E. (1998). Suicidal behaviors in vulnerable adolescents: Time trends and their correlates. *British Journal of Psychiatry, 173,* 154–159.

Ford, M., & Kroll, J. (1990). *Challenges to child welfare: Countering the call for a return to orphanages.* St. Paul, MN: North American Council on Adoptable Children.

Fraser, M. (1990). Program outcome measures. In Y. Y. Yuan and M. Rivest (Eds.), *Preserving families: Evaluation resources for practitioners and policymakers.* Newbury Park, CA: Sage.

Frick, P., Lahey, B., Christ, M., Loeber, R., Green, S. (1991). History of childhood behavior problems in the biological relatives of boys with attention-deficit hyperactivity disorder and conduct disorder. *Journal of Clinical Child Psychology, 42* (94), 445–451.

Frymier, J. (1988). Understanding and preventing teen suicide: An interview with Barry Garfinkel, M.D. *Phi Delta Kappan, 70* (4).

Gaudin, Jr., J. M., & Pollane, L. (1983). Social networks, stress and child abuse. *Children and Youth Services Review, 5,* 91–102.

Gelles, R. J. (1987). *Family violence* (2nd ed.). Newbury Park: CA: Sage.

Gillis, J. J., Gilger, J. W., Pennington, B. F., & Defries, J. C. (1992). Attention deficit disorder in reading-disabled twins. Evidence for a genetic etiology. *Journal of Abnormal Child Psychology & Psychiatry, 20,* 303–315.

Gordon, S. B., & Asher, M. J. (1994). *Meeting the ADD challenge: A practical guide for teachers.* Champaign, IL: Research Press.

Green, R. J. (1990). *Family violence* (2nd ed.). Newbury Park, CA: Sage.

Greenberg, L. S., Pinsof, W. M. (1986). Process research: Current trends and future perspectives. In L. S. Greenberg & W. M. Pinsof (Eds.), *The psychotherapeutic process: A research handbook* (pp. 3–20). New York: Guilford Press.

Groze, V., McMillen, J. C., Haines-Simeon, M. (1993). Families who foster children with HIV: A pilot study. *Child and Adolescent Social Work Journal, 10* (1), 67–87.

Grueling, J., & DeBlassie, R. R. (1980). Adolescent suicide. *Adolescence, 15,* 589–601.

Harlow, L. L., Newcomb, M. D., & Bentler, P. M. (1987). Depression, self-derogation, substance use, and suicide ideation: Lack of purpose in life as a mediational faction. *Journal of Clinical Psychology, 42* (1), 5–21.

Harrison, P. A., Hoffman, N. G., & Edwall, G. D. (1989). Differential drug use patterns among sexually abused adolescent girls in treatment for chemical dependency. *The International Journal of the Addictions, 24* (6), 499–514.

Hartman, A. (1978). Diagrammatic assessment of family relationships. *Social Casework, 59,* 465–478.

Henggeler, S. W., et al. (1998). *Multisystemic treatment of antisocial behavior in children and adolescents.* New York: Guilford Press.

Henggeler, S. W., Rowland, M. D., Pickrel, S. G., Miller, S. L., Cunningham, P. B., Santos, A. B., Schoenwald, S. K., Randall, J., & Edwards, J. E. (1997). Investigating family-based alternatives to institution-based mental health services for youth. Lessons learned from the pilot study of a randomized field trial. *Journal of Clinical Child Psychology, 26,* 226–233.

Henggeler, S. W., Schoenwald, S. K., Pickrel, S. G., Brondino, M. J., Borduin, C. M., & Hall, J. A. (1994). *Treatment manual for family preservation using multisystemic therapy.* Columbia, SC: Department of Health and Human Services.

Hepworth, D. H., Farley, O. W., & Griffiths, J. K. (1986). Research capsule. *Social Research Institute Newsletter.* Salt Lake City: Graduate School of Social Work, University of Utah.

Hudson, W. W. (1990). *The Multi-Problem Screening Inventory.* Arizona: WALMYR Publishing Co.

Husson, R. N., Comeau, A., Hoff, R. (1990). Diagnosis of human immunodeficiency virus infection in infants and children. *Pediatrics, 86* (1), 1–10.

Ingram, D., & Hutchinson, S. A. (1999). Defensive mothering in HIV-positive mothers. *Qualitative Health Research, 9* (2), 243–258.

Jellinek, E. M. (1960). *The disease concept of alcoholism.* New Brunswick, NJ: Hillhouse Press.

Johnson, H. C. (1988). Drugs, dialogue, or diet: Diagnosing and treating the hyperactive child. *Social Work Journal, 33,* 349–355.

Johnson, J. P., Nair, P., Hines, S. E., Seidan, S., Alger, L., Review, D., O'Neil, K., & Hebel, R. (1989). Natural history and serologic diagnosis of infants born to human immunodeficiency virus-infected women. *American Journal of Diseases of Children, 143,* 1147–1153.

Jones, G. D. (1997). The role of drugs and alcohol in urban minority adolescent suicide attempts. *Death Studies, 21,* 189–202.

Kaplan, C. & Shachter, E. (1991). Adults with undiagnosed learning disabilities: Practice considerations. *Families in Society, 72* (4), 195–201.

Keane, E. M., Eick, R. W., Bechtold, D. W., & Manson, S. M. (1996). Predictive and concurrent validity of the Suicidal Ideation questionnaire among American Indian adolescents. *Journal of Abnormal Child Psychology, 24* (6), 735–747.

Kirk, R. S., Reed, K., & Lin, A. (1996). *NCFAS: North Carolina Family Assessment Scale.* Adapted for New Mexico Family Preservation Family Support Programs.

Kovacs, M. (1980–1981). Rating scales to assess depression in school-aged children. *Acta Paedopsychiatrica, 46,* 305–315.

Kretzmann, J. P., & McKnight, J. L. (1993). *Building Communities from the Inside Out: A Path Toward Finding and Mobilizing a Community's Assets.* Chicago: ACTA Publications.

Landry, K., & Smith, T. (1998). Neurocognitive effects of HIV infection on young children: Implications for assessment. *Topics in Early Childhood Special Education, 18* (3), 160–168.

Lesar, S., & Maldonado, Y. A. (1997). The impact of children with HIV infection on the family system. *Families in Society, 78* (3), 272–279.

Lester, D. (1998). Adolescent suicide risk today: A paradox. *Journal of Adolescence, 21* (4), 499–503.

Lindergren, M. L., Byers, R. H. Jr., Thomas, P., Davis, S. F., Caldwell, B., Rogers, M., Gwinn, M., Ward, J. W., & Fleming, P. L. (1999). Trends in perinatal transmission of HIV/AIDS in the United States. *JAMA 282* (6), 531–538.

Lockhart, L. L., & Wodarski, J. S. (1989). Facing the unknown: Children and adolescents with AIDS. *Social Work, 34* (3), 215–221.

Long, K. A. (1986). Cultural considerations in the assessment and treatment of intrafamilial abuse. *American Journal of Orthopsychiatry, 56* (1), 131–136.

Lowenthal, B. (1997). Pediatric HIV infection: Effects on development, learning, and interventions. *Early Child Development & Care, 136,* 17–26.

Magura, S. (1981). Are services to prevent foster care effective? *Children and Youth Services Review, 3,* 193–212.

Magura, S., & Moses, B. S. (1986). *Outcome measures for child welfare services: Theory and applications.* Washington, DC: Child Welfare League of America.

Mannes, M. (1990a). Implementing family preservation services with American Indians and Alaskan natives. In M. Mannes (Ed.), *Family preservation and Indian child welfare.* Albuquerque, NM: American Indian Law Center, Inc.

Mannes, M. (1990b). Linking family preservation and Indian child welfare: A historical perspective and the contemporary context. In M. Mannes (Ed.), *Family preservation and Indian child welfare.* Albuquerque, NM: American Indian Law Center, Inc.

Mannes, M. (1993). Seeking the balance between child protection and family preservation in Indian child welfare. *Child Welfare League of America, 72* (2), 141–151.

Marin, B. (1991). Drug abuse treatment for Hispanics: A culturally-appropriate, community-oriented approach. In R. R. Watson (Ed.), *Drug and alcohol abuse prevention.* Totowa, NJ: Humana Press.

McCubbin, H., & Thompson, A. (Ed.). (1987). *Family assessment for research and practice.* Madison: University of Wisconsin.

McLachlan, F. C., Walderman, R., Birchmore, B., & Marsden, L. (1979). Self-evaluation, role satisfaction and anxiety in the woman alcoholic. *The International Journal of the Addictions, 14* (6), 809–832.

Merkel-Holguin, L. (1998). Implementation of family group decision making processes in the U.S.: Policies and practices in transition? *Protecting Children, 14* (4), 4–10.

Meyer, B. L. (1999). *Implementing actuarial risk assessment: Policy decisions and field practice in New Mexico.* In Twelfth National Roundtable on Child Protective Services Risk Assessment-Summary of Proceedings. Englewood. Colorado: American Human Association, 103–117.

Michaels, D., & Levine, C. (1992). Estimates of the number of motherless youth orphaned by AIDS in the United States. *Journal of the American Medical Association, 268,* 3456–3461.

Miller, B., Downs, W., & Testa, M. (1993). Interrelationships Between Victimization Experience and Women's Alcohol Use. *Journal of Studies on Alcohol,* (Suppl. 11), 115–123.

Miller, W., & Rollnick, S. (1991). *Motivational interviewing: Preparing people to change addictive behavior.* New York: Guilford Press.

MMWR Weekly. (Nov. 22, 1996). AIDS among children—United States, 1996. Available: http://www.cdc.gov/epo/mmwrhtml/00044515.htm.

Mofenson, L. (1994). Epidemiology and determinants of vertical HIV transmission. *Seminar in Pediatric Infection Disease, 5,* 252–265.

Mullen, E. J. (1988). Constructing personal practice models. *Social Work Research and Evaluation.* Itasca, IL: Peacock Publishers.

Nakken, J. M. (1989). Issues in adolescent chemical dependency assessment. In P. B. Henry (Ed.), *Practical approaches in treating adolescent chemical dependency: A guide to clinical assessment and intervention.* New York: Haworth Press.

Nash, J. K., & Fraser, M. W. (1997). Methods in the analysis of risk and protective factors: Lessons from epidemiology. In M. Fraser (Ed.), *Risk and resilience in childhood: An ecological perspective* (pp. 34–49). Washington, DC: NASW Press.

National Institute of Alcohol Abuse and Alcoholism. (1990). Alcohol and Women. *Alcohol Alert, 10* (Oct.), 1–4.

Nelson, D. E., Landsman, M. J., & Deutelbaum, W. (1990). Three models of family-centered placement prevention services. *Child Welfare, 69* (1), 3–21.

New Jersey Department of Human Services Division of Youth and Family Services. (1989). *A practice guide to caring for children with AIDS.* Trenton, New Jersey: Office of Policy, Planning and Support.

Oleske, J. (1987). Natural history of HIV infection II. In K. B. Silverman & A. Waddell (Eds.). *Report of the surgeon general's workshop on children with HIV infection and their families* (pp. 24–25). Washington DC: U.S. Department of Health and Human Services, Public Health Service.

Oxtoby, M. J. (1994). Vertically acquired HIV infection in the United States. In P. A. Pisso and C. M. Wilfert (Eds.), *Pediatric AIDS: The challenge of HIV infection in infants, children, and adolescents.* Baltimore, MD: Williams & Wilkins.

Patterson, G. R., Chamberlain, P., & Reid, J. B. (1982). A comparative evaluation of a parent training program. *Behavior Therapy, 13,* 638–650.

Pattison, E. M. (1974). The rehabilitation of the chronic alcoholic. In B. Kissen & H. Begletter (Eds.), *Biology of alcoholism: Vol. III. Clinical Pathology.* New York: Plenum Press.

Pierce, D. (1977). Suicidal intent in self-injury. *British Journal of Psychiatry, 130,* 377–385.

Pisterman, S., McGrath, P., Firestone, P., Goodman, J., Webster, I., & Mallory, R. (1989). Outcome of parent-mediated treatment of preschoolers with attention deficit disorder with hyperactivity. *Journal of Consulting and Clinical Psychology, 57,* 628–635.

Pollard, S., Ward, E., & Barkley, R. (1983). The effects of parent training and Ritalin on the parent-child interactions of hyperactive boys. *Child and Family Therapy, 5,* 51–69.

Prochaska, J., DiClemente, C., & Norcross, J. (1992). In search of how people change: Applications to addictive behaviors. *American Psychologist, 47* (9), 1102–1114.

Prosser, J., & McArdle, P. (1996). The changing mental health of children and adolescents: Evidence for a deterioration? *Psychological Medicine, 26* (4), 715–725.

Rapport, J. L., & Ferguson, H. B. (1981). Biological validation of the hyperkinetic syndrome. *Developmental Medicine and Child Neurology, 23,* 667–682.

Rigby, K., & Slee, P. (1999). Suicidal ideation among adolescent school children, involvement in bully-victim problems, and perceived social support. *Suicide and Life-Threatening Behavior, 29* (2), 119–130.

Rogers, M. F. (1985). AIDS in children: A review of the clinical epidemiologic and public health aspects. *Pediatric Infectious Disease, 4,* 230–236.

Rogers, M. F. (1987a). AIDS in children. *The New York Medical Quarterly, 21,* 68–73.

Rogers, M. F. (1987b). Transmission of human immunodeficiency virus infection in the United States. In K. B. Silverman & A. Waddell (Eds.), *Report of the surgeon general's workshop on children with HIV infection and their families* (pp. 17–19). Washington, DC: U.S. Department of Health and Human Services, Public Health Service.

Root, M. (1989).Treatment failure: The role of sexual victimization in women's addictive behavior. *American Journal of Orthopsychiatry, 59* (4), 542–549.

Rossi, P. H. (1992). Assessing family preservation programs. *Children and Youth Services Review, 14,* 77–98.

Rowe, M., & Ryan, C. (1987). *A public health challenge: State issues, policies and programs, I.* Intergovernmental Health Policy Project. Washington, DC: George Washington University.

Rzepnicki, T. L., Schuerman, J. R., & Littell, J. H. (1991). Issues in evaluating intensive family preservation services. In E. M. Tracy, D. A. Haapala, J. Kinney, & P. J. Pecora (Eds.), *Intensive family preservation services: An instructional sourcebook.* Cleveland: Mandel School of Applied Social Sciences, Case Western Reserve University.

Sandau-Beckler, P. (1999). *New Mexico Family Centered Tool Research Report.* New Mexico State University, Los Cruces.

Sandmaler, M. (1992). *The invisible alcoholics: women and alcohol.* Blue Ridge Summit, Pa: TAB Books.

St. Luke's Innovative Resources. (1994). P.O. Box 315, Bendigo, Victoria 3552, Australia; email: *stlukeir* 03 5440 Fax: 03 5440 1139.

Schachar, R., Rutter, M., & Smith, A. (1981). The characteristics of situationally and pervasively hyperactive children: Implications for syndrome definition. *Journal of Child Psychology and Psychiatry, 22* (14), 737–753.

Scott, G. B. (1987). Natural history of HIV infection I. In K. B. Silverman & A. Waddell (Eds.), *Report of the surgeon general's workshop on children with HIV infection and their families* (pp. 22–23). Washington, DC: U.S. Department of Health and Human Services, Public Health Service.

Seidman, L., Biedermans, J., & Faraone, S. (1995). Effects of family history and comorbidity on the neuropsychological performance of children with ADHD: Preliminary findings. *Journal of the American Academy of Child and Adolescent Psychiatry, 34* (8), 1015–1024.

Shannon, K. M., & Animann, A. G. (1985). Acquired immune deficiency syndrome in childhood. *Journal of Pediatrics, 106,* 332–342.

Shapiro, S. K., & Garfinkel, B. D. (1986). The occurrence of behavior disorder in children: The interdependence of attention deficit disorder and conduct disorder. *Journal of the American Academy of Child Psychiatry, 25,* 809–819.

Shekim, W. O. (1986). Dimensional and categorical approaches to the diagnosis of attention deficit disorder in children. *Journal of the American Academy of Child Psychiatry, 25,* 653–658.

Smith, D. (1976). Adolescent suicide: A problem for teachers? *Phi Delta Kappa, 57,* 539–542.

Stein, T. T., & Rzepnicki, T. (1983). *Decision making at child welfare imbalance: A handbook on practitioners.* New York: Child Welfare League of America.

Stroul, B. A., & Friedman, R. M. (1994). *A system of care for children and youth with severe emotional disturbances* (rev. ed.). Washington DC: Georgetown University Child Development Center, National Technical Center for Children's Mental Health, Center for Child Health and Mental Health Policy.

Tafoya, N. (1990). Home-based family therapy: A model for Native American communities. In M. Mannes (Ed.), *Family preservation and Indian child welfare.* Albuquerque, NM: American Indian Law Center, Inc.

Tompkins, T. L., Henker, B., Whalen, C. K., Axelrod, J., & Comer, L. K. (1999). Motherhood in the context of HIV infection: Reading between the numbers. *Cultural Diversity & Ethnic Minority Psychology, 5* (3), 197–208.

Toseland, R. W., & Rivas, R. F. (1984). *An introduction to group work practice.* New York: Macmillan.

Tracy, E. (1992). Defining the target system for family preservation services. In K. Wells and D. E. Beigel (Eds.), *Family preservation services: Research and evaluation.* Newbury Park, CA: Sage Press.

Tracy, E. M., & Whittaker, J. K. (1990). The social network map: Assessing social support in clinical practice. *Families in Society: The Journal of Contemporary Human Services, 71,* 461–470.

Tramontana, M. G., & Sherrets, S. D. (1985). Brain impairment in child psychiatric disorders: Correspondences between neuropsychological and C.T. scan results. *Journal of the American Academy of Child Psychiatry, 24,* 590–596.

Vance, J., & Elofson, P. (1998). Family group conferences: Implementation with Native American families. *Protecting Children, 14* (4), 19–20.

Velicer, W. F., DiClemente, C. C., Prochaska, J. O., & Bradenburg, N. (1985). A decision balance measure for assessing and predicting smoking status. *Journal of Personality and Social Psychology, 48,* 1279–1289.

Wagner, B. M. (1997). Family risk factors for child and adolescent suicidal behavior. *Psychological Bulletin, 121,* 246–298.

Weiss, G. (1985). Hyperactivity: Overview and new directions. *Psychiatric Clinics of North America, 8,* 737–753.

Wells, K., & Biegel, D. (1992). Intensive family preservation research: Current status and future agenda. *Social Work Research & Abstracts, 28* (1), 21–27.

Wheeler, B. L., Biase, D. V., & Sullivan, A. P. (1986). Changes in self-concept during therapeutic community treatment: A comparison of male and female drug abusers. *Journal of Drug Education, 16* (2), 191–196.

Winters, K. C., & Henly, G. A. (1989). *Personal Experience Inventory Test and Manual.* Los Angeles: Western Psychological Services.

Yandow, U. (1989). Alcoholism in women. *Psychiatric Annals, 19,* 243–247.

Young, E. B. (1990). The role of incest in relapse. *Journal of Psychoactive Drugs, 22,* 249–258.

Library and World Wide Web Resources

Compiled by Donnelyn Curtis
Director of Research Services
University of Nevada, Reno, Library

LIBRARY RESOURCES

Most of these library resources are in print format. Web-based subscriptions are listed in the library sections rather than in the Web sites sections if they are restricted. Depending on your affiliation with the library's parent institution, you may or may not be able to use library-provided Web resources from outside the library. Access by anyone who is within the library is generally allowed.

Background Sources:
Dictionaries, Encyclopedias, and Handbooks

These and other similar reference books can be found in the reference area of an academic or large public library. To browse for other social-work-specific background materials in a university library reference area, try the HV and HQ areas. In a public library reference area, browse the 360 section.

Barker, R. L. (1999). *The social work dictionary* (4th ed.). Washington, DC: NASW Press.
This volume provides social work definitions and identifies and describes organizations, trends, philosophies, and legislation relevant to social work. It gives concise definitions of terms as they are used by social work practitioners and offers a chronology of important events in the history of social work and the NASW Code of Ethics.

Contemporary world issues series. Santa Barbara: ABC-CLIO.
These specialized handbooks provide preliminary background information, including overviews, chronology, biographical information about important people in the field, lists of organizations, and annotated resource lists.

Selected titles:

Costa, M. (1996). *Abortion: A reference handbook* (2nd ed.).

Hombs, M. E. (1994). *American homelessness: A reference handbook* (2nd ed.).

Kinnear, K. L. (1995). *Childhood sexual abuse: A reference handbook.*

Kinnear, K. L. (1996). *Gangs: A reference handbook.*

Kinnear, K. L. (1999). *Single parents: a reference handbook.*

Kinnear, K. L. (1995). *Violent children: A reference handbook.*

Lerner, E. K. (1998). *AIDS crisis in America.*

McCue, M. L. (1995). *Domestic violence: A reference handbook.*

Moe, B. A. (1998). *Adoption: A reference handbook.*

Rafter, N. L. (1998). *Prisons in America.*

Encyclopedia of social work (19th ed., 3 vols.). (1995). (supplement, 1997). Silver
Spring, MD: National Association of Social Workers.
This is the only encyclopedia devoted entirely to social work. It contains
290 articles, some lengthy, and 142 bibliographies. In addition, it provides
a good overview of issues and activities in social work and social welfare,
serving as an excellent starting point for background information or a literature search. The one-volume supplement updates the encyclopedia.

Garland reference library of social science series. New York: Garland Press.
The formats of these titles vary. Some are straightforward bibliographies,
while others are encyclopedias or handbooks, providing background information and facts as well as sources for further information.

Selected titles:

Bingham, R. D. (1999). *Evaluation in practice: A methodological approach.*

Gilmartin, P. (1994). *Rape, incest, and child abuse: Consequences and recovery.*

Jacobson, C. K. (1995). *American families: Issues in race and ethnicity.*

Lester, B. M., Zuckerman, B., & Fitzgerald, H. E. (Eds.). (1999). *Children of
color: research, health, and policy issues.*

McRoy, R. G. (1999). *Special needs adoptions: Practice issues.*

Netting, F. E., & Williams, F. G. (Eds.). (1999). *Enhancing primary care of
elderly people.*

Rodwell, M. K. (1998). *Social work, constructivist research.*

Statistical Sources

American statistics index (ASI). Washington, DC: Congressional Information
Service (published since 1973).
The index volumes are bound separately from the abstract volumes,
which describe statistics that are published in other government docu-

ments. Chances are good that the actual source of the statistics can be found in the library if it is a government depository library. Some libraries will have cumulated volumes covering several years.

Chadwick, B. A., & Heaton, T. B. (1999). *Statistical handbook on the American family* (2nd ed.). Phoenix, AZ: Oryx Press.
American families are profiled in 350 tables, charts, and figures. The data are collected from federal and state government agencies, Gallup polls, professional journals, and research monographs.

Index to international statistics (IIS). Washington, DC: Congressional Information Service (published since 1983).
This subscription provides an index that includes abstracts for statistical publications of international intergovernmental organizations, including United Nations agencies. The publications that are indexed here may require the use of Interlibrary Loan.

Smith, J. C., & Horton, C. P. (1996). *Statistical record of black America* (4th ed.). Detroit: Gale.
This resource contains more than 1,000 statistical graphs, tables, and lists from a wide variety of private, commercial, and governmental sources on population, vital statistics, family, labor and employment, and education.

Statistical Reference Index (SRI). Washington, DC; Congressional Information Service (published since 1980).
SRI provides information about statistics generated by private sector organizations and state governments throughout the United States. Briefly-annotated index volumes direct users to abstract volumes that provide details about the publications, which will require some effort to obtain.

Statistical universe. Congressional Information Services. World Wide Web, and CD-ROM.
Statistical Universe (which includes *ASI, IIS, SRI,* and the *Statistical abstract of the United States*) is available on the Web and CD-ROM and provides some full-text access to federal and international statistics. It provides detailed abstracts, indexing, and locator information for all statistical reports of general research value issued by the federal government since the early 1960s. It includes direct links to all key statistical data available on federal agency World Wide Web sites as well as to reports collected by the publisher. The number and type of the latter reports will depend on the library's subscription choices.

U.S. Bureau of the Census. *Statistical abstract of the United States.* Washington, DC: Government Printing Office (annual, published since 1987).
This standard work for locating statistical information is also available online. It includes data from both private and government sources. Emphasis is on national data; however, many tables reflect state or regional data (look up "state data" in the print index to find the charts that differentiate among states). References in the print index are to chart number, not to page number. Often the original work from where the statistics were taken is cited.

Further Resources: Selected Bibliographies and Guides

The following are examples of the numerous specialized bibliographies of interest to social work researchers. To find a bibliography in an online library catalog, use the subject term with the subheading "bibliography."

AIDS bibliography. Bethesda, MD: National Medical Library (monthly, published since 1989).

Nordquist, J. (Ed.). *Contemporary social issues* series. Santa Cruz, Ca: Reference and Research Service.

> *Selected titles:*
>
> ———— (1996). *Asian Americans: social, economic, and political aspects: A bibliography.*
>
> ———— (1998). *The Asian American woman: social and economic conditions: A bibliography.*
>
> ———— (1997). *The health care crisis in the United States: A bibliography.*
>
> ———— (1999). *Native Americans: social, economic, and political aspects: A bibliography.*
>
> ———— (1997). *Race, crime, and the criminal justice system: A bibliography.*
>
> ———— (1998). *Violence against women: international aspects: A bibliography.*

Social welfare. Washington, DC: Government Printing Office (annual, published since 1994).

Identifying the Periodical Literature: Indexes, Abstracts, and Databases

Many of these indexes are available in both print and electronic format, usually through the World Wide Web, but sometimes on CD-ROM. The electronic version is often updated daily or weekly; print indexes are usually updated quarterly. These are specialized databases that a library may or may not have, depending on its budget and priorities. Many cross-disciplinary databases, though not listed here, can include citations and the full text of articles on social work topics.

Abstracts in social gerontology. Newbury Park, Ca: Sage Periodicals (published quarterly since 1990).
This resource gives abstracts for journal articles, books, pamphlets, government publications, legislative research studies, and other types of publications. It includes an author index.

CIJE (Current index to journals in education). Phoenix: Oryx Press (published since 1969).

RIE (Research in education) 1966–74. Washington, DC: Government Printing Office (*Resources in education*) (published since 1975).

ERIC. Available in many versions on the WEB and as a CD-ROM database, combines the *CIJE* and *RIE* indexes, which are still available in print versions that are updated monthly. The database contains references (with abstracts) to journal articles (indexed in *CIJE*) and ERIC Documents (indexed in *RIE*), and the full text of ERIC Digests, which summarize current issues. ERIC Documents include research reports and studies, conference proceedings, some dissertations and theses, and other non-journal literature of interest to those involved with education and children's issues. ERIC Documents are available in many libraries on microfiche.

PsycLIT, PsycInfo, Psychological abstracts. Washington: American Psychological Association (published since 1927).

The electronic versions are available on CD-ROM and the Web, with various search interfaces. *PsycInfo* is the expanded version of *PsycLIT,* containing abstracts of dissertations and other resources as well as the journal articles and book chapters that are abstracted in the latter product. In order to derive the greatest benefit from *Psychological abstracts, PsycInfo,* or *PsycLIT,* the *Thesaurus of psychological index terms* should be used.

Public affairs information service bulletin (PAIS). New York: Public Affairs Information Service (published since 1915).

The subjects that are covered in this index include crime, poverty, unemployment, divorce, work, women, culture, and race relations. It is also available in CD-ROM and on the Web, with various search interfaces.

Social sciences index. New York: H. W. Wilson (published since 1929).

This is an author and subject index to over 350 journals in the fields of anthropology, sociology, and related fields. A separate section at the end of each quarterly print issue indexes book reviews. It is also available on CD-ROM and on the Web, with various search interfaces.

Social work abstracts. Silver Spring: National Association of Social Workers (published since 1977).

Lengthy abstracts are organized in broad categories in the quarterly (and annually cumulated) print version, with author and subject indexes. The Web and CD-ROM versions can be searched by keyword and limited by dates.

Sociological abstracts, Sociofile. San Diego, CA: Sociological Abstracts (published since 1952).

This index/database includes abstracts to articles, papers presented at sociological meetings, books, book reviews, and bibliographies. *Sociofile,* the electronic version, is available on CD-ROM or the Web, with various interfaces. The print version is organized in broad subject categories with a subject index.

Women studies abstracts. Rush, NY: Rush Publishing (published since 1972).

This index, with abstracts, is available in print and electronically. It describes articles from a wide range of periodicals and incudes additional listings of articles not abstracted. The print version is organized by subject and updated quarterly.

Selected List of Current Journals

The best approach to finding articles to frame or support your research is to search by subject in one of the indexes listed above. But you may have an occasional need to browse through journals on a library shelf or online. Some academic libraries shelve their journals by call number (social work journals will often have call numbers that begin with HV or HQ; use the online catalog to get a call number for a specific journal). In libraries that shelve journals alphabetically, it helps to know some titles. Many of the journals listed below are available on the Web.

Addictive Behaviors
Administration in Social Work
Advances in Behaviour Research and
    Therapy
Affilia: The Journal of Women and
    Social Work
Aggression and Violent Behavior
AIDS Education and Prevention:
    An Interdisciplinary Journal
Alcohol Health and Research World
Alcoholism Treatment Quarterly
American Journal of Drug and Alcohol
    Abuse
American Journal of Family Therapy
American Journal of Orthopsychiatry
Aretê
Behaviour Research and Therapy
Behavioural Processes
The British Journal of Social Work
Canadian Social Work Review:
    Revue Canadienne de Service Social
Child Abuse and Neglect:
    The International Journal
Child and Adolescent Social Work Journal
Child and Family Social Work
Child and Youth Services
Child Care Health and Development
Child Maltreatment
Child Welfare
Children and Society
Children Today
Clinical Social Work Journal
Crime and Delinquency
Drug and Alcohol Dependence
Ethnic and Racial Studies

Evaluation and Program Planning:
    An International Journal
Families in Society: The Journal of
    Contemporary Human Services
Family Planning Perspectives
Family Process
Family Relations: Interdisciplinary
    Journal of Applied Family Studies
The Gerontologist
The Hastings Center Report
Health and Social Work
Hispanic Journal of Behavioral Sciences
Hospice Journal
Human Services in the Rural
    Environment
Indian Journal of Social Work
Information and Referral: The Journal
    of the Alliance of Information and
    Referral Systems
International Journal of Aging and
    Human Development
International Journal of the Addictions
International Social Work
Journal of Aging and Social Policy
Journal of Analytic Social Work
Journal of Applied Gerontology
Journal of Applied Psychology
Journal of Applied Social Psychology
Journal of Child and Adolescent
    Substance Abuse
Journal of Criminal Justice
Journal of Divorce and Remarriage
Journal of Family Issues
Journal of Family Social Work
Journal of Family Therapy

Journal of Family Violence
Journal of Gerontological Social Work
Journals of Gerontology: Series B,
    Psychological Sciences and Social
    Sciences
Journal of Homosexuality
Journal of Marital and Family Therapy
Journal of Marriage and the Family
Journal of Multicultural Social Work
Journal of Progressive Human Services
Journal of Research in Crime and
    Delinquency
Journal of School Psychology
Journal of Social Policy
Journal of Social Service Research
Journal of Social Work Education
Journal of Social Work Practice
Journal of Sociology and Social Welfare
Journal of Studies on Alcohol
Journal of Substance Abuse Treatment
Journal of Teaching in Social Work
Journal of Women and Aging
Journal of Youth and Adolescence
Marriage and Family Review
Mediation Quarterly: Journal of the
    Academy of Family Mediators
Omega: Journal of Death and Dying
Personality and Individual Differences
Policy and Practice (formerly *Public*
    Welfare)

Professional Development: The Journal
    of Continuing Social Work
    Education
Pubic Administration Review
Research, Policy and Planning:
    The Journal of the Social Services
    Research Group
Research on Social Work Practice
Residential Treatment for Children
    and Youth
School Social Work Journal
Smith College Studies in Social Work
Social Forces
Social Policy
Social Problems
Social Psychology Quarterly
Social Service Review
Social Work
Social Work Education: Development
    and Training for Social Care and
    Social Services
Social Work in Education
Social Work in Health Care
Social Work Research
Social Work with Groups
Suicide and Life Threatening Behavior
Youth and Society

WEB SITES (PUBLIC ACCESS)

Web sites have a way of vanishing. The sites listed below were selected in part for their longevity and their stability, but they may not always be available at the URL (Web address) given here. If an institution reorganizes its Web files or changes servers, you might get an error message when trying to find one of these sites. If one of them seems to have disappeared, utilize a single engine such as Alta Vista (http://www.altavista.com/) or Google (http://www.google.com/) to find its new location by searching for its name, which is less likely to change.

Data Sets and Statistics

The Annie E. Casey Foundation (http://www.aecf.org/kidscount/index.htm).
    KIDS COUNT, a project of the Annie E. Casey Foundation, is a national
    and state-by-state effort to track the status of children in the United States.

From this site you will be able to link to the latest annual KIDS COUNT Data Book, which measures the educational, social, economic, and physical well-being of children. Other statistical reports are available at this site as well.

Bureau of Justice Statistics (http://www.ojp.usdoj.gov/bjs/welcome.html). The Bureau of Justice Statistics (BJS), a component of the Office of Justice Programs in the U.S. Department of Justice, is the federal government's primary source for criminal justice statistics. BJS collects, analyzes, publishes, and disseminates information on crime, criminal offenders, victims of crime, and the operation of justice systems at all levels of government.

ChildStats.gov The Federal Web Locator is a service provided by the Center for Information Law and Policy (http://www.childstats.gov/). The Federal Interagency Forum on child and Family Statistics maintains this site, which provides state statistics and reports on children and their families, including population and family characteristics, economic security, health, behavior and social environment, and education.

FedStats (http://www.fedstats.gov/). More than 70 agencies in the federal government produce statistics of interest to the public. The Federal Interagency Council on Statistical Policy maintains this site to provide easy access to the full range of statistics and information produced by these agencies for public use.

ICPSR (http://www.icpsr.umich.edu/index.html). The Inter-University Consortium for Political and Social Research is located within the Institute for Social Research (ICPSR) at the University of Michigan. ICPSR provides access to a large archive of computerized social science data. Some of the data can be downloaded at no cost, while other data must be purchased. Universities that belong to the ICPSR get a substantial discount.

National Data Archive on Child Abuse and Neglect (http://www.ndacan.cornell.edu/). The Data Archive is a project of the Family Life Development Center in the College of Human Ecology at Cornell University. The mission is "to facilitate the secondary analysis of research data relevant to the study of child abuse and neglect. By making data available to a larger number of researchers, NDACAN seeks to provide a relatively inexpensive and scientifically productive means for researchers to explore important issues in the child maltreatment field."

U.S. Census Bureau (http://www.census.gov/). The Census Bureau of the U.S. Department of Commerce makes census documents available through this site. Choose "Publications" and then "Population" to get demographic and economic statistics.

Free Indexes and Databases on the Web

CORK Online Database (http://www.dartmouth.edu/dms/cork/database.html).
The Cork bibliographic database contains references (with abstracts) to over 13,000 journal articles, books, book-chapters, etc. on the subjects of alcoholism and substance abuse. The file is updated quarterly. It is available for searching through the Dartmouth College Library Online System. It is necessary to read the directions before beginning.

ERIC (http://ericir.syr.edu/Eric/).
This version of *ERIC* can be searched with three combinations of descriptors, keywords, author names, title words, or other features. The search can be limited by date of publication. The database contains references (with abstracts) to journal articles and ERIC documents on education and children's issues, published since 1966. Some full text is included in the database.

PIE Online (http://www.pie.org/mimhweb/pie/database/datasearch.htm).
The Missouri Institute of Mental Health sponsors the Policy Information Exchange. It is a comprehensive, searchable database of mental health policy related sports.

PILOTS Database (http://www.dartmouth.edu/dms/ptsd/PILOTS.html).
The National Center for PTSD (post-traumatic stress disorder) maintains this index to the worldwide literature on PTSD. Full citations and long abstracts are provided.

PubMed (http://www.ncbi.nlm.nih.gov/entrez/query.fcgi).
PubMed is the National Library of Medicine's search service that provides access to over 10 million article citations in MEDLINE, PreMEDLINE, and other related databases. The subject coverage is largely medical, with some allied health topics included. *PubMed* offers the option of purchasing articles or ordering them through Interlibrary Loan.

UnCover Web (http://uncweb.carl.org/).
UnCover is a database of references for articles in over 18,000 journals. It contains brief descriptive information for articles, which have appeared in the journals since 1988, allowing keyword searches of article titles and summaries. UnCover offers you the opportunity to order fax copies of the articles from this database.

Government Information Gateways

Federal Web locator (http://www.infoctr.edu/fwl/).
This service is provided by the Center for Information Law and Policy at Villanova University.

GPO access (http://www.access.gpo.gov/su docs/).
GPO, the Government Printing Office, provides organized and searchable access to the full text of government documents through this site.

U.S. federal government agencies directory
(http://www.lib.lsu.edu/gov.fedgov.html).
This site, provided by the Louisiana State University Library, provides organized access to the Web sites of all government agencies and sub-agencies,
listed by agency hierarchy. As stated, "This index is for people who know
where they want to go, but don't know the address."

State and local governments (http://lcweb.loc.gov/global/state/stategov.html).
The Library of Congress maintains this site, which provides links to state
government agencies.

U.S. depository libraries WWW home pages (http://drseuss.lib.uidaho.edu:80/
govdoc/otherdep.html).
Using these pages, researchers can find the nearest source of government
documents that are available on the Web.

Gateways for Social Workers

World Wide Web resources for social workers
(http://www.nyu.edu/socialwork/wwwrsw/).
This Web site is jointly sponsored by New York University's Ehrenkranz
School of Social Work and the Mount Sinai-NYU Medical Center and
Health System.

Internet social work resources
(http://www.smith.edu/libraries/subject/sswgen.htm).
The Smith College Libraries maintain this gateway site.

SWAN: Social Work Access Network (http://www.sc.edu/swan/).
The University of South Carolina School of Social Work provides this site.

Other Important Web Resources

Catalog of federal domestic assistance (http://aspe.hhs.gov/cfda/index.htm).
The Catalog of Federal Domestic Assistance Programs (CFDA) is a govern-
ment-wide compendium of all 1,412 federal programs, projects, services,
and activities that provide assistance or benefits to the American public.
It can be found in print form in libraries.

Green book (http://aspe.os.dhhs.gov/).
Listed under "Initiatives and Resources" at the ASPE site, the *Green Book*
consists of background material and data on programs within the jurisdic-
tion of the Committee on Ways and means of the U.S. House of Representatives. It is compiled by the staff of the Committee from many sources and
provides program descriptions and historical data on a wide variety of social and economic topics, including Social Security, employment, earnings,
welfare, child support, health insurance, the elderly, families with children,
poverty, and taxation. It is a standard reference work for those interested in
the direction of social policy in the United States. It can be found in print
form in libraries.

NASW online (http://www.naswdc.org/).

The National Association of Social Workers site provides information about current issues of national interest, publications of the NASW, and links to other sites.

Office of the Assistant Secretary for Planning and Evaluation (http://aspe.hhs.gov/).

The Web site of the Assistant Secretary for Planning and Evaluation (ASPE) of the U.S. Department of Health and Human Services is an excellent resource for social work researchers. This sizable site includes many research reports and other documents. An especially useful area is the *Directory of health and human services data resources* (http://aspe.hhs.gov/datacncl/ datadir/index.htm) that contains statistical reports on children and family, aging, health care, substance abuse, and mental health. The ASPE is also responsible for maintaining the *Green Book* and the *Catalog of Federal Domestic Assistance* (noted earlier).

Statistical Formulas

Pearson *r*

$$r = \frac{e - \dfrac{(a)(b)}{N}}{\sqrt{\left[c - \left(\dfrac{a^2}{N}\right)\right]\left[d - \left(\dfrac{b^2}{N}\right)\right]}}$$

where r = Correlation coefficient
a = Sum of values of x
b = Sum of values of y
c = Sum of values of x^2
d = Sum of values of y^2
e = Sum of values of x and y
N = Number of cases

t-test

$$t = \frac{Ma - Mb}{\sqrt{\left(\dfrac{(Sa)^2 + (Sb)^2}{Na + Nb - 2}\right)\left(\dfrac{Na + Nb}{(Na)(Nb)}\right)}}$$

where t = t value
Na = Number of cases in Group A
Nb = Number of cases in Group B
Sa = Sum of squares of raw scores in Group A
Sb = Sum of squares of raw scores in Group B

Mean

$$\bar{x} = \frac{\sum X_1}{N}$$

where Σ = scores added together
X_1 = score for subjects
N = number of subjects

Median

Given an ordered list of n values, the median equals the value at position $\frac{(n+1)}{2}$.
If n is odd, a single value occupies this position. If n is even, the median equals
the mean of the two middle values.

Standard Deviation

$$S = \sqrt{\frac{\sum (x-\bar{x})}{n-1}}$$

where S = sample standard deviation
n = sample population
$\bar{x}$ = sample mean
x = total scores

Chi-Square

$$\chi^2 = \sum \frac{(O-E)^2}{E}$$

where χ^2 = Chi-square value
O = Observed frequency
E = Expected frequency
Σ = Sum of (for all cells)

$$E = \frac{(R)(C)}{(N)}$$

where E = Expected frequency in a particular cell
R = Total number in that cell's row
C = Total number in that cell's row
N = Total number of cases

Probability Tables

Critical values of chi-square

df	.10 .20	.05 .10	Level of significance for a one-tailed test .025 Level of significance for a two-tailed test .05	.01 .02	.005 .01	.0005 .001
1	1.64	2.71	3.84	5.41	6.64	10.83
2	3.22	4.60	5.99	7.82	9.21	13.82
3	4.64	6.25	7.82	9.84	11.34	16.27
4	5.99	7.78	9.49	11.67	13.28	18.46
5	7.29	9.24	11.07	13.39	15.09	20.52
6	8.56	10.64	12.59	15.03	16.81	22.46
7	9.80	12.02	14.07	16.62	18.48	24.32
8	11.03	13.36	15.51	18.17	20.09	26.12
9	12.24	14.68	16.92	19.68	21.67	27.88
10	13.44	15.99	18.31	21.16	23.21	29.59
11	14.63	17.28	19.68	22.62	24.72	31.26
12	15.81	18.55	21.03	24.05	26.22	32.91
13	16.98	19.81	22.36	25.47	27.69	34.53
14	18.15	21.06	23.68	26.87	29.14	36.12
15	19.31	22.31	25.00	28.26	30.58	37.70
16	20.46	23.54	26.30	29.63	32.00	39.29

(continued)

Critical values of chi-square (continued)

df	.10	.05	Level of significance for a one-tailed test .025	.01	.005	.0005
	.20	.10	Level of significance for a two-tailed test .05	.02	.01	.001
17	21.62	24.77	27.59	31.00	33.41	40.75
18	22.76	25.99	28.87	32.35	34.80	42.31
19	23.90	27.20	30.14	33.69	36.19	43.82
20	25.04	28.41	31.41	35.02	37.57	45.32
21	26.17	29.62	32.67	36.34	38.93	46.80
22	27.30	30.81	33.92	37.66	40.29	48.27
23	28.43	32.01	35.17	38.97	41.64	49.73
24	29.55	33.20	36.42	40.27	42.98	51.18
25	30.68	34.38	37.65	41.57	44.31	52.62
26	31.80	35.56	38.88	42.86	45.64	54.05
27	32.91	36.74	40.11	44.14	46.94	55.48
28	34.03	37.92	41.34	45.42	48.28	56.89
29	35.14	39.09	42.69	46.69	49.59	58.30
30	36.25	40.26	43.77	47.96	50.89	59.70
32	38.47	42.59	46.19	50.49	53.49	62.49
34	40.68	44.90	48.60	53.00	56.06	65.25
36	42.88	47.21	51.00	55.49	58.62	67.99
38	45.08	49.51	53.38	57.97	61.16	70.70
40	47.27	51.81	55.76	60.44	63.69	73.40
44	51.64	56.37	60.48	65.34	68.71	78.75
48	55.99	60.91	65.17	70.20	73.68	84.04
52	60.33	65.42	69.83	75.02	78.62	89.27
56	64.66	69.92	74.47	79.82	83.51	94.46
60	68.97	74.40	79.08	84.58	88.38	99.61

Source: From Table IV of R. A. Fisher and F. Yates, *Statistical Tables for Biological, Agricultural, and Medical Research,* published by Addison Wesley Longman Ltd. Reprinted by permission of Addison Wesley Longman Ltd.

Code of Ethics, approved by the National Association of Social Workers (NASW), January 1, 1997, Section 5.02 Evaluation and Research

(a) Social workers should monitor and evaluate policies, the implementation of programs, and practice interventions.

(b) Social workers should promote and facilitate evaluation and research to contribute to the development of knowledge.

(c) Social workers should critically examine and keep current with emerging knowledge relevant to social work and fully use evaluation and research evidence in their professional practice.

(d) Social workers engaged in evaluation or research should carefully consider possible consequences and should follow guidelines developed for the protection of evaluation and research participants. Appropriate institutional review boards should be consulted.

(e) Social workers engaged in evaluation or research should obtain voluntary and written informed consent from participants, when appropriate, without any implied or actual deprivation or penalty for refusal to participate; without undue inducement to participate; and with due regard for participants' well-being, privacy, and dignity. Informed consent should include information about the nature, extent, and duration of the participation requested and disclosure of the risks and benefits of participation in the research.

(f) When evaluation or research participants are incapable of giving informed consent, social workers should provide an appropriate explanation to the participants, obtain the participants' assent to the extent they are able, and obtain written consent from an appropriate proxy.

(g) Social workers should never design or conduct evaluation or research that does not use consent procedures, such as certain forms of naturalistic observation and archival research, unless rigorous and responsible review of the research has found it to be justified because of its prospective scientific, educational, or applied value and unless equally effective alternative procedures that do not involve waiver of consent are not feasible.

(h) Social workers should inform participants of their right to withdraw from evaluation and research at any time without penalty.

(i) Social workers should take appropriate steps to ensure that participants in evaluation and research have access to appropriate supportive services.

(j) Social workers engaged in evaluation or research should protect participants from unwarranted physical or mental distress, harm, danger, or deprivation.

(k) Social workers engaged in the evaluation of services should discuss collected information only for professional purposes and only with people professionally concerned with this information.

(l) Social workers engaged in evaluation or research should ensure the anonymity or confidentiality of participants and of the data obtained from them. Social workers should inform participants of any limits of confidentiality, the measures that will be taken to ensure confidentiality, and when any records containing research data will be destroyed.

(m) Social workers who report evaluation and research results should protect participants' confidentiality by omitting identifying information unless proper consent has been obtained authorizing disclosure.

(n) Social workers should report evaluation and research findings accurately. They should not fabricate or falsify results and should take steps to correct any errors later found in published data using standard publication methods.

(o) Social workers engaged in evaluation or research should be alert to and avoid conflicts of interest and dual relationships with participants, should inform participants when a real or potential conflict of interest arises, and should take steps to resolve the issue in a manner that makes participants' interests primary.

(p) Social workers should educate themselves, their students, and their colleagues about responsible research practices.

AB design   A single-system design in which there is a comparison between the baseline (A) and an intervention period (B).

ABAB design   A single-system design that is also known as a withdrawal or reversal design where the AB design is duplicated in order to increase the validity of the results.

ABC design   A single-system design in which the baseline (A) is followed by one intervention period (B) and a second intervention period (C). Also known as successive intervention design.

Alternate form   A method of testing an instrument's reliability where different but equivalent forms of the same test are administered to the same group of individuals, usually close in time, and then compared.

Alternative hypothesis   A means of validating findings when analyzing qualitative data (also referred to as a rival or alternative hypothesis).

Anonymity   A condition in which the researcher cannot identify a given response with a given respondent.

Applicability   Whether or not a measuring instrument is appropriate and suitable for a particular type of problem.

Applied research   Research that produces practical outcomes and is directed at solving problems encountered in social work practice.

Authority   Referring to outside sources of knowledge.

Autocorrelation   The relationship between the outcome or dependent variable scores in single-system studies.

Availability sampling (convenience sampling)   A nonprobability sampling method where available or convenient elements are included in the sample.

Bar graph   A visual means of displaying data at the nominal level of measurement.

Baseline   Repeated measurement before the introduction of the intervention that allows the comparison of target behavior rates before and after the intervention.

Baseline comparison   A strategy for comparing the equivalency between experimental and comparison groups where the comparison group is composed of cases handled prior to the introduction to the program.

Bivariate measure   A method of measuring the relationship between two variables.

Case studies   A description of the application of an intervention.

Causal flowcharts   A visual means of representing causal connections of qualitative data.

Causality   A principle that involves meeting three conditions: first, two factors are empirically related to one another; second, the cause precedes the effect in time; and third, the relationship between the factors cannot be explained by other factors.

Celeration line   A means of predicting the dependent variable in single-system studies.

Client satisfaction survey   A design used to ask clients how they experienced or perceived a program.

Clinical significance (practical significance)   Significance level that is achieved when the specified goal of the intervention has been reached.

Closed-ended question   Questions that provide respondents with a fixed set of alternatives from which they choose.

Cluster sampling   A form of probability sampling that involves randomly sampling a larger unit containing the elements of interest and then sampling from these larger units the elements to be included in the final sample.

Coding   A means of organizing and collecting information so that it can be entered into a computer.

Cohort groups   A strategy for increasing the equivalency between experimental and comparison groups where the comparison groups move through an organization at the same time as those in the program being evaluated but do not receive program services.

Cohort studies   Cohort studies examine specific subgroups as they change over time.

Community forum   A public meeting or series of meetings where individuals are briefed on the issues and then asked for input—a form of purposive sampling.

Comparison groups   Subjects who receive another type of intervention or who receive no type of bona fide intervention and who have not been randomly assigned. Comparison groups can be used to increase the internal and external validity of group designs.

Confidence level   How often you would expect to find similar results if the research were repeated.

Confidentiality   A state in which the researcher knows the identity of the respondents and their associated responses but guarantees not to disclose this information.

Construct validity   A means of testing an instrument's validity; involves examining the extent to which an instrument measures a theoretical construct.

Contamination   The difficulty of distinguishing between the experimental and comparison groups, either due to contact between the subjects of each group or due to no clear distinction between the program experiences of the clients in each group.

Content analysis   A method of coding written communication to a systematic quantifiable form.

Content validity   A method of testing an instrument's validity that involves ensuring the content of the instrument corresponds to the concepts being measured.

Contingency table   A measure of association, also known as cross-tabulation.

Control group   Subjects who do not receive the intervention being evaluated and who have been randomly assigned.

Convenience sampling (availability sampling)   A nonprobability sampling method where available or convenient elements are included in the sample.

Copyright   Laws that apply not only to published material but also to in-house reports.

Correlation   A measure of association used with interval or ratio level data.

Correlation coefficient   A statistic that measures the extent to which the comparisons are similar or not similar, related or not related.

Cost-benefit analysis   Program costs compared with the dollar value of the program results; a ratio of costs to benefits is computed.

Cost-effectiveness study   Program costs compared to some measure of program output; a cost per unit is calculated.

Cover letter   Sent with a questionnaire to briefly describe the purpose of the study and the principle of confidentiality.

Criterion sampling   Selecting all cases that meet some criterion. A type of nonprobability sampling.

Criterion validity   The extent to which a correlation exists between the measuring instrument and another standard.

Cross-classification   A method of qualitative data analysis that creates categories by crossing one dimension or typology with another.

Cross-sectional design   A method of measuring behavior as it occurs at one point in time or over a relatively short period of time.

Cross-tabulation   A measure of association, also known as a contingency table.

Data (datum)   Information that is collected for research.

Deductive reasoning   A process of drawing conclusions from the general to the particular; opposite to the process of induction.

Dependent variable   The outcome variable that has been presumably affected by the independent variable.

Descriptive research   A process of recording and reporting phenomena; not primarily concerned with causes.

Descriptive statistics   A means of summarizing the characteristics of a sample or the relationship among the variables.

Developmental research (intervention research)   Research specifically focused on developing innovative interventions by actually using research to design the interventions, test their effectiveness, and modify them based on recommendations that emerge from testing.

Directional hypothesis (one-tailed hypothesis)   A hypothesis that specifies not only that there is an association between variables but also predicts whether the relationship is negative or positive.

Discontinuity   A difference in data levels between the baseline and intervention periods.

Discourse analysis   A way of understanding how the researcher's social context can influence how data are understood and analyzed.

Drifts   Trends that occur across the intervention and baseline periods.

Ecological fallacy   The danger of reaching conclusions in your study using a unit of analysis other than that used by the study.

Element   The item under study in the population and sample; in social work, a client system.

Emic   A system of organizing and developing categories of qualitative data that are derived from those being studied rather than constructed by the researcher.

Empiricism   Observation through the use of the senses.

Ethnography   A method of describing a culture or society.

Ex post facto design   Ex post facto ("after the fact") refers to designs where subjects already possess the independent variable of interest before the study begins.

Expected frequencies   Cross-tabulations that are what one might expect to observe according to probability.

Experience   A form of knowledge that includes firsthand, personal participation in events.

Experimental designs   Group research designs that randomly assign to the control group and experimental group.

Experimental group   In a program evaluation, the group that receives the intervention being evaluated.

Explanatory research   Studies directed at providing explanations of events to identify causes.

Exploratory research   A form of research that generates initial insights into the nature of an issue and develops questions to be investigated by more extensive studies.

Exploratory single-system design   A design focused on assessing an intervention's impact on a target behavior.

External validity   The extent to which research results are generalizable to the wider population.

Feasibility studies (needs assessment)   Another term for a needs assessment.

Feedback   An important way of testing the validity of data from interpretive studies and making certain that the data are understandable to and relevant to the participants in the research.

Feminist research   An approach to research that argues that a relationship is formed between the researcher and participant, which results in the formation of a constructed reality between them.

Fixed format   In computer programming, a format in which each code has its specific column assignment in each row of data.

Focus group   A group formed to help develop the research question, or as a form of non-probability sampling.

Follow-up   A second mailing can enhance the response ratio of mailed questionnaires.

Formative program evaluation   An examination of the planning, development, and implementation of a program.

Frame elicitation   A means of framing questions to elicit from subjects what they include in a particular topic or category.

Frequency distribution   A description of the number of times the values of a variable occur in a sample.

Front-end analyses (needs assessment)   Another term for a needs assessment.

Generalist social work practice   A form of social work practice taught in B.S.W. programs that involves practice with different-size client systems and uses a number of different interventions and practice roles.

Generalization   The application of research findings to other situations.

Generalize   The ability to apply the findings from studying the sample to the population.

Goal attainment scales (GAS)   Scales used in single-system studies that reflect the achievement of outcomes; they both set client goals and assess whether the goals have been met.

Group design   The effect of a variable or variables on another variable or variables for a number of different client systems or elements.

History   A threat to the internal validity; those events that occur, other than the intervention, to affect the outcome.

History-treatment interaction   A threat to the external validity.

Human diversity   The whole spectrum of differences among people, including but not limited to gender, ethnicity, age, and sexual orientation.

Human subjects committees   Committees that review the ethical implications of research.

Hypothesis   A probability statement about the relationships among certain factors.

Independent variable   The presumed causal variable in a relationship.

Inductive reasoning   The use of observation to examine the particular and then develop a generalization to explain the relationship among many of the particulars; the opposite of deduction.

Inferential statistics   A means to determine whether an observed relationship is due to chance or in fact reflects a relationship among factors; allows us to generalize the findings to the wider population.

Information-rich sampling (purposive sampling)   Picking cases from which you can learn about the issues central to the research question—the sampling method of choice in interpretive studies.

Informed consent   Subjects' permission, obtained after fully informing potential participants of their research role and the consequences of their participation.

Institutional review boards   Boards that review the ethical implications of research being conducted at that institution.

Instrumentation   A threat to internal validity; the way in which the variables are measured may change when measures are taken more than once.

Internal validity   The extent to which the changes in the dependent variable(s) are a result of the introduction of the independent variable(s) rather than other factor(s).

Interpretism   An approach to science that emphasizes the subjective, descriptive, inductive, and qualitative aspects of inquiry.

Interval measures   Measures that classify observations into mutually exclusive categories in an inherent order and with equal space between the categories.

Intervention research (developmental research)   Research specifically focused on developing innovative interventions by actually using research to design the interventions, test their effectiveness, and modify them based on recommendations that emerge from testing.

Intuition   A form of insight not based on specialized training or reasoning.

Key informant sampling   Picking someone in the community identified as an expert in the field of interest; a form of nonprobability sampling.

Level of measurement   The extent to which a variable can be quantified and subsequently subjected to mathematical or statistical procedures.

Likert scale   A common measurement scale consisting of a series of statements with five response alternatives.

Limited probability sample   A sample whose characteristics are compared with the characteristics of a sample drawn from a larger population, allowing some tentative generalizations of the findings to be made.

Line graph   A graph that uses a line to connect the data points.

Literature review   A resource for consulting with the written material relevant to the research problem.

Logical analysis   In qualitative data analysis, the process of looking at the relationships between the variables and concepts.

Longitudinal design   A study that tracks behavior over a significant period of time.

Margin of error   Measure of the precision the researcher needs.

Matching   A strategy for increasing the equivalency of experimental and comparison groups; certain characteristics thought to be important in impacting outcomes are selected, and these characteristics are equally represented in each group.

Maturation   A threat to internal validity; a change that is not a result of the intervention but of the subject's becoming more mature with the passage of time.

Mean   A measure of central tendency; the result of summing all values of the observations and then dividing by the total number of observations.

Measuring instrument   The method or means by which data are collected.

Median   A measure of central tendency; a value where 50% of the cases lie above the value and 50% of the cases lie below the value.

Missing values   Incomplete data.

Mode   A measure of central tendency; the value possessed by the greatest number of observations.

Monitoring client progress   Examine and reflect on client progress; used in practice evaluation.

Monitoring interventions   Examine and reflect on interventions used in practice evaluation.

Mortality   A threat to internal validity; subjects dropping out of groups, resulting in a lack of equivalency between the groups.

Multiple baseline design   A replication of the AB design where the same intervention is applied to two or more target problems, to two or more clients, or in two or more settings at different points in time.

Multivariate analysis   Involves examining relationships between more than two variables.

Multivariate measure   A method of measuring the relationship of two or more variables.

Needs assessment (feasibility studies and front-end analysis)   Questions concerned with discovering the nature and extent of a particular social problem to determine the most appropriate type of response.

Negative cases   A means of validating findings from qualitative research.

Negative correlation   A relationship between two variables; as the values of one variable increase, the values of the other variable decrease.

Neutrality   When the researcher does not seek a particular perspective in order to draw conclusions.

Nominal measures   Measures that clarify observations into mutually exclusive categories with no ordering to the categories.

Nondirectional hypothesis (two-tailed hypothesis)   A hypothesis that states there is an association between two or more variables but predicts nothing about the direction of that association.

Nonprobability sampling   The process of selecting a sample where each element in the population has an unknown chance of being included in the sample.

Normal distribution   A bell-shaped curve that is symmetrical; the mean, median, and mode are the same, and most of the scores cluster around the mean, median, and mode.

Null hypothesis   A hypothesis that there is no association between the variables.

Objectivity   The condition in which to the greatest extent possible, the researcher's values and biases do not interfere with the study of the problem.

Observation   A way of collecting information separate from philosophizing or speculating.

Observed frequencies   Frequencies in a cross-tabulation derived from the sample.

Observer reliability   The comparison of different administrations of the same instrument by different observers or interviewers.

One-group posttest-only design   A type of quasi-experimental group design.

One-group pretest/posttest design   A type of quasi-experimental group design.

One-tailed hypothesis (directional hypothesis)   A hypothesis that specifies not only that there is an association between variables but also predicts whether the relationship is negative or positive.

Open-ended questions   Questions that do not provide respondents with responses, leaving them free to formulate their own responses.

Operationalize   A means of specifying the manner by which the variable is to be measured.

Ordinal measures   Measures that classify observations into mutually exclusive categories with an inherent order.

Output   The final product obtained from submitting a computer program to the computer; this can be displayed on the screen or as hard copy (printout).

Overflow comparison groups   A strategy for increasing the equivalency of comparison and experimental groups where the comparison groups are those who are referred to a program but who cannot be served at that time.

Panel studies   Studies that look at the same set of people over time.

Participant observation   An observation method involving the observer's fully submerging himself or herself to become one of the observed group.

Participatory action research   An opportunity for the subjects' involvement in the research process—an approach to research that has several aims, all intended to empower participants.

Perfect correlation   A relationship between two variables where the values of each variable increase or decrease at the same rate as each other.

Pie charts   A visual representation of data used to show the relative contributions of each of the values to the whole variable.

Population   All possible cases that are of interest to the researcher.

Positive correlation   A relationship between two variables where, as the values of one variable increase, the values of the other variable also increase.

Positivism   An approach to science that adheres to the principles of objectivity, causality, deduction, collecting quantitative data, and producing generalizable results.

Posttest-only control-group design   A type of experimental design.

Power   The probability of correctly rejecting a null hypothesis.

Practical significance (clinical significance)   Significance level that is achieved when the specified goal of the intervention has been reached.

Practice evaluation   The type of research that assesses an individual social worker's practice.

Practice logs   A type of process recording where the practitioner keeps an ongoing record of their practice.

Preexperimental designs   Group designs that use comparison groups rather than control groups, or that use no type of comparison group or control group, and thus have limited internal and external validity.

Pretest/posttest comparison-group design   A type of preexperimental group design.

Pretest-posttest control-group design   A type of experimental design.

Probability sampling   The process of selecting a sample where each element in the population has a known chance of being included in the sample.

Problem-solving process   Specific steps in generalist social work practice.

Process recording (process analysis)   A written record of what transpired with a client system.

Program evaluation   A type of research concerned with the assessment of a program's overall functioning.

Provisionality   A scientific principle involving the realization that all scientific findings are tentative and that no ultimate truths can be established.

Pure research   Research centered on answering questions about human behavior to satisfy intellectual curiosity with little concern for the practical benefits that might result.

Purposive sampling   Another term for nonprobability sampling.

Qualitative   The nonnumerical examination of phenomena focusing on the underlying meanings and patterns of relationships.

Quantitative   The creation of categories of phenomena under study prior to investigation and the assignment of numbers to these categories.

Quasi-experimental designs   Designs that eliminate more threats to internal and external validity than preexperimental designs, and use comparison groups rather than control groups, and thus still have limited internal and external validity.

Quota sampling   A nonprobability sampling method that includes a certain proportion of elements with specific characteristics in the sample.

Random assignment   The process by which every subject has an equal chance of being assigned to a control group or the experimental group.

Range   A measure of variability; the distance between the largest and the smallest value.

Rapid assessment instrument (RAI) A standardized series of questions or statements to connect data in single-system studies.

Rates under treatment A type of secondary data that uses existing data from agencies to determine the needs of the community.

Ratio measures Measures that classify observations into mutually exclusive categories with an inherent order and equal spacing between the categories; the ratio measure reflects the absolute magnitude of the value (and has an absolute zero point).

Reactive effect The degree to which the researcher's presence affects the behavior being observed.

Reactivity (reactive effect) The problem of the observer's behavior inhibiting or affecting the subject's behavior.

Reductionism The extreme limitation of the kinds and numbers of variables to be considered when explaining or accounting for broad types of behavior.

Regression analysis A statistical analysis that allows an estimate of how much change in the dependent variable is produced by a given change in the independent variable or variables.

Regression to the mean A threat to external validity; the tendency of test scores to regress to the mean.

Reliability The extent to which a measure reveals actual differences in what is being measured, rather than differences that are inherent in the measuring instrument itself.

Replicate To repeat a study in order to determine if the same results are found.

Representative sample A sample that accurately represents the distribution of relevant variables in the population.

Research log Informal but systematic records of ideas and progress relating to a research study.

Research methods Means of systematically organizing observations and replicating studies.

Research proposal A paper proposing to undertake a specific type of research.

Response rate The proportion of the sample that responds to a questionnaire or interview.

Reversal design A design that is the same as an ABAB single-system design.

Rival hypothesis A means of validating findings when analyzing qualitative data (also referred to as an alternative hypothesis).

Sample A group of subjects chosen from the population.

Sampling A means of determining the subjects of the study.

Sampling error The extent to which the values of a sample differ from those of the population.

Sampling frame A list of all the elements in the population from which the sample is selected.

Scales A measurement technique that combines a number of items into a composite score.

Scattergram A means of plotting the relationships between two-interval or ratio-level data.

Science   A system for producing knowledge and the knowledge produced from that system.

Secondary data   Existing forms of information that have been previously collected.

Selection   A threat to internal validity; the possibility that the group of people selected for one group will differ from those selected for the other group.

Selection-treatment interaction   A threat to external validity.

Self-monitoring   A process in which a client collects data on his or her own behavior.

Semistructured interview   An interviewing situation in which the interviewer is freer to pursue hunches and improvise in asking questions.

Simple random sampling   A form of probability sampling in which the population is related as a whole unit and each element has an equal chance of being included in the sample.

Single-system design or study   The type of design used in practice evaluation.

Skewed distribution   A distribution in which most of the scores are concentrated at one end of the distribution rather than in the middle.

Split half method   Items on the instrument are divided into comparable halves.

Slopes   Trends that occur in the data within the baseline or within the intervention period.

Snowball sampling   A form of nonprobability sampling that identifies some members of the population and then has those individuals contact others in the population.

Social indicators   A form of secondary data collection that involves selecting demographic data from existing records to predict a community's needs.

Solomon four-group design   A type of experimental group design.

Standard deviation   A measure of variability that averages the distance of each value from the mean.

Standardized scales   Uniform scales that are tested extensively.

Static-group comparison design   A type of quasi-experimental group design.

Statistically significant   Characteristic of a finding when the null hypothesis is rejected and the probability that the result was due to chance falls at or below a certain cutoff point—usually 5%, or the .05 significance level.

Stratified random sampling   A form of probability sampling in which the population is divided into strata, and subsamples are randomly selected from each stratum.

Structured interview   An interviewing situation in which the interviewer knows ahead of time the questions to be asked and in many cases is simply verbally administering a questionnaire.

Structured observation   Behaviors are categorized prior to the observation according to their characteristics, including their frequency, direction, and magnitude. These categories can then be quantified.

Subjective   Reality as perceived by the subject; the researcher's biases and values are explicitly stated.

Successive intervention design   A design that is the same as the ABC single-system design.

Summative program evaluation   An assessment that determines whether goals and objectives have been met and the extent to which program efforts are generalizable to other settings and populations.

Survey research   Studies focusing on describing the characteristics of a group.

Systematic random sampling   A form of probability sampling in which every *n*th element of the sampling frame is selected for the sample.

Target problem scales   Scales used in single-system studies to track the changes in a client system's target behavior.

Task forces   Representatives of the agency or community, used to help formulate research questions.

Testing   A threat to internal validity; the effect the testing itself may have on the subject.

Test-retest   The repeated administration of the instrument to the same set of people on separate occasions.

Theories   Scientific descriptions and explanations of logical relationships among phenomena.

Time series design   A type of quasi-experimental design in which a number of measurements are made both before and after the intervention.

Transcribe   The act of writing down verbatim a recording of the interview.

Treatment diffusion   The act of ensuring that there are no interferences during the course of the evaluation that may affect either the equivalence of the groups or the representativeness of the sample.

Trend studies   Multiple samplings from the same population over months or years to monitor changes or trends.

Triangulation   A means of validating findings from qualitative research.

Two-tailed hypothesis (nondirectional hypothesis)   A hypothesis that states that two or more variables are associated, but does not predict whether the association is negative or positive.

Type I error   An erroneous rejection of the null hypothesis—the conclusion that a relationship exists between the variables when no relationship in fact exists.

Type II error   An erroneous failure to reject the null hypothesis—a failure to identify a relationship between variables.

Typical case sampling   The most often-used type of nonprobability sampling. Typical cases are sought using the literature, previous research, or consultation with relevant groups.

Unit of analysis   The situation or person who is the object of the study.

Univariate measures   Measures that examine variables one at a time.

Unstructured interviews   Interviews that are similar to conversations except that the interviewer and interviewee know that an interview is being conducted and the interviewee is privy to information of interest to the interviewer.

Unstructured observation   Observation that is used when little is known about the behaviors being observed and no categorization of the behaviors has been done before the interview.

Validity of a measuring instrument   The extent to which we are measuring what we think we are measuring.

Value   The quantitative measure attached to a variable.

Values   Beliefs about what is right and wrong.

Variable   Characteristic of a phenomenon; something that varies and subsequently has different values.

Vignettes   Hypothetical situations either drawn from a source or developed by the researcher for the purpose of eliciting certain responses from the participants.

Visual significance   A state that occurs when the visual presentation of results from a single-system study looks significant.

Withdrawal design   A design that is the same as an ABAB single-system design.

TO THE OWNER OF THIS BOOK:

We hope that you have found *Research Methods for Generalist Social Work*, Third Edition, useful. So that this book can be improved in a future edition, would you take the time to complete this sheet and return it? Thank you.

School and address: _____

_____

Department: _____

Instructor's name: _____

1. What I like most about this book is: _____

_____

_____

2. What I like least about this book is: _____

_____

_____

3. My general reaction to this book is: _____

_____

_____

4. The name of the course in which I used this book is: _____

_____

5. Were all of the chapters of the book assigned for you to read? _____

If not, which ones weren't? _____

6. In the space below, or on a separate sheet of paper, please write specific suggestions for improving this book and anything else you'd care to share about your experience in using this book.

_____

_____

OPTIONAL:

Your name: _____ Date: _____

May we quote you, either in promotion for *Research Methods for Generalist Social Work,*
Third Edition, or in future publishing ventures?

Yes: _____ No: _____

Sincerely yours,

Christine R. Marlow

FOLD HERE

NO POSTAGE
NECESSARY
IF MAILED
IN THE
UNITED STATES

BUSINESS REPLY MAIL

FIRST CLASS   PERMIT NO. 358   PACIFIC GROVE, CA

POSTAGE WILL BE PAID BY ADDRESSEE

ATTN: *Lisa Gebo, Social Work Editor*

**BROOKS/COLE/THOMSON LEARNING
511 FOREST LODGE ROAD
PACIFIC GROVE, CA   93950-9968**